Uncle John's
BATHROOM
READER®
PLUNGES
INTO
HISTORY
AGAIN

Uncle John's BATHROOM READER® PLUNGES INTO HISTORY AGAIN

The Bathroom Readers'
Hysterical Society

San Diego, CA

UNCLE JOHN'S BATHROOM READER
PLUNGES INTO HISTORY AGAIN

"Bathroom Reader" and "Portable Press" are registered trademarks
of Advanced Marketing Services, Inc. All rights reserved.

For information, write
The Bathroom Readers' Hysterical Society
Portable Press, 5880 Oberlin Drive, San Diego, CA 92121
e-mail: unclejohn@advmkt.com

Cover design by Michael Brunsfeld (brunsfeldo@comcast.net)

ISBN-13: 978-1-59223-261-1

Library of Congress Catalog-in-Publication Data
Uncle John's bathroom reader plunges into history again.
        p. cm
    Includes index
    ISBN 1-59223-261-2 (pbk.)
        1. World history—Humor. 2. World history. I. Bathroom
Readers' Hysterical Institute
(San Diego, Ca.)

PN6231.H47U54 2004
081'.02'07—dc22
                                                2004046438

Printed in the United States of America
First printing: September 2004
Second printing: March 2005
Third printing: August 2005
Fourth printing: July 2006
Fifth printing: November 2006

06 07 08 09 10   10 9 8 7 6 5

Project Team:

Allen Orso, Publisher

JoAnn Padgett, Director, Editorial and Production

Stephanie Spadaccini, Senior Project Editor

Amy Briggs, Editor

Sue Steiner, Editor

Frances Heaney, Editor

Victoria Bullman, Copy Editor

Robin Kilrain, Copy Editor

Jackie Estrada, Indexer

Michael Brunsfeld, Cover Design

Lois Stanfield, Interior Design and Composition

THANK YOU!

*The Bathroom Readers' Hysterical society
sincerely thanks the following additional
people whose advice and assistance
made this book possible.*

Jennifer Baldwin

Cynthia Francisco

Mary Lou Goforth

Gordon Javna

Dan Mansfield

Ellen O'Brien

Julia Papps

Sydney Stanley

Deborah Taylor

Jennifer Thornton

Connie Vazquez

THANK YOU
HYSTERICAL SCHOLARS!

The Bathroom Readers' Hysterical Society sincerely thanks the following people who contributed selections to this work.

Myles Callum

Jennifer Carlisle

Jennifer Crawford

Ian Fitzgerald

Kathryn Grogman

Deborah Hardin

Vickey Kalambakal

Martha Keavney

Diane Lane

Phillip Lollar

Christopher Lord

Jane Lott

Lea Markson

Graham Meyer

Arthur Montague

Ken Padgett

Bethanne Kelly Patrick

Debra Pawlak

Valerie Pell

Charyn Pfeuffer

William Dylan Powell

Lucian Randall

Terri Schlichenmeyer

Joyce Slaton

Stuart Smoller

Stephanie Spadaccini

Sue Steiner

Johanna Stewart

Diana Moes VandeHoef

Ana Young

CONTENTS

*Denotes extra-long articles suitable
for an extended sitting session.

INTRODUCTION

Finally.

We're finally there, yet again. The end of a fascinating journey and the culmination of our efforts as we finish a new book. It all comes down to (complete exhaustion?)—the introduction.

Three years ago we created our very first *Uncle John's Bathroom Reader Plunges Into History* (dare we call it a historic event?), and now we're very proud to present its creatively titled offspring *Uncle John's Bathroom Reader Plunges Into History Again*.

Anyway, in compiling our first book, we discovered that we had so many great stories, anecdotes, and tidbits that we couldn't squeeze them all in. It was an embarrassment of riches, if you know what I mean. Take a look at some of these gems and see what I'm talking about:

Typhoid Mary Quite Contrary　　Chanel No. 1
The Real M*A*S*H　　　　　　Move Over Babe Ruth
Let's Go to Greenland　　　　　The Coolest Man in History
Mona Lisa Caper　　　　　　　Carbine Williams
The Mighty Pen　　　　　　　The Queen's Dwarf

So we decided to create this book. We couldn't just let this great material fall through the cracks, could we? We hope you enjoy reading this as much as we did writing it for you.

So...bring your seatbacks to their full and upright or comfortably reclined positions. Make sure that those trays are up and locked, please turn off all electronic devices, and get ready for another fascinating, fun, and factual journey through time in *Uncle John's Bathroom Reader Plunges Into History Again*.

And speaking of time—it's getting late. We have other books to finish and start, and we all want to go home.

Enjoy!

Remember to always go with the flow,

> Uncle Al (the Bathroom Reader's Pal)
> and the Outhouse Staff, aka,
> The Bathroom Readers' Hysterical Society

P.F. (Post Flush) Visit our website at www.BathroomReaders.com

LONDON'S BURNING

*The biggest fire in British history was the Great Fire of
London, which, in 1666, destroyed 80 percent
of the old walled city—and, strangely, led to
anti-French and anti-Dutch riots on the streets.*

Poor old London was having a hard time of it in the mid-
1660s. In 1665, the dreaded plague swept through the city,
and in 1666, it was still going strong, claiming almost 70,000
lives. Of course, 17th-century London wasn't the most hygienic
place on earth—it was an overcrowded, smelly, ancient town built
of wood. It was *screaming* for a makeover.

BAKING HOT
On the night of September 2, 1666, the spark (literally) that led
to the re-creation of London ignited in a bread shop owned by
Thomas Farynor, the king's baker, on the appropriately named
Pudding Lane. The Farynor family, awakened by smoke, escaped
across the rooftops of neighboring houses. A maid, too scared to
run, stayed behind—and so became the first victim of the most
devastating conflagration the city has ever seen.

HOT ENOUGH FOR YOU?
At first, everyone thought it was just another fire; they happened
all the time in London, especially with all those wooden buildings
conveniently packed so close together. The famous diarist and
government official Samuel Pepys (we'll be hearing more from
him later) heard the alarm raised, but went back to sleep. Even
more dismissively, the mayor of London, Thomas Bludworth,
when called to the scene exclaimed, "Pish! A woman might piss it
out!" (They were a foul-mouthed lot in those days.)

LONDON WHEN IT SIZZLES
But soon enough it became clear that this was no ordinary fire.
High winds were helping the fire to spread, and by the morning,
when Samuel Pepys went on a morning walk to the Tower of London, he saw "pigeons...hovering about the windows and balconies

"Siamese Twins" Chang and Eng married two sisters and between them had 21 children.

till they burned their wings and fell down." With the fire spreading, Pepys sought out Mayor Bludworth and suggested that a firebreak be built by pulling down the houses surrounding the fire. Bludworth was appalled. "Who will pay for the rebuilding?" he cried.

Pepys then went over Bludworth's head and visited the king, Charles II, at Whitehall Place, a few miles away. The king ordered Bludworth to destroy as many houses as he could; but by then it was too late. The fire had taken hold and was destroying everything in its path. Pepys, in the meantime, went home to rescue what he could. He recalls how he dug a hole and buried "a parmazan [sic] cheese as well as my wine and some other things." Not weighed down by his collection of fine Italian cheese, Pepys then headed for the hills.

HOT UNDER THE COLLAR

It took the fire four days to burn itself out. The fire stopped only when it came up against the stone walls surrounding the city and when there were no more wooden buildings left to destroy. Four-fifths of the historic heart of London had gone up in smoke, from the Tower of London (singed, but intact) in the east to Fleet Street in the west.

In the end, the statistics looked like this:
- 13,200 houses were reduced to ashes.
- 84 churches were burned to the ground.
- 100,000 people, one sixth of the population of London, were now homeless.

The town was like one giant, smoldering refugee camp, with sooty-faced citizens camping out in parks and commons across the capital.

IN THE HOT SEAT

Everyone was tired, hungry, confused, and angry—and looking for someone to blame. The English never need much of an excuse to bash the French, and a rumor spread as quickly as the fire had that it was all a dastardly attack by Catholic France on Protestant England. The Dutch were also blamed (England was at war with the Netherlands at the time).

Before long, anyone with a foreign accent—or wearing clogs—was a target for the London mob. Things got so bad that the

America actually declared its independence from Britain on July 2, 1776...

Spanish embassy offered asylum to all foreigners in the city. To calm things down, a convenient scapegoat was found: a French watchmaker named Robert Hubert. He was an emotionally disturbed young man, and he readily confessed to starting the fire (even though everyone knew he hadn't). He was tried, convicted by a biased jury (which helpfully contained three members of the Farynor family), and hanged.

OUT OF THE ASHES

After all this excitement, the next step was to rebuild London. The king saw this as a golden opportunity to remake the capital as a world city, something to rival Paris or Rome. Commissions were established, committees formed, and plans drawn up for a city of stone with wide boulevards and sweeping vistas. Of course, this city was never built. But out of the muddle of competing schemes emerged Christopher Wren, a young architect with big ideas. His plans for rebuilding London so impressed the powers-that-be that he was given the plum job of rebuilding St. Paul's Cathedral.

The old, wooden structure of St. Paul's was in desperate need of repair before the fire. Not only was it crumbling to bits, but it was not exactly treated as a proper place of worship. During the week, it was used as a meeting place for lawyers and their clients, and as an indoor market. Worse, porters from the beer, fish, and flower wholesale warehouses on one side of the cathedral used it as a shortcut to the shops on the other side. Work on the new St. Paul's began in 1675. Although it took 35 years to finish, the magnificent cathedral is now one of the best-known symbols of Great Britain.

BUT WHO'S COUNTING?

Equally symbolic is the Monument, also designed by Wren. The stone column's 202-foot (61.5 m) height exactly replicates the distance from where it stands to where the fire began in Pudding Lane. Oddly enough, to date it has claimed more victims than the Great Fire of London ever did. At least nine souls have thrown themselves from the Monument since it was opened to the public in 1677; only four people are known to have lost their lives in the actual fire.

WHERE ARE THEY NOW?

The Neanderthals

Dear Uncle John,

My dad keeps saying that all the guys I date are like Neanderthals. Who are these Neanderthals? Are they cute, and where can I find some?

Mad at Dad

Dear Mad at Dad,

Neanderthals, or *Homo neanderthalensis*, appeared approximately 250,000 to 30,000 years ago and lived in an area bordered by Britain on the west and Iraq in the east—a big piece of territory. Neanderthals had large (like really large) noses, massive eyebrow ridges, big teeth, and no chins. These days, they'd be candidates for extreme makeovers.

Are your boyfriends mentally challenged? Neanderthals developed a reputation for having plenty of brawn but tiny brains. Actually, their brains were as large as Dad's—or any modern human's. Recently, science has given the Neanderthals credit for inventing the world's first "crazy glue," an adhesive made from birch pitch that the clever Neanderthals developed to attach flint knives to wooden handles.

These days, it's tough to date a Neanderthal because they haven't been heard from since they disappeared about 30,000 years ago. Some scientists theorized that modern humans have a bit of Neanderthal in them. But so far, DNA evidence indicates that Neanderthals aren't our ancestors and that these folks are extinct—completely gone—though obviously not forgotten by your dad.

The prolific author Isaac Asimov was a claustrophile—he **liked** small, enclosed spaces.

THESE TOOLISH THINGS

Anyone stuck behind bars without a file can tell you that there's nothing like the proper hand tool for the proper job. Here's what happened once our ancestors figured that out.

HAMMERHEADS
- Hammers have been around for millions of years—ever since folks smashed objects with heavy stones called "hammerstones."
- The earliest hafted hammers, hammers with wooden handles tied on, appeared about 6000–4000 B.C.
- Materials to make the hammerhead kept up with man's progress—from stone to flint to bronze. And, by the Iron Age (which began in about 200 B.C.), the hammerhead was a strong, handy tool that didn't change much until the modern age of steel alloys.
- That toolbox staple, the claw hammer, was designed by the Romans.

GETTING THE AX
- Like hammers, the first axes with handles date back to around 6000 B.C. They had blades of stone or flint.
- In 1000 B.C., axes were cast in copper or bronze.
- By the Iron Age, axes were cast with a hole to take a wooden handle.
- The Roman ax was much like the one we use today.
- Double-bladed axes, like those used by lumberjacks, have been popular for centuries.

OLD SAWS
- The first saws were pieces of flint with jagged edges; they were essential for cutting up an animal and removing its meat.
- The Bronze Age (about 3300–700 B.C.) brought saws with long, copper blades and teeth.
- The ancient Egyptians could saw stone with their copper saws; there are even saw marks on the Great Pyramids!

Hirohito, Japan's 124th emperor, was an internationally respected marine biologist.

PULLING FAT OUT OF THE FIRE

- Fire was fine. But how to pull food out of the fire before it burned? The answer came around 2000 B.C., in Europe, with the earliest pliers—nothing more than a couple of sticks, which soon evolved into crude tongs.
- By 500 B.C., blacksmiths had discovered the advantage of leverage, making pliers with long handles and short teeth for gripping—less effort for more grip.
- In Roman times, pliers did various jobs from pulling nails to cutting.

SCREWING AROUND WITH HISTORY

- Wooden screws were invented by the 5th-century-B.C. Greek philosopher Archytas of Tarentum. He is credited with inventing the pulley and—of all things—the baby rattle!
- By the 1400s, screws had gone metal, popping up on everything from armor to furniture.
- The screwdriver, as we know it, was historically documented for the first time in the 15th century in Germany—designed for use in carpentry.
- Screwdrivers gained ground in the 1850s, when metal screws were manufactured en masse.
- The namesake of the screwdriver with the little x on top was traveling salesman Henry M. Phillips of Portland, Oregon. He invented his "Phillips head" screwdriver in the 1930s to make car manufacturing go more smoothly. It took time to center a standard screw and screwdriver; so, Phillips designed a screw with an x on the head, which would center automatically. He made the x very shallow, so that once the screw was in place the screwdriver—even the automatic ones used by carmakers—would pop out instead of stripping the screw.
- The 1936 Cadillac featured Phillips screws.

WRENCHING DEVELOPMENTS

- The basic wrench is an American invention used as a lever for tightening or turning objects. The first basic wrench was patented in 1835 by Solymon Merrick of Springfield, Massachusetts.

The custom of coloring Easter eggs dates back to the ancient Egyptians and Persians.

- The huge pipe wrench, which bad guys wield in movies, was invented in 1870 by steamboat fireman Daniel C. Stillson. He got rich from the royalties.

DOING THE DRILL
- The first Stone Age drills were low-tech affairs, consisting of a stick with abrasive sand poured under the tip. Early drillers rolled the stick back and forth between their palms. And after a while—after a long while—the sand wore a hole into whatever they were drilling.
- In the 1400s, braces were used to hold objects on one side and poke holes into them on the other.
- The biggest drilling breakthrough came with the advent of the screw (see above), which let you drill a hole into something while removing the drilling residue.

FILE THIS
- The first known files were pieces of sharkskin. Superabrasive, they were used to smooth out rough surfaces of stone, wood, or bone.
- The first metal files were made of bronze, and the Romans used them to help sharpen their saws.
- Leonardo da Vinci once sketched a file-making machine, but he never took the time to build it (being a pretty busy guy already).

* * * * *

Hand tools discovered in northern Kenya in 1969 are estimated to be about 2,600,000 years old.

"One only needs two tools in life: WD-40 to make things go, and duct tape to make them stop."—G. Weilacher

"Men have become fools with their tools."—Thomas Elisha Stewart

They practiced the custom during their spring festivals.

THIS OLD HOUSE

William Winchester's repeating rifles may have tamed the Wild West, but they sure rattled his widow's spirits.

THE MEDIUM GIVES THE MESSAGE

By most accounts, Sarah Winchester was perfectly normal in 1862 when she married William Winchester. Hubby Will was the marketer of the Winchester repeating rifle used widely on the western frontier. And he was fabulously wealthy. But after the death of her infant child in 1866 and her husband's death in 1881, Sarah realized that money wasn't everything. Despite the shares of Winchester stock and cash she'd inherited—a windfall that gave her an income of roughly $1,000 (823 euros) a day—Sarah was so depressed and miserable that she went to a Boston spiritualist for help.

The Boston medium announced that Sarah's family died because of, essentially, bad karma. Ghosts of those killed by Winchester rifles were the culprits. Maybe because Sarah already felt guilty about those death-dealing rifles, she believed the ghost story. She didn't even argue when the spiritualist told her how to appease the angry spirits: The Winchester widow must move out West and build a mansion that would never be finished. As long as she kept on building, Sarah would stay alive.

WACKY HOME IMPROVEMENTS

Sarah fled New Haven, Connecticut, for the farming community of San Jose, California, in 1884. She settled into a small farmhouse, set up a séance room, and each night communicated with the spirits who told her what to build next.

The clatter of hammer and saws filled the house 24 hours a day. Sarah employed a legion of builders who worked in shifts for almost four continuous decades fulfilling Sarah's odd demands. The result was quite a piece of work: a rambling maze with stair cases that led nowhere, more than 2,000 cupboards (some only one inch deep), doorways that opened onto nothing, and balconies with no way to get to them.

Sarah installed five separate central heating systems—despite California's sunny, warm weather—and strung miles of wire connecting strange communication systems that no one knew how to work. She developed a fixation with the number 13: she built rooms with 13 windows each, 13 fireplaces in one suite, 13 gaslights on her chandelier, 13 holes in her kitchen drain, and so on.

At the end, her house boasted 160 rooms, 3 elevators, 6 kitchens, 40 bedrooms, 47 fireplaces, 17 chimneys, 10,000 windows, and 467 doors—but just 1 shower!

GOING TO THE MANSION IN THE SKY

Sarah Winchester died at age 83 in 1922, having lived the long life that her spirits had supposedly promised her if she kept building. For the next 16 years the house remained empty. But it was eventually converted into a popular museum, which draws thousands of visitors to San Jose. Ghost tours and nighttime flashlight tours titillate the tourists.

Some say the house is still inhabited. Staff and visitors have reported lights going on and off, and cold spots in certain rooms. Maybe it's vengeful spirits, angry that the building has ceased. Or maybe it's Sarah herself, trying to find that shower.

* * * * *

LAUGHING STOCK

Talk about poetic justice. In Puritan Boston in 1634, a carpenter named Edward Palmer built the first wooden stocks for public punishment. When he then submitted a bill for 1 pound, 13 shillings, and 7 pence, the town officials considered the amount extortionate. They not only fined him 5 pounds but also ordered the carpenter himself to "be sett an houre in the stocks," the first victim of his own handiwork.

The troll doll of the 1960s was also called the Dammit doll, after its creator, Joseph Dam.

BLACK LIKE HIM

*The book he wrote was so popular that when his neighbors in
Mansfield, Texas, found out about it, they hanged him in effigy.*

The movie *Black Like Me* was based on the autobiographical
book by the same name. In the preintegration days of 1959,
the author, a Texas-born white man named John Howard
Griffin, had himself injected with a chemical that makes skin turn
brown on exposure to the sun. What would possess a white man to
try to pass himself off as black?

Griffin had been part of the French Resistance in World War
II and had helped rescue Austrian Jews who were fleeing the Nazis.
When he returned home, he was appalled by the persecution of
blacks by whites. So Griffin shaved his head, disguised himself as
an African American, and set off for the Deep South to experience
firsthand what life was like for an African American male. He
spent six weeks hitchhiking and riding buses throughout the
South—and suffering indignity after indignity at the hands of
whites. This actually turned out to be one of the less interesting
interludes in an altogether fascinating life.

THE WRITER AS A YOUNG MAN

Griffin's mother was a classically trained pianist and piano teacher,
and his father was a radio personality. When Griffin was 15, he
wrote a letter to a French boarding school and offered to work in
exchange for tuition. After boarding school, he stayed in France
and worked in an insane asylum to help pay for further studies in
music and psychology. He devised a therapy for the inmates based
on Gregorian chants. He joined the Resistance as a medic at age
19. To help Jews escape, he disguised them as asylum patients,
even going so far as to put them in straitjackets.

When America joined the war, Griffin returned home to
enlist in the U.S. Army Air Corps. While stationed in the South
Pacific, he suffered severe head wounds in an explosion. Medics
left him for dead, but luckily the burial crew noticed that he was
still—just barely—breathing. Griffin's injuries had damaged his
sight, which worsened over the next few years. He returned to

France to finish his studies, but he was forced to go home when he lost his sight completely.

Griffin turned to writing. He dictated into a tape recorder then transposed his words on a typewriter. His first book (*The Devil Rides Outside*, 1952) about a man's attempt to resist a worldly life and live a spiritual one was part of an obscenity hearing before the Supreme Court in 1957. A bookseller was convicted for selling it because of its "sexually charged" content, but the Court overturned the conviction. After a while, life settled down. He wrote four more books, converted to Catholicism, remarried, and fathered two of an eventual four children. One day—all of a sudden—his eyesight returned. (We're not making this up.)

IT'S NOT ALL BLACK OR WHITE

It was at this point that he undertook the *Black Like Me* project, which started as a series for *Sepia*, a photojournalistic magazine that focused on African American culture. He wrote about how he was insulted, harassed, threatened, and not allowed to cash his traveler's checks. Drivers wouldn't let him off the bus to use a restroom or wouldn't let him off at his stop. He was turned away at restaurants and was kicked out of a public park because he was black.

The *Sepia* articles were eventually published as *Black Like Me* in 1961. A best seller in some parts of the country, it was definitely *not* well received in others. After he was burned in effigy in Mansfield, Texas, Griffin en famille moved to Mexico until things blew over. When the family returned to Texas nine months later, Griffin discovered that he was suffering from bone deterioration and tumors. He had 70 operations between 1960 and 1970. During that time he was appointed the official biographer of another Catholic convert and the author of *The Seven-Story Mountain*, Thomas Merton. Through it all, Griffin never stopped writing, teaching, and lecturing.

Even before Griffin died in 1980, rumors began to circulate that his illness was a result of the *Black Like Me* skin-darkening experiment. Griffin did not die of skin cancer or any illness related to the experiment. In fact, he'd been in poor health for most of his adult life. He died at age 60 from diabetes-related complications.

The Great Pyramid is made of 2.3 million limestone blocks.

FEARS AND PHOBIAS OF THE FAMOUS

Scared of spiders? Afraid of flying? You're not alone.

- If the idea of flying in an aircraft at several hundred miles per hour makes you queasy, you're in good company. Author Ray Bradbury—whose heroes rode around in spaceships—was afraid of flying. So were former president Ronald Reagan, French statesman Georges Clemenceau, and singer Johnny Cash. (Cash, we've heard, was also afraid of snakes.)
- The list of people afraid of cats includes a lot of famous and powerful men: playwright William Shakespeare and leaders Napoléon, Julius Caesar, Benito Mussolini, Alexander the Great, and Dwight Eisenhower.
- Composer Frédéric-François Chopin and author Hans Christian Andersen were both afraid of being buried alive. Anderson was so fearful that he had a sign that he set at the side of his bed when he retired for the night. The sign said he only *looked* dead.
- Scientist and serious ding-a-ling Nikola Tesla was afraid of pearl earrings on women and any hotel room number or floor divisible by three.
- Adolf Hitler was claustrophobic; so was Ronald Reagan. Surprisingly enough, magician Harry Houdini hated tight spaces, which makes his daring feats seem even more courageous.
- Austrian neurologist Sigmund Freud, who was bound to have at least one phobia, was afraid of ferns.
- Sir Laurence Olivier, arguably the greatest actor of the 20th century, had horrible stage fright.
- Indian nationalist Mahatma Gandhi was afraid of the dark.
- Industrialist Howard Hughes took his fear of germs to the extreme; it's been said that he'd burn his clothing if someone he met was ill. (Do you suppose he ever met actress Katharine Hepburn? She was afraid of fire.) Actress Joan Crawford was said to be afraid of germs, too.
- Director Alfred Hitchcock was afraid of eggs. "Blood is jolly, red," he once said. "But egg yolk is yellow, revolting."

JUST CRAZY ABOUT TRAINS

The mode of transportation that inspired a psychological disorder of its very own.

These days we think of trains as old-fashioned and sweet, safer and quainter than the carbon monoxide–spewing, metal monsters we pilot on the highway every day. But it wasn't always that way.

GETTING UP TO SPEED

The first railroad steam engine was built in England in 1804, but it took some time to put together a workable combination of car, track, engine, and fuel. By 1830, American locomotives were able to travel at the astonishing speed of 14 miles per hour. It took two more years for the top speed to reach 60 miles per hour. This may seem rather insignificant to us, but imagine if you'd never gone faster than a horse could gallop—30–45 mph at the most, with the high end being for the fastest horse breed, the thoroughbred. Like most people at the time, you'd feel that trains were shockingly fast and ferocious, belching smoke as they rolled over everything in their path. You, the newly minted passenger, might well be terrified—and with good reason.

MURDER ON THE ANY OLD EXPRESS

The first fatality connected with a passenger train was in 1830, when a British member of Parliament (MP) was run over on the train's opening day festivities. Lacking a whistle, brakes, or even a warning bell (frankly, getting the thing going was more of a priority than stopping it), the train rolled right over the MP as horrified partygoers looked on.

After that, train accidents were a near-daily occurrence. In America, where railroad magnates were pushing for the completion of the Transcontinental Railway, poor tracks, faulty trestles, broken signals, and exploding boilers were commonplace, causing untold numbers of accidents. By 1890, railroads were causing

10,000 deaths and 80,000 injuries a year! In one particularly gruesome incident, a Rhode Island train smashed into a riverbank, and
three of its coaches burst into flames. Newspapers reported the
carnage almost gleefully, describing how passengers were roasted
alive inside the cars.

Even scarier were the dangers of getting too close to the
tracks. Grade-crossing accidents were common—train tracks often
cut right through the center of towns, so panicky citizens would
have to cross directly over them. In just one year, 330 Chicagoans
didn't make the grade-crossing; ditto 124 New Yorkers.

NERVOUS WRECKS

Fearful passengers developed unusual symptoms: confusion, poor
memory, nightmares, sleeplessness, grumpiness, loss of sexual function, altered sense of taste and smell, weight loss—all symptoms
we recognize today as characteristic of classic psychological disorders. British doctor John Eric Erichsen described the syndrome in
1866, calling it "railway spine" and theorized that the damage
came from concussions to the spinal cord.

IT'S ALL IN YOUR MIND

Patients brought cases against the railroads, complaining that due
to being in railway accidents—or, in some instances, just witnessing accidents—they were unable to sleep, felt numbness in
their limbs, or couldn't perform their daily duties. Even with no
physical injury present, the sufferers of what was beginning to be
known as "railway neurosis" were usually rewarded with a financial
settlement.

Did railway neurosis really exist or were the plaintiffs simply
malingering? The railroads maintained the latter. But some began
to wonder—was it possible that an extremely frightening incident
could put such emotional pressure on humans that they could be
negatively affected afterward?

Practitioners in the then-novel field of psychology were
intrigued. Little did they know that they'd discovered what would
now probably be diagnosed as post-traumatic stress disorder (PTSD),
but now it's due to many more horrible and frightening events than
riding on a train.

GUERRILLA WARFARE PART 1

The beginnings of Army Special Operations in America

About 2,000 years ago, the great Chinese military strategist Sun Tzu argued in his book *The Art of War* that the way to defeat a more powerful enemy is to employ your strength to exploit his weaknesses. One way to do that is through guerrilla warfare. Guerrilla—Spanish for "little war"—describes a method of fighting an enemy that employs small groups of irregulars within areas controlled by the enemy. Guerrilla units attack the enemy's communications and supply lines and other small or isolated enemy units.

Chinese Communist leader Mao Zedong described tactics he successfully used against the Japanese during WWII in *On Guerrilla War*: "The enemy advances, we retreat; the enemy camps, we harass; the enemy tires, we attack; the enemy retreats, we pursue."

U.S. ARMY SPECIAL OPERATIONS

Special ops units are elite forces that engage in unconventional (i.e., guerrilla) warfare. Today, the U.S. Army relies heavily on elite units like the Rangers, Green Berets, and Delta Force to accomplish missions requiring smaller, more highly skilled and specialized units than found in the military in general. But guerilla units have been around for a long time.

The European wars of centuries ago were fought by assembling large formations and meeting the enemy on open ground—tactics that were unsuitable for America's limited manpower and vast wilderness. The history of U.S. Special Operations Units begins with the French and Indian War (1754–1763), in which France and England were fighting for control of North America. The objective was to harass the enemy till he decided to leave an area. Small, independent units were much more effective in pursuit of this goal.

ROGERS' RANGERS

The first and most famous of these units was known as Rogers'

When it was **first** established, the U.S. Supreme Court had 6 justices.

Rangers after their commander, Major Robert Rogers. The Rangers wore distinctive green outfits and practiced tactics called Rogers' Rules of Ranging, which the British considered unsporting, if not downright cowardly because they included sound advice such as, "If you are obliged to receive the enemy's fire, fall, or squat down, till it is over; then rise and discharge at them." Major Rogers hired men solely on merit and shocked regular commanders with his use of Native Americans and freed slaves.

Rogers's Rangers roamed the countryside between the New England states and Detroit, Michigan, attacking French army supply convoys and small units. They also sacked and burned French colonial homes and farms. These tactics were effective in forcing the French and their allies to abandon the countryside and concentrate their forces in Quebec City and Montreal (in eastern Canada), and in Detroit. The British and their colonial allies then concentrated their forces to lay siege to each city in turn until it fell and they could move on to the next. By the time Detroit fell, the British had control over all of North America.

THE SWAMP FOX

The greatest guerrilla fighter in the American Revolution was General Francis Marion. He formed Marion's Brigade in 1780, with 150 tattered and penniless patriots. None received pay, food, or even ammunition from the Continental army. But they still managed to terrorize the British Army in South Carolina and Georgia with a series of hit-and-run raids in the face of overwhelming odds. Marion and his men would strike swiftly and then vanish into the swamps. His tactics were so effective that he was nicknamed the Swamp Fox by one very frustrated British general. Later in the war, Marion and his men combined with larger, regular army forces to attack and defeat the British in South Carolina's big cities. In 1781, Marion rescued an American unit that was surrounded by British forces at Parker's Ferry, South Carolina, and received the thanks of Congress for his efforts. His victories eventually drove British forces out of South Carolina entirely.

For more in the series, see "Guerrilla Warfare Part 2"—The Civil War—on page 76.

To celebrate his victory over Roman general Pompey in 48 B.C., Julius Caesar gave a banquet...

THE GOLDEN AGE OF QUACKERY

Go ahead and scoff at the cure-alls and tonics concocted in the 1800s, but know this: taken in large enough quantities, they'd make people forget what ailed them.

You'd think our ancestors had cornered the market on gullibility. They'd take kickapoo juice, swamp root, ocean weed, or just about anything else to cure their ills. They must have been crazy! Or were they?

THE WAY WE WERE

In the 19th century, doctors were few and far between: which may have been a good thing, since medical practices weren't anywhere near an exact science. Patients took their chances: bloodletting, purging, sweating, and freezing were standard operating procedures. Blistering was also in vogue, based on the notion that a body could harbor only one ailment at a time. The theory was that the pain of raw blisters would drive out the pain of just about anything else. Many doctors carried a supply of acid and other skin scorchers. If they ran short, a hot poker from the hearth worked just as well.

ON THE CUTTING EDGE

Amputations were also popular; hence the nickname "sawbones" for doctors. There also was something called "trepanning" that involved drilling holes in the patient's skull to relieve pressure on the brain.

When electricity came into everyday use in the late 1800s, doctors quickly discovered the healthy jolt it could provide to their incomes. One doctor advertised a range of electric brushes, corsets, hats, and belts to cure everything from constipation to malaria.

IS THERE A DOCTOR IN THE HOUSE?

Calling the doctor was a last resort. In some communities, the doctor moonlighted as the local undertaker. Mothers, who made their own home remedies, did most of the doctoring. Sometimes an apothecary, who could grind together a more exotic medication, was consulted. But in the 19th-century spirit of unbridled and unregulated American capitalism, it wasn't long before Mom got a little mass-produced help from the medicine men.

Doctor Chilton offered a guaranteed "Fever and Ague Cure"; Doctor Rowell sold an "Invigorating Tonic...unrivaled as a cathartic"—a fancy name for a bowel loosener. One of the most successful medicine men was Doctor Ayer, who used saturation newspaper ads to create product demand, and mail order to meet it. No prescriptions were needed to buy Ayer's Cherry Pectoral for coughs, colds, asthma, consumption; Ayer's Cathartic Pills for constipation, dyspepsia, biliousness; Ayer's Sarsaparilla, a surefire blood purifier; or Ayer's Hair Vigor to put an end to gray hair.

OPIATE OF THE PEOPLE

Ayer and company had plenty of competition: Parker's Tonic was among the toughest, a cure for just about any internal ailment. The tonic definitely provided a quick fix—it contained 40 percent alcohol. For children's coughs, colds, and runny noses, Allen's Lung Balsam was a staple; for adult ailments there was Perry Davis's All-Purpose Pain-Killer. Doctor Thomas' Eclectic Oil was guaranteed to cure everything from a toothache (five minutes) to a backache (two hours) to lameness (two days) and deafness (two days). All of these tonics shared one characteristic: they contained opium. The Eclectic Oil was also laced with alcohol and chloroform.

SLIME FEVER SYNDROME

This army of humanitarians busily relieving the suffering of the masses contained a few charlatans and swindlers. Take the Killmer brothers, Andral and Joseph, for example. Doctor Killmer's U & O Meadow Plant Anointment allegedly eased suffering from more than 45 ailments—some of which he invented himself. Doctor Killmer's Swamp Root Kidney, Liver, and Bladder Cure worked its magic on pimples, diabetes, syphilis, and something called "internal slime fever." But best of all was Doctor Killmer's Ocean-Weed Heart Remedy, which was advertised to cure "sudden death." Maybe it worked. There's no record of anyone demanding a refund on the money-back guarantee.

MARKETING MAGIC
The Killmer brothers became millionaires, as did several other patent-medicine moguls. These "wholesale druggists" refined print media advertising, product packaging, and direct mail sales—all hallmarks of American mass-market retailing. Their free samples and revolutionary one-time-only introductory offers were very popular. They also came up with the discreet "plain brown wrapper" for milady's feminine products, many of which contained alcohol, opium, morphine, cocaine, and even arsenic (in some beauty aids).

But the newly minted millionaires couldn't have had as much fun as the hucksters who operated the traveling medicine shows that went from town to town like a small carnival, complete with bands, dancers, jugglers, magicians, and skit actors. The entertainment was free, but the inevitable hard sell of exclusive elixirs—a specially blended sarsaparilla, a balsam brew, or a genuine kickapoo cure-all—paid the bills.

SNAKE OIL IN YOUR FACE
Snake oil cures were very popular on the medicine show circuit until exposés by muckraking reporters decreed them to be not only useless but also lacking in authentic snake oil—about the same time that the term *snake oil salesman* took on its shifty connotation.

But that did nothing to stop the self-styled Rattlesnake King, Clark Stanley, from selling his snake oil at the 1893 World Columbian Exposition in Chicago. His routine was to kill and process the rattlesnakes right in front of potential customers.

THE GOVERNMENT GETS IN THE ACT
By the turn of the century, the great cure-all period was drawing to a close. Germs and bacteria had been discovered; bona fide medical doctoring was on the rise. There were pill-making machines that could turn out millions of pills daily, and some large wholesale drug companies were evolving into pharmaceutical giants and retail chains. In 1906 the federal Pure Food and Drug Act was passed; advertising codes of ethics and ingredient labeling weren't far behind.

Now the ailing public had to go to a drugstore to get their cure. The soda fountain—a fixture in most drugstores—served mineral water (which was thought to be curative) from carbonation machines. Though the medicinal connection withered away, when Prohibition was enacted, the soda fountain's success was assured—at least for a little while. Root beer and ice cream sodas were the order of the day.

Unfortunately, in the long run, soda fountains couldn't compete with the money brought in by shelves and shelves of mass-produced cold, headache, and heartburn relievers—to say nothing of the beauty aids, school supplies, canned goods, and batteries. Welcome to the drugstore of today.

* * * * *

WE'LL DRINK TO THAT

Why do people clink glasses before drinking alcohol with one another? This tradition started in medieval days when some people had the unfriendly habit of spiking wine with poison. To show that a drink wasn't poisoned, a host would pour part of the guest's wine into his own glass and drink it first. If the guest wanted to show that he trusted his host and that actual sampling wasn't necessary, he would just touch glasses when the host offered his glass for a sample. Hence, clinking glasses became a sign of trust. Now it's a toast to friendship and good health.

- The word alcohol comes from Arabic *al kohl*, which translates to *the essence*.

- Montana, in 1926, was the first state to stop its enforcement of Prohibition.

- Mississippi became the last state to repeal statewide Prohibition in 1966.

- Rhode Island never ratified the 18th amendment.

- An act of Congress designated bourbon as the United State's official spirit.

- An insatiable craving for alcohol is known as *dipsomania*.

HOLLYWOOD REWRITES HISTORY

*Nothing good on TV? Rent some of these classic movies
and see if you can spot the flubs.*

CAMELOT
Okay, so maybe the mythical kingdom of Camelot didn't really exist. But if it did, it probably didn't have a supply of flesh-colored bandages, like the one King Arthur (Richard Harris) is wearing on the side of his neck while stumbling through the forest looking for Merlin.

FIELD OF DREAMS
Ray Liotta plays Shoeless Joe Jackson as a right-handed batter. The experts know better: the real Shoeless Joe was a southpaw.

ONE MILLION YEARS B.C.
Raquel Welch and her cave woman friends are wearing false eyelashes, which was a fad when the film came out in 1966, but probably not the fashion in prehistoric days. But we could be wrong—that's why they call it *pre*-history.

THE SEARCHERS
Returning Civil War veteran John Wayne gives his niece a medal that he supposedly won in the war. In actuality, the Confederate Congress approved the design of a medal and a badge of distinction, but there's no record of one ever having been made. A small number of medals were made and awarded for certain battles, but of the few that were awarded by the end of the war, none were of the same design as Wayne's.

TORA! TORA! TORA!
When the Japanese planes fly over Oahu en route to Pearl Harbor, you can distinctly see a white cross that memorializes

---

...Titled *De Re Coquinaria*, it described the feasts enjoyed by the Emperor Claudius.

the first casualties of World War II; it was erected in 1962. A bit later, in the background, is Tripler Army Hospital, which was built after the war.

A BEAUTIFUL MIND
And for fans of the minutest minutiae, Alicia Nash (Jennifer Connelly), who plays a 1950s housewife to hubby mathematician John Nash (Russell Crowe), owns an orange Tupperware bowl that, according to at least one former Tupperware lady, was not introduced until the mid-to-late 1970s.

* * * * *

LIGHTS, ACTION—OOPS!

The Ten Commandments (1956)—a blind man is seen wearing a watch.
Easy Rider (1969)—Peter Fonda's watch changes from a Rolex to a Timex.
Rear Window (1954)—Jimmy Stewart's cast switches from his left to his right leg.
The Bible (1966)—Adam has a belly button.
Butch Cassidy and the Sundance Kid (1969)—Sundance fires off 17 shots from two six-shooters.
The Two Jakes (1990 sequel to *Chinatown*)—There's a shot in which star Jack Nicholson strolls past an ATM. Unfortunately, the film is set in the late 1940s, about 30 years before ATMs were installed in banks.
Pretty Woman (1990)—An usher calls Julia Roberts "Julia" instead of "Vivian."

FORBIDDEN LOVE

*Their story rivals Romeo and Juliet's for drama,
but the ending is a lot more gruesome.*

Once upon a time, before Spain existed, the area that's
now Spain and Portugal was composed of a number of
small kingdoms: Aragon, Castile, Catalonia, Leon,
Granada, and Portugal. Strong alliances were vital to these kingdoms to maintaining autonomy and avoiding wars. And what
better way to ensure the strength of an alliance than to marry
the heir to the throne of one kingdom to the daughter of the
ruler of another?

LOVE AT FIRST SIGHT

Portugal and Castile were in a permanent state of war. In 1340,
King Afonso of Portugal decided to form a union with the king of
Castile. King Afonso's son, Dom Pedro, needed a wife and a search
narrowed the choice down to Donna Constança, the daughter of a
Castilian nobleman.

When the bride arrived in Portugal, young Dom Pedro took
one look at her and thought, "Not bad." But then he saw—among
her ladies-in-waiting—the beautiful Inês de Castro and immediately was smitten.

HEAD OVER HEELS

Dom Pedro and Inês soon became lovers. By all accounts, they
conducted their affair very openly, making the king and the rest of
the court very unhappy; such openness between lovers was frowned
upon. And, to make things worse, Inês was his cousin. As a result,
the king ordered Inês to be exiled to Coimbra, more than 100
miles (161 km) away.

DUTY CALLS

Although his affections lay elsewhere, Dom Pedro couldn't forget
his duty to Portugal and, in due course, Donna Constança produced a son, Fernando of Portugal. In what romantics call divine
intervention, the future queen died in childbirth, and the way was

---

...Dick Syme, East Hampton's official whipper, was paid 3 shillings for each person whipped.

now open for the lovers. Dom Pedro, against the specific orders of his father and court advisors, moved in with Inês.

HEAD OVER THERE

Over the course of their affair, Ines had also borne children to Dom Pedro—four of them. But King Afonso wanted to preserve Fernando's claim to the throne. So, on the morning of January 7, 1355, after Dom Pedro had left to go hunting, three men entered the palace where the lovers lived and decapitated Inês.

Dom Pedro was so enraged at discovering that the love of his life had been killed by orders of his father that he went to war against him. But he made peace with the ailing Afonso when he realized that a civil war would make the kingdom vulnerable to takeover by the other kingdoms.

REVENGE IS SWEET—AND MESSY

There's more. When Pedro became king in 1357, he immediately went after Inês's killers. Of the three, one was lucky enough to escape. The other two were executed in a horrible fashion—they had their hearts removed while they were still alive.

In 1360, Pedro announced that he had secretly married Inês some years before (and had witnesses to prove it). In her honor, he ordered that two marble tombs be built in the Monastery of Alcobaça, one for himself and one for Inês. The two tombs were built so that the lovers lie feet to feet; so, when the time comes for them to rise and ascend to heaven, the first thing they'll see is each other.

BURIED IN STYLE

As soon as Inês's tomb was finished, her body was exhumed from her humble burial place and transported to her new marble tomb. Her funeral was attended by the whole royal court and countless commoners. The tragic story has inspired writers and poets throughout the ages: Voltaire, Victor Hugo, and maybe even William Shakespeare.

The word "daisy" comes from the Old English *daeges eage*, meaning "the eye of the sun."

TALKIN' TRASH

Uncle John is proud to present (ta-da!) the history of garbage.

For as long as there have been people, there has been garbage. The simplest way to get rid of something was to leave it where it lay and walk away, which is what many early cultures did, moving to a different location when the trash got too high or too unbearable. The Mayan people threw the things they couldn't reuse into what was an ancient version of a municipal dump. Some Bronze Age people simply made new floors by adding layers of clay when the old floors of their homes became too littered with debris. Ancient Jews near Jerusalem burned their refuse.

THE FIRST DUMPSTERS?
In 1757, Ben Franklin introduced America's first citywide street-cleaning service in Philadelphia, Pennsylvania, an idea that eventually made its way to New York and other cities. At about the same time, urban Americans started digging pits for their garbage, rather than simply tossing it in the streets or alleys. Privy pits, if they were dug deep enough, could do double duty as Dumpsters (if you'll excuse the puns). Larger pieces of junk, like the hulls of boats, could be used to build up the earth near rivers and streams to keep water at bay.

THIS? IT'S JUST AN OLD RAG!
Remember last week's grocery list? After you got home, you crumpled it up and used it to play wastepaper basketball. It's only paper, and paper is cheap, right? Well, that wasn't always so. Paper used to be made of cloth that was no longer good. Problem was, cloth was used until there was almost nothing left.

Cloth was a valuable commodity in the mid-1800s. Clothing was mended until it couldn't be mended any more, and even wealthy women were acquainted with a needle and thread. When an adult's article of clothing couldn't be mended one more time, a child's outfit would be made from it. Quilts and rugs were made from scraps, and the end of the line for Grandma's old dress was the ragman, who sold the rags to paper mills, newspapers, and bookmakers.

Wood pulp paper was developed in 1847. It made paper cheaper to manufacture. But within a few decades, there was so much wastepaper cluttering businesses and homes that paper recycling became common by the turn of the century—1900, that is.

THE ORIGINAL SACK DRESS

Before about 1910, Americans didn't throw away a lot because there wasn't much that was considered garbage. Aside from liquids and medicines in glass bottles, most food products and household items were sold in bulk. Pickles and dry goods like crackers were sold in barrels or crates; people bought only what they needed and empty crates would later be salvaged for everything from furniture to kindling.

Flour, chicken feed, and cornmeal came in colorful sacks that could become a dress for the lady of the house or clothes for the young'uns. Food scraps would be used in other dishes, given to servants, or fed to the livestock. Bits of paper and wood scraps kept the house warm with the fireplace roaring. Possessions that were still useful but no longer needed were stored or given to others to use—and broken things were fixed (what a concept!). Even ashes from the fireplace were used in making soap.

EARLY DUMPSTER DIVERS

As Americans became more affluent and began to discard more items, poor immigrants began making their livings scrounging for choice items that could be reused or sold. Trash became a class issue; specifically, garbage was something the lower classes used to make money. In 1919, the Chicago Juvenile Protection Association noted that scavenging children (who should have been in school) were pawing through trash—not to help their families, but to get spending money. Although in New York City, author and photographer Jacob Riis sadly noted boys who sorted trash for their families who lived in squalid shacks, built conveniently on the dump sites. (For more on Jacob Riis, see *Uncle John's Bathroom Reader Plunges into Great Lives*, pp. 142–144.)

THERE'S GOLD IN THEM THAR TRASH HEAPS

While scavenging kept families in poverty from going hungry or totally homeless, it began to play a smaller role in the history of trash as time went on. Laws were passed to prohibit dumping garbage at will—but most Americans ignored them and threw away their trash wherever it seemed convenient. Landowners saw dumping as a right and were resentful of reformers. Eventually, it became obvious that there was a major need for change. Ladies' groups in major cities lobbied city officials to ensure that municipal contractors did their jobs.

LET'S SEE IF IT FLOATS
But all that trash had to go somewhere. Dumping it in waterways, rivers, and in the ocean was what many cities did. And although it was a quick fix for the garbage problem, it was controversial almost from the beginning. Beaches were ruined, water was contaminated, and the smell had to have been unbelievable. Residents of Milwaukee, Wisconsin; Long Island, New York; and New Orleans, Louisiana started to complain. In many cases, garbage was dumped purposely in wetlands in order to shore them up or create new land.

BURN, BABY, BURN
In the latter part of the 1800s, many cities in Europe used incineration to get rid of garbage. The idea spread to America when a model incinerator was exhibited during Chicago's 1893 Columbian Exposition. Sanitary engineer Colonel William Morse delivered a paper, at the World's Public Health Congress during the Chicago World's Fair, singing the praises of the incinerator. Before the century was over, most big cities had installed them. Problem solved? Not exactly. The smell was oppressive, and there was considerable labor involved to keep them running.

Reduction, a method of chemically separating grease and water from trash, was tried, but that also failed because of the smell and the high cost. By the 1930s, sanitary landfills became the (cheaper) preferred method of disposal—and still are.

USE IT UP, WEAR IT OUT
So if you think you're doing something chic, modern, and environmentally friendly when you separate your aluminum cans from your glass bottles from your plastic from your newspapers, remember that recycling is nothing new. Rags became paper. A worn-out

The system was created by Dionysius Exiguus, also known as "Denis the Little."

leather harness became a new belt. Tires were recycled during World War II, as were household grease and scrap metal.

And you know that great recycling bin idea? George Waring Jr., New York City's commissioner of street cleaning, thought of it first. In 1896, he instituted a program for New Yorkers to separate their trash into three containers to maximize reuse of what was useable, and to make money for the city.

Still think you're doing something modern when you recycle? Maybe not, but you're doing something good—and that's a notion you can't discard.

* * * * *

"I have a cat named Trash. In the current political climate it would seem that if I were trying to sell him (at least to a Computer Scientist), I would not stress that he is gentle to humans and is self-sufficient, living mostly on field mice. Rather, I would argue that he is object-oriented."—Roger King

ANOTHER WARING WITH A GOOD IDEA

Wisconsin engineer Stephen Poplawski set out to invent a gadget to make his favorite drink, a malted milk shake. He got the patent for his "vibrator" in 1922. With "an agitating element mounted in the bottom of a cup," it was eventually renamed "blender" and did a nice business in soda fountains.

Enter bandleader Fred Waring, who was looking for a way to mix *his* favorite drink—the daiquiri. Fred and his partner, inventor Fred Osius, improved on Poplawski's mixer and called it the Waring Blender. It looked like Poplawski was one-upped until his company was bought by John Oster in 1946. Oster engineers added a few extra touches and the Osterizer was born.

Beginning in the late 1950s, in what was called "the Battle of the Buttons," the humble blender went from the two speeds of "low" and "high" through "chop," "grate," "liquefy," and so on, until in 1968 a housewife could buy a blender with as many as 15 different buttons.

THE MIGHTY PEN

Novel ways that changed the world. There are books that explain history—obviously we love those around here—but what about books that make history?

OLIVER TWIST

The Times: Victorian England's workhouses put poor people to work in return for housing and food (but deliberately not enough to content them with their lot in life—the idea was to get them out and looking for jobs). Workhouses were grim prisons that punished people for their poverty, which middle-class society claimed came from laziness, immorality, and weakness. Young children weren't cut any slack, either. Factory owners looking for cheap labor apprenticed workhouse children as young as eight and paid them little more than room and board—while working them up to 16 hours a day.

The Author: Charles Dickens was 12 years old when his carefree childhood came to an end because his father couldn't pay his debts and was sent to prison. The boy left school to help support the family and worked long hours in a boot-blacking factory. He returned to school when his father received an inheritance that freed him from debtor's prison. But Charles Dickens never forgot his close brush with a life of drudgery. Protecting oppressed children became his mission in life. In 1837, his second novel, *Oliver Twist*, took on the subject of the exploitation of poor children living in the workhouses.

The Tale: Oliver's mother dies in childbirth, and he becomes a workhouse orphan. The orphans are cruelly starved, and when Oliver Twist politely asks for more food, he's branded a troublemaker and treated even more harshly. Sent to work for an undertaker who beats him, Oliver escapes to London. There he falls victim to a criminal gang that uses boys for pickpocketing and burglary. Oliver's good character (and a lucky inheritance) helps bring him a happy ending.

The Change: The novel was so popular that nearly everyone in England and America came to know of Oliver's troubles—and through him, the plight of any child trapped in the workhouse system. The book fueled a reform movement that gradually forced the government to pass laws protecting children from harsh working conditions. Before *Oliver Twist*, the Poor Law of 1834, which Benjamin Disraeli called an announcement that "poverty is a crime," had instituted the workhouse system. After the novel was published, the plight of hungry, working children could no longer be ignored—even though it still took decades for workhouses to completely disappear.

UNCLE TOM'S CABIN

The Times: In 1850, slavery was a way of life in the Deep South. There, African Americans worked without pay on large plantations, on small farms, and in factories, suffering from overwork, punishment, and a lack of decent living quarters. They also lived in fear of being sold. Southerners claimed that slaveholders tried to keep families together, but the painful reality was that children of slaves were often separated from their families and never saw them again.

The Author: Harriet Beecher Stowe was a New England writer who was also the mother of seven children. She'd visited the South, had seen slavery firsthand, and had found it cruel—but it was a personal tragedy that led her to write a book about it. Stowe's 18-month-old son Charlie had died from cholera, and she was still grieving when she heard a story about a fugitive slave escaping to Canada with her baby so it wouldn't be sold away from her. Stowe felt immediate empathy and began writing a novel that included the story of a slave mother desperate to keep her child. In 1852, *Uncle Tom's Cabin, or Life Among the Lowly* was published.

The Tale: The story's hero is Uncle Tom, an elderly slave who is about to be sold because of his owner's debts. Tom's friend and fellow slave Eliza takes her baby and makes a harrowing escape to Canada, but Tom stays behind. Tom is bought and sold again, ending up under the thumb of Simon Legree, a cruel overseer who mistreats slaves: "Use up, and buy more's my way." Tom is a good

---

Romans did not eat sitting up—that was considered extremely bad manners.

Christian who forgives the evil Legree—even for the beating that eventually kills him.

The Change: *Uncle Tom's Cabin* may not have been subtle literature, but it was an instant best seller. In its first year of publication, 300,000 copies were snapped up. "Tom-mania" became the order of the day. Fans sang and played Uncle Tom songs, trotting off to a theater or traveling show to see a stage version.

Today the phrase *Uncle Tom* is a pejorative term for a black who gives undue subservience to a white person. In his own time, the character sparked so much will to fight that the book is often included in lists of causes of the Civil War. Tom's fictional sufferings polarized the country. Uncle Tom fans became abolitionists, furious at the slaveholders and willing to fight to end slavery. When President Lincoln met Harriet Beecher Stowe in 1864, he summed it up by saying, "So you're the little woman who made this big war."

THE JUNGLE

The Times: At the turn of the 20th century, U.S. capitalism was king. American companies were free to advertise and sell their products without any inspections or interference from the federal government. When it came to food, the rule was buyer beware, which could make eating a risky proposition. For example, during the Spanish-American War, spoiled meat treated with dangerous chemicals was sold to the U.S. Army. What the soldiers called "embalmed beef" is estimated to have killed 3,000 enlisted men.

The Author: Upton Beall Sinclair was born into a family of extremes. His mother was the daughter of a well-to-do railroad executive. His father was an alcoholic and salesman who could barely keep his family in low-class boarding houses. Whenever Dad drank the rent money, Mom took young Upton home to her family, where they lived it up in luxury. Like Dickens, young Sinclair knew what it was like to go from being comfortable to being desperate. He too vowed to help the poor.

Taking an assignment for a Socialist newspaper, Sinclair showed up in Chicago to research the experiences of immigrant workers in the stockyards. The idealistic and pro-Socialist author

Romans ate in a reclined position on couches around the table.

wanted to bring to the world's attention the exploited workers who suffered and died in dangerous conditions. And while he was at it, he threw in some choice descriptions of the unsavory practices of the meat-packing industry. His angry novel was published in 1906.

The Tale: Jurgis Rudkus brings his family from Lithuania to Chicago to find the American dream. Jurgis gets a job in the stockyards, where his dream becomes a nightmare. Even with the entire family working, they can't get out of poverty so bleak that it kills Jurgis's wife and son.

The meat-packing houses are described as gruesome places: rats and their droppings are shoveled into sausage makings, dirt and guts from the floor are made into "potted ham," and workers falling into rendering vats are sometimes unnoticed until they emerge as lard!

The Change: *The Jungle* was a sensation—though not exactly the one Sinclair wanted. President Theodore Roosevelt received 100 letters a day demanding reforms in the meat-packing industry. *The Jungle* made Roosevelt feel a little queasy himself; he called upon Congress to pass a law establishing the Food and Drug Administration, which set up federal inspection standards for meat.

Thanks in large part to *The Jungle*, Congress passed the 1906 Pure Food and Drug Act. But the socialism that Sinclair was pushing didn't take hold. He'd intended to make the public fighting mad, but instead, his readers were gagging. "I aimed at the public's heart," he later wrote, "and by accident hit it in the stomach."

* * * * *

"There are books of which the backs and covers are by far the best parts."—Charles Dickens's character, Oliver Twist

"Common sense is seeing things as they are; and doing things as they ought to be."—Harriet Beecher Stowe

The Circus Maximus (for horse and chariot racing) could hold up to 250,000 people.

MISSION IMPOSSIBLE

Saving the forgotten soldiers of World War II

Nearly everybody knows about the bombing of Pearl Harbor. But few folks know about the bombing of Clark Field in the Philippines that happened only hours later. The French resistance is legendary—especially in bad movies. So where are the movies about the heroes of the Filipino resistance? And while Hitler's concentration camps deserve their worldwide infamy, did you know that Allied troops in Philippine POW camps suffered starvation, torture, and outright murder?

If World War II in the Philippines is neglected in the history books, it was worse while the battles actually raged. Thousands of the USAFFE (United States Armed Forces in the Far East) figured they'd become "the forgotten."

NO MAMA, NO PAPA, NO UNCLE SAM

Within weeks of Pearl Harbor, the Japanese Imperial Army pushed American and Filipino troops out of Manila. They were forced to the jungles of the Bataan Peninsula and the Island of Corregidor where they were cut off from supplies. Hungry and suffering from tropical disease, the troops were promised by the commanding General Douglas MacArthur that "thousands of planes" with food, medicine, and reinforcements were on their way. But no help had arrived by March when MacArthur was ordered to leave and set up a command in Australia.

MacArthur promised, "I shall return." But the soldiers were cynical about promises. They already had a song that went in part:

No Mama, no Papa, no Uncle Sam
No aunts, no uncles, no nephews, no nieces
No pills, no planes, no artillery pieces
And nobody gives a d—

By April, Allied losses and the lack of supplies in Bataan were so bad that General King, the local commander, ordered the surrender of more than 70,000 troops (Filipinos and Americans)—the

The Villa Romana del Casale has famous mosaics showing Roman girls in bikinis.

largest American army in history to surrender. Having made plans to accept the surrender of about 25,000 soldiers, the Japanese were overwhelmed with POWs.

THE HIKE

Food, water, and housing for all the unexpected prisoners were never supplied. Less fortunate than the men on Corregidor who surrendered a few months later, the exhausted, sick men pouring out of the Bataan jungles were force-marched through the heat on what survivors called "the Hike." History named it the Bataan Death March after thousands of USAFFE soldiers died from deprivation, disease, or simply execution; all stragglers were killed. Prisoners who reached the squalid prison camps alive realized that hunger, thirst, sickness, and brutal treatment would now be routine.

Imperial Army soldiers had been trained to commit suicide to save their families from the "dishonor" of surrender. Ready to take their own lives, they had little concern for the lives of a dishonored enemy. Still, deadly as they were, Philippine POW camps weren't extermination camps—not until December 1944.

By then the Allies were winning battle after battle and MacArthur was making good on his promise to "return." Japanese commanders of POW camps were given the option of killing their prisoners rather than return them to the Allies. On December 14, guards at Palawan prison camp, fearing defeat, herded nearly 150 prisoners into bunkers and set the bunkers on fire.

A SECRET MISSION

MacArthur's forces invaded the Philippines in January. As they advanced, word reached General Kreuger of the Sixth Army about the Cabanatuan POW camp north of Manila, where 516 British and American prisoners still survived. Many of them were survivors of the Hike. Kreuger ordered a rescue mission.

But how to do it? Cabanatuan was 30 miles (48 km) inside enemy lines and heavily guarded. Surprise was essential: the Americans had to take control before the guards had time to kill the prisoners. But the prison was on open ground, and Caucasian U.S. soldiers didn't exactly blend in with the Filipino community. And if the raid was successful, how could they move the prisoners out of enemy territory? The survivors in Cabanatuan were living skeletons who could barely walk.

But after all those soldiers had suffered, Kreuger refused to let the men of Cabanatuan die. To accomplish his mission impossible, the general called on the Rangers.

NO MORE MULE SKINNING

The Sixth Army Rangers started out as "mule skinners," leading mules that packed heavy artillery through the mountains of New Guinea. The army decided pack mules were obsolete, but they kept the guys—sending them to train under Lieutenant Colonel Mucci. Under Mucci's tough regime, homegrown farm boys became experts at hand-to-hand combat, bayonet and knife fighting, and marksmanship—elite fighters.

Mucci asked for volunteers who would, "die fighting rather than let harm come to those prisoners." Every single Ranger volunteered. And on January 28, 1945, they set out on their liberation mission. Guiding them secretively through rice paddies and cogon weeds were the Alamo Scouts (a Sixth Army outfit that gathered intelligence behind enemy lines) and Captain Eduardo Joson's group of Filipino guerrillas. The Scouts would provide information on the prison layout and the number and positions of the guards. Joson's guerillas would cover the Rangers during the attack and—if all went well—on the return to base camp too.

GO DIRECTLY TO JAIL

After close calls with enemy patrols and acquiring plenty of blisters, 120 Rangers and their guides ended their march successfully five miles from Cabanatuan. But Scouts brought bad news of heavy Japanese activity in and around the prison. A surprise attack and safe escape seemed more impossible than ever.

Then salvation appeared in the form of Captain Juan Pajota. The USAFFE guerilla captain had learned that the Rangers planned the prison break that night. Pajota and his men had arrived to help, but the Captain warned the Rangers to wait 24 hours, since many of the Japanese would be moving on. Mucci didn't like a delay, but he eventually agreed to it—and to some of Pajota's more unusual ideas too.

Sundiata founded the great trading empire of Mali in the 13th century.

JAIL BREAK

On the evening of January 30, Filipino guerillas cut the phone lines to Manila. Captain Joson and Captain Pajota's combined forces of about 300 Filipino guerillas blocked the east and west ends of the road that passed the POW camp, isolating the camp from enemy forces. But as the Rangers crawled the last mile through an open field, they knew the guards would spot them.

Suddenly, a P-61 night fighter or "black widow" buzzed Cabanatuan POW camp. The plane (Pajota's idea) had been requested by Mucci. While the Japanese guards stared up at the sky, wondering if the plane would crash, the Rangers crawled into position.

They divided up, some going to the main front gate and hiding until the others reached the back entrance, where signaling shots were fired. Then locks were shot off and the Americans moved inside the prison, guns blazing. They quickly overwhelmed the guards and the raid went like clockwork—until the evacuation.

Hearing gunfire and sure they'd be murdered, many POWs hid. Others, out of touch for years and nearly blind from starvation, didn't recognize the Ranger's uniforms or weapons. Some POWs fled at the sight of their saviors; a few believed it was a trick and refused to go anywhere.

Pushing some prisoners toward freedom and carrying others, the Rangers hustled them to a site where Filipino civilians waited with Pajota's final gift—ox carts pulled by tamed carabao (water buffalo) for the prisoners to ride in. As Filipino guerillas bravely held off the Japanese, and the Scouts stayed behind to fight off any retaliating Japanese, a strange band of prisoners, carabao, and former mule-skinners traveled all night to the safety of the Allied front lines. About 1,000 people, including the U.S. Army, Filipino guerrillas, and unarmed Filipino civilians, had worked to set them free, producing one of the most spectacular rescues in military history.

Eventually 272 American survivors of Cabanatuan sailed into the San Francisco Bay. Greeting them were crowds massed on the Golden Gate Bridge. As the former POWs sailed under the bridge, the cheering crowds tossed gifts (coins, show tickets, and even lingerie) down to the deck of their ship. These heroes of the Philippines hadn't been forgotten after all.

Confucius (551–479 B.C.) was also called Kong Zi, or "Master Kong."

PARADING THROUGH THE AMERICAS

The first parade may have been a hunting party returning to its cave, laden with fresh meat. Certainly that would have been cause for celebration.

1700S: *ERIN GO BRAGH!*

"Ireland forever!" The first St. Patrick's Day Parade was held in New York City in 1762 or 1766. Given the rather "fluid" nature of postparade celebrations, confusion over the exact date is no surprise. The 1766 date sticks out for officialdom, though, because it was the first of the parades when a military unit led off.

Today, more than 150,000 participants march down Fifth Avenue every March 17. The Ancient Order of Hibernians is there and, marching along with them to the cadence of drums and bagpipes, are 30 Irish county societies and Irish nationalist groups of almost every stripe. The pride, the pageantry, and the color—who needs floats?

1837: FAT TUESDAY

Mardi Gras came to New Orleans in 1743, but it wasn't until 1837 that New Orleans had its first official Mardi Gras parade. Early on, Mardi Gras was celebrated with costume balls by the well-to-do and chaotic street revelry by the lesser mortals, everyone wearing masks. Bands played on most main street corners, and in 1835, the first float appeared. Maybe the float was what started the official organizing of the celebrated parade. In any case, the Mardi Gras Parade never looked back.

1886: THE CANYON OF HEROES

The ancient Romans had laid out a very specific route for victory marches in Rome. When New Yorkers decided they needed one too, they chose Wall and Broad streets, in the financial district, maybe because it was the only area that could provide instant decorations—tons of wastepaper and ticker tape.

The first ticker-tape parade was for the dedication of the Statue

---

Crossing the Gobi, Genghis Khan's troops survived by drinking their horses' blood.

of Liberty in 1886, a spur-of-the-moment affair so enjoyed by New Yorkers that they decided to do it again and again...and again.

Since then, ticker tape has deluged political leaders, victorious generals, sports champions, and individual heroes. The all-time multiple ticker-tape honoree, as might be guessed, is the New York Yankees. By 2000, they had seven parades to their credit. Among individuals, Commander Richard E. Byrd had three and Amelia Earhart had two. Pioneer flyers and astronauts have been honored many times. Then there's the parade puzzler—in 1910, former president Theodore Roosevelt was honored with a parade upon returning from an African safari. He must have brought back some pretty remarkable trophies.

1890: COMING UP ROSES

Parades are about celebration and color. Some, with luck, are also about profit. The Valley Hunt Club of Pasadena, California, wanted to show the world—or at least the colder regions of the United States—the warmth and fertility of Southern California. So was born the Tournament of Roses in 1890, a parade followed by sports competitions, held on New Year's Day.

At first, the Rose Parade was just an introduction to the main events, exciting happenings like ostrich races—once even a race between an elephant and a camel. In 1902, organizers tried a college football game. Alas, Michigan mashed Stanford, 49-0, which was hugely embarrassing to the Californians. The organizers made a $3,000-plus (over 2,400 euros) profit that year, but it would be 16 years before they'd try a football game again. By then, the Rose Parade had become the main event, attracting tens of thousands of onlookers to watch its magnificent flower-decked floats and marching bands.

1901: MUM'S THE WORD

The Swedes and the English brought the mummer tradition to the United States, most specifically to the Philadelphia, Pennsylvania, area. Groups of men (no women allowed!) presented costume plays, going from house to house reciting their parts in hopes of some reward: money or some kind of seasonal treat.

Nearly every January 1 since 1901, they've paraded through the city in outrageous costumes and in three main divisions:

Chess is a descendant of an Indian game known as "Chatur-Anga," played in the 7th century.

clown, fancy dress, and string band. ("Oh, Dem Golden Slippers" is the song that the string band is best known for.) Participation is now open to all ages and sexes. More than $400,000 (330,497 euros) in prizes is up for grabs each year, but the prizes don't nearly cover the expense of putting together a winning string band, which can run to a cool $150,000 (almost 124,000 euros).

1905: HERE COMES SANTA CLAUS

The legendary Canadian department store—Eaton's, in Toronto, Ontario—started their annual Santa Claus Parade (featuring one float) in 1905 to attract customers to the store. As it happened, the thousands who jammed Toronto's Yonge Street (for more on this incredible street, see pp. 381) for the parade took their Christmas shopping business to an archrival because, with Santa installed on the premises, Eaton's was too crowded for comfortable shopping. (Needless to say, the competition loved the parade.) Eaton's kept at it anyway, for more than 75 years, retiring from the parade business in 1982.

Today, its more than 1,700 participants ride on more than 24 floats and march in more than 24 bands. And Toronto's Santa Claus Parade is proud to call itself the longest parade in North America.

1924: MIRACLE ON 34TH STREET

In the 1920s, the first-generation immigrants who worked in Macy's department store in New York City wanted to celebrate their new American holiday—Thanksgiving—with the kind of festivals they loved in Europe. So they dressed up as clowns and sheiks and knights and cowboys, borrowed 25 live animals from the Central Park Zoo, and marched from 145th Street to 34th Street, along with floats and bands, to the delight of 250,000 onlookers.

The big balloons that the parade is famous for debuted in 1927—Felix the Cat among them. The parade was canceled during World War II but resumed in 1945—and was televised (in New York) for the first time that year. Today, the balloon count hovers around 25 and includes—depending on the year—Jeeves (of Ask Jeeves), Kermit the Frog, and (is he still around?) Barney.

Betsy Ross's pew was next to George Washington's at Philadelphia's Christ Church.

1932: SAMBA CITY

The Portuguese in Rio de Janeiro who wanted to celebrate Carnival took to the streets, wearing gaudy, sequined costumes and dancing to bands. In 1932, in an effort to quell the mob scene, the city turned Carnival into a parade, with bands, floats, dancers, harlequins, clowns, and spectacular samba clubs. The Carnival Parade is now the highlight of a three-day festival that attracts people from throughout the world.

1958: GUNG HAY FAT CHOY!

"Happy Chinese New Year!" Almost every great parade can trace its traditions back centuries—some to the Druids, others to the old gods. But when it comes to reaching back to ancient roots, it's hard to beat the Chinese. Their new year's celebration can be traced back thousands of years, almost into prehistory.

Even so, the most elaborate Chinese New Year Parade in North America didn't come into its own until 1958 in San Francisco, when the local Chinatown Chamber of Commerce took over the arrangements. The parade (usually held in early February) consists of all the traditional hoopla done up properly in Chinese cultural motif, with firecrackers popping all along the parade route. For pure awe, it's Gum Lung, a 200-foot (61-m) dragon, drawn through the streets by 100 members of White Crane, a San Francisco martial arts group.

NOT EVERYBODY LOVES A PARADE

The citizens of ancient Rome loved the victory parades of their successful generals. These were affairs with strict rules, blending religion, feasting, and politics. One custom, as part of each parade, was to enchain the defeated ruler and march him or her along the parade route, then execute the luckless soul. Among defeated rulers was Cleopatra, and she definitely *didn't* love a parade. When she heard she was to be the star attraction of Octavius's victory parade through Rome, she opted for the asp.

* * * * *

"Parades should be classed as a nuisance and participants should be subject to a term in prison."—Will Rogers

King Edward "the Confessor" was so named because of his construction of Westminster Abbey.

BILLY, DON'T BE A HERO

How one man's life was ruined—just because he saved the life of the president of the United States.

On September 22, 1975, Oliver "Billy" Sipple was walking by San Francisco's Saint Francis Hotel where a crowd of about 3,000 people was hoping to catch a glimpse of President Gerald Ford. As Sipple moved toward the front of the crowd, the president emerged and started walking toward a waiting limousine. Suddenly, the middle-aged woman standing next to Sipple pulled a pistol out of her raincoat and pointed it in the president's direction. Without thinking, Sipple grabbed the woman's arm just as her finger squeezed the trigger. His action threw off Sara Jane Moore's aim just enough to cause her to miss her intended target; the bullet flew wide of its mark and into the side of a building. Sipple wrestled the woman to the ground, and he prevented her from getting off a second shot by shoving his hand into the firing mechanism.

A MAN OF ACTION

The instinct had come naturally to Sipple; he was an ex-marine who'd fought in Vietnam. The 33-year-old Sipple had been wounded in action and given an honorable discharge in 1970. Since his release, he'd been in and out of Veterans Administration (VA) hospitals. At the time of the assassination attempt, he'd been listed as 100 percent disabled on psychological grounds and had been living on his veteran's disability pay between jobs.

RELUCTANT HERO

Sipple's heroism made him an instant celebrity-hero. The media didn't have to dig too deeply to find out that Billy Sipple was a homosexual, even though he was still "in the closet," and no one outside his small circle of friends knew of his sexual orientation—including, and especially, his parents.

Billy managed to keep that closet door closed for a few days—

Poland is named for the Slavic tribe Polane.

until a radical gay activist named Harvey Milk (who was publicly assassinated three years later, but that's another story) took it upon himself to out Sipple, to "help break the stereotype of homosexuals" and to show the world that gay guys could be tough guys too.

So whether he wanted to or not—and he didn't—Sipple became the poster boy for the gay liberation movement. Prominent San Francisco columnist Herb Caen published the Sipple story, as did six other newspapers. One of them was the *Detroit Free Press*, the newspaper in Billy's hometown. As a result, his parents were harassed by their neighbors; the next time Billy called home, his mother hung up on him. When Mrs. Sipple died in 1979, his father still refused to have any contact with him.

ALL DOWNHILL FROM THERE
Sipple sued the seven newspapers, but the suits were dismissed. Sipple's alcoholism worsened. He was fitted with a pacemaker, his weight ballooned up to 300 pounds, and he became paranoid and suicidal. In 1989, at age 47, he was found dead in his $334 a month apartment—where the walls were plastered with newspaper accounts of his heroism on that day in 1975. He'd been dead for two weeks.

The last person who saw him alive said Sipple had been to the local VA hospital that day because he'd been having trouble breathing, but that the hospital had turned him away. It was never determined whether Billy Sipple had died by his own hand, from alcohol poisoning, or from that breathing problem the VA wasn't interested in. And no one cared enough to find out.

AMONG MY SOUVENIRS
Even though Billy was never invited to the White House to shake the hand of the man whose life he saved, a framed letter from the White House was found in his room.

> *I want you to know how much I appreciated your selfless actions last Monday. The events were a shock to us all, but you acted quickly and without fear for your own safety. By doing so, you helped to avert danger to me and to others in the crowd. You have my heartfelt appreciation.*
> — *President Gerald Ford, September 25, 1975*

Before his victory at Hastings, William the Conqueror was called "William the Bastard."

HIS FAME LINGERS ON

Today, the outing of Billy Sipple is a topic covered in journalism school. The questions that are asked are just as pertinent today as they were 30 years ago:

Was it appropriate to report details of his private life? Did the gay community in San Francisco take unfair advantage of Sipple in celebrating his heroism?

* * * * *

THE MURDER OF HARVEY MILK

The man who outed Billy Sipple was the first openly gay person elected to the San Francisco Board of Supervisors. He was instrumental in the passage of San Francisco's first gay civil rights ordinance and was politically buddy-buddy with the mayor, George Moscone. Their nemesis was Dan White, a conservative ex-cop and the only member of the board who voted against the civil rights ordinance.

White had been so incensed by the passage of the ordinance that he resigned from the board. When he tried to get himself reinstated, he met a brick wall instead of a welcome back. On November 27, 1978, inside city hall, Dan White shot and killed both Harvey Milk and Mayor George Moscone.

Everyone expected a murder one conviction. When the verdict came down as manslaughter (part of Dan White's defense centered around his instability due to eating too much junk food), it was followed by gay riots. The riots in turn were answered by the San Francisco Police Department with an unprovoked attack on the city's gay neighborhood, the Castro district. Dozens of people were injured, and a bar, the Elephant Walk, was nearly destroyed. Its owners sued the city, and in a historic judgment, they were reimbursed for all damages incurred.

The "Twinkie Defense" became common parlance for someone who suffered from a diminished mental capacity due to the consumption of too much sugar.

Dan White was paroled in 1985 and committed suicide shortly afterward.

William the Conqueror was the result of his father's affair with a tanner's daughter.

A BRUNCH OF REBELS

*The great generals of history always claim that soldiers march
on their stomachs. The same can't be said for rebels.*

Rebels are always quick to point out that you can't make an omelet without breaking some eggs. But history has shown that not a single rebel leader was an experienced fry cook or chicken farmer, so what did they know? No wonder so many rebellions have been monumentally scrambled screwups!

BANG-UP OMELETS

The Gunpowder Plot of 1605 was hatched in a London alehouse called the Duck and Drake. Guy Fawkes and a gaggle of coconspirators were planning to break their eggs with enough gunpowder to level half of London. The "eggs" they had in mind were the king, his lords, and elected members of the House of Commons. The "frying pan" was to be the House of Lords on the opening day of Parliament. Once Fawkes broke the eggs, his gang was supposed to lead a popular uprising in the countryside. Unfortunately, there was a "fox" in their "henhouse."

Or was it a rat? Tipped off about the plot, authorities snagged Fawkes in the cellar of the House with 36 barrels of gunpowder. Curiously, although the conspirators had been forewarned their jig was up, they still went ahead with it.

KEEP YOUR INGREDIENTS DRY—OOPS!

Some of the rebels managed to escape into the countryside, where they settled in with muskets and pistols to wait for a showdown. But their powder was wet—that darn English weather!—so they put it near an open fire to dry. Unlike Fawkes's powder, *theirs* exploded. One conspirator was killed and another was blinded; the capture of the dazed remnants was no more difficult than cleaning up a Teflon frying pan. All met a savage end—and the only eggs broken were their own.

ANCIENT NINJA: SEPARATING THE MEN FROM THE MYTH

You've seen these men in black everywhere, usually in a group, threatening a movie hero. But how much do you really know about the dark warriors of feudal Japan? It's time to separate the men from the myth.

1. The ninja were a clan of evil assassins for hire.

Myth! In the movies, ninja are portrayed as evil mercenaries crawling out of the woodwork to make sashimi out of the good guy. In reality, they were mountain people of Japan who were systematically harassed by the samurai ruling class 400 years ago. Mostly they farmed. For self-defense when outnumbered, the ninja created a fighting system called Ninjutsu, "the art of stealth." When money got tight the occasional ninja would sell his skills. These few renegades created the stereotype of ninja as the warrior killer.

2. One ninja could sometimes defeat five soldiers.

Fact! Ninja specifically trained to fight more than one opponent. But they considered escape a victory. Their big-city oppressors outnumbered them, so training involved "dirty" fighting tactics that would scare or injure adversaries just long enough for ninja to get away. The samurai were trained in one-on-one fighting against an opponent who actively engages, not a slippery man in black who kicks you in the toe and disappears. Ninja learned to get the job done quickly. A ninja boxing match wouldn't make a good spectator sport: one pokes the other in the eye and climbs a tree.

3. All ninja were male.

Myth! Lady ninja were called *kunoichi*. Occasionally, some wielded swords like the men, but most often, they were trained as spies and messengers to help gather information that could help their clan. Kunoichi used the illusion of helplessness to their advantage, wielding secret weapons like sashes, fans, combs, and umbrellas when forced to fight. On occasion, they

---

It was ordered in 1085 by William the Conqueror.

assassinated unsuspecting "suitors." They even carried a bag of little, bladed finger gloves that gave them the equivalent of iron press-on nails of death!

4. Ninja practiced black magic and had supernatural powers.
Myth! While ninja may have appeared magical, they put their pajamas on one leg at a time, just like everybody else. In battle, though, they used this legend to frighten their enemies. The height of ninja activity was during the 1600s; but by the 1800s, most ninja action involved farming or looking for work. Yet ninja buzz kept growing through art, theater, and word of mouth. By the 1900s, ninja were portrayed as practically superhuman.

5. Ninja always wore black.
Myth! In real life, ninja dressed for the job at hand; they usually looked like everyone else. When sneaking into an enemy lair, they wore the uniforms of their adversaries to trick them. By the Edo Period (1603–1867), their exploits were famous enough to hit the Kabuki theater. Taking the stealthy reputation of the ninja into consideration, Kabuki troupes decided to portray ninja the same as stagehands—dressed all in black so as not to be seen by the audience. Henceforth, all ninja were portrayed in black.

6. Ninja in training walked through fire, stood under freezing waterfalls, and dangled themselves over cliffs.
Fact! Nature played a big role in ninja culture. Taking on the aforementioned tasks was said to both bring one closer to nature and help one eliminate personal fear. Training began in childhood so that as children grew they could use their skills if necessary.

7. Practicing ninja walk among us today.
Fact! As Japan's Edo period wore on, the ninja became less secretive. There were no feudal wars left to fight. Ninja masters wrote books, opened schools to teach others, and became scholars. And their fighting became world famous. In the 1980s, the American film *Enter the Ninja* set off a brief ninja craze in the United States, and lots of schools opened (some more authentic than others). There are thousands of practicing ninja in the United States today.

The Bayeux Tapestry (actually an embroidery) measures over 230' long and 20" wide.

ROCKING HORSES

If you think dancing is for sissies, the battlefield ballerinas of Vienna will change your mind.

We couldn't pass up a story that combines Genghis Khan, Hannibal's elephants, the Nazi SS, General Patton, and fine equestrian traditions. They all come together in the story of Vienna's magnificent dancing Lipizzan stallions.

CRISS CROSS

We'll start with Hannibal's elephants and Genghis Khan. Vilano horses from the mountains of Spain were well known for their strength at least as far back as the days of Julius Caesar. These big guys carried Hannibal's warriors across the Alps alongside those famous elephants. Then, someone got the bright idea of crossing Vilanos with the Barb horses (whose ancestors carried Genghis Khan and his hordes from Asia). The result was the Andalusian horses of Spain. If all this Alps crossing and horse crossing makes your eye cross, be patient—we've almost got our dancing horses.

In 1580, Charles, Archduke of Vienna, founded a stud farm at Lipica (also called Lipizza) a village in Slovenia close to the Italian border. There, using the Spanish bloodstock, the Archduke created strong, graceful horses that are born dark in color but whose coats gradually lighten to a brilliant, snowy white—the Lipizzan breed. At about the same time Austrian royalty also founded the Spanish Riding School in Vienna to teach classical horsemanship. The horses used and bred at this school became exclusively the Lipizzan.

GETTING THEIR KICKS IN BATTLE

By the 1600s, Lipizzans were a must-have for both the aristocracy and the military because of their speed, endurance, and strength. But it was their ability to leap that made the horses state-of-the-art battlefield equipment.

Ground troops quaked with fear when confronted by a Lipizzan's powerful kicks called "airs above the ground." These airs included a *courbette*, where horses reared on their hind legs

---

The Bayeux Tapestry depicts the Norman invasion of England and the events that led up to it.

and jumped. The *croupade* was fancier, with a leap that had them tucking their legs up in midair. The *capriole* was the most dazzling feat: a horse leapt into the air with its forelegs drawn under its chest; then, from midair, it kicked out violently with its hind legs. A Lipizzan could make a ballet star look clumsy.

THE PERFORMANCE OF THEIR LIVES
Fast forward to World War II in 1945. Germany was losing the war, and the Allies were bombing Vienna. Hoping to save his Lipizzan stallions, the director of the Spanish Riding School, Colonel Alois Podjahsky, relocated them to St. Martin in Upper Austria, 200 miles (322 km) away. No bombs were falling in St. Martin, but food was scarce. The Lipizzans might have wound up in local casseroles if the U.S. Army hadn't arrived in Upper Austria at about the time the horses did.

An American officer recognized the travel-worn Lipizzans. He sent word about them to the headquarters of U.S. general George Patton, who was a horse lover and a competitor in the equestrian Olympic event in 1912. When Patton came to view the horses, Podjahsky had the animals put on the show of their lives—a show that *saved* their lives. Patton was so impressed that he made the stallions protected wards of the U.S. Army. But the breed was still in danger of destruction if no mares survived.

THE CAVALRY RIDES TO THE RESCUE
During World War II, the Nazis had moved the Lipizzan mares and foals to a stud farm in Hostau, Czechoslovakia. An American soldier, Colonel Charles H. Reed of the Second Cavalry Brigade (it was a mechanized cavalry by then), looking for information on Allied prisoners held at Hostau, also learned of the horses whereabouts. The information came from a captured German general who worried that the Russians might destroy the Lipizzan mares or ship them to the Soviet Union.

When General Patton heard that the classic horses were in danger, he sent word to Reed: "Get them. Make it fast!" Reed complied. He sent a courier to arrange a surrender at Hostau—where Germans were eager to give up to Americans rather than face the Russians. And Reed launched a lightning strike against

Hitler's SS troops, who wouldn't surrender and tried to block his plans. But the SS was quickly overwhelmed.

On April 28, 1945, the American entry into Hostau, according to Reed, was a "fiesta," rather than a battle. Allied prisoners lined the streets, and surrendering German troops welcomed the American soldiers with salutes and an honor guard. As for the horses, 300 Lipizzans were rescued and were, ironically, protected by the U.S. Army when Nazi SS troops attacked Hostau. By May 7, the war in Europe was over, and arrangements were being made to return the horses to the care of Alois Podjahsky and the republic of Austria.

A TALL TAIL

Colonel Reed's account of the rescue of the Lipizzan breed differs in one respect from the traditional version. According to Reed, Patton ordered the rescue of the mares in Czechoslovakia before he saw the stallions in St. Martin. Reed claimed that when Disney made a movie of the rescue, *The Miracle of the White Stallions*, the performance of the horses was emphasized to make the story more dramatic.

However it happened, it's thanks to the U.S. Cavalry that one of the oldest European breed of horses still performs at the Spanish Riding School. As the magnificent animals leap to their battle-worthy airs, audiences from around the world come to watch—from a safe distance.

* * * * *

- The Lipizzan is a long-lived horse; 30 to 35 years is their average life span.

- Lipizzans are usually born black and change slowly, through a period of from 6 to 10 years, to their final, pure white color.

- Occasionally, a Lipizzan colt is born pure white, but they are rarities. In the days of the Hapsburg royalty, white colts, when they grew older, were used to pull royal vehicles.

Alfred, king of England (A.D. 849–899), is the only English king called "the Great."

IT'S A DOG TAG'S LIFE

The history of military identification tags.

O nly 58 percent of the soldiers killed in action during the American Civil War were positively identified. Soldiers' had a legitimate concern that if they were killed, their families would never know what happened to them—other than that they were missing in action. Each soldier started writing his name on a piece of paper or a handkerchief and pinning it to his clothing before going into battle. Some soldiers went to the trouble of carving small wooden disks with their names on them, then drilling a hole in the disk and hanging the disk from their necks with a piece of string. Others made their own ID tags by grinding off one side of a coin and then etching their name on it.

Voila! The first ID tags—not called dog tags yet, though.

IF YOU MAKE IT, THEY WILL BUY

Eventually, retail merchants started producing and selling metal disks to soldiers. During the Civil War, *Harper's Weekly Magazine* advertised "soldier's pins" made of silver or gold and etched with the soldier's name and unit, but some soldiers still made their own ID tags by grinding off one side of a coin and then etching their names on it. Dogs wore similar identification tags, so it wasn't long before soldiers began referring to their ID tags as dog tags.

DOGGY DOG TAGS

The history of tags for dogs goes back to Thomas Jefferson, who wrote the first dog-licensing law for his home state of Virginia— not because dogs were leaving "presents" on his lawn, but because dogs were killing his sheep. The idea was to identify the dog's owners and make them pay for the sheep they'd killed.

By the 1850s, most localities had dog-licensing laws that required dogs to wear a collar with the owner's name and license number. Eventually, small wooden or metal disks were used and referred to as dog tags.

STANDARD ISSUE
By the 1890s, the U.S. Army and Navy were experimenting with metal identification tags for recruits. During World War I, each French soldier wore a bracelet with a metal disk called a *plaque d'identité* that was engraved with the soldier's name, rank, and formation. When America entered the war in 1917, all soldiers were issued two aluminum tags that were stamped by hand with their name, rank, serial number, unit, and religion. The tags were suspended from their necks by cord or tape.

HEARST IS THE WORST
In the 1930s, when the government was considering ways to assign Social Security numbers, someone whose name is lost to history suggested that the numbers be stamped on a metal plate and worn like a dog tag by civilians. The idea was quickly shot down by the powers that be. But that didn't stop Franklin D. Roosevelt's adversary, William Randolph Hearst, from claiming during the very heated 1936 election campaign that the Roosevelt administration was planning to require everyone to wear dog tags.

THE GREATEST DOG TAGS
World War II dog tags were rectangular with rounded ends and a notch at one end (now stamped by machine). It was rumored that the notch was put in the tag so that the tag could be placed in a dead soldier's mouth to hold it open so that gasses would escape and the body wouldn't become bloated. Fortunately, the truth was a lot less gruesome. The stamping machine required a notch to hold the blank tag in place while it was being stamped. The tags were first made of brass and later of a corrosion-resistant alloy of nickel and copper. By the end of the war, all tags were made of stainless steel. They were suspended from the neck by a rope, a beaded chain, or a stainless steel wire with a plastic cover.

THOROUGHLY MODERN DOG TAGS
During the Vietnam War, new stamping machines were used, and the notch was eliminated. Soldiers started taping their tags together so that they wouldn't make any noise and give away their position. By the end of the war, rubber covers were issued to keep the tags silent. A soldier often put one tag in his boot, in case his

body were dismembered so that normal means of identification were impossible.

IRAQI ARMY ISSUE
American-style dog tags are a worldwide phenomenon, thanks to the post-WWII export of blanks and stamping machines by the United States. In fact, during the two Persian Gulf wars, Iraqi soldiers wore dog tags that were identical to their American counterparts—except that the printing was in Arabic.

HIGH-TECH DOG TAGS FOR HUMANS
The soldier of the future will wear dog tags that hold a microchip containing his or her medical and dental records, and which will be called a Personal Information Carrier (PIC). The U.S. Marines have developed their own version, called the Tactical Medical Coordination System (TacMedCS) that can pinpoint the location of a wounded soldier using the Global Positioning System (GPS).

DOG GONE?
As for the original dog tag wearers—dogs, that is—pet owners these days are having microchips implanted in Max's neck to store an identification number that can be read with an external scanner.

Some day humans might be implanted with microchips at birth, which will allow them to be located and which will have the capacity to store massive amounts of personal information. If our descendants aren't careful, they'll end up like dogs on an electronic leash. George Orwell may have had the date wrong, but not the concept.

* * * * *

THANKS, MOM!

According to William Manchester's book *American Caesar*, Colonel Douglas MacArthur's mother wrote a letter on behalf of her son to General Pershing, suggesting that it was time for him to be promoted to general.

"Panama" is a native word that means "plenty of fish."

BAD TRIP

*The CIA's Electric Kool-Aid Acid Test
and how it went horribly wrong.*

For decades rumors have swirled around the CIA's testing of lysergic acid diethylamide (LSD) in the 1960s. In seeking a knockout drug weapon, did the CIA slip substances to unsuspecting patsies? The answer is yes. And Frank Olson was the man who paid the heaviest price.

BEHIND CLOSED DOORS
The Olson family—Alice, Frank, and their three young children—lived an all-American, idyllic life in Frederick, Maryland. But unbeknownst to everyone, Frank had a secret life: developing ways of efficiently distributing deadly strains of diseases during bacteriological warfare for the Special Operations Division (SOD) of the army's Chemical Corps.

LAB RATS
While Frank Olson was busy creating ways to hide delivery systems in shaving cream and bug spray cans, a CIA researcher and official, Dr. Sidney Gottlieb, was developing very different weapons with his team, called MK-ULTRA. For years Gottlieb had been studying the use of narcotics such as cocaine and mescaline, hoping that he could come up with a pharmacopoeia of substances that could be used as tactical weapons. In the early 1950s he believed he had found something that might work—lysergic acid, aka LSD. LSD seemed perfect for Gottlieb's purposes. It was colorless, odorless, and capable of reducing sane people to babbling, disoriented idiots.

EVERYBODY MUST GET STONED
Besides conducting experiments at universities and prisons, the MK-ULTRA team tested LSD on themselves, slipping it into each other's food and drinks without warning. But Gottlieb wasn't interested in LSD's effects on willing subjects; he needed to know how average folks would react when fed the drug without their knowledge.

An official census of Panama City in 1610 listed 548 citizens and 3,500 African slaves.

Gottlieb's bosses had put the kibosh on furtive civilian experiments, but Gottlieb had a better idea. Every year the MK-ULTRA team met up with the SOD (Frank's group) for a brainstorming weekend. These were men who worked around hazardous chemicals all the time. Surely it would be okay to doctor *their* cocktails.

EXPERIMENT IN ERROR

Two days into the meeting, November 19, 1953, Gottlieb struck. He gathered a group together—eight colleagues including himself and Olson—and made everyone a cocktail. Twenty minutes later he let them in on his little secret: their drinks were spiked.

Within an hour, Olson began acting strangely. He was paranoid, convinced there was a CIA plot to discredit him. He wept, laughed, ranted, and howled. Gottlieb was nonplussed. None of his test subjects had acted this way before. And it went on and on. The next morning, all the other unwitting trippers had come down, but Frank was still disturbed and fearful. Not knowing what else to do, Gottlieb allowed him to return home.

TUNED-IN, TURNED-ON, DROPPED-OUT

A new Frank Olson came back to his family. Instead of the loving and cheerful husband and father, Frank was suspicious and depressed. Gottlieb took responsibility. He sent Olson to a Manhattan psychotherapist who for years had administered LSD to his patients in order to study its effects on sex and addiction. Dr. Harold Abramson tried to talk Olson down—the patient was holding forth on the CIA's plans to get him, humiliate him, and slip him drugs to keep him awake. He was afraid he'd be made to disappear; he heard voices and believed that agents were waiting everywhere to arrest him.

Stymied, Abramson and Gottlieb agreed Olson should be put in a psychiatric hospital. Just before he was to be admitted, Olson was sharing a hotel room with a CIA scientist who'd brought him to New York. In the middle of the night, just nine days after Frank ingested the LSD, the agent awoke in time to see Frank Olson dashing across the room and crashing through the window. By the time the agent was able to reach the window and look a long 10 stories down, Frank Olson was dead.

COVER UP EXPOSED

CIA officials soon found out what had happened. In the interest of national security, they elected to cover it up. Alice Olson was told that her husband had died of a "classified illness," and she received two-thirds of his salary as a pension. The CIA admonished Sid Gottlieb but didn't halt his experiments—instead they ordered that LSD be tested instead on street prostitutes and other people who they figured wouldn't much be missed if they went astray. The LSD experiments continued for 10 more years.

But Frank Olson's unusual death didn't remain a secret. In December 1974, the *New York Times* broke the story of the CIA's mind-control experiments, and eventually it was revealed that at least one subject had died after being fed LSD. The Olson family realized that subject was Frank. They told his story to the national media, winning a $750,000 settlement in 1976—and a personal apology from President Gerald Ford.

* * * * *

WATCH WHAT YOU SAY!

World-famous conductor Pierre Boulez was detained by police for one of his critical remarks about classical music—over two decades after his comment.

Swiss police awoke Boulez from the gilded bed of his five-star hotel in Switzerland in December 2001, interrogated him, and confiscated his passport because his name was on a suspected terrorist list.

Apparently, when he made the critical remark in the 1960s that "all opera houses should be blown up," his name was placed on a government watch list and never removed. Boulez was in town at the invitation of a classical music festival.

SIR FRANCIS FAKE

*No one ever called Sir Francis Drake a liar, but, then,
not many people know he rigged the history books.*

The Spanish danced in joy and the English wept in sorrow when they heard that Sir Francis Drake was dead. In his lifetime he achieved a lot more than fifteen minutes of fame. But curiously, by his own doing, he may have lost credit for his greatest achievement.

WIN SOME, LOSE SOME

As history has evolved, Sir Francis already has a lot going for him. First off, he was the second seaman to sail around the world—Magellan had been the first, some 50 years earlier. Drake took three years to do it (1577–1580), but it was no mean feat in those days: imagine traveling 38,000 miles (61,155 km) in a flimsy wooden boat. Later, he commanded the English fleet that destroyed the Spanish Armada (1588). Drake was a man dedicated to queen and country, and he didn't do too badly for himself along the way.

WHO ARE YOU CALLING A PIRATE?

When he was 12 years old, Sir Francis was apprenticed to a merchant shipping firm, and by the time he was 20, he was captaining a three-masted 50-ton ship. The year 1571 found him raiding Spanish ships in the Caribbean and the Gulf of Mexico. In 1573 his raids, undertaken without official authority, netted nearly as much as 20 percent of Queen Elizabeth's annual revenues.

MISSION IMPOSSIBLE

By 1577, Drake was cursed by the Spanish and applauded by the English. This was the year he set off on the voyage that he hoped would truly make his name.

Like a lot of monarchs of the day, Good Queen Bess (Elizabeth I) had aspirations of empire. Unfortunately, the Spaniards, Portuguese, and Dutch did too, and they had already staked out the South and Central Americas, Mexico, and the Indies. Bess decided that the best way to get in on the action was to find a shorter trade route, which meant finding the

Byzantine architects created the largest domes ever built in the ancient world.

Northwest Passage, a sea route through America from the Pacific to the Atlantic. Drake was *secretly* assigned to find the passage from the Pacific side and claim it for England.

Once Drake made it into the Pacific, he gleefully robbed Spaniards all along the coast from Chile to California. His ship became so treasure-laden he had to throw out his ballast to make room for loot. Then, for several months he seemed to drop off the edge of the world, at least until he turned up in the Indies and Philippines, eventually to make his way around Africa and back to England in 1580. Where had he been for those months? Maps, logs, artifacts, and Indian legends indicate that he was pursuing his secret mission, but the evidence is all circumstantial.

A skilled sailor and superb navigator (and in the opinion of some, a villainous pirate), Drake was also a man who observed the niceties. On his ship, the *Golden Hind,* he set a good table. And, as if he knew his 1577 adventure would last three years, he took along a small orchestra for entertainment.

He treated his crew so even-handedly that the sailors adored him. Of course, their devotion may have also stemmed from the fact they knew they'd share in the booty at voyage's end. They knew Drake to be a man of his word too; when he told them they'd hang if they breathed a word about the secret voyage, they knew he meant it.

ALWAYS THE GENTLEMAN

If there was any doubt about that threat or of Drake's qualities as a captain and a gentleman, the case of Thomas Doughty put it to rest. Doughty was an arrogant dandy with connections in the queen's court. He sailed with Drake in 1577, but even before the ships left Plymouth, England, he was instigating mutiny and general discord. Drake put up with his nonsense all the way across the Atlantic.

Finally, at Port St. Julian, near the treacherous uncharted Straits of Magellan at the southern tip of South America, Drake got fed up with young Mister Doughty. He charged him with treason, administered a quick and proper trial, and sentenced him to death. Ever the gentleman, Drake shared a last meal with Doughty and permitted the condemned man to choose the manner of his own execution. Doughty chose the ax—beheading was regarded in those days as a more dignified way to die than by hanging.

The most famous example is St. Sophia, built by Justinian and Theodora in Constantinople.

Because Drake expected repercussions upon his return to England, he meticulously recorded Doughty's case in his logs. The part about the "secret mission" was an addendum for the Queen's eyes only. (The papers reside in the British archives in secretary of state Walsingham's secret intelligence files.) Drake's primary issue with Doughty had to do with the Northwest Passage—the secret mission. Doughty threatened to talk, and Drake was, on penalty of death, sworn to secrecy. Whether he found the passage or not, Queen Elizabeth didn't want the world to know that Drake was even looking for it.

LIAR, LIAR
Being the first Englishman to sail around the world made Drake an instant public hero. And, he also enriched his financial backers. What no one knew about was where else Drake had sailed in his secret attempts to find a Northwest Passage.

From Drake's return in 1580, in a display of remarkable deviousness, maps and logs of the voyage were altered to indicate that Drake had sailed no farther north than 48° latitude (the U.S.–Canada border). Drake wasn't the first to fake a map. (Spain's King Phillip had done it to understate sailing distance and scam an extra 1,000 miles of territory from the Portuguese.) Drake's actions were just as deliberate.

Drake had the mapmakers add about 1,500 miles to the west side of the North American continent. He identified a fine Pacific Coast base for future English ships but placed it 10 degrees south of its actual location, a 600-mile variance. He did the same with river mouths and islands. Drake had sailed uncharted seas and he was obliged to keep them that way.

FOR THE RECORD
In later years, Drake may have had second thoughts, as bits and pieces of his actual discoveries began to emerge, most often as obscure insets on maps, nothing else. Those privy to the secret mission eventually died, including Drake. Most written records that would confirm the truth were lost or destroyed. The maps were forgotten.

But those old maps were still kicking around, right up until nearly the end of the 20th century when, finally, someone

Ferdinand Magellan was the first person given credit for sailing around the world.

very familiar with the Pacific Northwest coast gave them a hard look.

DA DRAKE CODE

The old maps, drawn with informed instruction from Drake, showed he had traveled as far north along the coast as 58° latitude, the southern part of Alaska. Drake's code, moving everything 10° south, was broken. In reality, Drake had identified Cape Flattery, Vancouver Island, and the Queen Charlotte Islands. He'd traveled the Inner Passage between the island chains and the British Columbia mainland. He'd mapped the twin delta of the Fraser River, as well as the Columbia River where it empties into the Pacific.

BEARING WITNESS

Other evidence also gave hints of Drake's achievement. At least one native tribe on the coast affirmed to Captain Cook that, according to their legends, other white men had come from the sea generations before him. Add to that, the fact that Elizabethan artifacts have shown up on Oregon's coast, as well as a crude land-based structure used by Elizabethan mariners to determine longitude.

For a 16th-century sailor to have completed Drake's perilous journey up the coast, and to have thrown in a trip around the world and some diligent pirating en route, would be tantamount to an astronaut making it to the moon in a hot air balloon.

Quite a man was Sir Francis Drake. Sure, there was a touch of larceny, but there was a lot more of boldness, skill, and diplomacy. And now he just might be acknowledged as one of the foremost explorers of Elizabethan times.

* * * * *

WHY, YOU...YOU...DOMESTIC PERSON!

In the 16th century, no woman took offense at being called a "hussy"—it was perfectly respectable. The word was derived from the short form of the Middle English *huswif*, which simply meant a housewife. Only a century later, the word had come to mean "a lewd or brazen woman" or "a saucy or mischievous girl."

THE AMERICAN PLAGUE

The ships that delivered African slaves to their cruel fate in the New World carried something else: a disease that Africans were immune to.

As early as 1647, a mosquito-borne yellow fever epidemic became known as the American Plague when it struck the Massachusetts Bay Colony. It was probably transported via vessels from the West Indies, which suffered an outbreak of the epidemic the same year. The stricken were confined to bed with high fevers, aching limbs, and the yellow skin and eyes that gave the virus its name. Back then, no one knew its cause. All they knew was that almost everyone who got it ended up perishing horribly: coughing up vile black fluid and bleeding copiously from every orifice. The Massachusetts Bay outbreak eventually died down, but yellow fever continued to pop up in the New World with terrifying regularity, even in the most cosmopolitan of cities.

PHILADELPHIA FLEEDOM

In the hot, dry summer of 1793, doctors in Philadelphia, Pennsylvania (America's national capital at the time), noticed an increasing number of patients who complained of nausea, black vomit, lethargy, and yellow skin coloration. When prominent physician Dr. Benjamin Rush (a signer of the Declaration of Independence) realized that the illness was yellow fever and advised locals to leave the city if they could, they fled by the thousands.

This might sound as if the doctor were encouraging the spread of the disease, but yellow fever spreads more quickly in crowded areas. The more mess, muck, crowding, and filth, the more mosquitoes bred, and in a city, the more people they have to bite. So in reality, evacuation was a good idea.

The city's library, churches, and newspapers shut their doors. The national government disbanded. Husbands abandoned families, and children left aged parents helpless and alone. Those who

In ancient Sparta, weak babies were left exposed on hillsides or taken away to become slaves.

remained shut themselves in their houses and refused to see anyone. They burned tobacco and gunpowder to keep away infection, chewed garlic or kept it in their pockets in hopes it would have an antibacterial effect, and they covered handkerchiefs in vinegar to breathe through if they had to leave home.

LIFE AND DEATH

With doctors stymied as to the fever's cause and remedy, the disease continued to spread in waves around the crowded, dirty city. Prominent residents were affected as often as the poor: no less a personage than Alexander Hamilton came down with the illness, and George Washington and Thomas Jefferson were forced to vacate their Philadelphia homes.

Before long, thousands of the stricken lay dying while carts waited to carry them to shallow graves. Once the fledgling nation's largest and most cosmopolitan city, Philadelphia had lost almost 10 percent of its population to the disease by the time the fever subsided in 1800. And the city never regained its previous stature—particularly after the nervous politicians deserted it for Washington, D.C.

Similar outbreaks followed in New York and other big cities. In New Orleans, Louisiana, more than 8,000 people died in the summer of 1853; in 1878, almost 20,000 Southerners died of the illness. It became commonplace to leave cities in the summer to escape to cooler and safer countryside climates.

Other than advising patients to escape their cities, doctors didn't know how to halt the disease. To stop its spread, they tried burning disinfectants, burning the dead, and quarantining ships. Hoping to contain an 1888 epidemic in Florida, the postmaster general fumigated mail leaving the state by locking it in train cars with burning sulfur. Nothing seemed to work. That is, until Dr. Walter Reed came along. After thousands of workers died from malaria, yellow fever, and other diseases while building the Panama Canal at the end of the 19th century, the U.S. Yellow Fever Commission began to research the disease. While stationed in Cuba, Dr. Reed discovered in 1900 that the virus was carried by the *Aedes aegypti* mosquito. Within a year, mosquito-eradication programs had wiped out the disease in America for good. A yellow fever vaccine would not be developed until 1937.

THE "RELAX, THIS WON'T HURT A BIT" AWARDS

Dentists get a bum rap: they just want to help us, and all we do is bad-mouth them! Uncle John joins in the fun with these diabolical dental awards.

To honor the history of the many suffering dental patients of the past, Uncle John offers the "Relax, This Won't Hurt a Bit Awards." These awards should remind dental-phobes to relax—it could be a lot worse.

If going to the dentist isn't your favorite pastime, consider this: you could have lived back in the Middle Ages when the dentist was a barber-surgeon who performed bloodletting to fix a toothache. "Great Gigs of History" on page 448 tells you more about the job of barber-surgeon, as well as the story about the reputed origin of the trademark red and white barbershop poles.

Humans have always experienced dental problems. Modern dentistry dates from the mid-1800s. For more about this, see "Return of the 'Relax, This Won't Hurt a Bit' Awards" on page 233. But now, let's look at how earlier civilizations dealt with dental distress.

The ancient Greeks, Romans, and Egyptians all used various toothache remedies, including extractions. Many ancient civilizations believed that toothaches were caused by a "toothworm" twisting inside the tooth. To get rid of both the worm and the ache, a delicious concoction of boiled spiders, eggs, and oil were applied to the tooth. It almost makes novocaine sound appealing.

WORST TOOTHPASTE AND MOUTHWASH AWARD
This was a tough decision since several nominees were so worthy. The ancient Greeks prized white teeth, especially among men. To get a bright smile they used pumice, talcum, emery, granulated alabaster, powdered coral, and iron rust on their teeth. (It was

---

The earliest ancient Egyptians buried their dead in small pits in the desert.

the rust that got them nominated.) The great Greek physician Hippocrates gave his patients a concoction made of three mice and a burned rabbit's head to brush with.

But the award goes to ancient Rome, where they cleaned their teeth with powders made from ground antlers, hooves, crabs, eggshells, and lizard livers. Ancient Rome also gets kudos for the worst mouthwash, a "medicinal rinse" of human urine.

WEIRDEST TOOTHACHE CURE AWARD

An ancient Chinese cure favored garlic as a toothache remedy, mixed with horseradish and human milk, which were then made into a paste. Not a bad idea, huh? But then the paste was rolled into pills and stuck up the patient's nostril on the side opposite the toothache.

But the Chinese dentists were on to something. There is evidence of acupuncture treatment in China to combat the pain of toothaches as early as 2700 B.C. By A.D. 659, the Chinese were filling cavities with a mixture of silver, tin, and mercury—something very close to the silver amalgam still used extensively in modern Western dentistry.

But it was the Roman physician Pliny the Elder (A.D. 23–79) who created a prescription that really impressed the judges: "To stop toothache bite on a piece of wood from a tree struck by lightning." He suggested, "Touch the tooth with the frontal bone of a lizard taken during the full moon." He also suggested that his patients find a frog by the light of the full moon, spit into its mouth, and say, "Frog, go and take my toothache with thee!" Pliny wins. After that cure, nobody else is in spitting distance.

DON'T QUIT YOUR DAY JOB AWARD

Scary as those barber-surgeon dentists might have been, it was probably even tougher when they weren't around. Barber-surgeons weren't always available to people in rural areas of colonial America. Many colonists turned to other teeth specialists, or even friends and neighbors if they had a toothache. Silversmith and revolutionary Paul Revere, in fact, was an amateur dentist whom many colonists visited. Revere did fillings and cleanings and made bridges and false teeth.

The heat and dryness of the sand dehydrated the bodies quickly, creating natural mummies.

COSMETIC DENTISTRY AWARD

Some cultures didn't have a clue about how to treat tooth disease, but they did know beauty when they saw it. The Mayans in Mexico, for example, decorated their teeth with inlays of precious metals and gems. But Uncle John's cosmetic dentistry award goes to Chinese women during the second and third centuries A.D. who dyed their teeth pure black with a mixture of natural chemicals derived from plants and resin. It actually ended up protecting the teeth from decay. And you could have a nice black smile for the rest of your life!

DIRTY ROTTEN SCOUNDREL AWARDS

This one was easy. It goes to "the tooth-drawers" who roamed from town to town throughout the 18th century in Europe and America. On entering a new town, they would gather a crowd and brag about their pain-free work. Picking a "volunteer" from the audience, the tooth-drawer would gently open the person's mouth, and in a matter of seconds, pull out a bloodied tooth; the volunteer swore there was no pain. Of course, the volunteer was a shill—and the already extracted tooth, covered in animal blood, had been hidden in the tooth-drawer's hand all along.

After the crowd saw how gentle the tooth-drawer supposedly was, he had real customers—who writhed in agony as the tooth-drawer yanked and jerked, sometimes breaking the victim's jaw or worse. But the crowd didn't hear the cries of the real patients because the tooth-drawers were accompanied by noisy musicians once the actual procedures began so the patients' cries were drowned out. Then the tooth-drawers quickly left town—before infection set in.

By A.D. 300 there were more than 900 public baths in Rome.

A GRAVE MISTAKE

*The commonly held belief that Mozart was buried
penniless, in a pauper's grave, is bunk.*

Fans of classical music know that Wolfgang Amadeus Mozart died without a cent to his name and was buried, without any mourners, in an unmarked mass grave, the site of which is lost to the world, right? Well, actually...no.

DIGGING UP THE TRUTH

Austria's ruler, Emperor Joseph II, was a miser, and he forced his miserliness on his subjects. He was also greatly concerned with improving hygiene. These two motives were behind a decree he issued in 1784 that closed all cemeteries within Vienna's city limits and mandated burial in cloth sacks in mass graves. The plan was both to save wood (on coffins that just rotted anyway) and to improve hygiene (by getting decomposing bodies out of Vienna, where they might contaminate the groundwater).

Mozart died in 1791, seven years after Joseph II's decree. Legend states that Mozart was buried without ceremony, mourned by no one. In fact, Mozart's funeral took place in a chapel in St. Stephen's Cathedral in Vienna, where, reports indicate, the crowd must have numbered at least 16. Also, his Masonic lodge held a special ceremony for him, and 4,000 mourners attended his memorial service in Prague. It's true that no mourners attended his burial, but that was customary—mourners didn't attend *any* burials in Vienna at the time.

The detail about his grave being unmarked is the only one that has some credence. The emperor's decree stated that any monuments to the dead were to be placed along the cemetery walls, not next to a gravesite itself. This was because a grave would be reused after the body decomposed, and the ground would quickly get too crowded with monuments if every burial were marked.

The part about his being penniless? That's not completely true, either. It's true that Mozart had no *cash*, but that was because he spent money as quickly as he earned it.

In fact, the only part of the story that's really true is that Mozart was dead. We can be pretty sure about that one.

Wealthy Romans had lavish bathing habits: men might bathe in wine; women in milk.

NO NUTS, NO GLORY!

Forget Van Gogh; he only lost an ear. It was the great castrato Farinelli who gave up everything for art. Well, almost everything.

Carlo Broschi was a man who *really* suffered for his music. Known to the world as the great opera singer Farinelli (1705–1782), he was castrated as a young boy to prevent his exquisite singing voice from ever breaking. But before you start feeling too sorry for the songsmith, it's worth bearing in mind that Farinelli was showered with wealth and adulation throughout his career. And even with a couple of pieces missing from his repertoire, he still managed to make beautiful music with the ladies.

THE UNKINDEST CUT OF ALL

The practice of castrating men (making them into eunuchs) arose around 3,000 years ago. Castration was usually inflicted on slaves who worked in the harem of a king or powerful ruler; the object was to ensure that they could not father children. It involved the removal of the testicles only (!), and a castrated singer like Farinelli, though sterile, was often able to perform in a lady's boudoir as well as on the stage.

Eventually, the demand for castrated men ran out, except in one area: music. The 17th and 18th centuries were a golden age of eunuchs in classical music. Especially in Italy, where boys became castrati, or "the castrated ones." The special thing about these little fellas was that they were altered just before reaching puberty, so that their voices never broke. Boys who were promising singers were selected, given the snip, and then sent to special schools for vocal training.

THE CUTTING EDGE OF FAME

From 1599, castrati were allowed to sing in the papal choir. They proved to be so popular that a whole type of music theater was invented for them, known as opera seria, from which modern opera partly developed. While a castrato's voice always kept its high, childlike pitch, it was delivered with the power of a fully grown man. A castrato could soar effortlessly up and down vocal registers, belting out tunes like a diva on helium. Castrati could also perform all manner of vocal tricks, such as holding a single note for a full minute. Audiences loved it, and the castrati were the rock stars of their day, complete with rampant egos, fawning flunkies, adoring fans, and obliging groupies. And the biggest star of all was Farinelli.

Farinelli, unlike many other castrati, was not from a poor background. Indeed, his father, Salvatore, was the governor of the region around Naples, in southern Italy. Young Carlo displayed vocal talent as a child. And so, some time between his seventh and eighth birthdays, little Carlo said goodbye to part of his anatomy—and hello to a singing career. After studying with the greatest vocal masters of the day, Carlo, now renamed Farinelli after one of his patrons, made his debut in 1720, aged 15. From then on in it was nonstop fame and fortune for the next 17 years. After conquering Italy with triumphant performances in Naples, Rome, and Bologna, Farinelli toured Europe in his early 20s, billed as "the Singer of Kings," due to his having performed for most of Italy's many princes and minor royalty. King Louis XV of France fell under his spell, as did the British public. Farinelli was paid huge fees to perform, either onstage or in private audiences. All in all, life was pretty good for our hero.

THE REIGN IN SPAIN

But then, Farinelli gave it all up. Maybe life on the road with wealth, adulation, and amorous women isn't all it's cracked up to be; but in 1737, at the age of 32, Farinelli announced he was quitting the stage to become the private court singer to King Philip V of Spain. Farinelli had originally visited Spain as part of his European tour, but he was so affected by the king's emotional response to his singing that he decided to stay on.

It turns out that he got much more than he bargained for. Philip V was a manic-depressive, and once he'd latched onto Farinelli and his singing, he wouldn't let go. The king claimed that he could only get to sleep if Farinelli serenaded him. So, the castrated crooner was hired to sing the same set of songs to his patron every night *for the next ten years.*

Farinelli was at the Spanish court for 25 years in total, outliving two monarchs. In that time he acquired great wealth and

---

In 1890 (the "Gilded Age") the average annual income was $380, well below the poverty line.

even more political power: Philip trusted the Italian artist so much that Farinelli eventually became one of the kings most trusted advisors.

In 1759, Farinelli quit Spain and retired to Bologna, Italy, where he lived out his remaining years composing and playing music, receiving famous guests, such as Mozart, and using his great wealth to fund many charitable causes.

GETTING THE AX
In 1870 Italy finally outlawed the creation of castrati. In 1902, and again in 1904, phonograph recordings were made of Alessandro Moreschi, the last surviving Italian *castrato*, but he was by then old and ill and his voice was shot. We will probably never know what a true *castrato* in his prime sounded like—something that young Italian boys should praise the Lord for every day of their prepubescent lives.

* * * * *

WHISTLE WHILE YOU WORK

James Abbott McNeill Whistler isn't nearly as famous as his painting *Arrangement in Grey and Black: Portrait of the Painter's Mother* or "Whistler's Mother" as it's commonly known. McNeill's famous painting, on display at The Detroit Institute of Arts, illustrates the raw talent and hard work that made him one of history's great painters. But in his day he wasn't without his critics.

In 1878, art critic John Ruskin attacked one of McNeill's paintings, accusing him of "throwing a pot of paint…in the public's face." Rather than sloughing it off, he sued Ruskin for libel—and won. He wasn't awarded court costs, however, and the damages consisted of only a single token farthing! The lawsuit ended up driving McNeill into bankruptcy and giving Ruskin a serious résumé bruise.

A MATCH MADE IN HEAVEN

*Gin and vermouth: how two of chemistry's more bilious concoctions
merged to become the immaculate martini. It's a miracle.*

Perhaps the achievement draws its perfection from the addition of ice, or maybe it's the olive. Then again, it might be the ritualistic mystique attached to its preparation and consumption, a kind of Japanese tea ceremony—only made in America. One thing is certain, the martini has risen far above the lowly station of its chief components, as it's sipped reverently in chic bars throughout the world.

GIN IS IN
Gin began its life around 1650 as a medicine for kidney disorder, presumably because kidney disorders were considered worse than cirrhosis of the liver. Created by a Dutch doctor from clear alcohol and oil of juniper berries, gin soon became the rage in England. It could be made at home, was cheaper than beer, and, in those days, was probably less toxic than the local water. Within a century, Londoners were knocking back 11 million gallons a year, or so the history books say.

Another century passed. By then a few sober heads had prevailed in England, and gin was priced out of the reach of the masses. Fortunately, its quality—that is, its dryness—improved, and it became the drink of choice in English high society. Out in the colonies, where quinine was imbibed to counter malaria, the English used gin as a mixer to neutralize quinine's abominable taste. Today, the tonic water that goes so well with gin contains fewer than 20 milligrams of quinine; you'd have to drink at least 30 gin and tonics a day to get the recommended dose to cure your malaria.

But something else happened in the 19th century: gin found its way to the Americas.

THE VERMOUTH STORY
Sweet vermouth came on the scene in Italy in the 18th century.

...who arrived sporting a $15,000 diamond collar.

Mostly, vermouth was a medicinal wine-based brew used to hide the bitter taste of wormwood, which was a supposed cure for intestinal worms. With the addition of herbs, spices, and sugar—lots of sugar—vermouth became a primo pre-pasta aperitif at the best Italian dining tables. Dry vermouth was a later French version, distinguished by the use of a dry white wine base. Given the French passion for food, dry vermouth quickly made its way into recipes.

FROM COAST TO COAST
So, back in the 19th century, the stage was set in America for the martini. Where and when it premiered is still debated. First, a San Francisco bartender is said to have mixed a special drink for a traveler bound for the town of Martinez, California. Then, there's a Martinez bartender who is said to have whipped up a special drink for a local gold prospector. The name has also been connected to the Martini vermouth company, later called Martini & Rossi, which had been making vermouth since 1829. And finally, in 1912, a New York bartender named Martini is said to have created a drink combining equal parts gin and vermouth. Whether he plopped in an olive or an onion is lost to history or, at least, to the land of urban legends.

POUR ME ONE, WILL YOU, DARLING?
During pre-Prohibition days, the martini cocktail became the alcoholic symbol of America's upper classes, absolutely essential in chic drawing rooms across the nation. Picture *The Thin Man's* sophisticated and glamorous Nick and Nora Charles knocking back more than a few in their stylish New York City apartment.

Prohibition and cheap gin made it easy for Nick-and-Nora wannabes to acquire the habit. Americans, like the English of centuries before, discovered that gin was easy to manufacture; they called it "bathtub gin" for a reason.

REQUIEM FOR VERMOUTH
Almost to a drinker, martini experts wanted dry, drier, and driest. The addition of vermouth nose-dived. The quest for dryness may not have been the only reason vermouth fell out of favor. Vermouth, the one in the seven-to-one martini, was now being manufactured from a base of the cheapest white wine available,

goosed up with lots of herbs and spices. In Prohibition days, the bathtub gin could kill you. In more modern times, the vermouth could leave you feeling as if you should be dead.

007, LICENSE TO SWILL

The biggest boost to martinis had to be fictional spy James Bond, though some purists think he corrupted the drink by adding two parts vodka to six parts gin—shaken, not stirred. Bond single-handedly reasserted the martini's masculinity, until the untimely death of the three-martini, tax-deductible business lunch.

THE SHAPE OF THINGS TO COME

Martinis in the 1990s took a form that sometimes didn't see a drop of gin, vermouth, or, for that matter, vodka. But it held onto its marquee status as the symbol of cool and prosperity among 20- and 30-somethings, even though it was transformed. Now, the more exotic the mix the better: tequila martinis, scotch, rum, crème de menthe, curaçao, sambucca, anisette; a dash of grenadine, a hint of Angostura Bitters, or lychee nuts, for heaven's sake! The only real evidence of a traditional martini anymore is the shape of the glass.

Except, of course, for the purists.

* * * * *

STAR BILLING

The noble martini has stood the test of time. Franklin Roosevelt's personal martini shaker holds a place of honor in the Franklin D. Roosevelt Presidential Library and Museum. Of any president's martinis, his were considered to be the worst: no two the same and most often made with whatever was at hand.

As a martini aficionado, FDR had presidential company: Herbert Hoover, Richard Nixon, Gerald Ford, and the senior George Bush are all on record as martini men. Among other personalities who enthused over the drink were Dorothy Parker, William F. Buckley, George Burns, and Mae West.

This "house for dung" has its own name: a stercorary.

THE EXPERIMENT THAT FAILED

*For 13 years, selling liquor was illegal in the United States.
How did American citizens handle that? Yankee ingenuity, my friend.*

HOW DRY WE ARE

In December 1917, Congress passed the 18th amendment prohibiting the manufacture, importation, sale, or consumption of alcohol. By January 1919, thirty six states had ratified the amendment, which went in effect on January 16, 1920. In the greatest capitulation to moral reform ever known, the country outlawed liquor. The United States went dry. Americans would henceforth be sober, and all of the problems caused by overimbibing—wife beating, child abuse, gambling, bankruptcy, and prostitution among them—would vanish. Or so the reformers said.

January was the month when the United States as a *nation* officially went dry. But Prohibition did not happen overnight. It was imposed gradually from county to county and state by state. The truth is that saloons, bars, and liquor stores closed down on January 16—and by January 17, the bootleggers and speakeasies had swung into operation. Since everyone knew that Prohibition was coming, liquor prices had been skyrocketing for months, and there was money to be made.

WE DELIVER

A friendly neighborhood bootlegger was more than happy to supply the alcohol that the government denied its citizens. It might be imported from across the border, or even from Europe. Bootleggers would bring bottles to your home or business hidden in baby carriages, fruit crates, or even brown paper bags. They also supplied the speakeasies or "speaks"—bars that operated in secret.

Such an operation required a network of smuggling, transportation, and protection services. Criminal gangs had experience in these areas, having run illegal gambling joints and brothels for years, and Prohibition was the best thing that ever happened to them. It transformed them into a powerful criminal network.

The first law on record, about 2100 B.C., was made to ban witchcraft.

"JOE SENT ME"

Hidden in restaurants, basements, apartments, mansions, farm-houses, or behind stores, the speakeasy was where you went for newfangled cocktails and entertainment. To get in, you knocked on the door and waited for a small door panel to slide open. A pair of eyes checked you out, but after you whispered the password like "Joe sent me" or flashed a club card or token, you were generally given entry.

Restaurant kitchens made perfect speakeasies, since they were already hidden from public view. Work crews gutted the cooking areas and brought in bars and intimate tables. Hidden panels and false walls hid the liquor. Extra doors and secret escape routes were installed. Slot machines were installed, and musicians were hired. Stick a piano player in the corner and voila!—instant speakeasy.

Since they were already operating illegally, many speaks served minors and unescorted women. The local police were paid handsomely to look the other way; graft was a major expense for the speakeasy owner.

A NATION OF LAWBREAKERS

The phrase *Noble Experiment*, by which Prohibition commonly became known, grew out of a 1928 campaign speech Hoover gave in which he described it as a "great social and economic experiment—noble in motive."

Did Prohibition have an effect on the nation's morals? It did, but not the one those reformers had hoped for. Before Prohibition, there were 15,000 bars in the city of New York. Early in the dry era, at least 32,000 speakeasies filled the gap. And every ordinary guy or gal who went into one for a drink was now breaking the law and a criminal. And don't forget all those now-organized and businesslike gangs. Al Capone, the criminal Bill Gates of his era, was making $60 million a year from liquor sales. According to some accounts, Al Capone controlled all of the 10,000 speakeasies in Chicago by 1930.

BUT SERIOUSLY, FOLKS

Prohibition, clearly a dismal failure, ended on April 7, 1933. The 18th Amendment was repealed by the 21st Amendment. But if you feel you missed out on all the fun, you can still join the

---

Until 1819 in the United Kingdom, felling a tree illegally was punishable by hanging.

Prohibition Party. With several hundred members nationwide, it's working hard to bring back the good old days. You can check it them out at www.prohibition.org.

* * * * *

THE NOT-SO-SOBER FACTS

An article that ran in *Repeal* magazine in 1931 counted 222,225 speakeasies in the United States, but it also said that the real number was probably double that.

Following are some samples of the figures (before doubling):

New York: 42,000
Illinois: 40,000
Pennsylvania: 20,000
California: 15,000
Massachusetts, Michigan, and New Jersey: 10,000 each
Wisconsin: 7,500
Ohio: 5,000
Kansas: 1,000
Wyoming, Idaho, and Washington, D.C.: 500 each

* * * * *

WHAT'S IN A NAME?

Both *bootlegger* and *speakeasy* were coined in the 1800s.

A *bootlegger* was someone who smuggled illegal whiskey in his tall boots.

Speakeasy is from "spake aisy," Irish and British dialect for "smuggler's den."

Redhanded—having blood on your hands—is a Scottish legal term that dates to 1432.

THE CAT'S PAJAMAS

Some 1920s lingo has survived the decades—terms like
"swanky," "sugar daddy," "nifty," "pipe down,"
"killjoy"—and "that's no baloney." But then there are
the ones that even Gramps might not remember.

Bearcat: A hot-blooded girl

Bell bottom: A sailor

Big six: A strong man (from the new, powerful six-cylinder engines)

Billboard: A flashy man or woman

Breezer: A convertible

Brillo: Someone who lives fast and spends money freely

Butt me: Give me a cigarette

Button shining: Close dancing

Cake-eater: A ladies' man

Charlie: A man with a moustache

Choice bit of calico: An attractive female

Corn shredder: A man who's an awkward dancer

Dog jock: A man who walks his wife's dogs

Face stretcher: An older woman trying to look young

Father Time: Any man older than 30

Fig leaf: A one-piece bathing suit

Fire alarm: A divorced woman

Fire extinguisher: A chaperone

Go chase yourself: Get lost, scram

Goofy: In love, attracted to

High hat: A snob

Jack: Money

Mop: A handkerchief

Oliver Twist: A good dancer

Once in a dirty while: From time to time

Panther sweat: Whiskey

Petting pantry: A movie theater

Priscilla: A girl who prefers to stay home

Prune pit: Anything that's old-fashioned

Sharpshooter: A young man who spends a lot and dresses well

Sheba: A woman with sex appeal

Sheik: A man with sex appeal

Spill an earful: Talk too much

Struggle buggy: The backseat of a car

Ten minutes: An exceptionally tough (hard-boiled) man

At birth Genghis Khan was named Temujin, which means "blacksmith."

GUERRILLA WARFARE PART 2

The Civil War

The hit-and-run tactics of guerrilla-style warfare were further refined with the use of cavalry units during the Civil War. Men on horseback with revolvers and repeating rifles could surprise and outgun much larger infantry forces who were mostly armed with muskets. Then, they could withdraw quickly and disappear into the wilderness.

MOSBY'S RAIDERS

Colonel John S. Mosby led a band of Confederate soldiers behind Union lines in northern Virginia. Because of his ability to hit the North's supply lines and then disappear into the countryside, he was given the nickname "the Gray Ghost." He so dominated the area militarily that it became known as Mosby's Confederacy.

In 1863, he and 29 of his men captured Union general Edwin H. Stoughton at the Fairfax Court House. Legend has it that the general was roused from his bed with a slap on the rear end. On another occasion, Mosby nearly captured the train on which Union general Ulysses S. Grant was traveling.

Mosby and his men were paroled at the end of the Civil War. He supported his former adversary, Ulysses S. Grant, when he ran for the presidency in 1868 because Mosby believed that Grant was the best man to restore the South and heal the union. Because of Mosby's distinguished war record, he was encouraged by Southern leaders to run for elective office but he declined. Later, President Rutherford B. Hayes named him the consul to Hong Kong and he served in that post with distinction. Mosby practiced law in San Francisco after his return to private life.

QUANTRILL'S RAIDERS

William C. Quantrill led a band of pro-slavery raiders in Kansas and Missouri before the Civil War. After the war started, he and his men were sworn into the Confederate army, and he was given the rank of captain.

Edward IV was the tallest English monarch at 6'3".

In 1863, Quantrill led his 300-plus followers in a violent attack on Lawrence, Kansas, burning the major buildings and killing or executing between 150 and 200 men and boys in the town. Later that year, Quantrill and his men disguised themselves in Union blue to launch an attack on the Union's outpost at Baxter Springs, Kansas.

Quantrill's brutal tactics earned him a reputation as a cruel and vicious leader. The Northern generals were determined to stop him, and in 1865, in a surprise attack by Union guerrillas, Quantrill was shot. He died a month later, at the age of 27.

JESSIE'S SCOUTS
Union general John C. Fremont organized a special ops group called "Jessie's Scouts," named after his wife, the former Jessie Benton. They often wore Confederate uniforms and operated in western Virginia and the Shenandoah Valley where they conducted raids on communications and supply lines and carried out assassinations.

IT AIN'T OVER TILL IT'S OVER
At the end of the Civil War, Confederate President Jefferson Davis and other Southern leaders wanted to continue the fight as a guerrilla war, but most of the Confederate generals opposed them, including Robert E. Lee, who considered that course of action to be dishonorable.

Many of the men who had fought with Mosby and Quantrill were unwilling or unable to return to civilian life. They became some of the era's most notorious outlaws. Members of Quantrill's Raiders included Jesse and Frank James, Cole Younger and his brothers, and the Dalton gang.

For more in the series, see "Guerrilla Warfare Part 3"—The U.S. Army Rangers during WWII—on page 142.

Robert Baden Powell once wrote a serious book on how to recognize German spies by their walk.

WILD ROSE

What if Ian Fleming had written Gone With the Wind?
It might have looked something like the real-life story of
Rose Greenhow, the ultimate Dixie chick.

Rose O'Neal Greenhow was a Southern belle if ever there was one. Her delicate white skin and jet-black hair, her fine features, her charm, and her well-spoken intelligence made her the toast of Washington, D.C. She was brought up there by a maiden aunt and was introduced into the high-society circles where she would spend all her glamorous life.

She was courted by politicians and other well-connected fellows, but in 1835 at the age of 18 she married a quiet, unassuming physician and settled down to married life. But fate had something more dramatic in store.

Belle's husband worked in the State Department, and through him she met the leading politicians and high-ranking military officers of the time. One close friend was Senator James Buchanan, who would later be elected president in 1856.

INSIDER TRADING

In 1857, her husband was killed in a fall. Not long after, one of her daughters died of an illness. Rose took to wearing widow's black, and even though she was soon surrounded by eligible suitors again, she never changed that custom. Rose had been raised as a Southern aristocrat, and she made no secret of her Confederate sympathies. As war loomed, she became a passionate secessionist. Because Belle moved in high political circles and had access to powerful men, she could socialize with Northern and Southern leaders alike.

A young Confederate soldier, Thomas Jordan, realized that she was perfectly placed to be a Confederate spy, and could report to General P. G. T. Beauregard, who was already one of her many friends. (It was Beauregard who personally fired the first cannon when Confederate and Union forces fought at Fort Sumter in South Carolina.) All Beauregard wanted from Rose Greenhow were the Union Army's battle plans.

The oldest known sample of a chewing gum was found near Ellos in western Sweden in 1993.

This might seem like a tall order, but Wild Rose (as she'd been called since she was a girl) was up to it. In July 1861, Rose invited a friend of hers, Senator Henry Wilson, to dinner and wondered aloud how the government was planning to defeat the rebels. The senator happened to be chairman of the Committee on Military Affairs; he accommodated his charming hostess by giving her a copy of the battle order and marching routes, which he'd received from General Irwin McDowell. She read and absorbed the information, and sent a friend, a Mrs. Duval, to General Beauregard with the information that "McDowell with 55,000 men will advance this day from Arlington Heights and Alexandria on to Manassas via Fairfax Court House and on to Centreville."

Beauregard lost no time preparing a surprise attack, and the result was the first Battle of Bull Run, in which the Union Army was overrun.

WHITE HOUSE LEAK

In August of the same year, Rose was able to provide some more interesting information: the complete plans of the fortifications of the city of Washington, D.C. Every mule and every musket was accounted for. The Confederates were delighted, but the Union realized that information was getting out. After the fiasco of Bull Run, the new commander, General George McClellan, proposed to do something about the leak. He hired Allan Pinkerton, of the Pinkerton National Detective Agency, to find out where the leak was coming from.

PINKERTON GETS HIS WOMAN

Pinkerton discovered that Rose was somehow involved, and he set out to catch her—personally. He trailed her through the streets, hid in bushes to look through her windows, and eventually observed her receiving military information from a young officer who seemed to be in love with her (and who later committed suicide). Even though Rose realized she was in danger, she stayed in Washington to warn her own network of agents—mostly society friends—that the game was up. As a result, Pinkerton arrested her.

A search of her house soon revealed the amazing extent of her activities. She had a network of some 50 agents, mostly

---

The well-chewed, 9,000-year-old gob of honey-sweetened resin still contained tooth marks.

women. She also had a large store of love letters from highly placed men she'd evidently been carrying on affairs with in order to extract the information that Beauregard and the Confederate forces needed. Since nobody knew what to do about the situation, Wild Rose was simply placed under house arrest. Her contacts extended to the cabinet of President Abraham Lincoln, and the potential for scandal was so huge that secret pressure was exerted to have her released.

Meanwhile, she'd become a celebrity in the North, thanks to newspaper articles, and crowds gathered every day outside her house. Her guards soon fell under her spell—she had them running errands for her—so the government felt forced to move her to a real prison. There she spent five uncomfortable months, accompanied by her eight-year-old daughter, while still managing to send coded messages out.

OH, WHAT A RELEASE IT IS!
Eventually, the authorities decided to give up and send her south to Virginia; it was a triumphant journey. The Unionists gave her a military guard of honor, and thousands came to cheer her. Rose drank champagne along the way, and she greeted the adoring Southern crowds who met her at the other end by pulling from her bosom a large Confederate flag—that she'd managed to sew together in her spare time in prison (this woman could do *anything*!). She was then taken to dine with President Davis, who had some new ideas for her.

HOBNOBBING WITH THE MONARCHS
Rose became a diplomat, traveling to Europe to plead the case of the Confederacy in London and Paris—where she met Queen Victoria and Emperor Napoléon III. She dashed off a book of prison memoirs, which became a best seller in England, and once again she was the queen of society. But her heart was still in the South, and in September 1864, she went on her last, heroic journey. She'd apparently negotiated a last-ditch secret agreement with Great Britain and had to carry the news back to President Davis that the British were prepared to enter the war against the Union. She also had $2,000 (1,652 euros) in gold—royalties from her book.

GUTSY TO THE END

The British merchant ship, the *Condor*, was a fast vessel, but it ran into a storm as it tried to run the Union blockade off Wilmington, North Carolina. Wild Rose demanded to be put down in a lifeboat, and accompanied by a few adoring officers, she tried to get to shore. At the mouth of the Cape Fear River, the storm capsized the vessel and Belle drowned—although some say it was the weight of the gold that dragged her down.

The whole South wept for her, and she was buried with full military honors, with thousands of soldiers following her coffin. Those who saw her drowned body said she was more beautiful in death than any living woman they had ever seen.

And the question will always remain—would the outcome have been different if Great Britain had stuck its great nose into America's Civil War?

* * * * *

GET OUTTA HERE!

The word "ostracize," meaning "to exclude from society," is from the Greek *ostrakizein*, "to banish by voting with potsherds (pot shards)," from *ostrakon*, "a piece of earthenware, a potsherd."

Ostracism was practiced in ancient Athens to get rid of any citizen whose power was considered dangerous for the liberty of the state. Each voter wrote on a shard the name of a person he wanted to banish, and a man whose name turned up often enough was sent away, normally for a period of ten years.

Venetian gondolas must be painted black unless they belong to a high official.

THE FIRST
GOLD DIGGER

The life and times of a lucky guy who blew it all.

Califonia schoolchildren all know the story: Captain John Sutter owned the land where gold was discovered in 1848, kicking off the famous Gold Rush. But what brought Sutter to California? Was it a premonition of greatness; did he sense that fortune was about to shine on him?

Actually, he was on the lam.

RUNNING FROM THE PAST

Sutter owed a lot of money in his native Switzerland and was about to be thrown into debtors' prison. In 1834 he abandoned his wife and four children and left the country. A few years later in Hawaii, he borrowed money, hired some native servants, and hooked up with a woman named Manaiki. They packed up everything and in 1839 sailed for California, which was still a part of Mexico. John Sutter became a Mexican citizen.

Sutter met with the provincial governor and did some fast talking, exaggerating his military record and his solvency. He must have spoken well: he was appointed a militia captain and *alcalde* (mayor)—and given nearly 50,000 acres in the Sacramento Valley to settle. He named his little universe New Helvetia (New Switzerland).

SUTTER IN THE GUTTER

As you may have already guessed, Sutter was not a particularly stand-up guy. His new role as a kind of feudal master brought out the worst in him. He employed local Indians, keeping them at work by force when necessary, and locking them up at night. Whippings and executions were performed when necessary, and when he needed more laborers, Sutter sent his private "army" into the foothills to capture unwilling workers from the Nisenen tribe.

Sutter borrowed more money to add land to his holdings. He

The word "Khan," as in "Genghis Khan" and "Kublai Khan," means "the ruler."

also drank heavily and chased after women. While Sutter kept Manaiki at his New Helvetia fort, acquaintances reported that he enjoyed the charms of many Nisenen and Miwok women, willing and otherwise.

THE PAST CATCHES UP WITH HIM
Meanwhile, news of the gold discovery reached Switzerland and Frau Sutter. She sent one of their sons to California, at which point Sutter, who was heavily in debt, signed over his property to the son, mainly to stall foreclosure, and took off with an Indian mistress. Sutter's wife and other children showed up the next year, but by then, there was little for them to enjoy of Papa's empire. Most of his employees had left to search for gold in the mines. Gold seekers overran Sutter's land, slaughtered his herds, and stole whatever food, tools, and lumber they found.

Sutter moved his original family to a smaller piece of land that he thought he owned, but the courts of the new state of California disagreed and he lost that home as well. By 1865 the California legislature voted him a pension because, quite honestly, his poverty was an embarrassment. When that money ran out, Swiss Family Sutter moved to Pennsylvania, where he died.

* * * * *

BANKRUPT

Many people view bankruptcy as an admission of failure, but the excusing of debts has been around since the time of Moses. The Jewish law provided for a period, every seven years, where all debts were excused and the slate wiped clean. Jewish lawmakers knew that keeping people under heavy debt forever would only cause their overall economy to diminish. By excusing debts periodically, their economy grew because people had more money to put back into its growth.

GOLD RUSH GALS

*How various women, respectable and not, made their
living in California's Gold Rush territory.*

When gold was discovered in California, men rushed
there from all over the world to get rich. For the most
part, they left their wives and sweethearts behind.
According to the 1850 census, California was 93 percent male;
in the mining country it was more like 97 percent. What sort of
women made up that tiny female population? Here's a sample:

RESPECTABLE ENTREPRENEURS
Forced to barbecue for themselves, the men in California missed
home cooking more than anything else. Some savvy wives realized
they could profit from this situation. One woman baked 1,200 pies
a month and sold them to the prospectors, raking in $18,000 over
a couple of years. One Señora Pérez served up dozens of plates of
tortillas and beans to the hungry miners and earned more than
$50 a day—about four times what her customers were making
mining for gold.

SUPERWOMAN, circa 1849
Luzena Wilson realized there was gold in them thar guys when a
miner offered her $10 for the biscuits she served to her family.
While her husband panned for gold, Luzena cooked. She charged
a dollar for each meal, and pretty soon had hundreds of customers. Her husband, no dummy, gave up mining to help her
cook and keep a boardinghouse. Eventually the couple invested
all their new savings in barley, stored it in their new house
and—in a nasty turn of luck—was wiped out by a flood that
soaked and sprouted the grain.

   That's okay. Luzena started over, building her own tables out
of boards and stakes, and cooking again. She was even more successful this time around and soon had bags of gold dust hidden in
the oven at night and thousands of dollars stashed in her mattress.

   Then the Wilsons bought a hotel. This time, within a year, a
fire wiped them out. Mr. Wilson went to work baling hay, and

Luzena went back to cooking in mining camps again...and ended up owning yet another hotel. This one they kept, and years later they retired in style.

THE OTHER WAY TO A MAN'S HEART (AND WALLET)

French was the ethnicity of choice among prostitutes in California. Whether they were from Bangor, Maine, or gay Paree, all the best hookers claimed to be French. Maybe the women thought it made them more exotic (even though, when the ratio was 33 men to one woman, who needed an accent?).

Loose women tended bar in the saloons and served as bankers in gambling halls, where their very presence unsettled the men. Not having seen a woman in months, men from the mines would drink more, gamble foolishly, and let themselves be shamelessly fleeced when urged on by femme fatales.

THAT'S ENTERTAINMENT

Female actors, musicians, and dancers also flocked to California, charging more per performance than they could get anywhere else. Strolling musicians with guitars and tambourines could earn hatfuls of gold by strumming sentimental songs like "Home, Sweet Home" for lonely miners. Child star Lotta Crabtree got her start at age six touring the mining camps where her song-and-dance act was rewarded with bags of gold dust thrown at her feet.

Women appeared onstage in California as soon as the stages were built. The Eagle Theatre in Sacramento opened in 1849, and customers paid $3–$5 (2.4 to 4 euros) a ticket to goggle at Elizabeth Ray, the only woman in the company. Few could understand her thick New Zealand accent, but they didn't care. She was a female, and that was all it took.

San Francisco had legitimate theater too, and soon ballerinas, operatic singers, chanteuses, actresses, and scandalous dancers like Lola Montez were all over the new state. Miners paid for tickets in gold nuggets and dust, and box office profits boomed. That's show biz.

A: The original profession of both men was doctor.

ONE POTATO, TWO POTATO...

Ten things you probably never knew about potatoes and Ireland.

1. No one in Ireland or most of Europe had even heard of potatoes before the 1600s. Spuds, which originated in South America, arrived in Europe via English and Spanish explorers.
2. Potatoes grew prolifically in the rocky, boggy Irish soil. Enough potatoes could grow on a half-acre (0.2 hectares) to feed a family of six.
3. You can live on potatoes. All you need to add is a little buttermilk or fish, and maybe some cabbage, for fat and vitamin A. As a diet, it's duller than dirt, but it does keep you alive.
4. Although packed with nutrition, you need a lot of potatoes if they're the main course. Workingmen ate around 14 pounds (6 kg) of spuds daily to stay healthy and active.
5. By the 1840s, about 3 million people in Ireland were eating potatoes for breakfast, lunch, and dinner.
6. Potatoes kept people so healthy that the poor produced more babies than ever before. Fifty years after the potato was introduced to the island, Ireland's population had doubled. Coincidence? We think not.
7. In 1845, a third of the total tilled land in Ireland was devoted to growing potatoes.
8. In 1845, a fungus named *Phytophthora infestans* attacked the potato crop. Leaves turned black, new spuds withered, and those already grown turned black, soft, and smelly. Those 3 million, mostly poverty-stricken folks who depended on potatoes suddenly had nothing to eat. Only potatoes, the foodstuff of the poor Irish, were affected; other crops grew just fine, but only the rich could afford them.
9. The Irish Potato Famine (also known as The Great Famine and The Great Hunger) lasted until 1851.
10. No one knows for sure how many people died during the Great Famine, but historians now put the number at between 500,000 and 1,100,000. Another million left the country, many for the United States.

Hawaii's flag displays a Union flag as part of its design.

CHANEL NO. 1

You've heard that clothes make the man?
Meet the suit that made the woman.

Gabrielle "Coco" Chanel was born in Samur, France, in 1883. Her life got off to a rocky start. Her mother died shortly after Gabrielle's birth, and her father took off, abandoning the five Chanel children. Gabrielle was raised in a local Catholic orphanage until she came of age, at which point the nuns found her a job at a local boutique, the House of Grampayre.

TALENT WILL OUT

The little shop assistant honed her skills as a seamstress, and soon she had a faithful following of customers who came directly to her for alterations. She also worked at a tailor shop once a week. And in addition to her two day jobs, did some moonlighting as a café and concert singer for a few years. She used to sing one of those sad French songs about a poor girl who lost her little dog, Coco—that's where her nickname came from.

WITH A LITTLE HELP FROM *MES AMIS*

She did very well in the male companionship department: two of her lovers—a military officer and an English industrialist—bankrolled her first millinery shop in Paris in 1909. It didn't take her long to establish herself as a leading fashion designer.

In 1920, Chanel borrowed an idea from Charles Frederick Worth, the founding father of French couture. Worth had created the first woman's suit with a masculine shirt combo back in 1869, believe it or not. Chanel's version was made up of a cardigan jacket, skirt, and shirt. At the time, women were starting to join the workforce—and even to drive automobiles. Her designs emphasized clean, flowing lines with plain colors—usually gray, beige, and navy—and fabrics associated with menswear: knit and wool jersey.

THE SUIT

What made a Chanel suit so remarkable wasn't simply the boxy design, exquisite fabrics, or the perfect hand-sewing, but the practical details. The suit was designed to be worn loose in the belly to accommodate the average woman's figure. The slim skirt didn't pull or crease when a woman moved around. A ribbon was sewn into the waist of the skirt to keep a blouse properly in place, and a side zipper made getting in and out of the skirt more efficient. The hemline was progressive for the time, since it made women's ankles visible. The collarless jacket, made of light fabric weighted down by a gold chain, resembled a cardigan-style sweater. Both the suit jacket and the skirt featured coordinating trim—typically braided—and lining.

At the time, the Chanel suit was truly a couture creation, only accessible to the wealthiest of women, who had the funds to go to Paris for up to seven (count 'em, seven) fittings. The high price tag didn't curb the public's enthusiasm for her designs though.

The first perfume named for a designer, the ever-classic Chanel No. 5, was introduced in 1923. The late 1920s saw the introduction of classic Chanel designs—the little black dress and the cardigan jacket. In the 1930s Samuel Goldwyn hired her to dress some of his stars. She also developed a line of costume jewelry inspired by the Art Deco movement. Sales and her success continued unabated until WWII and the Nazi occupation of Paris, which cast a pall on the fashion business—among other things.

NAUGHTY, NAUGHTY
An affair with a Nazi officer during the German occupation of France hurt her popularity and sales suffered, but Coco staged a comeback in February 1954. *Life* magazine ran a four-page spread that raved about Chanel's comfortable style and the following month, a navy blue Chanel suit appeared on the cover of French *Vogue*. She also appropriated clothing styles worn by men and introduced sports clothes for women including bell bottom pants and pea jackets. Chanel fever had struck once again. In 1969 Katharine Hepburn played her in the Broadway show *Coco*.

CHANEL, UPDATED
When Coco Chanel died in 1971, her custom suits were fetching as much as $12,000 (10,000 euros). Several of her assistants assumed command of her design house, but sales stagnated until Karl Lagerfeld stepped in as chief designer in 1983. Lagerfeld

catered to a younger clientele, while keeping Chanel's signature sense of modernity, style, and silhouette intact. In 1991, he successfully paired the Chanel jacket with trendy denim miniskirts. In 2001, he designed his entire fall couture collection without a single skirt; he liberated the jacket as a stand-alone symbol of Chanel style.

Through decades of hit-or-miss trends, the Chanel suit has stayed the course on the catwalk. At an average of $5,000 (4,000 euros) for a ready-to-wear suit (the vintage pieces can fetch more), the Chanel suit still claims a unique place in the history of fashion. Start saving, girls.

* * * * *

CHERCHEZ LA FEMME

Some revealing Chanel quotes:

"Fashion is made to become unfashionable."

"Fashion has become a joke. The designers have forgotten that there are women inside the dresses. Most women dress for men and want to be admired. But they must also be able to move, to get into a car without bursting their seams! Clothes must have a natural shape."

When a young woman asked Chanel, "Where should one use perfume?" she answered, "Wherever one wants to be kissed."

"I don't understand how a woman can leave the house without fixing herself up a little—if only out of politeness. And then, you never know, maybe that's the day she has a date with destiny. And it's best to be as pretty as possible for destiny."

"Nothing goes out of fashion sooner than a long dress with a very low neck."

"In order to be irreplaceable one must always be different."

THE NIGHT YOU COULDN'T GET A TAXI IN PARIS

Because that was the night the taxis carried the soldiers to the front.

During WWI, Germany and France had only been at war since August 3, 1914, but by late August, Germany already had a war plan that called for the capture of Paris within six weeks. As the day approached, German aircraft began dropping leaflets on the city announcing their imminent arrival. On August 30, German aircraft bombed Paris and killed two civilians.

By early September, the Germans were within 30 miles (48 km) of Paris, so close that they could see the top of the Eiffel Tower. The exhausted French and British armies had retreated to the south. The French government cleaned out their Paris offices and moved to Bordeaux. About a third of the population went with them. Those Parisians who stayed began preparing for a state of siege.

TAXI! TAXI!

On September 6, 1914, with the help of the Brits, the French pushed the Germans back and halted their advance at the Marne River. But the tired Allied soldiers couldn't hold off the enemy for long. A British officer wrote of his troops, "I would never have believed that men could be so tired and so hungry and yet live." Reinforcements were needed. The French Army's 7th Division had 6,000 troops ready to join the attack—but no way to get them to the front lines.

Desperate to save his city, General Joseph Gallieni, the military governor of Paris, had a brilliant idea. The order went out that all Parisian taxis and drivers were to meet at the Esplanade des Invalides. As word got around, passengers in Parisian taxis found themselves unceremoniously deposited on the street. About 600 vehicles, including trucks, limos, and a racing car or two, showed up.

The Afghan hound, a hunting dog and pet, originated not in Afghanistan but in ancient Egypt.

DRIVING OFF INTO THE SUNSET

The taxis hustled to the railway station, where each loaded up with five infantry soldiers. At dusk on September 7, the drive to the front began.

The hitch was that the drivers had to make their way without auto lights so they wouldn't be spotted and bombed by enemy aircraft. And bombs weren't the only problem. The Renault taxis were high-off-the-ground vehicles with tiny engines; they were slow, and some broke down altogether (oh, for a couple of Humvees!). And since water was in short supply, most taxi drivers were given rations of wine for their journey. Combining wine with the lack of headlights, it was amazing that some soldiers got to the front at all.

But they did. The operation, remembered as the Taxis of the Marne, was a huge success. Most taxis made two trips, taking about 6,000 men to reinforce the beleaguered French and British troops. With the help of those reinforcements, the First Battle of the Marne was won, and Paris was saved. The Germans not only didn't advance any farther—by September 11, they were forced into full retreat.

* * * * *

PHOOEY, I WOULDN'T PAY A NICKEL FOR THAT JUNKER!

Can you spot the three words of German origin in the above title? They're "phooey," "nickel," and "junker."

A short list of other German words in English:

carouse	poltergeist
cookbook	protein
hamster	quartz
hoodlum	waltz
iceberg	wunderkind
noodle	yodel
ouch	zigzag
plunder	zinc

Why call it an "Afghan?" Because it developed its present traits in the mountains of Afghanistan.

HOLLYWOOD REWRITES HISTORY: *TITANIC*

The story of how the "unsinkable" ocean liner hit an iceberg on the night of April 14, 1912, and sank— with various rewrites, intended or not.

The Rewrite: Jack (Leonardo DiCaprio) tells Rose (Kate Winslet) that he and his father used to go ice fishing on Lake Wissota in Wisconsin.
The Facts: The man-made lake wasn't created until 1917, five years after the *Titanic* sank.

The Rewrite: Jack talks about drawing and selling portraits on the Santa Monica Pier and proposes that he and Rose could "ride on the roller coaster till we throw up."
The Facts: The pier was built in 1909, but the roller coaster wasn't up and running until at least 1916.

The Rewrite: The woman we know as "the Unsinkable Molly Brown" (Kathy Bates) is called Molly during the trip.
The Facts: Margaret "Maggie" Brown didn't get her nickname until after the sinking, when the media started referring to her as "the Unsinkable Mrs. Brown" and "Molly."

The Rewrite: The distress signal that the radioman sends out is unintelligible—definitely not Morse code.
The Facts: There is an urban legend afoot that the *Titanic* was the first ship to use the new SOS code to signal distress and that a nearby ship didn't understand the signal—and therefore didn't come to the *Titanic's* rescue. This is untrue. The real radioman alternated signals between the old CQD (which stood for "seek you, danger"), the new SOS (selected because of its distinctive dot-dot-dot dash-dash-dash dot-dot-dot, *not* because it stood for "Save Our Ship" or "Save Our Souls"), and MGY (the *Titanic's* code name).

In 1946, the U.S. Marines were called to subdue a prison riot on Alcatraz Island.

The Rewrite: After the rescue, the survivors mill around under a green Statue of Liberty.
The Facts: The statue is made of copper; it took nearly 70 years of natural aging for it to turn green. Since it was erected in 1886, it should have still been copper brown in 1912.

The Rewrite: The most titanic distortion of facts was committed against First Officer William Murdoch, who is portrayed as an incompetent hysteric who shoots two passengers and then himself.
The Facts: According to eyewitness accounts, Officer Murdoch was a true hero. Not only did he guide passengers to lifeboats and throw deck chairs overboard for those in the sea to cling to, but he also gave his own life jacket to a passenger and, like any upstanding officer, went down with his ship.

The portrayal caused such an uproar in Murdoch's hometown of Dalbeattie, Scotland, that 20th Century Fox vice-president Scott Neeson visited the town to deliver a personal apology to William Murdoch's 80-year-old nephew. Producer-director James ("I'm king of the world!") Cameron never apologized.

* * * * *

DRAMA KING

Ancient Greek dramatist Aeschylus, aka "the Father of Tragedy," was born in 525 B.C. in the Greek city of Eleusis. At that time, "plays" consisted of little more than a single actor on stage reciting lines, while a chorus of actors and dancers accompanied him from the wings. Aeschylus took the novel step of introducing a second actor to the proceedings, and so the whole idea of drama was born. So, if you want to know who's responsible for *Days of Our Lives*, Aeschylus is the man to blame! In all, he wrote more than 90 plays, but only seven have survived. They are *The Suppliant Women, The Persians, Seven Against Thebes, Prometheus Bound,* and the *Oresteia* trilogy.

LET'S GO TO GREENLAND!

Such excitement! Viking ships, dramatic climate changes, mysterious mass disappearances—have we found the site for the next Survivor season? Or the next extreme vacation spot?

Greenland, the world's largest island at more than 800,000 square miles (2 million square km), isn't quite a country. It's officially part of Denmark; but it does have its own capital (Nuuk) and its own official language (a local version of Inuit or Eskimo).

LIVING ON THE EDGE

Greenland has something else: extremely inhospitable conditions. During the course of its history, the island has been repeatedly abandoned by people who tried to settle it, something that never happened in Canada, Siberia, or other Arctic regions. Maybe it's due to the fact that every square inch of Greenland is covered with a mile-thick sheet of ice.

If it's covered with all that ice, why on earth is it called Greenland? The famous Viking, Erik the Red, discovered it and named the island Greenland to attract settlers. In A.D. 986, he established a Norse outpost there, with the settlers arriving by ship from neighboring Iceland.

Approximately 5,000 years before the Vikings arrival, Greenland had been inhabited by two different tribes. Little is known about them because for some unknown reason they abandoned Greenland and it remained uninhabited for something like 3,000 years.

The Thule people, who are the ancestors of the modern Canadian Inuit arrived at about the same time as the Vikings, in the 10th century. They brought two new aids to survival: the kayak and the dog sled.

In A.D. 1000, Erik's son, Leif Eriksson, brought the first European settlers; Greenland quickly became a Christian settlement, and the church quickly became the main landowner. The church also took an active part in Greenland's international trade,

---

Marco Polo dictated his *Travels of Marco Polo* to a fellow inmate in a Genoa prison.

exporting such unique items as walrus ivory, polar bear pelts, and snow-white falcons to Europe.

TROUBLE ON THE MAINLAND

By the 12th century, the Norse colonies were well established, and conducted regular trade with Europe on their own account. There were pirates prowling the seas, but the foreign trade ships that sailed to and from these remote colonies were under royal protection from the powerful kings of Norway, which officially claimed Greenland in 1261. When Norway united with Denmark in 1380, Greenland first came under Danish rule. Even though the farming settlements were completely reliant on outsiders for their link to the rest of the world, trade was evidently working out for the Greenlanders. But in the 1400s, something went horribly wrong. As the Black Death swept through Europe in the 1300s, trade between Norway and Greenland faltered; around 1380, it stopped completely.

HEY, WHERE'D EVERYBODY GO?

For at least 80 years, nobody at all from the outside world made it to Greenland, and the Greenlanders themselves had no oceangoing boats to attempt the journey in the other direction. When Scandinavian mariners made contact again, they found that the colonies were empty. Some time between 1480 and 1500, the settlements in Greenland ceased to exist. Nobody knows exactly what happened to the settlers. Modern archaeological methods show that the most likely culprit was the weather.

Climate change in the Arctic isn't a new phenomenon. The "green land" that Erik the Red had found became less and less green over the centuries. The winters grew colder and the summers became shorter, until, perhaps, the settlers reached a point where they couldn't grow enough food to keep their livestock alive over the winter. Did they join the Inuit and abandon their useless farm buildings?

POSSIBLE FORWARDING ADDRESS

There's a theory, popular in Greenland itself that the Norse settlers left for America. Although many experts reject the idea, there's some evidence to support it. The remains of what could have been a Viking ship were found in Cedar Rapids, Iowa, in

1866. Two stones with Scandinavian runic inscriptions are supposed to have been found in America, one of them next to a Mandan Native American village in North Dakota. The Mandan became famous in the 19th century as the "European Indians" because of their European looks and the fact that their culture possessed some Christian legends (such as Noah and the Flood). These elements could possibly match up with a small emigration of Norse settlers from Greenland.

BACK IN GREENLAND

The union between Norway and Denmark ended in 1814; Greenland remained with Denmark. Missionaries, scientists, whalers, and explorers rediscovered it, ushering in the first attempts by adventurous foreigners to reach the North Pole overland. There were some new Scandinavian settlements in the 18th century, but things didn't change much until the 20th century, when the modern world suddenly arrived in the shape of the United States Air Force.

During World War II, the USAF saw Greenland as a strategically important location and built a number of bases there, including Thule Base in the far north. The Pentagon decided to keep these facilities operating during the cold war, expanding Thule in 1953 and keeping nuclear weapons there from 1968 on.

HOME RULE

In the 1970s, Denmark granted Greenland home rule after a growing body of protest over Denmark's control of the government. A few years later, Greenland joined the European community, only to withdraw in 1982 because the citizens wanted more control—this time over their economy. Until the 1900s, the economy was based on seal hunting, but the seals eventually migrated north. Fishing is a major economic activity, but it only employs about a third of the population. The bitter climate makes farming next to impossible. Which doesn't leave too many options for survival. But, hey, what about tourism? If you don't mind year-round ice and snow, how would you like to share your beach holiday with walrus and polar bears this year?

Let's all go to Greenland!

The line of succession to the British throne includes 60 people.

BATHROOM SAFETY

Close the door and have a seat. You're in one of the most dangerous places in the house.

Your bathroom looks pretty innocent, doesn't it? A toilet with a few inches of water. A bathtub made for relaxing soaks or quick, refreshing showers. Wrong. Maybe you ought to call for backup before you "go" next time.

DON'T EVER TAKE A BATH AGAIN

What could be better for sore muscles or a sore psyche than a hot soak in a steamy bubble bath? Well, you can forget about it if you want to live a long and healthy life.

- Leader of the French Revolution Jean-Paul Marat was stabbed in the bathtub by a woman who supported the opposition.
- Agamemnon, Greek army commander during the siege of Troy, was also slain in the bathtub.

DON'T EVEN THINK OF GOING NEAR THE TOILET

- Edmund II, king of England, was stabbed from beneath as he sat on a privy.
- Some reports say that another "king," Elvis Presley, died while on the toilet.
- And in case you're thinking you can hold it instead, that's not such a good idea, either. Danish astronomer Tycho Brahe died because he waited too long and his bladder burst.

JUST STAY AWAY ALTOGETHER

- Fleeing his killers, King James I of Scotland was assassinated in a bathroom.
- British kings didn't fare much better: King George II was discovered by his valet, dead on the floor of his bathroom. King Henry III was killed by a fanatical friar on his way out of the loo.
- Roman emperor Elagabalus was slain in a latrine by his own troops.
- Architect Louis I. Kahn was found dead in a bathroom at New York City's Pennsylvania Station, his identity unknown for days.

Scotland's Balmoral Castle, a residence of Her Majesty the Queen, is now a wedding venue.

THE COOLEST MAN IN HISTORY

Willis Haviland Carrier improved the quality of life for millions of people. He was the genius who invented air-conditioning.

I n the dark, hot days "B.C." (Before Carrier), people tried all sorts of creative methods to keep cool. In India, they used to take wet grass mats and put them over the windows. The evaporating water would then absorb the heat of the room and make it a few degrees cooler inside. Roman emperors ordered snow to be brought down from the mountains. (Romans without the resources of an emperor could buy their own snow at a shop.) Around A.D. 1500, Leonardo da Vinci built a water-driven fan to cool the bedroom of his patron's wife. (For more about Leonardo's inventiveness, see page 465.) In the 1830s, a Florida doctor who was worried about his patients' body temperatures getting too high rigged up buckets of ice above their beds and blew air over them. None of these methods were particularly effective— although the snow probably made a refreshing snack.

THE CARRIER OF GOOD NEWS

In 1902, Willis Carrier, a young engineer fresh out of Cornell University, was faced with a problem. A publishing company in Brooklyn, New York, had found that the humidity of the air in their printing plant was affecting the size of the paper they were printing on. It was making color printing (which had to be done by running the same piece of paper through the presses multiple times) undependable and wasteful. At the time, Carrier was work- ing for the Buffalo Forge Company, which manufactured heating and ventilation equipment. The year before Carrier had made a splash by saving the company $40,000 (33,000 euros) in money lost to fixing inefficient heating installation.

Carrier knew that when liquids evaporate they remove heat from and cool the air. He devised a system using ammonia and artesian well water as the evaporating liquid. The gas that was cre- ated when the mixture evaporated in a room and cooled the air was recovered and piped outside so that it would release its heat and turn back into a liquid. The liquid was then piped back into the room so that the process could start over again.

A COLD FRONT SWEEPS AMERICA

Once the word got out about Buffalo Forge's techniques for temperature and humidity control (which was called "air-conditioning" starting in 1906), all kinds of businesses got their own. Air-conditioning was used in industries as diverse as textiles, tobacco, and pharmaceuticals. All the while, Carrier was making small improvements to the technology to make it safer and more efficient.

In 1914, Buffalo Forge made the phenomenally stupid move of eliminating Carrier's division of the company. Carrier and his colleagues went it alone and, in the early 1920s, invented an improved refrigerating machine to put in their air conditioners. It used a new kind of compressor and a safer refrigerant than ammonia, the industry standard. Carrier Engineering Corporation started producing the smaller, more efficient (and nontoxic) air conditioners and quickly broke into a new market. When the J. L. Hudson Company bought an air conditioner in 1924 for the basement of their Detroit, Michigan, department store, it was the first air conditioner used specifically for personal comfort.

Air-conditioning for comfort really took off in the next few years, when it began to appear in movie theaters. Theaters in Los Angeles, Houston, Dallas, and New York were the first to take up the technology; then, every theater wanted air-conditioning. Most advertised it as being as much of an attraction as the movies playing, which sometimes might not have been far from the truth. Snow- and icicle-covered lettering on signs promised patrons an environment that was 20 degrees cooler inside. Air-conditioning was now accessible to everyone.

IN THE COMFORT OF YOUR OWN HOME

When World War II was over, air-conditioning began to find its way into private homes and cars, until gradually, it became standard in both. Unsurprisingly, its popularity grew faster in the hottest places. In 1966, Texas became the first state to have half its homes air-conditioned. By the end of the decade, Florida and Louisiana also passed the 50 percent mark. Some scholars claim the increase in comfort that comes from air-conditioning can be credited with reversing the South's decades-long trend of population loss, which turned around in the 1960s, just as air-conditioning became more prevalent.

A number of studies have ascertained that productivity is greatly enhanced by air-conditioning in the workplace. Of course, a number of studies have also shown that taking an afternoon nap also improves productivity, but companies have yet to start routinely offering their employees pull-out beds. Oh, well. One out of two isn't bad.

* * * * *

TEFLON FINALLY PANS OUT

On April 6, 1938, Roy Plunkett, an employee of DuPont, was experimenting with cooling gases. One day he left some tetrafluoroethylene gas in a container, and upon returning the next day, he noticed it had turned into superslick waxy substance with impressive properties. Teflon was born. But no one at DuPont ever thought about how it might be applied to consumer stuff.

Nevertheless, there was enough of it floating around for Frenchman Marc Gregoire to start using it in the early 1950s on his fishing tackle to minimize sticking and tangling. When his wife wondered if the Teflon might keep her eggs from constantly sticking to the pan, Marc performed a test. When he found out how well it worked, he went into business.

He was selling over a million pans a year, when a United Press International (UPI) foreign correspondent, Thomas Hardie, came across one at a friend's house. Knowing a good thing when he saw one, Hardie had Gregoire ship him 3,000 Teflon-coated pans. After a mailing of samples to 100 department stores that produced no results, Hardie went straight to Macy's in Herald Square, New York City, just before Christmas 1960. The 200 pans that Macy's ordered sold out in two days.

The Guinness Book of World Records declares Teflon the slipperiest substance on the planet.

In 1619, a Dutch ship brought slaves to British North America for the first time.

YOU SHRED IT, WHEAT!

A lot of 1930s slang grew out of the emerging swing era and the sad days of the Depression, with a little Chicago mob thrown in for good measure.

Abercrombie: A know-it-all

Abyssinia: I'll be seeing you

All wet: No good

Ameche: A telephone (after Don Ameche, who starred in 1939's *The Story of Alexander Graham Bell*)

Big It: A conceited person

Blow your wig: Become very excited

Bouncing Betty: A car, especially a Ford

Brodie: A mistake

Cat: A fan of swing music

Chase yourself: Get lost!

Check or checker: A dollar

Chicago overcoat: A coffin

City juice: A glass of water

Clam-bake: Wild swing music

Copper: A policeman

Crumb: A loser

Dead hoofer: A bad dancer

Drag a hoof: Dance

Egg: A crude person

Frog-skin: A dollar

Grounder: A cigarette picked up off the ground

Hit a flick: Go to a movie

Hot squat: The electric chair

Hump: A cigarette (probably after the camel on a pack of Camels)

In your hat!: I don't believe that!

Jack: Money

Jungle: A hobo camp

Mitt me kid!: Congratulate me!

Off the boat: Out of style

Off the cob: Corny

Pearl diver: A dish washer

Pip: An attractive person

Suds: Money

Sweet patootie: An attractive woman

Wet sock: A social misfit

Veteran's Day (Armistice Day) is the holiday celebrating the end of WWI.

DANCING FOR DOLLARS

Dance marathons started out as innocent fun but wound
up as grim as the Depression that ended them.

Post–World War I America was in a mood to break all records: popular events included endurance kissing and hand-holding contests, eating marathons, and flagpole sitting. A guy named Shipwreck Kelly became a national celebrity after sitting atop a flagpole for 7 days, 13 hours, and 13 minutes. When someone challenged Bill Williams to push a peanut up Pike's Peak with his nose, he agreed. It took him 30 days, and he won $500 (415 euros) for the feat. It all had to do with the mood of the day. But nothing caught the public's fancy as much as dance marathons.

A CRAZE IS BORN

The birth of U.S. dance marathons can be traced to early 1923 when, inspired by a record set in Britain a few weeks earlier, Miss Alma Cummings took to the floor of the first American dance marathon, which was held in New York City's somewhat seedy Audubon Ballroom. Cummings wore out six male partners over the next 27 hours and set a world record. Within a week, a French college student broke that record. A few days later, Cummings retook the title, which was soon broken again, this time by a Cleveland, Ohio, salesgirl. The challenge was on.

A few weeks after Cummings's win, a Texas dance hall owner got the brilliant idea of charging spectators admission (25¢ during the day, $1 at night). He gave his first winner—Miss Magdalene Williams—a prize of $50 (42 euros). On April 16, Cleveland's Madeline Gottschick beat Williams's record with a time of 66 hours. Within days, that record was broken three times. On June 10, Bernie Brand danced for 217 hours (more than 9 days) and went home with $5,000 (4,151 euros) in prizes.

In just a few months in 1923, the dance marathon craze had swept the nation and the world. And so it continued throughout the 1920s.

The Romans believed in numerous household gods and spirits.

THE DOWNBEAT

The deaths of a few supposedly healthy young people—including 27-year-old Homer Morehouse from heart failure after 87 hours of dancing—brought some unwelcome attention. Officials banded together with church groups (who saw the marathons as immoral) and movie theater owners (who saw the marathons as competition) to try to stomp out the fad. Critics called the contests "dangerous, useless, and disgraceful," and they even likened them to the dancing manias of 14th-century Europe.

TAKE A LOAD OFF

In an effort to save their golden goose, promoters added rest periods during which the dancers could lie down on cots, take hot showers, or have their injuries seen to. Some even let dancers take a short walk outside, but eating still was done while dancing, at chest-high buffet tables set up mid-floor. The length and spacing of rest periods varied from contest to contest: 15 minutes every hour, 11 minutes out of every 90 minutes, and so on. Another change was that couples versus individual contestants became the norm. But a dancer wasn't stuck with one partner for the duration. If your partner gave out, you could dance solo for a set amount of time while seeking another, healthier partner in the group. Now, thanks to rest periods and partners who could hold you up while you slept, a marathon could last for weeks. But watching a dance floor full of droopy couples wasn't going to hold the crowd's attention, so vaudeville skits were added. So were professional dancers, who worked the crowd and posed as good guys and bad guys, like modern-day pro wrestlers.

A marathon that started with 100 contestants would dwindle to the hard core after a week or two. The remaining couples would drag themselves across the floor, but at specific times the emcee would make an announcement, and the dancers would be expected to run a 10-minute footrace or perform an all-out foxtrot or tango—the losers of which would be eliminated.

TALK ABOUT DEPRESSING

Marathons were well established by the arrival of the Depression in 1929, and they became the perfect escape. If you could scrape together the admission, you could come in out of the weather and

They included Cardea, the goddess of hinges, and Forculus, god of the door leaves.

be entertained; if you were young and strong enough, you could enter and try to win a few thousand dollars. Even if you lost, you'd be well taken care of while you lasted: three square meals, snacks, and medical teams to treat your injuries and give you rubdowns.

Of course, you could be mistreated, too, by "grinds"—show employees whose job it was to prod contestants who fell behind, or generally harass the dancers to keep things exciting. Promoters staged weddings and fights and it was hard to differentiate between what was staged or genuine. But there was plenty of real drama: sleep-deprived dancers suffered hallucinations and delusions, hysteria, and bouts of temporary amnesia.

THE DANCE IS ENDED

By the mid-1930s, the contests had lost their glitter. What had been lighthearted entertainment became a struggle for survival, and it showed. Dance marathons weren't fun anymore. The country was in a Depression in more ways than one. The marathoners, once viewed as respectable and plucky, were now viewed as being no better than the vagrants who traveled the country looking for food or work. They became a reminder of the failed American dream; a symbol of just how low the country had fallen.

One by one, states and cities across the country banned dance marathons. The shows continued on a small scale until the mid-1940s, but their heyday had long passed. Danceathons gave way to walkathons, which gave way to skateathons, which birthed the roller derby. But that's another story.

* * * * *

According to *The Guinness Book of World Records*, the longest dance marathon was won by Mike Ritof and Edith Boudreaux at Chicago's Merry Garden Ballroom. The couple "danced" for seven months, from August 29, 1930, to April 1, 1931. The grand prize was $2,000 (1,664 euros).

THE REALLY DEPRESSING GREAT DEPRESSION

How bad was it?

No economic collapse in American history even comes close. The Great Depression was America's longest and most severe economic crisis. The economy has grown in every decade in U.S. history—except for the decade of the 1930s.

HOW LOW CAN YOU GO?

While October 29, 1929, the day the stock market crashed, is recorded as Black Tuesday, it was just part of a long, downward spiral that went on for weeks. In the 10 weeks between September 3 and November 13, 50 percent of all stock value was lost. But that wasn't the bottom; stocks went even lower in subsequent years. For example, by 1932, General Motors shares, which had traded at $500 a share, were selling at $10. And General Motors was one of the few companies that still managed to make money every year during the Depression.

WELL-KNOWN LOSERS

Among the investors who lost everything were Clarence Birdseye, who'd sold his frozen foods company and put everything into stocks; William C. Durant, founder of General Motors, who lost more than $40 million in personal fortune; and Winston Churchill, a big investor in the American stock market.

BUDDY, CAN YOU SPARE A JOB?

In the rosy days of 1929, the average rate of unemployment was just 3.2 percent. The following year, it was 9 percent. And the layoffs continued until, by March 1933, unemployment was at a whopping 33 percent. In manufacturing, unemployment was 46 percent. Those who kept their jobs had their wages and hours cut.

Broadway Melody won the best picture academy award in the second Oscar awards in 1929.

OFFICES FOR RENT: CHEAP, GREAT VIEW

Between 1930 and 1932, 85,000 businesses closed. Classic auto-makers like Essex, Pierce Arrow, and Auburn went bust. The Empire State Building opened on May 1, 1931. It was the tallest building in the world, but it was only one-third occupied, so it was nicknamed the Empty State Building. The only thing that kept it out of bankruptcy was the revenue from tourists who paid to go to the observation decks on the top. The release of the first *King Kong* movie, in 1933, probably didn't hurt business either.

YOU COULDN'T BANK ON IT

In 1930, 1,300 banks failed. In 1931, 2,000 more folded. In all, 11,000 of the nation's 24,000 banks closed their doors. There was no federal insurance on deposits at the time, and people lost their entire life savings when their banks collapsed.

Farm prices fell, and 1931 marked the beginning of seven straight years of a severe drought in the plains. Huge dust storms blew away the fertile topsoil. In one immense dust storm, on May 11, 1934, 300 million tons of topsoil were blown right off the farmland of the plains; that's as much dirt as they had to dredge to form the Panama Canal. The storm had far-reaching effects: it was called a black blizzard because streetlights had to be turned on in Boston, New York, and Washington, D.C. in the middle of the day.

NO KICKS ON ROUTE 66

The Dust Bowl, that parched region of the Great Plains, blew peo-ple away too. More than 18 percent of Oklahomans left the state, many following Route 66 to California, where the nickname "Okie" was no compliment. By 1936, one of every four farms in the Dust Bowl had been abandoned. In 1932, 60 percent of North Dakota farms were auctioned off, along with their equipment and furniture, because of unpaid mortgages and back taxes. In one day in 1932, one-fourth of the land in rural Mississippi was auctioned off.

HAVE WE GOT A DEAL FOR YOU

When Franklin Roosevelt was sworn in as president in 1933, he immediately instituted a series of job programs to put people back to work. The Civilian Conservation Corps took 500,000 unemployed, young men to camps in the forest to plant trees. They received work clothes, room and board, and $30 per month—of which they were allowed to keep $5 for themselves. The rest was sent home to the young men's parents.

FDR's New Deal programs built dams, post offices, and schools. Artists were hired to paint murals and writers to write plays. The Work Progress Administration (WPA) laid down 650,000 miles of highways and streets, and built 124,000 bridges. But a lot of jobless people were still out there: at no time did the New Deal programs employ more than a third of them.

The New Deal tried to raise wages and prices by having the government set them on every transaction. Enforcement was strict, with fines and imprisonment for violations. In April 1934, a dry cleaner was jailed for three months for charging 35 cents to press a suit rather than the 40-cent price fixed by the government's dry cleaning code.

FAKE-OUT

By early 1937, things were looking up. Unemployment, though still in double digits, was down. Stock prices and production levels were up. Then on October 19, 1937, the stock market crashed again— almost as severely as it had in October 1929. It continued to slide throughout 1938. What had happened? In 1936, Social Security taxes were withheld from paychecks for the first time. But none of these monies were paid out. (The first Social Security checks would not be sent until 1940.) The removal of this buying power caused a decrease in consumer spending and shrank the economy. Unemployment rose to 22 percent. It was a depression within the Depression.

It wasn't until 1943, in the middle of World War II, with millions of young men in the military and wartime production steaming ahead, that unemployment returned to the lows of the late 1920s.

A SOCIAL SECURITY POSTSCRIPT

A woman named Ida Mae Fuller hit the Social Security jackpot. Ms. Fuller, of Vermont, received the first Social Security check ever on January 31, 1940. She had been in the system two years and had paid in $22.00. Ida Mae lived to be 100 and ended up collecting $22,000 in Social Security benefits.

Go-go boots, popular in 1965, originated in the collection of André Courreges, a Parisian designer.

YE OLDE MONEYLENDER

*"Neither a borrower nor a lender be." That's what
Shakespeare said. But nobody's ever listened.*

oney is old—around 10,000 years—and the desire to
have more of it is just as old. The first form of currency
exchange was the barter system, which dates back to
prehistory. In those days, phrases like, "I'll trade you four chickens
for a haircut," were commonplace.

Soon after bartering began, there came a time when the trade
wasn't even, and both parties knew that arrangements were
required. Voilà! The history of the loan was born.

I OWE EWE
Writing began as a way to record who owed what to whom.
Around 3100 B.C., the Sumerians (who lived in what is now Iraq)
realized that using letters and numbers to record transactions was
more efficient than counting tokens.

Lending a few ewes here and there was common in small
farming villages. A farmer who lent out an ewe counted on the
borrower giving him help if he needed it in the future. But as the
Sumerians organized the world's first big cities, they found that
folks needed written records. Lenders couldn't afford to trust to a
stranger's future goodwill.

MOO-LAH
The Sumerians were also the first to charge interest. Their word
for "interest" was *mash*, the same word used for a baby cow. Back
in good old Sumer, a financial portfolio consisted mostly of cattle.
If you loaned someone a herd, you suffered a temporary loss. And
during that time, some of the cattle would give birth. So when
time came for repayment, the borrower would return the herd
along with the extra mash born in their care. The baby cattle
made up for the value of the time and loss of wealth on the part of
the borrower.

This Sumerian system wasn't just the birth of interest. It was also an early example of how wealth creates more wealth since—in theory anyhow—you could just loan out your herd and get a bigger one returned to you.

YOU CAN BANK ON IT

Early banks (3000–2000 B.C.) were nothing more than a safe place to keep valuables such as grain; they were usually located at a temple or other important building.

Banks really liked the Sumerian idea of interest! In fact, the first laws regulating interest originated in Mesopotamia. Hammurabi, who ruled Mesopotamia from 1792 to 1750 B.C., declared that a maximum of 33.5 percent could be charged on grain exchanges and 20 percent on silver.

Private bankers emerged in ancient Greece around 500 B.C. or so. Called *trapezitai*, after their trapezoid-shaped tables, they set up shop near popular public places to get business. These sidewalk-sale moneylenders were common for centuries in public squares across the Mediterranean and Middle East. They became famous—or infamous—after the Bible described Jesus overturning the tables of moneylenders in the square at the Temple of Jerusalem.

JOLLY OLD PAWNBROKER

In Europe, from the 13th to 17th centuries, the Church also outlawed loaning money and charging interest (called "usury" in its early days). But lenders managed to make money in other ways. One way was by utilizing the oldest organized financial institution on the planet: pawnbroking, which began in China around 3000 B.C. Pawnbrokers held something of value and loaned money in return for it. Borrowers paid back the money to get their stuff.

The laws against usury didn't stop pawnbrokers from gaining a stronghold in early Europe. The Old French word *pan* is the same as their word for cloth, from the Latin *pannus*. This probably comes from commoners pawning the only thing they owned in times of emergency—their clothes. The nursery rhyme *Pop Goes the Weasel* is about pawning tailoring tools for beer money in England (a weasel was a tailor's tool; to pop was to pawn). Pawnbrokers even had their own saint. Saint Nicholas of Myra (yes, *that* St. Nick!) watched over financial commitments and obligations.

"PEZ" is short for "pfefferminz," the German word for "peppermint."

PAPER OR PLASTIC OR SHEEP?

Back in the Sumer days, domestic animals such as cows, camels and sheep had been the first type of currency. Since they were tough to carry in your pocket, as were bags of precious metals such as gold it's no surprise that regional paper currencies developed, with different countries using different forms of currency.

The earliest recorded foreign exchange transaction was in 1156, when two brothers traveling from Genoa to Constantinople borrowed cash from the office in Genoa. Arriving at their destination, they repaid the loan at a higher price in the currency of Constantinople. Soon, foreign exchange transactions became a way for lenders to make money—and to get around those dratted usury laws that kept them from charging interest.

The ability to lend and borrow was much easier after cows were replaced with paper currency. But some people think borrowing got a tad *too* easy after plastic credit cards came along.

THE CARD GAME

Frank X. McNamara of New York invented the credit card in the 1950s. Frank ran the Hamilton Credit Corporation during a time when most people paid cash for everything. Gas stations and department stores issued charge cards. But if you wanted to fill up your Ford, buy some neckties, have lunch, pick up your kid's birthday present and surprise your wife with roses, you'd need five or six charge cards.

One day, after having lunch and about to pay the check, McNamara realized he didn't have any cash. Blushing, he called his wife to bail him out. It was then that he had the bright idea that one credit card could be used to pay several merchants. He started Diner's Club, the first independent credit card. By the end of the year, 20,000 people were using it. But McNamara sold his interest in the business in 1952. He thought credit cards were just a fad!

CREDIT WHERE CREDIT IS DUE

Having a third party figure out how credit-worthy you are is a relatively new idea. Back in the 1800s, most credit purchases were made at the general store. If you bought bread or socks on credit, the store clerks wrote it down on a piece of paper worn on his wrist, known as a "cuff."

Jackie Kennedy popularized the pillbox hat and wraparound glasses in the early 1960s.

German merchants who gave out goods on credit compared their notes on clients in "mutual protection societies." In the 1830s, someone came up with the idea of doing this for a living. Through franchising, credit agencies began popping up everywhere; no longer just for business owners, they now served the general public too.

As telephones, fax machines, and the Internet developed, it became easier to tell someone they probably shouldn't buy that Corvette in Miami until they paid their dry cleaning bill in Jersey. Unfortunately, reporting often got sloppy. Governments have fined these businesses millions of dollars for giving notoriously inaccurate reports (up to one-third of all credit reports contain errors) and then charging consumers to see if their information is correct.

The big business of borrowing and lending goes on. If you're over your head, take a deep breath and consider this: at one point, Donald Trump racked up $900 million (700 million euros) in personal debt and $3.5 billion (3 billion euros) in business debt.

* * * * *

- The mortgage loan is more than 2,500 years old (not the same loan, thank goodness, just the idea).
- The largest loan ever was issued in 2002 from the International Monetary Fund to the government of Brazil: $30 billion (approximately 25 billion euros).
- European colonists who noted the Native American use of shells as currency used the phrase "shell out" first.
- When Danes living in Ireland between A.D. 800 and 900 didn't pay their poll tax on time, the locals would slit their noses with a knife; hence the phrase "pay through the nose."
- The Incas of Peru did not use money. Having built the largest nation of their time, the Incan people possessed staggering amounts of wealth but made little fuss of it. Citizens paid taxes through labor.
- According to the *Guinness Book of World Records*, a woman in Sweden has the largest piggy bank collection in the world: more than 5,000, from all over the world!

The Slinky toy was made of an 87-foot piece of wire, 3" in diameter and 2" high.

KNOCKING 'EM DEAD IN POUGHKEEPSIE

For about 30 years, a whole world of stage shows and stars appeared every day but Sunday across America. In those halcyon days, a few hours of fun cost only a nickel. And it was worth every penny.

The origin of the term vaudeville may stem from a popular satirical song style that originated in the valley of Vire (Vau-de-Vire), France. Another theory claims the term stems from *voix de ville*, slang for "songs of the town." Regardless of its origin, Vaudeville emerged in 1890s America as a new form of pure family entertainment.

The Industrial Revolution had concentrated larger populations in towns and cities. The workers wanted inexpensive and inoffensive entertainment on a regular basis. Variety shows often were too coarse for women and children. If you wanted half-naked showgirls or risqué jokes, you could try Minsky's Burlesque House down the street. For a cheap afternoon with the kiddies, you couldn't beat a vaudeville theater.

SOMETHING FOR EVERYONE

The shows featured around eight 15-minute acts free of off-color jokes and guaranteed squeaky clean (but not necessarily stellar) entertainment.

Dancers showcased the latest steps from the big city; magicians performed old, familiar tricks. There were comedians with funny accents, young girls with big, feathery hats and off-key voices, adults dressed like children pretending they were in school, jugglers, minstrels in burnt-cork makeup, families of bell ringers, serious actors performing bits of Shakespeare, drunken dogs (yes), and acrobats.

THE ROAD TO THE PALACE

Life on the vaudeville stage meant a life on the road. Performers crossed the country in trains and wagons for most of the year, playing two, three, up to five shows a day, and spending a few days

Harry Belafonte was the first black Grammy winner.

at each stop. Untested new acts underwent trial by fire: performers might be pelted with rotten fruit, cheated out of wages, or stranded in the boonies.

Seasoned vaudevillians worked the theater circuits. The constant travel was just as bad, but a circuit guaranteed you at least one performance in the next town. Popular acts worked the better circuits and larger cities, and the ultimate triumph was to appear at the Palace Theater in New York City. From there, star performers often went on to Broadway shows or the movies.

WHAT, AND GIVE UP SHOW BUSINESS?
Whether your act was star quality or stinkeroo, you still had to endure the same boardinghouse beds and food when you were on the road. In some places, the bedbugs ate better than the vaudevillians. Restaurants were usually closed by the time performers got out of the theaters, so they were forced to eat at the boardinghouse, where the spaghetti might be seasoned with questionable ingredients. As George Burns once (or probably more than once) said, "The only thing worse than working in vaudeville is *not* working in vaudeville."

ALL WASHED UP
Vaudeville lost a huge share of its audience to the movies; although, for a while, theaters featured both a vaudeville show and a moving picture for one low price. But by the time the talkies arrived, vaudeville was all but dead. Movies were cheap; live shows were costing more and more to produce. Theaters replaced their stages with screens, and an era came to an end.

FAMOUS PEOPLE WHO APPEARED IN VAUDEVILLE
Vaudeville was a venue for the superstars of the day—famous entertainers and sports stars people read about in newspapers but would never have gotten to see in person without vaudeville.
- Ballerina Anna Pavlova and dancer-choreographer Martha Graham (but not together).
- Lillie Langtry, royal mistress and English actor, who was the first to demand a carpet in her dressing room (to protect her skirts from the dirty floors).

Horse racing originated in Central Asia among nomadic tribesmen around 4500 B.C.

- Serious thespians such as Sarah Bernhardt and Maurice Barrymore did short plays. Maurice's daughter Ethel Barrymore also performed in vaudeville (his great-granddaughter Drew Barrymore never has).
- Sports stars such as heavyweight champ "Gentleman" Jim Corbett and baseball star Ty Cobb made appearances.

Some other famous folks got their start on the vaudeville stage.

- Brother-and-sister dance team Fred and Adele Astaire first took to the stage when Adele was eight and Fred was six or seven. Since they were underage, they weren't allowed to play the big, fancy theaters in New York City because of child labor laws; the smaller theaters looked the other way.
- Dancer (yes, dancer) James Cagney, whose big break came when he replaced Archie Leach in a dancing trio called Parker, Rand, and Leach. Archie changed his name to Cary Grant and went to Hollywood.
- Movie stars Rudolph Valentino, Al Jolson, Bob Hope, Charlie Chaplin, Marie Dressler, Ed Wynn, Danny Kaye, and the Marx Brothers.
- One of Mae West's vaudeville routines involved a dress with a trick strap that would break, revealing at least one of her best features; it was the original "wardrobe malfunction."
- Will Rogers performed rope tricks, and W. C. Fields was a juggler. Neither one of them uttered a word during their first few years on the stage.
- Early TV stars like Jack Benny, Milton Berle, and Jimmy Durante got their training in vaudeville. George Burns and Gracie Allen did too; George went through many partners, including a singing seal, before finding Gracie.
- Child performers Rose Louise Hovick (who grew up to become stripper Gypsy Rose Lee) and her sister, actor June Havoc, got their starts in vaudeville.
- Judy Garland, who later became famous as Dorothy in *The Wizard of Oz*, started performing when she was two years old with the Gumm Sisters (her real name was Frances Gumm). *Wizard* costar Bert Lahr (the Cowardly Lion) dropped out of school at age 15 to perform in comedy skits. Scarecrow Ray

Bolger began his showbiz life as a dancer, and Tin Man Jack Haley sang ballads—all in vaudeville.

- TV star Buddy Ebsen (*Beverly Hillbillies, Barnaby Jones*) was a vaudeville dancer too. Ebsen was the first choice to play the Tin Man in *The Wizard of Oz*, but the powdered aluminum brushed on his face as makeup got into his lungs and nearly killed him. Jack Haley was called in as a replacement.
- Houdini, the magician and escape artist, was a struggling performer until he hit the vaudeville circuit.

* * * * *

2,360 YEARS AND 15 MINUTES OF FAME

One of the Seven Wonders of the World, the Temple of Artemis in Ephesus (located in modern Turkey) was burned down by an arsonist in 356 B.C. When the firebug was captured he admitted that he'd committed the crime so that his name would be recorded in history.

The arsonist was executed and to thwart him, it was ordered that his name be erased from records and never mentioned again. But despite all the precautions, the criminal got his wish. As the destroyer of the temple, Herostratus is remembered as one of the most notorious arsonists in history.

GRAVE NEWS

- Kernels of popcorn have been found in graves of pre-Columbian Indians in South America.

- Dice have been found in the graves of ancient Assyrians in Nineveh (now Mosul, Iraq)

- In ancient China, horses and vehicles were buried alongside human bodies to indicate that the dead person had wealth and high status.

THEATER OF THE ABSURD

Some of the most unique acts that ever graced the vaudeville stage.

The Cherry Sisters: The sisters were actually billed as "America's Worst Act." And they didn't seem to mind—until after a show at Hammerstein's Theater in New York City in 1896, when a reviewer compared their singing to "the wailings of damned souls." When the review was reprinted in their hometown (Des Moines, Iowa) newspaper, the sisters sued for libel. They lost the case after performing their musical act in court, thus establishing the protection of "fair comment and criticism" as part of libel law.

Evelyn Nesbit: She was billed as a dancer, but she couldn't dance much. Her husband, Harry K. Thaw, had murdered her former lover, architect Stanford White, at a very public party. And so, in 1913, Evelyn was raking in $3,500 a week for being a beautiful instigator who people liked to gawk at.

Fink's Mules: Don't laugh. They played the Palace. And both Judy Garland and Milton Berle claimed to have shared a bill with them.

Nelson's Cats and Rats: Comedian Fanny Brice headlined on the same bill as this act in Chicago, when one of the rats escaped and snuck into her dressing room. Nelson, the animal trainer, recaptured the naughty rodent in time for the next show—when said rat carried an American flag onto the stage.

Orville Stamm, the Strongest Boy in the World: Orville played the violin while an English bulldog hung from his bow arm. For his finale, Orville would lie on his back with a small piano on his stomach. The pianist stood on Orville's thigh (and supposedly bounced up and down while he played). Thus accompanied, the boy sang "Ireland Must Be Heaven, 'Cause My Mother Came from There."

Paul Swan: A ballet dancer billed as the "Handsomest Man in the World," Swan performed his dances dressed only in very short pants.

Peg Leg Bates: Peg Leg's leg had to be amputated after an accident at a cotton mill when he was 12, but that didn't stop him from dancing. Peg Leg was a headlining tap dancer in both the black and white vaudeville circuits. He stayed active through the television era, when he appeared on the *Ed Sullivan Show* 21 times.

Toots Paka: Accompanied by Joseph Kekuku and the steel guitar he invented, Toots started the first Hawaiian entertainment craze back in 1910.

The 12 Speed Mechanics: Assembling a Ford automobile on stage in two minutes flat—now *that's* entertainment.

* * * * *

TIGER THEATER

Most tigers are shy by nature and prefer to avoid humans. Except for the tigers in the Sundarbans near Calcutta. They actually seem to like to attack humans, and have been reported to swim the Ganges and attack fishermen in their boats.

Since the mid-1980s, however, humans have been "attacking" back; they've set up realistically clothed, electrified mannequins to give an aggressive tiger a shock in the hopes that a jolt will teach the animal to give humans a wide berth.

Because tigers almost always attack from behind, field workers have been wearing masks on the backs of their heads to confuse the animals, and deaths by tigers in the Sundarbans have declined.

So, those tigers you see in the zoo? Get a good look. Just watch your back and don't stand too close.

WHERE ARE THEY NOW?

The Etruscans

Dear Uncle John,
I've heard that the Etruscans were the original party animals. I'm giving a party next week and want it to be as much fun as an Etruscan bash.
Hostess with the mostest

Dear Hostess,
The Etruscans knew how to live well, but exactly what their parties consisted of is lost to history. First, they had a unique language (scholars are still scratching their heads over it as opposed to reading it). Second, their buildings were made of wood—so the only artifacts to examine are their tombs.

If you were throwing a funeral, Uncle John could help. Tombs of wealthy Etruscans were filled with gorgeous, personalized coffins; shiny black, pottery (called *bucchero*); and metalwork: everything from fine weaponry to intricate gold jewelry. Tomb walls were brightly painted and depicted scenes of everyday life to special events.

The Etruscans were either native Italians or, possibly, eastern immigrants (from Greece or Turkey). They reached the height of their power in the 6th century B.C., when they ruled much of Italy. The Romans conquered them in the 4th century B.C. After that, their civilization died a slow death. One of the last mentions of them is in the 1st century B.C., when the Etruscan soothsayer Spurrina told Julius Caesar to "beware the ides of March."

What fascinates Uncle John the most is the Cloaca Maxima, the famous sewer that still serves modern Rome. It's believed that Etruscan engineers drained the marshy ground under what was to be the Roman Forum in about 625 B.C. Today, most of the original stonework has been replaced by concrete.

One of their most important contributions may have been bringing their Italian wines to the beer-drinking natives of France. It's true that the ancient Etruscans were known for living well. And their descendants still are—in Tuscany, which is named for them.

When and where was the wheel was invented? Around 4000 B.C., in Mesopotamia (now Iraq).

THE FIRST GREAT ECOLOGICAL DISASTER

These days we're used to reading accounts of giant oil spills, massive radioactive material releases, and various other disasters. But, back in 1967, the Torrey Canyon *oil spill was a new phenomenon.*

March 18, 1967. The captain of the *Torrey Canyon* didn't have a care in the world. His vast tanker was filled with Persian Gulf oil that would fetch a pretty price when he reached England. He allowed his attention (and his ship) to drift, paying little attention to where he was headed. He was brought back to reality by a sharp crack and a series of alarming grinding noises: the *Torrey Canyon* had smashed into rocks just off the British coast in the English Channel, ripping open more than half of the tanker's bottom.

WHAT A MESS

The impact released 30,000 tons of oil almost immediately, which drifted up the channel and slimed the coasts of England and France. Stunned and horrified, officials began soaking up the coastline oil with straw, but they couldn't settle on a method for stopping the flow of oil from the damaged *Torrey Canyon*.

Within a week, approximately 146,600 barrels of crude oil leaked out of the stranded vessel. The oil settled on the coast of West Cornwall, befouling about 100 miles of British coastline. On March 26, the *Torrey Canyon*'s strained structure finally gave way, this time releasing a torrent of 366,500 barrels of oil. The slick drifted into the Bay of Biscay, where it would remain floating on the sea like a giant Rorschach inkblot for the next two months.

THAT WASN'T THE WORST OF IT

All told, approximately 120,000 tons (or 860,000 barrels) of crude oil were released. But even worse than the oil slicks themselves

---

The first Egyptian movie, *Leila*, was made in 1927.

were the cleanup methods that were used—at the time, virtually no one was experienced in combating industrial disasters at sea.

The French cleanup crew used large quantities of chalk in an attempt to absorb the oil. Instead, the chalk made the oil sink to the bottom where the tarlike clumps of oil damaged living conditions for bottom-dwelling organisms. Manual cleanup methods, like bulldozing oily sand from the beaches, worked better. But the main British response was truly tragic. Hoping to disperse the oil, British officials sprayed 10,000 tons of noxious detergent all over the oil-clogged waters. Ironically, the detergent proved to be much worse for the local flora and fauna than the oil itself. It killed off millions of plants and sea creatures, including a rare species of hermit crab that hasn't reappeared since.

KA-POW!

Finally, on March 28, the British decided that it was impossible to tow the ship to shore and stem the ongoing leaks. Their solution? They would bomb the ship, sink it, and burn up the remaining oil, which had formed a 35-mile-long, 20-mile-wide slick around the ruined tanker. For the next two days, the Royal Navy bombarded the vessel with thousands of pounds of napalm, sodium chlorate, and aviation fuel, introducing still more contaminants into British waters as the stubborn vessel refused to sink. Only when the *Torrey Canyon*'s last reserves of oil had leaked into the water did the ship give up the ghost and go down.

THE AFTEREFFECTS

Coastline exposed to detergents sprayed on the water took up to a decade to return to normal, while other oil-stained coastline recovered and reestablished a healthy biological community within five to eight years. Approximately 25,000 birds were killed by the disaster, as well as untold numbers of sea creatures.

An investigative body assigned to identify ways to minimize future oil tanker disasters recommended the use of double-hulled ships and improved crew training. And emergency personnel learned a lot about the proper response to such a massive disaster. Good thing, too—*Torrey Canyon* would prove in time to be not a one-of-a-kind tragedy, but the harbinger of a brand new, all-too-common, man-made catastrophe.

FORGOTTEN FIRSTS

*Uncle John has regaled his readers with really important firsts like
the first toilet paper, the first bathroom, the first hotel with a bathroom,
and so on. But now that we've finished our business in the bathroom,
let's step outside and look at a few important non-bathroom firsts.*

FIRST PERSON WITH A WAR
NAMED AFTER PART OF HIS ANATOMY

The War of Jenkins's Ear is one of the more colorfully named con-
flicts in history. Under the 1729 Treaty of Seville, the British had
agreed not to trade with the Spanish colonies. To verify the treaty,
the Spanish were permitted to board British vessels in Spanish
waters. After one such incident in 1731, Robert Jenkins, captain
of the *Rebecca*, claimed that the Spanish coast guard had boarded
and searched his ship in the West Indies. Next, according to
Jenkins, one Captain Juan de Leon Fandino tied him up and cut
off his ear with a sword. But if Jenkins's claim were true, it stands
to reason that the English had probably been up to *something*.

A PICKLED HEARING

And indeed they were. As it turns out, the Spanish had had to
endure years of attacks from British privateers. By the fourth decade
of the 18th century, the British were feeling sufficiently confident
about their standing in the New World to start looking for an
excuse to begin throwing their weight around. The Spanish apparently gave it to them by separating an English sea captain from one
of his ears. In any case, when Jenkins returned to England, with his
ear pickled in a bottle, it caused quite the sensation. In 1738,
Jenkins was summoned to appear before the House of Commons
and produce the ear, which he did. The English believed that the
Spanish must be taught a lesson—they simply couldn't be allowed
to run around cutting off Englishmen's ears! So the British prime
minister, Robert Walpole, declared war in October 1739.

A month later the British Admiral Edward Vernon captured the
silver exporting town of Porto Bello, New Granada (now Panama).
The victory made two lasting contributions to history. The London
street Portobello Road was named in honor of the event, and at a

---

The houses of Mark Twain and Harriet Beecher Stowe stand side by side in Hartford, CT.

dinner honoring Admiral Venron, the future British national anthem, "God Save the Queen," was performed in public for the first time.

Neither side gained any significant territory, and the war eventually petered out until it later merged into the War of Austrian Succession.

FIRST PRESIDENT TO GET FULL-TIME SECRET SERVICE PROTECTION

On the evening of the same 1865 day that President Abraham Lincoln established the Secret Service (originally tasked with preventing the counterfeiting of money), John Wilkes Booth assassinated him at Ford's Theatre. This prompted Congress to begin thinking about adding presidential protection to the duties performed by the Secret Service. But all they did was *think* about it, because it wasn't until 1894 that the Secret Service began informal, part-time protection of President Grover Cleveland—a full 13 years after the 1881 assassination of President Garfield.

There was still no full-time Secret Service protection for the president of the United States; it would take a third presidential assassination, the murder in 1901 of William McKinley, for the Secret Service to finally assume full-time responsibility for protecting the president. Two operatives were assigned full time to the White House detail to guard McKinley's replacement, Theodore Roosevelt.

FIRST SCREEN STAR WITH A "STAGE NAME"

Fans of John Wayne may know that he came into this world with the less than he-man moniker Marion Morrison. Lucille Le Sueur spent her entire 50-year acting career under the name Joan Crawford, which was selected as the winner of a nationwide publicity contest to rename MGM's newest star. But the first star to have her name changed to enhance her appeal to movie audiences was one Theodosia Goodman from Cincinnati, Ohio. The studio, perceiving the name to be too long or too dull, sought a new name that would capitalize on her dark, exotic looks. It's said that studio execs played around with the words *death* and *Arab*, and came up with Theda Bara.

FIRST AMERICAN TO FACE
THE JAPANESE IN COMBAT IN WWII

One morning in December 1941, Ray Buduick, a lawyer in Honolulu, Hawaii, decided, as he so often did, to take his tiny, light plane up for a Sunday spin. As he headed out toward Pearl Harbor, he was a tad surprised to find the western skies dark with Japanese fighter aircraft, Zeros, all bearing down on him. They riddled the lawyer's plane with machine-gun fire. Buduick banked sharply and managed somehow to make a safe landing in the midst of one of the greatest airborne attacks in history. In the process, Ray became the first American to face the Japanese in combat, however inadvertently, during the World War II.

* * * * *

AND THE BEAT GOES ON

Writer Jack Kerouac (*On the Road*) had done his bit in World War II and, like a lot of other vets, had come home weary in body and in spirit. He first defined himself and his contemporaries in a conversation in 1948, "You know, this is really a beat generation." The name stuck.

Ten years later, when San Francisco was at the epicenter of the beat movement, *San Francisco Chronicle* columnist Herb Caen coined the word *beatnik*. (This was after Sputnik, when everything was getting the tagged-on suffix: nudnik, neatnik, and so on.)

The beats hated it. When Kerouac next saw Caen, he told him, "You're putting us down and making us sound like jerks… Stop using it." But it was too late—the media latched on to the word with glee.

Baudouin I (Belgium) was Europe's longest reigning monarch at his death in 1993.

BLUE BELLE

She was only 16, but she was one amazing little southern belle.

In 1738, British major George Lucas, his wife, and two daughters left Antigua in the West Indies and sailed to South Carolina to take possession of three plantations that he'd inherited. The following year, Major Lucas returned to Antigua to rejoin his army regiment. The eldest daughter, 16-year-old Eliza, was left in charge of Mrs. Lucas, who was an invalid, her toddler sister, and the management of the three plantations (including 20 slaves). Eliza acted as schoolteacher to her sister and also taught the slave children to read (although it was illegal at the time).

While other young women were tempted by nearby Charleston's social life, Eliza Lucas was more interested in plants. The Lucas family was land rich but cash poor. Rice was the main cash crop, but it wasn't doing well. Eliza had seen indigo grown in the West Indies, and she thought it could do well in South Carolina, so she had her father send her some seeds.

TURNING BLUE TO GREEN

Indigo, a plant in the pea family, produces a deep navy blue, color-fast dye (which Levi Strauss would later use to color his denim). Eliza's first crop was killed by frost; the next year, worms ate the crop; then production of the dye was sabotaged by her dye master. But Eliza persevered.

By 1744, she'd produced a quality grade of indigo and had interested the British government in purchasing it for use in dark-blue uniforms. Eliza Lucas became the first American planter to successfully cultivate indigo and produce a marketable dye. She shared her success too, giving seeds to her neighbors. From the late 1740s until the 1770s, indigo was the number one crop in South Carolina. Just before the Revolution, the colony was shipping one million pounds a year. As a result, the South Carolina low country was wealthier per capita than any of the other colonies.

The American Revolution caused the collapse of South Carolina's indigo export business; after the war, the British

---

Biggest army: the China's People's Liberation Army, with 2.2 million personnel as of May 2000.

imported indigo from their West Indian colonies. But for 30 years Eliza Lucas's experiments had helped sustain the South Carolina economy.

RAISING KIDS FOR THE RED, WHITE, AND BLUE
When she was 22, Eliza married Charles Pinckney, a widower twice her age (but it was a love match). They had two sons and a daughter. Eliza continued her agricultural experiments, reviving another interest of hers: silkworm culture. She even made a silk gown for the queen of England. When her husband died of malaria in 1758, Eliza, at 36, again had to apply her business and agricultural skills to managing property.

The American Revolution ruined sales for her plantation's main cash crop, but Eliza Lucas Pinckney supported the cause by loaning money to the South Carolina government. Both her sons fought in the Revolutionary War. Her son Charles was one of the drafters of the Constitution, and her son Thomas served as governor of South Carolina.

When she was 70 years old, Eliza Lucas Pinckney developed breast cancer. Seeking out the best doctors, she traveled to Philadelphia, where she died on May 27, 1793. At his own request, George Washington served as one of her pallbearers.

* * * * *

WRAP IT UP
Aluminum foil might never have been discovered but for the need to protect cigarettes from moisture. In the 1920s, when the price of aluminum dropped, Kentucky-born Richard S. Reynolds (the nephew of tobacco king R. J. Reynolds) created a tobacco wrap to replace the tin-lead sheets currently used. Two decades later his company, Reynolds Metals, came out with the lightweight, non-corrosive aluminum foil that we find it hard to live without.

REJECTS OF THE CONSTITUTION

*In order to form a more perfect union,
these ideas were tossed into history's circular file.*

For four months in the summer of 1787, fifty five men met in Philadelphia, Pennsylvania, and set about constructing a national government from the ground up. They produced the U.S. Constitution, the oldest written constitution still in use anywhere in the world. Delegates to that Constitutional Convention brainstormed and debated wildly different ideas on the form and function of the federal government.

DAY ONE

James Madison, Edmund Randolph, and the other Virginia delegates came early to Philadelphia. On the convention's first day they introduced the so-called Virginia Plan, a framework for a strong, central government that they'd crafted in long sessions at Philadelphia's Indian Queen tavern. The small states didn't like it and put forth the New Jersey Plan, which would give each state an equal voice in the new government—and which was voted down. Alexander Hamilton came up with his own plan, the Hamilton Plan, which was too monarchical for most—and which was also voted down. By September 8, 1787, the Great Compromise had been reached, and the Constitution was turned over to a Committee of Style and Arrangement. Ultimately, delegate Governeur Morris (that's his name, not his title) wrote the final draft. In the months of debate and discussion, all sorts of ideas were put before the convention and debated. Imagine the U.S. government if these ideas had been adopted!

ARE THREE HEADS (OF STATE) BETTER THAN ONE?

Some of the convention's hottest debates concerned the makeup of the executive branch. Elbridge Gerry, of Massachusetts, and others who feared that a single president could become entirely too kinglike, proposed that there should be a committee of three

The first Rotary Club was started in Chicago on February 23, 1905.

presidents. This triumvirate would be composed of one president from the northern states, one from the middle states, and a third from the southern states. Voting at the Constitutional Convention was by states; three states voted for this type of presidency, but seven voted against.

KING OF THE USA
Alexander Hamilton argued for a president for life. He wanted the president to serve indefinitely, so long as he exhibited "good behavior." Hamilton worried that ex-presidents would wander the country "like ghosts," pining for their former glory—and stirring up trouble. Newspapers circulated the rumor that King George III's second son was going to be offered the job of king of the United States.

MR. SECRETARY
At the other end of the power spectrum, Roger Sherman of Connecticut suggested that the president's role would be little more than that of a clerk; a simple administrator to make sure the laws Congress passed were implemented.

FREE REIGN
Ben Franklin didn't think the president should receive a salary; he fretted that a salary would attract greedy men to the office. George Washington may have taken Franklin's words to heart. When he was elected, he refused the $25,000 (20,000 euros) salary, asking only for reimbursement of expenses.

By 2001, the president's salary was $400,000 (326,000 euros). But in 2000, the presidential candidates spent a total of $343 million (279 million euros) seeking a $400,000 (326,000 euros) a year job—something even Ben Franklin could never have foreseen!

SEVEN-YEAR HITCH
One rejected notion was that the president should serve one seven-year term, with no option of reelection. Thomas Jefferson, in France at the time, wrote to James Madison that he thought the president should be limited to one term of office. (But when Jefferson became president, he changed his mind—and he was elected to a second term.)

THAT WOULD BE A CONGRESSIONAL RECORD

The Constitution provides that the House of Representatives have no more than one representative for every 30,000 persons, with a minimum of one per state. The idea was to keep the House close to the people. The numbers of elected representatives in the House continued to grow according to census figures until 1910, by which time there were 435 members. After the 1920 census, there were battles over apportionment. The final result was that Congress voted, in 1929, to limit the number of representatives to the existing 435. But if the original maximum ratio of one representative per 30,000 people still applied, a small city would have to be built on Capitol Hill to hold them all. After the 2000 census, there would have been 9,400 members of the House. Try to get anything done with a crowd *that* big!

OTHER IDEAS BURIED IN THE POLITICAL GRAVEYARD

With major battles brewing in the convention between the large and small states, George Read of Delaware called for state boundaries to be erased and state governments eliminated. Getting into the spirit of compromise, Ben Franklin, then president of the Pennsylvania Executive Council, generously offered to deed large chunks of Pennsylvania to New Jersey and Delaware to equal things out.

The delegates, all from Eastern states, saw the potential future power of the Western states. A proposal was floated that the number of Western states never be allowed to outnumber the Atlantic states. It lost by just one vote.

Although James Madison is now known as the Father of the Constitution, many of his proposals were soundly rejected. He wanted Congress to set up a national university and thought Congress should have the power to veto laws passed by state legislatures.

UNCONVENTIONAL WISDOM

The entire discussion of the future Constitution was held in secret. The doors of the meeting hall were guarded. No strangers (and certainly no reporters) were admitted, and members were cautioned not to discuss the proceedings with outsiders—something Ben Franklin had to be reminded of often.

WHAT ABOUT BILL?

The original Constitution had no Bill of Rights (the first 10 amendments to the Constitution). James Madison initially thought a Bill of Rights was unnecessary, but he ended up writing and proposing 12 amendments. The first two, dealing with congressional pay raises and reapportionment, were not approved. The now famous First Amendment—protecting freedoms of religion, speech, assembly, press, and petition—often argued today to be the most important because the founders had put it first, was actually the Third Amendment in Madison's original draft. The Bill of Rights was ratified and became part of the Constitution in 1791.

A NO-SHOW

Rhode Island, which had long been nicknamed "Rogue's Island" and known as "the traditional home of the otherwise minded," boycotted the Constitutional Convention entirely.

* * * * *

DON'T BE A SOAR LOSER, BEN

Benjamin Franklin wanted the turkey, not the eagle, to be America's national symbol. In a letter to his daughter, he wrote, "For my own part I wish the Bald Eagle had not been chosen the representative of our country. He is a bird of bad moral character. He does not get his living honestly. You may have seen him perched on some dead tree near the river, where, too lazy to fish for himself, he watches the labor of the fishing hawk; and when that diligent bird has at length taken a fish, and is bearing it to his nest for the support of his mate and young ones, the Bald Eagle pursues him and takes it from him...The turkey is a much more respectable bird and withal a true original native of America."

CAN I GET THAT IN WRITING?

The first writing utensil ever used was most likely a finger dipped in berry juice or blood to mark images on cave walls. Here's how we've progressed.

- Penlike devices were first used c. 3500 B.C. by Sumerians, who used sharpened twigs to etch their script into wet clay tablets, which were hardened in ovens.

- Around 2800 B.C., Egyptians used the first real pens. They were fashioned from wild reeds filled with dyes or a mixture of ash, fat from boiled donkey skin, and musk oil (to mask the smell of the donkey fat). The pens were tilted to slowly release the dye with each stroke.

- The Greeks started using reedlike pens in 1296 B.C.

- The ancient Chinese used brushes made of rat hair to paint pictograms in 1000 B.C.

- Europeans in 6 B.C. used quills: dried wing feathers—from swans, turkeys, and geese—filled with dyes. The practice of writing with quill pens spread to North America. For hundreds of years the quill pen was the only way to write.

- The discovery of a huge graphite mine during the 1500s in England led to the creation of marking stones, known today as pencils. Not as popular as pens, the stones were square-cornered sticks of graphite wrapped in string. They were chunky and awkward to use, didn't produce nice penmanship, and dirtied the user's hands. By the late 1700s almost all the graphite in the mine was used up.

- Frenchman Nicolas-Jacques Conté found a way to make pencil lead by mixing graphite powder with clay and baking it. This is similar to the method used today to make pencils.

- In 1780 Englishman John Mitchell invented the first machine-made, steel pen points (to be dipped in an inkwell), and in 1830 another Englishman, James Perry, refined the design.

The Kalashnikov AK-47 (and variants of it) has been used in more than 75 wars.

- By the beginning of the 19th century, people were getting tired of dipping their pens into inkwells or sharpening their pencils. Two British inventors, S. Mordon and J. I. Hawkins, created the first mechanical pencil in 1822, while other inventors went to work making a pen with a reservoir to hold ink. The first practical fountain pen was patented and produced in New York by Lewis Edson Waterman in 1884.

- In 1858, a Philadelphia inventor patented a pencil with a rubber eraser, and in 1888 Massachusetts inventor John H. Loud came up with the world's first ballpoint pen.

- Fiber-tip pens with coarse wool felt tips were used in the 1940s, but they weren't much more than crude applicators of ink. In 1962, Yukio Horie of Tokyo Stationery Company created the first official felt-tip pen. The marker was made of fine nylon ground to a point and was fed ink from a reservoir in the pen.

- In 1964 the felt-tip pen came to America with the creation of the Sharpie marker. It was made by Sanford Manufacturing Company and became the first permanent marker that could write on any surface.

* * * * *

LITERARY CRITICISM

Acting was Jacqueline Susann's original vocation until she decided to try her hand at something new. It turned out to be a good move; Susann's book *Valley of the Dolls*, one of her first attempts at writing, hit number one on the *New York Times* Bestseller List. Readers devoured her steamy and seedy tale of Hollywood, drugs, and decadence. The critics, on the other hand, weren't impressed. Gore Vidal once quipped that: "She doesn't write; she types."

But one literary critic, Douglas Watt, received firsthand feedback for his negative criticism. When Watt trashed Susann's first book *Lovely Me*, Susann tracked Watt down at the glitzy New York hangout Sardi's and slugged him in front of everyone.

UNCLE JOHN'S WEDDING AND BEDDING AWARDS

Hot times with the ancients.

The Egyptians were naturals at it. The Greeks deified it. The Romans, like with everything else, overdid it.

DOING WHAT COMES NATURALLY AWARD

In guiltless ancient Egypt, there was no false modesty. The gods not only approved of lovemaking, they indulged in it themselves. Egyptian gods, in fact, weren't above a bit of necrophilia: the chief god, Osiris, and his wife-sister, Isis, conceived their child *after* Osiris was murdered. What was good enough for the gods was fine for mere mortals too—even if they were dead: male mummies were equipped with an artificial phallus for use in their (hopefully active) afterlife. Incest like that of Isis and Osiris preserved the pharaoh's royal line. Commoners, though they might see a niece and an uncle marry, had family values more in line with modern times. Adultery, for example, was frowned on and could be used by a wife as grounds for divorce.

When it came to families, bigger was better. A pregnant woman was a respected woman, and if she delivered sons, she was a successful wife, treasured by her husband. Since family was the spice of love life in Egypt, and life was short (with an average life span of 35 years), couples got down to baby making right away. Girls were married at the age of puberty, about 13 or 14. Men usually married as soon as they could support a family. Helping them start the family "business" were Egyptian physicians, who recommended aphrodisiacs such as onions or pomegranates—or, for the wealthy, pearls dissolved in wine.

FRISKINESS-IS-NEXT-TO-GODLINESS AWARD

In marriage and family customs, the ancient Greeks in Athens also followed the ways of the gods. Unfortunately Zeus, the chief god, and his wife (and once again, sister), Hera, were a sadly dysfunctional couple. Zeus had the bad habit of falling in love with women other than his wife. And Hera had the bad habit of becoming insanely jealous and destroying Zeus's girlfriends if she could.

Respectable married women didn't just stay home to take care of their families and children—they literally stayed in the house or courtyard and were rarely allowed to leave. This made the wives as jealous as Hera, presumably because Athenian guys were as free-wheeling as Zeus.

The seclusion and relative powerlessness of wives led to an abundance of mistresses in Athenian life. It also led to the creation of a class of women known as the hetaerae, courtesans paid to entertain hubbies on the loose. The gorgeous and brainy Aspasia, who may have started out as a *hetaera*, was the exception to all the rules. Pericles, the leader of Athens during its golden age as a democracy, scandalized Athens when he left his wife and took up with Aspasia (without benefit of marriage). She could hold her own with great minds like Socrates—and the smaller minds in Athens disliked her for it.

But Athens remained a man's world. And Greek men in ancient times didn't send flowers or candy or Hallmark cards. They didn't strive for an enduring love between the sexes or consider it a path to happiness. In fact, some scholars believe that when Athenians thought of love at all, they considered it a kind of passing madness that was a punishment of the gods.

OVERDOING IT AWARD

The Romans adopted a lot of Greek culture, including their gods. Zeus and Hera became Jove and Juno; they had new names but kept to their bad old ways—by Jove! Roman adultery was officially a crime only if a married woman was involved. An unfaithful married man was his wife's problem. But a husband who had a faithless wife was required by law to divorce her—and empowered to kill her. In theory, an aristocratic Roman wife had to be modest and devoted to her home, hearth, and husband. Okay, so much for theories.

The reality was that Rome's wealth was built on conquered empires and foreign wars. So, Hubby often traveled far from home on warring or business—leaving the little woman in charge. Women lived longer too; as Rome became wealthier, so did many widows. Women gradually gained more authority and the freedom to do whatever they liked. And they liked to party. Emperor Augustus became alarmed at his pleasure-seeking subjects, so he passed an often-ignored law against adultery—then had to exile his daughter, Julia, for breaking it!

Unsurprisingly, Romans became more jaded and wilder as time went on. By the time the sadistic emperor Caligula came to power in A.D. 37, orgies were giving Rome a bad name. Slaves were provided for X-rated entertainment. And it didn't help matters that Caligula included his favorite racehorse, Incitatus, at his parties. Roman orgies became legendary for their decadence—and may have inspired more bad Hollywood movie scenes than any other aspect of history.

* * * * *

KISS ME, I'M A GOOD GIRL

According to *Isaac Asimov's Book of Facts*, "A conventional sign of virginity in Tudor England was a high exposed bosom and a sleeve full to the wrists."

SO THAT'S WHERE "SUCKING FACE" COMES FROM!

"Kissing seems to be unknown" among the Tinguian people of the Philippines, wrote anthropologist Fay-Cooper Cole in 1922. "But a similar sign of affection is given by placing the lips to the face and drawing the breath in suddenly."

HOW DID THE VIRGIN ISLANDS GET THAT NAME?

According to legend, in the fourth century, Saint Ursula was on a pilgrimage. Her entourage included 11 ships, each filled with 1,000 virgin acolytes. However, Ursula was martyred when she refused to marry a Hun leader. (The exact number of and fate of her followers in not recorded.) A church was built in their honor in Cologne, Germany. And the story goes that Columbus, who discovered the Virgin Islands during his second voyage in 1493, was reminded of Ursula and her virgins and, as a result, named the islands the Virgins.

More than 1,000 different languages are spoken on the African continent.

WHERE ARE THEY NOW?

The Sumerians

Dear Uncle John,

I've heard that people called Sumerians invented civilization. Is that true? Who were these people, and can you help me find some of them? I'd like to civilize my younger brother.

Searching Sis

Dear Searching Sis,

The Sumerians created the first known urban civilization in around 3500 B.C. in Mesopotamia. Sumerians are considered a mysterious people because they spoke a language different from all other languages. They built up great city-states, and the names of their cities—Ur, Kish, Uruk, and Eridu—do sound different.

The Sumerians were firsters: the first to use a system of irrigation in the fields and the first to use a pictorial system of writing called cuneiform. On wet clay tablets with reed styli, they wrote down everything from bookkeeping records to *The Epic of Gilgamesh*—the oldest written story on Earth. Sumerians also invented wheeled carts, mathematical symbols, and a system of math based on the number 60 (which apparently makes calculus look easy). In their leisure time, they even created a calendar based on the lunar month.

After about 1,000 years of being thousands of years ahead of their time, the Sumerians lost their cities to the Akkad king Sargon (who only sounds like a baddie from *Lord of the Rings*), who in turn lost the city-states to Hammurabi, who presided over the Golden Age of Babylon. But the Sumerian religion and culture were adopted by their conquerors, and some of their influence survives to this day. (Just look at that calendar on your wall divided into months.) To find the "cradle of civilization" in ancient Mesopotamia, and meet the descendants of the Sumerians, travel to the area between the Tigris and Euphrates rivers in the present-day country of Iraq.

The full name of soprano Maria Callas was Cecilia Sophia Anna Maria Kalogeropoulos.

THE YANKS ARE COMING!

*When the Yankees burned Toronto in 1813,
they actually did the Canadians a favor.*

Back in early 1812, life along the American-Canadian frontier was relatively wide open and peaceful. Locals on both sides of the border traded back and forth. No one had to declare their goods, and even if they had wanted to, there was no one to whom they could do so. Marriages back and forth were also an important part of cross-border traffic.

So imagine the chagrin of the locals when the British (who governed Upper and Lower Canada at the time) and the Americans went to war.

GOD BLESS AMERICA

In April 1813, the two mighty nations chose to clash in a muddy little settlement on the shores of Lake Ontario. An American force led by Major General Henry Dearborn attacked the city of York (now Toronto), Upper Canada's capital.

On paper, York was a well-defended garrison town. It had an imposing fort, lots of supply storehouses, enough red-coated regular British soldiers to march around impressively, and a citizen-militia that numbered about 300. It looked like Major General Dearborn had his work cut out for him. But by the end of the day, Dearborn had prevailed. In fact, much to his surprise, his forces were welcomed as liberators in more ways than one.

DON'T POINT THAT UMBRELLA AT ME

What Dearborn didn't know was that Upper Canada's stalwart militia was never exactly gung ho, even in peacetime. In a sense, they were draftees. The British demanded militia service of every male settler between the ages of sixteen and sixty. The service required one day of attendance annually, a day when the men gathered and marched in motley formation—usually wielding umbrellas and sticks because real weapons were at a premium.

Blue chip, meaning a company with high-value stock, originates from poker's highest-value chip.

Militia day was probably as close as Upper Canadians came to a national holiday. It was also an excuse for a monumental, 19th-century-style drunken binge.

ENDING WITH A BANG
It was as much the Canadian lackadaisical sense of duty as a series of mishaps that won the day for Dearborn and Company. First, a British contingent got lost and showed up to do battle at the wrong place. Then the defenders of York accidentally blew up their own ammunition dump. Shocked (and probably somewhat deafened), the British troops hastily left town, and the militiamen, who hadn't been all that enthused about the whole business in the first place, returned to their homes, farms, and places of business.

LET'S MAKE A DEAL
The merchants of York quickly cut a deal with Dearborn to prevent looting of private property. To that end, they graciously helped the Americans clean out the government storehouses, then they watched placidly as the "invaders" put the empty government buildings to the torch. The famous Burning of York was far more selective than Canadian history books have indicated. Local businesses were left untouched.

THE HONORABLE THING
Back then, prisoners of war were considered an inconvenience: They had to be fed, guarded, and sometimes treated for wounds—not the sort of activity that conquering heroes wanted to get involved in. So when an opposing army captured a prisoner, the prisoner was offered a "parole of honor" conditional on not bearing arms again. Paroles of honor were used as late as the American Civil War, at least during its early years. Both sides always respected these paroles, and they could not be lifted except by mutual agreement.

For the Canadian militiamen, paroles of honor were a way out of fighting the War of 1812—especially at seeding time for farmers and potential profiteering time for merchants, which it was.

Remember when Major General Dearborn landed in York, and the local militia roll counted about 300 men? By the time he left a few days later, he had issued nearly 1,400 paroles of honor. Folks had come from miles around—by foot, horse, wagon, and canoe—all the way to the capital to get their free passes out of the war.

THE ANTICLIMAX

Even though the British regulars had moved on and most citizens had paroles in their pockets, Dearborn was forced to reinvade York that July, this time to defend America's honor. It seems that during the intervening months, some enterprising Canadians had been confiscating crops, animals, goods, and machinery, brazenly stating they were doing so with approval of the Americans. Dearborn showed up to set the record straight and bring the villains to justice. It didn't happen though: The thieves hid their booty and fled into the bush until Dearborn left. The second invasion lasted only a day without a shot being fired.

The War of 1812 continued—minus the lucky parolees of honor—and York returned to the weightier prewar issues, like what to do about citizens who let their pigs run loose on the streets.

* * * * *

WAR OF THE NOSES

For centuries, warriors have used aromatherapy in battle. The fearsome Spartans of ancient Greece burned a potent mixture of sulfur that would float around a city they were about to destroy. Myrrh was carried into battle by a number of ancient warriors. The Scots used fragrant thyme in their tea to give them courage, and Samurai warriors often used Japanese koh incense to make their armor smell like the sweet smell of victory.

Apple pie at the "first Thanksgiving"? Not likely. There were no apples in 1621 Plymouth.

CARBINE WILLIAMS

The ex-con whose weapon helped win World War II.

S hots rang out on July 21, 1921. The sheriff of Cumberland County and his deputies had just destroyed a liquor still in the mountains of North Carolina when a volley of gunfire from the woods killed Deputy Alfred Pate. Three men were spotted at the site before the raid began. One of them, the owner of the whiskey still, David Marshall "Marsh" Williams, was charged with murder. He pled guilty (though he always claimed he was innocent, and there were conflicting stories of where he was when the shots were fired).

NOT MAKING LICENSE PLATES

Williams had always had a talent for machinery, especially firearms. While serving out his 30-year sentence in the Caledonia Correctional Institute, his talent got noticed. He was eventually put to work fixing farm machinery. Warden H. T. Peoples and Williams developed a relationship of mutual trust—a lot of trust. After the talented prisoner was given a job in the machine shop repairing guards' weapons, the warden let Williams take the next step: designing guns. This is where Williams made a semiautomatic rifle that worked on the short-stroke gas piston system. A gas piston was located under the middle of the rifle's barrel. When the gun was fired, the gases from the ejected bullet exploded and propelled the piston violently to the rear. The slam of the piston initiated a slide-bolt action in the gun and automatically loaded another bullet into the ejection chamber.

LIGHTENING THE BURDEN ON G.I. SHOULDERS

After eight years in prison, Williams went home and started working on more designs and getting patents. The folks at the Winchester gun company noticed and hired him as a weapons designer.

Meanwhile, in 1941, war was looming, and the army had a problem. The traditional M1 rifle, or Garand rifle, weighed about 10 pounds (5 kg). These were too cumbersome for medics, radio operators, vehicle drivers, and officers—basically, any troops who

---

Apples are not native to North America; they came from Europe and West Asia.

weren't frontline riflemen. These "second-line" troops usually carried the M1911A1 .45-caliber handguns. At 3 pounds (over 1 kg) loaded, the handguns were lightweight, but they didn't have the range or firepower needed for defense.

So the army held a competition to design a lightweight, semi-automatic shoulder weapon, which Winchester intended to win by providing a lightweight carbine. (Carbines, developed for cavalry troops, were shorter than standard rifles.) It was Marsh Williams who suggested using the short-stroke piston system he'd developed in prison. The result was the M1 carbine.

It weighed in at 5 pounds, 7 ounces (2.5 kg); some well-stocked purses are heavier. But its accurate range and firepower was much greater than any pistol. The army accepted Winchester's design less than three months before December 7, 1941, when the Japanese attacked Pearl Harbor and the United States went to war.

KEEP IT SIMPLE, STUPID

The first M1 carbines were delivered to the army in 1942. Six million would be produced by 1945. Standard issue during World War II, and used in Korea and even Vietnam, the carbine became "the war baby," the most produced small arms weapon in American military history. (The Soviet Kalashnikov AK-47 is the most produced small arms weapon in military history.)

The M1 took on mud, rain, rust, and rough treatment—and kept on shootin'. General Douglas MacArthur, head of the United States Armed Forces in the Far East, called the M1 carbine "one of the strongest contributing factors in our victory in the Pacific."

THEY'RE SHOOTING IN HOLLYWOOD

Postwar, Marsh Williams got a new nickname. Now he was known as Carbine Williams. He kept designing guns well into old age, and he eventually held more than 50 patents for gun improvements. He made a small fortune—and lost it again with bad investments and hard living.

Williams even traveled to Hollywood to see a movie being made. Starring Jimmy Stewart, it was about a convict serving time for murder—a convict whose gun designs helped the Allies win World War II. The movie was called *Carbine Williams*!

NOW YOU'RE COOKING WITH GAS!

While G.I. Joe was fighting the good fight, the kids at home were managing to keep their spirits up—as any Judy Garland musical of the day will prove. In fact, the word "teenager" was coined in the 1940s. Here are some slang terms from the era that those newly named teenagers tossed back and forth.

Aquarium: A house or apartment

Bagpipe: Someone who talks too much

Beagle: A hot dog

Beat: Broke

Boogieman: A jivester

Brighty: Very smart

Brush: A moustache

P.C.: A boyfriend (for Prince Charming)

Buzz: To kiss

Cogs: Sunglasses

Crazy: Wonderful

Date bait: A good-looking girl

Dead presidents: Money

Deadly: Wonderful

Deuce of haircuts: Two weeks

Drooly: A cute and popular guy

Eye: A detective

Fall: To be convicted of a crime

Gas: To engage in idle conversation

Gobbledygook: Inflated, unintelligible language

Hardware: Glitzy jewelry

Herd: A pack of Camels

Hinges: Elbows

Ivory-dome: An intellectual

Jackson: A form of address like "Buddy" or "Mac"

Jump: To dance to swing music

Old hat: Out of style

Rolling: Wealthy

Roost: A house or apartment

Slide your jive: To talk freely

Squirrel fever: A romantic urge

Tumble: To dance

Wack: An eccentric person

Whiffle: A crew cut

Yank: A dentist

GUERRILLA WARFARE
PART 3

The U.S. Army Rangers during World War II

In 1942, the 1st Ranger Battalion was created after Major General Lucien Truscott convinced General George C. Marshall, the army chief of staff, of the need for large, all-volunteer, and highly trained commando units that could be used for special operations. "Rangers Lead the Way" was and is their motto.

THE DEVIL'S BRIGADE

The Devil's Brigade, also known as the 1st Special Service Force, was a Canadian-American unit trained in mountaineering, airborne, and close-combat skills that operated mostly in Italy and France. They excelled at close-quarters combat with numerically superior forces.

At Monte la Difensa, Italy, they wiped out a strategic enemy defensive position high atop a mountain surrounded by steep cliffs. They got their nickname from a captured diary of a German officer who wrote of the American commandos (whose faces were camouflaged in black paint for the nighttime raid), "The black devils are all around us every time we come into line and we never hear them."

DARBY'S RANGERS

The 1st Ranger Battalion was named after their commander, Lieutenant Colonel William O. Darby. They first saw action during the invasion of North Africa, at the Battle of El Guettar, where U.S. forces handed legendary German general Erwin "the Desert Fox" Rommel his first solid defeat. During the invasion of Sicily, Darby led his Rangers in an attack on the town of Gela. Darby's men suffered heavy losses, including one platoon that was completely wiped out. During a counterattack by Italian tanks, Darby and one of his captains took control of a captured antitank gun, knocking out several of the tanks and forcing the surrender of more than 200 Italian soldiers.

RUDDER'S RANGERS

The 2nd Ranger Battalion was commanded by Lieutenant Colonel James Earl Rudder and is best known as the unit that scaled the cliffs at Point du Hoc during the D-Day invasion. Their mission was to neutralize a battery of six 15 mm coastal artillery pieces that were capable of hitting the Allied ships participating in the invasion. The Rangers hit the beach and immediately began scaling the cliffs with rope ladders, while under constant rifle and machine-gun fire from the Germans on the cliffs above. Once they made it to the top of the cliffs and eliminated the Germans, they were shocked to find out that Allied intelligence had been faulty. The guns had obviously been removed sometime before the invasion. Two hundred and twenty men attempted the climb up the cliffs. After the Germans were routed, only 90 Rangers were still battle-ready.

MERRILL'S MARAUDERS

Named after their leader, Brigadier General James Merrill, the 5037th Composite Unit (Provisional) operated in the Burmese jungle. The United States was supporting China by supplying them with war materials, but when the Japanese occupied Burma, they cut off the land route. The Marauders' mission was to pave the way for the construction of the Ledo Road—a connection between the Indian railway and the old Burma Road to China— and capture Myitkyina Airfield, the only all-weather landing strip in northern Burma.

Merrill's Marauders traveled more than 1,000 miles (1,600 km) in extremely dense jungle destroying Japanese supply lines, disrupting communications, and defeating the Japanese in 35 separate engagements. Every member of the Marauders was awarded the Bronze Star.

For more in the series, see "Guerrilla Warfare Part 4"—*the Green Berets—on page 237.*

ISLAND HOPPING

Cruising the Caribbean for a sunken treasure trove of history.

The islands of the Caribbean stretch from just south of Florida to just north of Venezuela. That's 1 million square miles (about 2.5 million square km) of land and sea, 30 million people, and 500 years of recorded, but little-known, history.

GETTING BETTER IN THE BAHAMAS

By 1700, piracy was big business in the Bahamas. Drinking, rioting, and plundering pirates ruled the port of Nassau. Law-abiding citizens fled to other islands. In 1718, the English king George I, perhaps thinking, "it takes a thief to catch a thief," appointed Captain Woodes Rogers as the Bahamas's first royal governor. Rogers was a former pirate, or more precisely, a privateer—a pirate who had permission from a government to plunder and pillage ships of other countries. The king ordered Rogers to clean out the pirates: Rogers solved piracy by pardoning 2,000 pirates. The newly pardoned pirates were then commanded to hunt down the *really* bad characters. Rogers's motto was also the official motto of the Bahamas until 1973: "Piracy Expelled, Commerce Returned." (The new motto, adopted when the Bahamas became independent of Great Britain, is a blander "Forward, Onward, Together.")

During Prohibition, the Bahamas brewed up business in the form of bootleg whiskey and rum; the Nassau waterfront was one giant liquor warehouse. The most infamous rumrunner was sea captain Bill McCoy, whose liquor was of such high quality that it led to the expression "the real McCoy." When Prohibition ended in 1933, the Bahamian economy stagnated, until the early 1960s when tourism boomed following the closure of Cuba to American visitors.

A LOVE-HAITI RELATIONSHIP?

In October 1492, Columbus discovered the Bahamas and thought he was in Asia. His flagship was the *Santa María*. Sailing on westward on Christmas Day 1492, the wheel of the *Santa María* was handed to a cabin boy. The rest of the crew, having partied hearty

The Caribbean ABC islands: Aruba, Bonaire, Curaçao.

for Christmas, was asleep. The inexperienced boy failed to recognize a submerged reef and ran the ship aground off the north coast of what is now Haiti. Columbus and his men had to abandon ship. Timbers salvaged from the *Santa María* were used to build the Europeans' first settlement in the Western Hemisphere. It was named Puerto de Navidad, Spanish for Christmas Port. Columbus left 39 men behind at the fort and returned to Spain with the *Niña* and the *Pinta*. A year later, Columbus returned and found the fort burned to the ground. There was no sign of the men except for four skeletons.

MALE BONDING IN JAMAICA
Ian Fleming, the creator of the character James Bond (Agent 007) wrote all of his 13 novels in the home he called Goldeneye, on Jamaica's north coast. Bond, James Bond, was also the name of the author of a book describing the birds of Jamaica.

THE VIRGIN ISLANDS: A BARGAIN AT ANY PRICE
Until 1917, the U.S. Virgin Islands were owned by Denmark. During World War I, the U.S. government feared that Germany would use the islands for U-boat bases and bought the islands from Denmark for $25 million (21 million euros), the highest price the United States had ever paid for land.

The man who won the design competition for the U.S. Capitol building was William Thornton, a sugar planter from the tiny British Virgin Island of Jost Van Dyke. Thornton also helped Thomas Jefferson design the buildings of the University of Virginia.

HOT AND COLD ABOUT NEVIS
The hot, tropical island of Nevis is named for snow. *Nieves* is the Spanish word for the cold, wet stuff. In 1493, Columbus named the island thinking the clouds on the mountaintop looked like the snow on the Pyrenees.

Alexander Hamilton, first secretary of the U.S. Treasury and the man on the $10 bill, was born on Nevis in 1755.

MARTINIQUE EXPLODES!
On May 18, 1902, the town of St. Pierre on Martinique was the most up-to-date town in the Caribbean. But early that morning,

two explosions thundered from Mt. Pelée. The volcano split in half. It spewed a cloud of ash, poisonous gas, and lava that ran down the mountainside at 250 miles (402 km) per hour. The lava vaporized everything in its path. In two minutes, 30,000 people were killed. In St. Pierre, the one lucky survivor was a prisoner in the town's underground jail cell. His escape from death was rewarded with a pardon. He later became a sideshow attraction in Barnum and Bailey's circus.

GUADELOUPE: A GOOD DEAL

The Seven Years' War between Great Britain and France was ended with the Treaty of Paris in 1763. The French had lost that war and gladly gave up their interest in all of Canada in exchange for little Guadeloupe. Guadeloupe was a valuable sugar island, and as the French philosopher Voltaire said, Canada was just "a few acres of snow."

DINNER IN DOMINICA

The word "Caribbean" comes from the Spanish *caribal* meaning "cannibal." The early Spanish explorers believed that the native people they called "Caribs" ate human flesh. Like some South American native peoples, they may have devoured people. But this was only on special occasions, such as after a raid on another tribe, which they would celebrate by eating one or two of their prisoners of war. Although a few Caribs still survive on the island of Dominica, within 50 years of Columbus's arrival, most of another group of native people, the Taino, had become extinct through warfare, disease, and intermarriage with Europeans. Of native Taino culture, only the hammock remains. The Taino people invented the hammock, which comes from a Taino word.

CURAÇAO

Curaçao has the oldest Jewish synagogue in continuous use in the Western Hemisphere; it was built in 1732. Jews came to the Dutch-owned island in the 1650s seeking religious freedom.

SAINTS IN THE HOOD

St. Martin: The value of the Caribbean islands kept European powers battling for ownership during the colonial era. But in a

---

The first published American woman writer was Anne Bradstreet, in 1650.

unique method of dispute resolution, the Dutch and the French agreed to divide the island of St. Martin between them. According to the traditional story, in 1648, the line of demarcation between the two nations was decided by a footrace. A Frenchman and a Dutchman, starting in the center of the island, walked around the coast until they met again. France got a bit more land because the Frenchman was quicker. (His sports drink of choice was wine. The Dutchman chose gin, which may have slowed his pace.) They line they marked still holds to this day. The island known as St. Martin (French)/Sint Maarten (Dutch) is still half French, half Dutch.

St. Lucia: Two St. Lucians have won the Nobel Prize. Author Derek Wolcott won the 1992 Nobel Prize for Literature. Sir W. Arthur Lewis won the 1979 prize in economics.

St. Bart's: Saint-Barthélemy (known to all as St. Bart's) was named for Columbus's brother, Bartholomew.

St. Kitts: For unknown reasons, the French brought African green velvet monkeys with them to St. Kitts as pets. The island now deals with their 35,000 descendants.

NAME-DROPPING IN PUERTO RICO

The first governor of Puerto Rico was Juan Ponce de León. He didn't discover the Fountain of Youth there, either.

* * * * *

IT'S NOT SO TRIVIAL

- The Caribbean Sea is the fifth largest body of water with a total area of 970,000 square miles.
- The largest island in the Caribbean is Cuba.
- The barrier reef off the coast of Belize is almost 185 miles long, making it the largest barrier reef in the western hemisphere.
- Jamaica has 120 rivers, including the Rio Grande in Port Antonio, which is the white river through which James Bond waded in *Doctor No*.
- Grenada produces the widest variety of spices in the world. Grenada also grows a third of the world's nutmeg.

Her book was *The Tenth Muse Lately Sprung Up in America*, a volume of poetry.

FROM BARBOCOA TO BRIQUETTE

No, this isn't an exotic route on the Oriental Express,
it's the history of barbecue!

Once primitive man discovered fire, it can't have been too long before someone accidentally dropped a chunk of meat onto an open flame and discovered meat tasted a lot better cooked than it did raw. The discovery of barbecue sauce would take a little longer.

LEGALIZE POTS

Even though our forefathers lacked propane-fired stainless steel grills, they managed to get along fine with just an open flame. During the Middle Ages, the use of iron pots in Europe became widespread, and Europeans discovered the ease of using large pots to boil meat, usually with vegetables and often with dumplings or pasta. Iron also permitted cooks to construct permanent or semi-permanent cooking devices, so that cooking and heating could take place indoors. Other cultures, like the Chinese, evolved similarly—away from cooking over direct heat and toward a "low and slow" method.

BBQ BY ANY OTHER NAME WOULD TASTE AS SWEET

By the beginning of the Renaissance in 1453, the low-and-slow method had been all but forgotten in Europe. When Columbus arrived in Haiti in 1492, he saw the Taino Native Americans cooking fish and wild game hung on a wooden structure over coals. The Taino word for the wooden structure sounded to the explorers like *barbacoa*.

Some have claimed that the word *barbecue* is actually derived from the Louisiana French *barbe à queue*, translated as from whiskers to tail (ostensibly a description of how a barbecued animal is roasted), but the *Oxford English Dictionary* rejects this folk etymology as "an absurd conjecture." And they're usually right.

O BRAVE NEW WORLD, THAT HAS
SUCH PULLED PORK IN IT

When the Spanish explorers returned to Europe with this new
cooking method, word quickly spread across Europe, with the help
of the recently invented printing press. Shortly thereafter, de Soto
and other explorers of present-day Florida brought swine from
Europe. The swine quickly spread throughout the American
Southeast, and soon a delightful marriage of cooking method and
pig would be born.

The first barbecues were held as social activities by wealthy
plantation owners. After George Washington laid the cornerstone
of the Capitol in 1793, the assembled group dined on a barbecued
500-pound ox. William Henry Harrison attracted 30,000 voters to
one colossal barbecue in Virginia. Slaves were often the cooks at
barbecues and they took barbecue with them when they moved
north after the Civil War.

COOK 'EM, COWBOY

In the late 1800s, during cattle drives out West, cowboys had to
be fed. The cattle barons didn't want to feed them good meat, so
disposable cuts were used. The main choice was brisket, a tough,
stringy piece of meat. Resourceful cowboys learned that if you left
this brisket to cook for a long period of time at low heat, it would
be more palatable.

Meats were cooked for hours over trenches filled with wood.
The wood smoke flavored the meats and the slow and low-heat
cooking method made the barbecue tasty and easy to eat, even
without a full set of teeth. (Cowboys weren't renowned for their
dental care.)

OLD KING CHARCOAL

In the 19th century, barbecue was a staple at church picnics and
political rallies. A barbecue was a popular and inexpensive way to
lobby for votes and an easy way for different social classes to mix.
Political organizers would provide barbecue, lemonade, and typically a bit of whiskey for the men.

The next big breakthrough on the barbecued meat front was
the invention of charcoal—by none other than Henry Ford. He
hit upon charcoal as a way to get some commercial use out of the

He was sentenced to five years' hard labor on the rock pile at Sing Sing Prison.

piles of wood scraps heaped up as a byproduct of his car-assembly operation. His friend Thomas Edison designed the first charcoal plant on a site selected by a Ford relative, E. G. Kingsford. In 1950, Ford Charcoal was renamed the Kingsford Product Company. Kingsford is still the leading manufacturer of charcoal in the United States.

BARBECUE TRIVIA

- Henry Ford rigged one of his cars to barbecue meat using engine heat. He and Thomas Edison used to drive out to the country, cooking their food along the way and then stopping for a picnic.
- George Stephan, an employee of Weber Brothers Metal Works, invented the kettle grill in 1951 from two metal bowls. It allowed indirect cooking with a vent system for airflow.
- More than 77 percent of all U.S. households own a barbecue grill and nearly half barbecue year round and use their grills five times a month.
- The Fourth of July is the most popular holiday weekend for barbecuing, followed by Labor Day and Memorial Day.
- The most popular foods to barbecue are, in order, hamburgers, steak, hot dogs, and chicken breasts.
- Half of all marshmallows eaten in the United States were toasted over a barbecue grill.
- A hibachi is the grill of choice in Korea.
- The first-known barbeque grills were found at Knossos, on the Greek isle of Crete around 5000 B.C.
- Lexington, North Carolina, lays claim to the title of "Barbecue Capital of the World."
- Among the most common different ways to phrase it: BBQ, Q, Cue, Bar-B-Cue, barbie, barbecue, barbeque, and barbique.

THE SUN KING DIET

*Are you struggling to lose those love handles and shed
some extra pounds? Take a hint from the Sun King of
France, and don't worry about it! Eat, eat!*

King Louis XIV (1638–1715), known as the "Sun King,"
imposed absolute rule over France and fought a series of
wars in an effort to impose absolute rule over the rest of
Europe. His reign was the longest in European history, and during that period, he pretty much got whatever he wanted. His
passions included art, music, women, and enormous quantities
of food. You can bet this monarch didn't watch his carbs, count
his calories, or monitor his fat intake. But if we can trust the
many portraits of him, Louis somehow managed to keep his
weight in relative check and stayed fit throughout his life. He
lived to be just two days shy of 77—no mean feat in the days of
what might be called "voodoo medicine."

THE MAN WHO HAD EVERYTHING
Louis XIV lived *well*. The king had enough servants and followers
to attend to his every whim. There were attendants whose only
responsibility was to apply his perfume in the morning and others
who were solely in charge of his bath, his clothing, or his every-
other-day shave. Guards at his favorite palace, Versailles, were
posted at the dozens of magnificent fountains that decorated the
grounds; their job was to whistle, as a signal, when the king
approached so that the waterworks could be in all their glory
when he passed.

He had dozens of mistresses as well as sycophants of both gen-
ders to tell him amusing stories and keep him laughing despite any
bad news he might encounter on the political front. And there
were people aplenty to make sure that his beloved hunting
grounds were bursting with stags and game birds.

LIVE TO EAT
Louis not only liked hunting game, he liked *eating* it. The famines
that swept through France during his reign didn't slow his appetite.

His main meals included bowls of four different kinds of soups, a whole bird (a pheasant, partridge, chicken, or duck—whatever game was in season) stuffed with truffles, a huge salad, some mutton for good measure, a couple of large slices of ham, a pastry or three, raw fruit, and to finish, compotes (fruit desserts cooked in syrup) and preserves. (Jam at that time was eaten straight up by the royalty and gentry; only peasants spread it on toast.)

Madame Françoise de Maintenon (whom Louis XIV married in secret late in his life) said that if she ate half as much as he did she'd be dead in a week.

DINING AS A SPECTATOR SPORT

Louis always awoke at 8:30 a.m. After he was bathed, coifed, and dressed, he had an uncharacteristically light meal: a breakfast of broth. During breakfast, about 100 of the king's closest friends (all men) were invited to join him.

Lunch was served promptly at 1:00 p.m. The king usually dined alone in his bedroom at a table facing the windows. Sometimes men of the court would be admitted and sometimes the queen. But the evening meal was the main event. The king was joined by the queen and the royal family's princes and princesses. In addition, a large crowd of spectators (usually numbering in the hundreds) was herded into the antechamber of the king's suite for the privilege of watching him and his family eat.

Since the Middle Ages, eating in public was considered to be a display of authority—and Louis XIV was not one to turn his back on ritual or a chance to display his power and wealth. This *grand couvert* (grand service), as it was called, was practiced every day, without fail. With each new course came a new procession of officers of the household to serve the dishes. The elaborate ritual was so well choreographed that the meal only took about 45 minutes. When the meal was over, the king retired. Louis always dined at 10:00 p.m. and was in bed by 11:00 p.m. Forget what your mother told you about not going to bed on a full stomach!

GOT ORANGE JUICE?

Versailles was about 13 miles (21 km) from Paris—a sizable distance for serving someone who expected instant gratification. So the palace had to be reasonably self-sufficient to be able to provide the luxuries the king required. Louis was especially fond of orange juice; so he kept more than 1,000 orange trees, in silver tubs, at Versailles, some in each room of the palace. The tubs were on wheels, so they could be easily carted outside in the sunshine. He grew more than 500 kinds of pears—another favorite fruit—in his garden. Pineapples and coffee beans, exotic fare in the 17th century, were grown in the vegetable gardens. Wheat was also grown on the grounds, to provide ample flour for the hundreds of loaves of bread the bakers turned out each week.

SNACKS, ETC.
And if the "normal" feasting wasn't excessive enough, three times a week court receptions known as *soirées d'appartement* were held. A buffet table was loaded with coffee, hot chocolate, wine, and liquor, in the aptly named Abundance Salon; another table in the Venus Salon held desserts of every imaginable sort. To burn off some of those calories, there was dancing in the Mars Salon. And special festivities scattered throughout the year accompanied weddings and the arrival of foreign dignitaries. These grand occasions usually lasted for several days. The festivities featured, of course, a lavish banquet with dozens of courses of meats, seasonal vegetables, fresh fruits, and mountains of pastries. Such a bacchanalian feast was followed by a dress ball and an opera.

SUPERSIZE ME!
But the king wasn't the only glutton in the land. The ladies of court were expected to eat, drink, and be merry—but especially to eat. The king hated people who refused food. No skinny women allowed! Size-wise, the fashion of the day was double chins, big bottoms, and buxom bosoms.

Even in childbirth (during which women of the court were expected to behave as if they had no physical pain), they were encouraged to drink liquor and eat large amounts of exceptionally rich food.

Needless to say, such overindulgence killed lesser men than the king. And most found consuming huge quantities of food and drink, even for one meal, extremely uncomfortable. Ladies tried to conceal unwanted food in the folds of their skirts, and gentlemen were known to drop hunks of meat on the floor.

For some, enemas were a fashionable antidote to the gargantuan meals. But it's not clear how Louis managed to keep his boyish figure. As anyone who's ever tried to lose weight knows, there's no free lunch. Maybe the artists who portrayed him were trying to flatter him; maybe he was fatter than they let on. At any rate, when an autopsy was performed on the late Sun King, he was found to have a huge stomach and bowels more than twice the usual length.

* * * * *

BLACK TUNIC, AND DON'T FORGET YOUR SWITCHBLADE

In medieval England, hosts did not provide knives at the table—dinner guests were expected to bring their own. Forks were not used in England until the 18th century; for a long time before that, use of a fork was considered unmanly, an Italian affectation. In France, King Louis XIV was the first host in Europe to provide complete sets of dinnerware for his guests. Visitors to his palaces would no longer have to provide their own utensils.

SOME LAST THOUGHTS ABOUT FOOD

"The rich would have to eat money if the poor did not provide food."—Russian proverb

"The next time you feel like complaining, remember that your garbage disposal probably eats better than 30 percent of the people in the world."—Robert Orben

"If you reject the food, ignore the customs, fear the religion and avoid the people, you might better stay home."—James Michener

"Old people shouldn't eat health foods. They need all the preservatives they can get."—Robert Orben

THE KING'S CHAMPAGNE

Champagne used to be France's favorite red wine.
Nonbubbly red wine, that is. It was King Louis XIV's
gout that turned it into what we know today.

I n 17th century France, the rich drank a lot of imported
Spanish wine. But as far as the local product was concerned,
the two most famous wine-making regions were Burgundy and
Champagne. While both made red and white wines, red wine
made up the bulk of the wine produced in both regions. Red
champagne had the best reputation, but the burgundy winemakers desperately wanted to destroy that reputation in order to
make *their* red wine into the number one product. Everybody said
that champagne tasted better, so they came up with a novel idea:
they would tell people that their wine was better from a health
point of view.

WINE WARS

Starting in the 1650s, Burgundians published a series of pamphlets
in Paris to explain how much healthier it was to drink burgundy,
basing their arguments on the rather sketchy medical understanding of the time. This started an exchange of attacks and counter-
attacks between the makers of burgundy and champagne that
went on for decades.

FOR MEDICINAL PURPOSES ONLY

Burgundy PR didn't seem to make much of a difference until
1693, when King Louis XIV got a new doctor, Guy-Crescent
Fagon. Louis suffered from all kinds of ailments, including gout,
which everybody knew was caused by drinking red wine—but
which the burgundy pamphlets claimed was caused specifically by
too much red champagne. Dr. Fagon was up with all the latest
ideas, and as soon as he got the job of royal physician, he
announced a radical new treatment: no more champagne.

May 16, 1975: Junko Tabei of Japan was the first woman to reach the summit of Mt. Everest.

RX FOR XIV

Louis was not pleased, and he only went along with the advice because he saw it as his duty to France. Nobody else in the court was pleased either, since it meant that they would all have to stop drinking champagne too; they would all have to drink whatever the king drank. This, Dr. Fagon announced, would be burgundy, even though he recognized that champagne was "much more agreeable." In fact, the burgundy was to be mixed with a special medicinal mixture of herbs and spices, in order to drive away the "acid from the melancholy humor" (one of those crazy 17th-century medical beliefs).

The king glumly accepted the prescription; the court went along with it. And before long, the whole of France got the message: the king had stopped drinking champagne because there was something wrong with it. In other words, everything the people from Burgundy had been claiming for years must be true.

YOU CAN'T KEEP A GOOD WINE DOWN

Fortunately, the Champagne winemakers had a Plan B. Their white wine had been modestly successful, too, although it did have one small problem. It tended to be a bit fizzy, due to secondary fermentation, especially when it was put in bottles. (This is natural for wine that's not killed by pumping poison gas through it to stop fermentation, as happens with all wine that's industrially bottled today.) It keeps on fermenting, in fact, until you drink it. In Italy and Greece, you can still find home-produced white wine like this in country areas: cloudy, yellow, and just a little bit fizzy on the tongue.

MORE BUBBLES PLEASE—WE'RE BRITISH

Coincidentally, glass making was developing around this same time, and in England, which had the most advanced methods for industrial bottle production, the champagne wine producers struck gold. The English bought white champagne in barrels and bottled it themselves in good-quality airtight bottles, with proper corks imported from Spain. They discovered that very soon this procedure would create enough gas, through natural fermentation, to make the bottle go "pop!" when opened. The people in Champagne had seen the little bubbles as one of their main problems, and if they'd known about the poison gas method, modern champagne would never have been invented. But when they learned that the crazy English actually *liked* the bubbles, history took another course.

VOILÀ, AS THEY SAY

The Champagne folks knew they had the right grapes and the right recipe, but two things bothered them. Since the wine was still fermenting when it was ready to drink, it produced muddy sediment in the bottom of the bottles, as well as that now-popular bubbly gas. Also, they didn't want to rely on other people bottling their wine. So, they came up with something that solved both problems.

They developed their own bottling method whereby they wait until enough secondary fermentation has taken place to produce the gas that's necessary for the fizz. It was to turn the bottles around so they slant with the necks pointing downward and all the sediment slides down into the neck. In 1816 Madame Clicquot developed a key technique for removing troublesome sediment. Over time the process was refined. Today champagne producers freeze the necks of the bottles with ice. The wine inside the neck freezes, too. The bottle can then be opened, the plug of ice containing the sediment can be removed, and a fresh cork can be put in. The cork is then wired, to keep it in. By fine-tuning this process, the Champagne winemakers found a way to produce a wine with the maximum possible amount of fizz, but no sediment at all. Bingo! From their murky, yellow, fizzy local wine, they had produced something clear, brilliant, and, yes, sparkling.

I'LL DRINK TO THAT!

The champagne makers had the last laugh. Research shows that their brand is up there with Coca-Cola in terms of global recognition. French champagne can still rely on its rock-solid international luxury image. This time around, it has no serious competition.

Ransom E. Olds, not Henry Ford, created the assembly line in 1901. Ford improved on it.

RING-A-DING-DING

Whether it's made of reeds, iron, or gold,
it's tough to say, "I do" without it.

The wedding ring is the product of dozens of cultures and several centuries of marital evolution. The circle, always a symbol of eternity, has no beginning or end. So the circular ring was a natural as the symbol of lasting union between a bride and groom. But the history of the wedding ring hasn't been all hearts and flowers.

IT'S THE MONEY, HONEY

Around 2800 B.C. in Egypt, money was molded as a ring. Ancient Egyptian marriage ceremonies involved placing the money on the bride's finger to show that she now possessed the wealth of the groom's family.

In ancient Rome, a similar custom evolved. Roman families kept wealth in strongboxes. New brides were given the keys to the strongboxes on a ring. Today's wedding rings are derived from those ancient wedding customs.

CHRISTIANITY COMES A-ROUND

Oddly enough, many in the Christian church looked upon early wedding rings with contempt. Rings were seen as crude and pagan. Puritans in the American colonies believed all jewelry was sinful waste, so they traded "wedding thimbles," which were, at least, useful. (But tenderhearted wives often cut the bottoms out of their thimbles and made rings of them anyway.)

It took a scandal before the church gave wedding bands a "ring-ing" endorsement. The scandal arose because wedding rings could be made of hemp, reeds, or other cheap materials; worn-out rings were replaced every year or so. Eventually, shifty-eyed young men began presenting fair ladies with rings and promises of eternal love that *both* fell apart quickly. Finally, the bishop of Salisbury published a law in 1217 saying that if you gave a girl a ring in front of witnesses, it was a binding marriage contract. After the bishop laid down that law, most Christian sects embraced the wedding ring.

George magazine was founded by John Kennedy Jr.; its first cover featured Cindy Crawford.

ON THE ROCKS
Romans sealed matrimony with an iron ring (iron symbolized the strength of love), even though they found that the iron rings rusted. Later, when gold gained popularity, they may have had a gold ring for special occasions and an iron ring (sometimes with a key) for around the house. More contemporary Romans used gold exclusively.

Silver was popular for a time during the Renaissance, but eventually, the English and Irish helped set the "gold standard." Folklore even suggested that a marriage could be deemed unlucky or legally invalid if the ring weren't gold. If a couple couldn't afford a gold ring, somebody lent them one for the ceremony.

When Archduke Maximilian I of Austria gave Mary of Burgundy a diamond engagement ring in 1477, diamonds became the wedding stone of choice. They symbolized luck, happiness, and magic. Both ancient Greeks and Romans thought of diamonds as "tears of the gods." And a diamond's indestructibility is a fine symbol of everlasting love. After 1870, the discovery of huge diamond caches in South America ensured that more grooms could afford to buy their sweeties diamond rings.

LOVE IN VEIN
In the 16th and 17th centuries, a fashionable woman might wear her wedding ring on her thumb. Later, it became popular to place the ring on the fourth finger of the bride's left hand, or the right hand, depending on what country you were from. A romantic legend concerning the left-handed tradition explains that the fourth finger of your left hand contains the vena amoris, which runs straight from your finger to your heart. (Alas for romantics, there's no scientific proof that the vena amoris exists.)

THREE-RING CIRCUS
And we can't forget engagement rings. During the Middle Ages, gimmal rings were *en vogue*; a gimmal ring was a combination of two or three rings that could be worn as one ring or separated. One was given for engagement, the other was held by a witness, and the third was the wedding band.

In the 1700s and 1800s, gemstone "betrothal rings" were popular. They were sometimes crafted so that the first initials of the stones spelled out words. A ring for a Diane, for example, might have held a diamond, an iolite, an amethyst, a natrolite, and an emerald. But that fad passed (which was probably just as well for guys buying rings for an Elizabeth or a Chlothilde).

As for the groom's wedding ring, this custom of the 1900s is still in its infancy. The groom's ring may be a result of the 20th century's two World Wars. A soldier shipped overseas had a ring to remind him of the loving wife waiting for him back home.

* * * * *

- Before acquiring fame and fortune, Sonny and Cher were wed with engraved $10 (8 euro) stainless steel rings. Cher lost hers. But 26 years later, shortly after Sonny Bono's death, a construction worker found the ring and returned it to Cher, after hearing her talk about it on Jay Leno's TV show.

- Queen Victoria gave out more than 50 rings at her wedding.

- All diamonds are more than 100 million years old, and they can be up to 3 billion years old.

- Jennifer Lopez lost a wedding ring (from Cris Judd) while filming *Gigli*. The ring's cost? More than $30,000 (24,700 euros). Nobody owned up to seeing it—sort of like *Gigli* itself.

- Two months' salary is the spending guideline established by industry experts for an engagement ring. These experts, of course, sell engagement rings for a living.

- 74 percent of all brides receive a diamond engagement ring and 60 percent participate in the selection of their ring.

- The average cost of an engagement ring is $3,165.

- Saturday, the most popular American choice for a wedding day is, according to English folklore, the unluckiest day to marry!

TAKE MY WIFE...
PLEASE!

*Let's say you're an 18th-century British peasant, and you
and your wife just aren't getting along anymore. What do
you do? Divorce her? Too expensive. Kill her? Too risky.
Oh, well, looks like you'll have to auction her off.
Welcome to the wacky world of wife selling!*

HARDY HAR-HAR
Hands up all of you who've read Thomas Hardy's classic of 19th-century British misery, *The Mayor of Casterbridge*. You know, the one where everybody dies and life is shown to be a pointless parade of squalor, pain, and death? You haven't gotten around to reading it yet? Well, it's worth filling you in on a key plot point, namely, that the main character, Michael Henchard, sells his long-suffering wife at a public auction. Surely not, you cry! Not in civilized old England. Thomas Hardy must have made it all up. Well, we're here to tell you that it's all true. Right up until the early 1900s, husbands in Britain were able to offer their wives to the highest bidder.

GOING, GOING...
The Golden Age of wife selling was between 1780 and 1850, when some 300 wives were sold (and that's just those that appeared in the record books—doubtless many more spouses were gotten rid of more quietly).

One of the earliest recorded wife sales took place in 1733, in Birmingham, central England. The local paper of the day records how "Samuel Whitehouse...sold his wife, Mary Whitehouse, in open market, to Thomas Griffiths. Value, one guinea [about one English pound]." As part of the deal, the paper comments, Griffiths was to take Mary "with all her faults." Another wife, in 1801, was put up for sale by her husband for one penny. Not surprisingly, this bargain sparked a frenzied bidding war among the locality's lonely farmers, and Mary eventually went for five shillings and sixpence. One husband even managed to off-load his old lady for eighteen pence and a quart of ale. An even luckier chap managed to trade in his other half for a full barrel of beer!

CATTLE CALL

As if the act of being auctioned off wasn't bad enough, the method in which wives were sold really rubbed salt into the wound. Wife-selling deals always followed the same very public ritual. First, the wives were led to the local market square with halters around their necks, just like cattle for sale. Then they were made to stand on an auction block, while their husbands-not-to-be began taking bids. A crowd would usually gather, and proceedings would be accompanied by much jeering and joking from the local peasantry. Once a deal was struck, all the interested parties, and most of the crowd, would retire to the local tavern to celebrate the successful transaction.

PRETTY CIVILIZED AFTER ALL

It all seems pretty distasteful, doesn't it? But it's not entirely what it seems. Far from being ritually humiliated by the whole thing, most of the wives on sale were there willingly. In fact, almost all sales took place with the agreement of both husband and wife. It was impossible for ordinary folk in Britain to get divorced. It was a difficult and expensive procedure—around $20,000 (16,256 euros) at today's prices. So, instead, unhappily married couples had to find another way to untie the knot. Wife selling killed two birds with one stone—it was the quickest of quickie divorces, plus it provided some live street theater for the local community. The authorities hardly approved of the practice, but they turned a blind eye to it, seeing as it kept the rabble amused.

THE GOOD OLD DAYS

In the vast majority of cases, the wife was sold to an existing lover for a nominal fee, which was agreed upon by all parties beforehand. By tradition, the husband would then use this fee to buy drinks for everyone in the local inn—including his ex-wife and her new husband.

Anyway, with all the pain, anguish, and huge costs that accompany most modern divorces, who's to say those ale-swigging, wife-swapping English peasants didn't have the right idea all along?

Early Hula Hoop: Egyptian children played with hoops of dried grapevines 3,000 years ago.

LOVE AND SILVERWARE

The Oneida Community wasn't the first, or last,
American group to practice free love and communism.
But it might have been the most successful.

The 19th century was a golden age in America for utopian communities—model societies based on religious or social ideals. One of the longest-lived of these experiments was the Oneida Community, founded by an ex-minister named John Humphrey Noyes.

SUCH A PERFECTIONIST

Noyes had been asked to leave Yale Divinity School in 1834 after he began preaching the doctrine of Perfectionism—a school of thought that held (counter to Calvinist dogma) that it was possible for Christians to completely free themselves from sin. In the late 1830s, Noyes organized a Perfectionist community in Putney, Vermont, under a system he called "Bible Communism." Gossip about some of the community's unorthodox practices drew the attention of authorities, and Noyes and his followers thought it best to relocate. They moved to Oneida, New York, where they founded a new commune in 1848.

THANKS FOR SHARING

In the Oneida Community, under Bible Communism, property was held in common and labor was shared by all. Children were raised communally. Members spent much time in Bible study and religious discussion. To help rid themselves of spiritual failings, members underwent "mutual criticism" sessions, during which their faults were pointed out by a committee or by the entire group. But sexy things were shared as well—Oneida's alternative lifestyle also featured something Noyes called "complex marriage."

Noyes held that monogamous marriage and the nuclear family structure went against God's rules of unselfish love for all humankind. He also believed that sex was not simply a procreative act but a sacred expression of love that could bring one closer to God. As he wrote to a friend in 1837, "In a holy community, there is no more reason why sexual intercourse should be restrained by law, than why eating and drinking should be—and there is as little occasion for shame in the one case as in the other." To that end, he instituted complex marriage, which meant that every man in the community was considered to be married to every woman.

HOT COMPLEX ACTION?

So how sexy was complex marriage, really? It wasn't the orgiastic free-for-all that some prurient outsiders imagined. Intercourse was regulated to a large extent by community leaders, who discouraged couples from forming exclusive attachments. Men and women were generally free to accept or reject a sexual proposition, which had to be communicated by a go-between. Jealousy was a no-no. A tradition called "ascending fellowship" required young men and women to pair up with their spiritually superior elders for instruction and mentoring. Noyes himself often initiated girls into sexual intercourse, sometimes when the girls were as young as 13.

ANTICLIMACTIC, TO SAY THE LEAST

How did the Oneidans prevent unplanned pregnancies? Noyes developed a form of contraception he called "male continence"—basically, a prohibition of ejaculation. Men were taught to master this (undoubtedly frustrating and not always effective) technique before they were allowed to have sexual relations with fertile women. In the mid-1860s, Noyes, who had been studying Darwin's theories, began a kind of eugenics program called "stirpiculture," in which reproduction was regulated by Noyes or a committee. Apparently, Noyes had a high opinion of his own genes, since he fathered nine of the breeding program's babies himself.

HEARTBREAK HOTEL

Did complex marriage mesh well with human nature? According to Spencer Klaw, author of *Without Sin: The Life and Death of the Oneida Community*, "At Oneida, as in the outside world, love and sex could still be a source of great anguish." Letters and diaries researched by Klaw reveal that people fell in love and felt jealousy despite their best efforts. Some resented the rule of ascending fellowship and wanted to be freer to choose their lovers. However, Noyes's followers did their best to make complex marriage work. And the lifestyle had benefits aside from variety and guilt-free sex: Male continence freed women from unwanted pregnancy, and skill at lovemaking was prized. According to Hilda Herrick Noyes, a grandniece of Noyes, "The men prided themselves on giving the women their orgasm."

THEY SAY OUR LOVE WON'T PAY THE RENT
Yet another unusual aspect of the Oneida Community, as far as utopian communities went, was its financial stability. After an early failed attempt at raising fruit, the community found success in a number of ventures, including the manufacture of beaver traps, silk thread, and flatware. By the mid-1860s, the community was making a profit, and by the 1870s, it was running mills and factories that were staffed by hired outsiders as well as Oneidans.

GOOD POLYAMORISTS MAKE GOOD NEIGHBORS
The community's domestic arrangements continued to draw criticism from religious leaders, but the Oneidans' integrity, piety, and industry won them the approval of their neighbors and business partners. Tourists from all over the United States and Europe came to visit the commune, and most came away with the impression of a happy, healthy, and well-ordered group. At its height, the Oneida Community had more than 300 members.

TROUBLE IN PARADISE
But by the late 1870s, serious internal dissension was weakening the community: Many of the younger members lacked commitment to the Oneida ideals. And a rebellious faction rejected Noyes's attempt to pass leadership to his son Theodore and demanded changes in complex marriage and other traditions. As the community struggled to resolve their problems, a group of clergymen mounted a campaign to have Noyes prosecuted on criminal charges for his sexual practices. Fearing jail, Noyes fled to Canada in the summer of 1879.

Eyeglasses were invented in Europe in A.D. 1286.

THE FALL OF COMMUNISM

Soon afterward, the community stopped practicing complex marriage. Some members married each other legally and formed conventional families. Next, communism was abandoned; and in 1881, the still-profitable Oneida Community was incorporated as a joint stock venture. Today, Oneida, Ltd. (as the company was renamed in 1935), is the biggest manufacturer of stainless steel and silver-plated flatware in the world. So, the silverware you give someone for a wedding gift may well be historically linked to a group who famously rejected monogamy. Just one of life's little ironies.

* * * * *

WINE, WOMEN AND SCENT

Over the centuries, many aromatic aphrodisiacs have been used for varied purposes. It's been said that Cleopatra helped seduce Anthony by dousing the sails of her boat in rose oil—a potent aphrodisiac. The smell of jasmine oil is said to produce a high and bring out wild passion. And during the Middle Ages, lavender was called the "Herb of Love." The smell of ginger, too, was said to spice up the love life.

All of this socializing worked up a thirst, though. Both the Romans and Greeks added violet leaves to their wine for a little extra fragrance. The Benedictines added angelica to their liquor, and the Spanish added chamomile to their sherry. Clary sage was used to fortify beer, which produced an especially invigorating euphoria followed by an especially cruel hangover.

The earliest household and beauty products also made widespread use of aromatic herbs. The ancient Romans put lavender in their bathwater, with its clean, fresh smell, hence the name lavender from the latin lavare ("to wash").

Sprigs of sage, rosemary, lavender and other fragrant plants were often tied inside clothing during 15th century Europe as a primitive deodorant.

The ancient Egyptians used the fragrant oils of cedar wood, myrrh, and other aromatic herbs to embalm their dead.

THE PAINTED LADY

How a lady and her hat scandalized Paris.

I n 1905, a painting shown in Paris shocked the public. Critics reviled it; religious and conservative moralists made speeches against it. The artist who painted it was vilified as a "wild beast" and a victimizer of women. But the painting could hardly be called pornographic. It wasn't even a nude; it was only a portrait of a fully clothed woman with hat.

THE EXHIBIT
While a group of nontraditional painters prepared for a fall exhibit in Paris, their president, Monsieur Jourdain, urged them not to show *Woman with Hat.* Jourdain considered himself a forward thinker who fought against the narrow-minded traditions of France's powerful art establishment. But he also knew trouble when he saw it. He warned the group that this modernistic work, by a struggling artist named Henri Matisse, would ruin their exhibition.

THE WILD BEASTS
When Le Salon des Independants opened its doors and Parisians got their first look at *Woman with Hat,* they either howled with laughter or gaped in horrified shock. The entire exhibition was derided. Matisse's painting became the star clown in a three-ring joke. The verdict of the public, and most of the art critics, came ´n´loud and clear. *Woman with Hat* was outrageous "barbouillage et gribouillage" (smears and scribbles). It was called barbaric. It was an insult to women as well as to art. Matisse and the rest were nothing but *fauves*...wild beasts.

THE PAINTING
Woman with Hat was a portrait of Matisse's wife, Amelie, wearing an enormous, feathered hat. Critics thought the portrait looked strangely unfinished and crude. What shocked them most were those odd, clashing colors that decorated the feathers of Madame Matisse's hat and illuminated her face. Parisians might be sophisti-

---

The earliest known written music for guitars was written by the Troubadours around A.D. 1100.

cated, but this painting confused and repelled them. Amelie Matisse was a respectable brunette, but in the portrait she sported brick red hair, an unnatural slash of dark green creasing her forehead, and mint green shading on the bridge of her nose. How could a man paint his wife in such a fashion? Rumors began to fly that all was not well in the marriage of Henri and Amelie.

THE PAINTER

For Henri Matisse, the scandal was just another dark episode in a painful struggle. Born in Bohain, a poor unlovely, industrial town in northern France, Henri was already a lawyer when he dismayed his working-class parents by deciding that art was his life's true calling. Painting never came easily to Matisse; he studied constantly. When he failed to break into the prestigious mainstream of French art, his family labeled him an embarrassment with no talent. But Henri, uncertain and depressed as he was, had bigger worries than rejection. By 1905, he was 35, a married man with three children—and he was broke.

He'd pinned his hopes on the 1905 exhibition. A hardworking perfectionist, Matisse believed that at last he was bringing something new and valuable to art—the joy of bright color. He painted *Woman with Hat* to communicate his own emotions and, he hoped, the soul of his subject. Matisse didn't portray the true colors of nature because he was determined to paint the colors of the heart.

THE MODEL

Amelie Matisse was a rebel with a cause, and her cause was her hubby's genius. Madame Matisse might not know art, but she knew Henri; whatever he did had to be great. Born in Toulouse in southwestern France, Amelie took Henri to her birthplace. When she showed her husband—a child of the cold, gray north—the hot colors of the south, she changed their lives, and the future of painting, forever.

Henri kept going back to the exhibit, fretting over the jeers and insults. But Amelie stayed at home. She never lost faith in *Woman with Hat*. The world must change; she would not! And sure enough, slowly, the world changed.

THE BUYERS

Two American art lovers, Gertrude Stein and her brother, Leo, visited the exhibition again and again, mostly to see *Woman with Hat*. They knew it was a complete break with tradition, but while others were horrified, they were impressed. A week before the exhibition closed, Leo offered to buy the painting for 300 francs. Henri could hardly wait to get rid of the unlucky canvas. His morale and his funds were very low. But Madame Matisse held out for 500 francs. The extra 200 would buy their daughter's clothing for the winter. She told her husband to sit tight.

Amelie's faith in the painting proved justified. *Woman with Hat* became a turning point for Matisse. Leo Stein not only paid the 500, but he and Gertrude also promoted Henri Matisse among the people they knew (along with another artistic upstart named Pablo Picasso).

THE LEGACY

The artists of Le Salon des Independants eventually took on the term *wild beast* with pride, calling themselves the fauve movement. The fuss over *Woman with Hat* made Matisse famous as well as notorious, and he became a leader of the French avant-garde. In time, the world became excited by Matisse's revolutionary vision of art. Critics praised him as the creator of modern painting, the liberator of color. In fact, Matisse was so famous and well loved, that some young artists found him too respectable, too bourgeois.

As for Madame Matisse, she later said that she was at her best in crisis, "when the house burns down." It never surprised her that the world came around to her point of view. Years after her death visitors at the San Francisco Museum of Modern Art still cluster around her portrait, the delightful *Woman with Hat*.

* * * * *

PETER, PETER, WALLET EATER

Peter I (1672–1725), aka Peter the Great, came up with inventive and thoroughly annoying ways to raise revenue. He taxed or imposed fines on births, funerals, hats, beehives, firewood, drinking water, and beards.

The first U.S. victory of WWI was the Battle of Belleau Wood in 1918.

STARVING FOR THEIR ART?

The musical geniuses of 18th-century Vienna were hugely gifted—but, as any artist knows, talent won't pay the rent!

If you were a musician in the 18th century, Vienna was the place to be. It's still known as *Musikstadt Wien*—"Vienna, the City of Music." And back in the day, you could hear just about any kind of music of the time: Italian opera, abstract instrumentals, serious string quartets—even violin pieces played by musicians holding their instruments upside down. During a span of about 50 years in the mid-to-late 18th century, Beethoven, Haydn, and Mozart all called Vienna home. But was there enough money to go around to *pay* all these superstars?

WORKING FOR A SONG

An average musician's salary was shockingly low during the 18th century, even compared with today's standards. Back then, musicians lived hand to mouth—if they survived at all. Still, music was extraordinarily important in everyday life in 18th-century Vienna.

Organ-grinders on street corners played bits of symphonies. In almost every coffeehouse, you could hear accomplished musicians playing instruments and singing operas. And if you didn't play an instrument and sing pretty well, you were not considered an educated or cultured person. You probably wouldn't get invited to many parties, either, if you couldn't add something to the entertainment. Instead of watching TV, middle-class people went to the theater or opera almost every day. So, if music mattered so much, and talented musicians mattered even more, why weren't they compensated accordingly?

Well...who would pay? The church employed musicians in their choirs and even commissioned composers to write original pieces for special masses. Mostly, though, it was the aristocracy who could afford to employ full-time musicians, and they weren't all that generous. Musicians might have been part of an aristo-

---

The first merry-go-round was seen at a fair in Philippapolis, Turkey, in 1620.

cratic or royal entourage, but they weren't considered equals and, therefore, weren't treated very well.

MONEY, MONEY, MONEY
Wolfgang Amadeus Mozart (1756–1791)

Mozart was probably the best paid of his contemporaries, but that didn't keep him solvent. By the time most kids are learning to color inside the lines in kindergarten, Mozart, at age six, could play the clavier, violin, and organ, and could read and improvise music. His gift astounded people, who would pay the price of admission for one of his concerts as much to see the tiny boy as to hear the music.

In his young adulthood, Mozart pulled down 450 florins a year for his gig as music director for the archbishop of Salzburg—an extremely secure and lucrative position for a young musician. For writing the opera *Così fan tutte* (1790) later in his life, Mozart received about 900 florins, about twice what his contemporaries would have been paid, because, by this point, he was well known and well liked. He also made money from commissions for new operas, ticket sales from his concerts as a pianist, royalties from publishers, and fees for piano lessons.

He wasn't rolling in dough, but he averaged about 1,000 florins a year. This was outrageously good for a musician at the time. To put this into perspective, Mozart's brother-in-law Franz Hofer drew only about 20 florins a year as twelfth violinist at St. Stephen's Church back in 1787.

No matter what he earned, Mozart famously lived beyond his means. If he hadn't died young, he would likely have made even higher earnings (collecting royalties from his compositions)—but who knows if he would have managed to balance his budget?

WHAT WOULD YOU DO IF I SANG OUT OF TUNE?
Ludwig van Beethoven (1770–1827)

A one-time pupil of Mozart's and a superstar in his own right, Beethoven got an early start in music too. His father was a popular singer in the court orchestra, so Ludwig learned the ropes early on. But he was no wunderkind like Mozart. His career didn't really take off until he was in his late teens. His "Moonlight Sonata" was written when he was at the ripe old age of 31.

Wealthy patrons and the nobility sponsored Beethoven throughout much of his life. But they didn't always treat him well, almost never paid him enough, and weren't terribly reliable sources of income. Many times in his life Beethoven was flat broke. At times, he earned his daily bread by giving piano lessons. In 1800, he made the grand sum of 600 florins.

When he began to lose his hearing as a young adult, he stopped performing because he couldn't stay on key. But he kept composing; some say his best works were completed once he was deaf. Beethoven never even heard his *Ninth Symphony* performed—the piece hailed by many critics as one of the greatest pieces of classical music ever written.

AT LEAST THE COSTUMES WERE CUTE
Franz Joseph Haydn (1732–1809)

Haydn, another great composer of the classical period, found himself going from job to job, even in his childhood. He started out as an eight-year-old choirboy in St. Stephen's Cathedral in Vienna. He kept hitting the high notes for another nine years, when puberty finally stole his soprano voice. After that, he struggled to make a living as a freelance musician. Having little money to pay for lessons, he was virtually self-taught.

Haydn served under the patronage of three successive princes of the Esterházy family of Vienna. The second, Prince Miklós József Esterházy, was a great lover of the arts and was especially fond of music. But Prince Miklós József worked Haydn to the bone. Haydn wrote symphonies, operas, marionette operettas, masses, chamber pieces, and dance music for the prince's entertainment. He also had to rehearse and conduct performances of his own and others' works; coach singers; oversee the music library; perform as an organist, violist, and violinist; and make sure the other musicians kept out of trouble. Whew!

Despite the long hours, Haydn didn't bring in the big bucks. In 1761, he earned 400 florins, plus 180 for expenses, a year. He got a raise, in 1764, to 600 florins, plus 180 for expenses. And when he took on another duty as organist in 1779, he received an additional 180 florins in goods—altogether, about 1,000 florins in one year.

But Haydn probably didn't complain about his pay: His brother Johann Evangelist was a tenor in the Esterházy choir and

---

The first blood transfusion was performed on Nov. 14, 1666, by Richard Lower of London.

earned only 25 florins a year, plus room and board. The prince did lend Johann a snappy green jacket with red cuffs to wear during performances, though.

FLORIN AFFAIRS

So, just how much was a florin worth in the 18th century anyway? It's near impossible to adjust the cost of living over the span of 150 years and make the conversion from florins to dollars or euros to boot. But think about this: Civil servants' wages at the time ranged from 8,000 to 20,000 florins a year for relatively high positions, to about 700 to 1,000 florins a year for low positions (say, clerks). If you were filthy rich—in other words, among the nobility—your annual income was anywhere from 100,000 to 500,000 per year.

So musicians were paid about as much as civil servants; the brilliant ones got about as much as low-level government officials. Remember the guy who took your picture when you got your driver's license? He makes about as much as the genius who wrote the opera *Don Giovanni*.

* * * * *

BAD BUSINESS

The inventor of the telephone, Alexander G. Bell, offered to sell his invention to Western Union. The commitee that was formed to review Bell's proposal had this to say:

> The telephone is named by its inventor A. G. Bell. He believes that one day they will be installed in every residence and place of business. Bell's profession is that of a voice teacher. Yet, he claims to have discovered an instrument of great practical value in communication which has been overlooked by thousands of workers who have spent years in the field. Bell's proposals to place his instrument in almost every home and business is fantastic. The central exchange alone would represent a huge outlay in real estate and buildings, to say nothing of the electrical equipment. In conclusion the committee feels that it must advise against any investment in Bell's scheme. We do not doubt that it will find users in special circumstances, but any developments of the kind and scale which Bell so fondly imagines is utterly out of the question.

Whoops!

Fidelio was Beethoven's only opera.

LET THERE BE LIBRARIES

Andrew Carnegie was no saint—just ask anyone who worked for him. But he was considered the patron saint of libraries.

A ndrew Carnegie was a Scottish immigrant whose family moved to Pittsburgh, Pennsylvania, when he was 13. His first job was as a bobbin boy, a kid who handles spindles in a cotton factory. Then, he got a job as a messenger, and next, he started working his way up at the Pennsylvania Railroad. As he got older and his talent with money became apparent, his mother mortgaged her house to provide him with some seed money for investments. Andrew parlayed his stake into a small fortune. He started his steel business, and in 1901, sold it to J. P. Morgan for $480 million (390 million euros).

SHREWD, BUT NO SCROOGE

Carnegie was always a big believer in charity. In 1889, he wrote an essay called "The Gospel of Wealth," in which he proposed that it was the responsibility of the wealthy to share their fortunes for the betterment of the people. But he didn't just believe in throwing money into the wind, either. So, in his later days, he pondered how he could do some good without wasting his money. A childhood mentor, wealthy retiree Colonel Anderson, provided his inspiration.

Colonel Anderson owned hundreds of books. He let neighborhood kids browse his shelves on Saturday afternoons, take books home, and come back for more—just like a library. That was how Carnegie got his childhood education, and he was ever grateful.

CHECK THIS OUT

Carnegie built Pittsburgh a grand library in 1899. One library might have been philanthropic enough for most men, but Carnegie was a library-building machine—2,509 in all. He built them in every state in the United States except Rhode Island. He built them in the United Kingdom too, including his hometown

The Dead Sea Scrolls were found in 1947 by Bedouin shepherds looking for a stray goat.

of Dunfermline, Scotland. He built them in Canada, New Zealand, and Australia—even Fiji.

By the time of his death, Andrew Carnegie had given away 90 percent of his fortune. And his name didn't appear above the entrance of any of his libraries. Instead, there was the simple inscription: "Let There Be Light."

* * * * *

BOOK TRIVIA

- In 1998, American Sir Paul Getty bought a first edition of Geoffrey Chaucer's *Canterbury Tales* for $7.5 million. The purchase broke the previous record for most expensive book in the world, $5.3 million paid in 1987 for a 1455 Gutenberg Bible.
- According to the Guinness Book of World Records, the most money ever paid for a musical manuscript was $4.1 million for a volume of Mozart symphonies. It was written in his own handwriting! At 508 pages, it was sold at the Sotheby's auction to an anonymous buyer in 1987.
- The world's smallest printed book is less than a millimeter long and less than a millimeter wide. That's one-sixth the length of a housefly. It's a copy of Chekhov's 1884 short story *Chameleon*, 30 pages long with 11 lines per page.

MAKING MONEY WITH BOOKS

When it comes to making money on books, first editions are a good place to start. Below are some sample first-edition values.
- Tom Clancy's *The Cardinal of the Kremlin* (1988), $25
- John Grisham's *The Pelican Brief* (1992), $25
- Anne Rice's *Interview With the Vampire* (1976), $500
- Kurt Vonnegut's *Slaughterhouse Five* (1969), $1,500
- J.R.R. Tolkien' s *Lord of the Rings* Trilogy (1954, 1954, 1955), $20,000
  Ian Fleming's *Casino Royale* (1953), $12,000
- Ernest Hemingway's *To Have and Have Not* (1937), $1,000
- Carolyn Keene's *The Secret of the Old Clock*, (Nancy Drew, 1930), $1,500
- Robert Frost's *A Boy's Will* (1913), $15,000
- Mark Twain's *Adventures of Huckleberry Finn* (1885), $3,000

Rob Roy was Scotland's "Robin Hood."

MORE MIGHTY PEN

Changing the world one page at a time.

THE GRAPES OF WRATH

The Times: During America's Great Depression of the 1930s—as if the country's financial ruin weren't enough—years of drought and overfarming turned the fertile Great Plains into a desert nicknamed the Dust Bowl. Crops failed and farms were deserted as desperate families piled their belongings into vehicles and headed west to California where agriculture was big business. But as thousands of these workers migrated (they were nicknamed "Okies" after the dust bowl state of Oklahoma) to California, they found only poorly paid seasonal work picking crops. They wound up moving from harvest to harvest as migrant farmworkers.

The Author: The novelist who immortalized the plight of the dust bowl immigrants was John Ernst Steinbeck. Born in 1902, Steinbeck grew up in Salinas, California, a farming community. Though he grew up in town, he was no stranger to farm work and often spent his summers doing manual labor on local ranches. But after graduating from high school in 1919 and spending time in Stanford without getting a degree, Steinbeck deserted his home state for New York. He arrived in the Big Apple in 1925, determined to make his mark as a freelance writer.

If Steinbeck had succeeded, he might never have written his historic masterpiece. But the young writer couldn't get a darned thing published. Feeling that "the city had beat the pants off me," Steinbeck returned home where he was more comfortable and began writing about the people and the land he knew best.

In 1936 Steinbeck wrote a series of articles for the *San Francisco News* called "Harvest Gypsies." He lived among California's Dust Bowl migrant workers and described the people and the conditions that he found. Steinbeck reported that many migrants lived in filthy camps with no sanitation, in shelters made from trash, weeds or quilts. He wrote that hardworking men who had once owned small farms, shops, or grocery stores now toiled in California fields all day for starvation wages. And he wrote of

---

Mummies have been found all over the world, including Alaska, Italy, Australia, and Japan.

watching families cope when their children died from lack of proper medical care and nourishing food. Steinbeck wrote that some of what he'd discovered left him "with a sorrow weeping cannot symbolize." That sorrow fueled his 1939 novel, *The Grapes of Wrath.*

The Tale: The Joad family packs up their truck as dust storms force them out of Oklahoma and off the land they've farmed for generations. The hardworking Joads go to California planning to start over, but they find themselves competing for jobs that pay virtually nothing with thousands of other Okies. The resourceful family survives and even helps others worse off than themselves. But they and those they meet, in the midst of California's large food harvests, are constantly battling starvation.

At one migrant camp, violence erupts when sheriffs put down a strike over the price paid for picking peaches. Joad's oldest son, Tom, kills a deputy and is forced to flee. He promises to devote himself to improving the lot of the migrants. The book's controversial ending finds the family taking shelter from a winter storm along with a boy and his sick, starving father. The Joads' daughter, who has just lost her infant son, nurses the father to save his life.

The Change: Within two months, *The Grapes of Wrath* was a number-one best seller. In 1940, it was awarded a Pulitzer Prize, and the film based on the novel won an Academy Award the following year for director John Ford. In 1962, John Steinbeck won the Nobel Prize for his entire body of written work, with *The Grapes of Wrath* generally accepted as his masterpiece.

Readers were shocked by the plight of the Joads, and the book launched a fierce debate about the problems of migrants and farmers. The book was branded a pack of lies by an Oklahoma congressman and banned in places like Kern County, in the heart of California farm country. However, after reading Steinbeck's work, President Franklin Roosevelt called for an improvement in conditions for migrant farm workers. The government held hearings and made agricultural labor reforms. Laws like the Farm Securities Act, which provided housing for migrants, were expanded by popular demand. Thanks to *The Grapes of Wrath*, there were increased inspections of grower-owned labor camps and government aid was no longer denied to migrants who refused to accept farm jobs at starvation wages. The book and the movie also brought new support for unions and a decent minimum wage. By the time *The Grapes of Wrath* was published, war in Europe was creating orders for U.S. goods and weapons. The improving economy allowed many Okies to take steady, nonagricultural jobs. But, even after times changed, the struggles of the fictional Joads remained an American symbol of the dignity of the working poor.

ONE DAY IN THE LIFE OF IVAN DENISOVICH

The Times: The Gulag, a Russian acronym for the Chief Directorate of Corrective Labor Camps, was a system of Soviet penal camps established after the Communist takeover by Lenin, and it expanded when Joseph Stalin came to power in the late 1920s. Stalin branded anyone who disagreed with his rule "an enemy of the people." Snatched from their homes in the dead of night, millions of political and religious dissidents became prisoners called zeks.

In the Gulag (which had prison camps everywhere from remote Siberia to the center of Moscow) zeks were used as forced labor to log forests, mine gold, and build everything from railroad tracks to apartment buildings. Millions of prisoners died, worked to exhaustion in freezing cold without proper food, clothing, shelter, or medical care. From 1929 to 1953, more than 20 million zeks endured forced labor camps, while Stalin's censorship of Soviet news, arts, and literature kept the true facts of the Gulag from the West.

The Author: Aleksandr Isayevich Solzhenitsyn, a decorated captain in the Soviet army, was arrested during World War II. Censors had discovered that his letters to a friend contained a few insults about "that man with the mustache" who, the censors rightly figured, was Big Boss Stalin himself. Solzhenitsyn was subsequently sent to the Gulag for eight years (a comparatively light sentence).

When his sentence was up in 1953, instead of being allowed to return home, Solzhenitsyn was exiled to eastern Kazakhstan. There, for three years, he taught high school math and spent every spare moment on his first love—writing.

The teacher turned out poems, stories, and even a short novel based on his Gulag experience, *One Day in the Life of Ivan Denisovich*. Solzhenitsyn carefully buried the manuscript in jars; if the wrong people read it, he'd be doomed. Finally, in 1962, after

Stalin had been dead for nine years, the new Soviet leader, Nikita Khrushchev allowed the publication of *One Day in the Life of Ivan Denisovich* in Soviet Russia.

The Tale: The day begins with reveille at 5 a.m. and ends at lights-out for Ivan Denisovich Shukhov, a simple carpenter unjustly imprisoned in Siberia. His goals are simple. He tries to stay warm enough, despite working in subzero temperatures with inadequate clothing. He tries to avoid illness, despite the lack of proper medical attention. He stays out of trouble and under the radar of the sadistic guards who treat prisoners cruelly. But mostly, Shukhov uses every tactic possible to get enough food; the starvation rations leave him constantly hungry. Shukhov has no interest in the politics or ideology that have led to his imprisonment. This one day, like all the 3,653 days of Shukhov's sentence (his 10-year sentence includes three extra days for leap years) is devoted to survival.

The Change: Once it was published, Solzhenitsyn's short, unsentimental, and straightforward depiction of brutality in the Gulag caused a furor. Foreigners in Russia read it, and soon there was an international uproar. Soviet authorities had never even admitted the Gulag existed. But now other former zeks found the courage to come forward. The Siberian cat was finally out of the bag.

One Day in the Life of Ivan Denisovich gave reformers of the Soviet Union proof of its evils. Even defenders had to admit that the Soviet government had committed terrible crimes against its own people. After Khrushchev died, a new regime tried to go back to the old ways and silence all criticism of the state. But they couldn't quiet Solzhenitsyn who was now a world celebrity (eventually winning the Nobel Prize for Literature).

Friends helped the author smuggle new manuscripts out of the Soviet Union—including *The Gulag Archipelago*, a detailed history that showed how many people had suffered in Stalin's gulag. For twenty years, beginning in 1974, Solzhenitsyn was banished from the Soviet Union to Vermont in the United States. But he finally returned home in time to see the mighty Soviet Union fall—a process that had been launched with his small novel about one prisoner's "ordinary" day.

A 1947 ad for Barbasol Lotion Deodorant referred to body odor as "Athletic Aroma."

THE FALL OF
THE WALL

The East German government called the Berlin Wall "the Anti-Fascist Protection Barrier." But the machine guns along its length were pointed inward, toward East Berlin, not outward.

Shortly after midnight on August 13, 1961, the city of Berlin was cut in two. Soviet and East German troops moved in and ringed the city. Train service between the two cities was stopped. Telephone lines were cut. Streets connecting East and West were sealed off. The construction of the Berlin Wall had begun. The people of East Berlin were being locked in.

EAST SIDE, WEST SIDE
At first, the wall consisted of barbed wire, concrete barriers, and tanks. When complete, it was 100 miles (161 km) of pure concrete, 10 to 13 feet (3 to 4 meters) high. It extended 28 miles (45 km) through the heart of Berlin and some 70 miles (113 km) around the city to isolate West Berlin from the rest of East Germany, which surrounded it.

The wall was painted white, not to make it prettier, but to make it easier for border guards to see and shoot at anyone attempting to climb over it. A second wall was built 100 yards (91 meters) to the east of the first wall. In the no-man's-land (known as the Death Zone) between them were 293 watchtowers, along with searchlights, killer guard dogs, self-firing guns, and land mines. Over the years, the wall was rebuilt three times to make it harder and harder to breach.

THE GREAT ESCAPES
- The greatest number of escapes from East Berlin took place in the first two years while the wall was being fortified.
- One East German butcher fashioned bulletproof protection by strapping hams, roasts, and sausages around his body. While he was hurling himself over the barbed wire, the meat absorbed the bullets.

In Africa, Jane Goodall studied chimpanzees; Dian Fossey studied mountain gorillas.

- If a building was on the boundary line, people escaped by throwing mattresses out windows and then jumping from second- or third-story windows. (First-floor windows had been bricked up early on.) Some parents threw their children out windows on the eastern side into firemen's nets on the western side.
- One man threw a hammer and line from the roof of a building in the East over the wall and, with his wife and young son, slid down it in a homemade chairlift. So many people used stout rope thrown over the wall (and held by someone on the other side) that East Germany banned the sale of any rope sturdy enough to hold a human being.
- East Germans used Berlin's ancient sewer system to escape— until the authorities cemented the manhole covers shut.
- One woman created Soviet uniforms for herself and three friends. They saluted the East German guards and walked through the checkpoint unquestioned.
- In 1979, two families with eight people sewed together bits of fabric, made a homemade hot-air balloon and flew to safety on the other side. In response, the East German government limited the sale of lightweight fabrics such as nylon.
- Tunnels were dug all over East Berlin. One ingenious tunnel started in a mausoleum in an East Berlin cemetery. "Mourners" would enter the crypt—and never exit. In 1962, NBC TV funded a tunnel from Bernauer Street in East Berlin to Schoenholzer Street in West Berlin. They filmed the escape of 56 refugees, before flooding shut the tunnel. Another tunnel, the escape route for 57 people, was 430 feet (131 meters) long and took six months to build. Yet another began in a backyard outhouse in East Berlin and ended in a bakery on the western side.

Estimates vary widely, but between 5,000 and 16,500 people escaped East Berlin by outwitting the wall—and the border guards. Some 246 hopefuls are known to have died trying, and approximately 3,200 people were arrested for attempting escape—and either sentenced to death or imprisoned for life. (Because of the extreme secrecy of the East German government, the exact number may never be known.)

THE FIRST CRACK IN THE WALL

By the late 1980s, the Communist governments of the Soviet Union and East Germany were near collapse. In May 1989, Hungary started cutting down the barbed wire fence along its Austrian border. East Germans vacationing at Hungary's lakes saw their opportunity. That summer, 5,000 people a week escaped to West Germany via Hungary and Austria. On September 10, 1989, Hungary completely opened its border with Austria. East Germans began streaming through, and by the end of the summer, 50,000 had fled East Germany.

The floodgates to freedom had opened. On November 4, 1989, Czechoslovakia opened its borders to tens of thousands of fleeing East Germans. All this fueled massive unrest in East Germany: antigovernment demonstrations were held, and the East German Communists ousted their leader.

THE WALL COMES TUMBLING DOWN

The East German government tried one last effort to stem the rush of people to the West. Late on November 9, 1989, as a post-script to a long news conference, an East German spokesman announced that, beginning immediately, the borders between East and West Germany and East and West Berlin would be open to travel unconditionally.

Within hours, stunned and disbelieving crowds had gathered at the wall. When people crossed the border checkpoints without being shot at, the celebrations began. Berliners hugged relatives they hadn't seen in 28 years. Masses of people took hammer and chisel, then sledgehammers, to the wall.

East Berliners marveled at the abundance in the West Berlin shops. The city of West Berlin gave each East Berliner $60 (49 euros) in "welcome money." One man returned library books that he had borrowed from the American library in West Berlin the day before the wall went up—only 28 years overdue. The world media turned out in droves to cover the weeks-long party at the wall.

By December 3, the Communist government in East Germany was ousted. In March 1990, East Germans voted their country out of existence. Germany was officially reunited on October 3, 1990.

The Chinese character for "money" originally represented a cowrie shell.

THE WORLD WIDE WALL

Today, very little of the Berlin Wall is left. The official demolition began on June 13, 1990. Small segments of the wall still stand in three locations, and the rest of the wall's course is marked by a double row of cobblestones. Some segments of the wall were recycled for road building.

Pieces of the wall are displayed in Washington, D.C.; at the libraries of former presidents Nixon, Reagan, and George H. W. Bush; at the Seattle Center; and, most improbably (or maybe not), in the men's restroom of a downtown Las Vegas casino. There, the once feared and hated Berlin Wall serves as the backdrop to a row of urinals. A nice spot for a little revenge.

* * * * *

- There were three checkpoints that were given names based on the phonetic alphabet. The Helmstedt checkpoint was called Alpha, the Dreilinden checkpoint was Bravo, and the checkpoint at Friedrichstrasse got the name Charlie.

- Although the wall was over 103 miles long, only a small section of it was painted with graffiti—the two-mile area between Checkpoint Charlie and the Brandenburg Gate. The rest was plain unadorned concrete.

- There are 80 known deaths of people who died while attempting to cross the Berlin Wall between 1961 and 1989. The last death occurred just nine months before the wall fell on November 9, 1989.

- Germany was reunited on October 3, 1990.

London's Post Office still gets letters sent to 221B Baker Street asking for Sherlock Holmes's help.

SEEING RED

The color red has meant a lot of things to a lot of people over the ages.

Today, you might say that red is the color of passion: think red lingerie in a red light district. Among colors, it's a natural magnet. If you want to get noticed, wear red. If you drive a red car, it's more likely that you'll get a speeding ticket.

Here's how red has been perceived and used by a variety of cultures that came before the days of red clown noses and the highway patrol.

RED FOR FERTILITY
In the ancient world, neolithic hunters thought red was the most important color because they believed it had life-giving powers: their cave painters drew animals in red ocher or iron oxide to represent their fertility. Ancient Egyptians rubbed the bodies of their dearly departed with red ocher, to give them a "lifelike" and fertile appearance in the hereafter. Brides in ancient Rome wore red wedding gowns as a symbol of love and fertility. Red wedding dresses and veils are still popular in parts of Asia, and it's not for nothing that some American brides and grooms enter their churches or temples walking on a red carpet.

RED FOR POWER
In medieval royal courts, red was the color of the monarchy. Only the ruling class could wear the color. (Purple was also reserved for VIPs; both red and purple required expensive dying techniques, so only the wealthy and powerful could afford the dyed fabrics.) Wearing of red by kings, queens, judges, and even executioners symbolically announced that these individuals had power over life and death.

RED FOR PROTECTION
Red bed clothing was customary in the Middle Ages in Germany to protect against "red illnesses," like rashes, fever, and miscarriages. Also in the Middle Ages, red amulets were worn as charms to protect against the "evil eye."

The Great Wall of China was actually four walls that were rebuilt and extended at different times.

RED FOR COURAGE AND VICTORY

Native American tribes used red war paint, presumably because of its likeness to blood. It was mostly intended to frighten opponents. But it was also believed to endow its wearer with power and strength, so that he might defeat his enemies more readily and be less afraid to die in battle. Weapons were decorated in red as well—the Creek tribe, for example, painted their clubs red to make them more effective in battle. The red paint in this instance, was mostly the blood from butchered animals.

Most experts agree that the term "redskin" was coined by the pale-skinned American colonists as a comparison of skin color. But there is also a school of thought that it originated with the colonists who first saw Native Americans wearing red war paint. There's a third group, that bears mentioning, too; they believe "redskin" originated with Old West hunters who sold the bloody scalps of tribespeople.

Red animals are also held in esteem among Native Americans. Possessing a particular animal—or a part of one—would supposedly endow a person with the powers and attributes of the animal. The Iowa tribe used the red crests of ivory-billed woodpeckers (now thought to be extinct) to ornament their ceremonial pipes. The red feathers signified power and victory over enemies, and the warriors believed they were drawing in extra courage along with the smoke.

RED FOR PROFIT

The Oaxacan people of Mexico claimed fame with cochineal red, processed from *Dactylopius coccus*, a kind of beetle that grows only on a particular type of cactus, which they raised on plantations. As many as 70,000 insects are required to process just one pound (0.5 kg) of dye. Cochineal was, at one time, the most important Indian dye in North America. It was greatly prized by Europeans and became an important source of trade that, temporarily, brought much wealth to Oaxaca. So, it was no surprise that the Spanish took over the cochineal plantations after their conquest of Mexico. (For years, the Spaniards had traded the processed cochineal as a grain—not realizing it came from an insect.)

Cochineal became such a staple of the British textile industry that it was used to dye the British army uniforms—you've heard, perhaps, of the redcoats?

The first English historian was a scholarly monk called The Venerable Bede (c. 672–735).

WHERE ARE THEY NOW?

The Phoenicians

Dear Uncle John,

I am a big fan of the color purple—my clothes are purple, ditto my hair and car. Somebody told me that long ago there were purple people. Who were they, how did they turn purple, and where are they now?

Purple people seeker

Dear Purple People Seeker,

From the coastal cities of the area that is now Lebanon and Syria came a seafaring, trading nation that the Greeks called Phonikes, or "Purple Men." There are disputes about the origins of the Phoenicians, who spoke a Semitic language resembling Hebrew and called themselves Canaanites.

The Phoenicians lived on dry land, so they turned to the water for their living. In about 1200 B.C., they built a seafaring empire with outposts throughout the Mediterranean and North Africa. Merchant and yachting skills made Phoenicia one of history's most influential nations. Trading in luxury goods, Phoenicians created fine metalworks, ivory carvings, and dyed textiles. They got their fame (and their colorful name) from a purple dye extracted from the glands of a shellfish, *Murex trunculus*. It took 10,000 shellfish to produce a single gram of the dye, so, only aristocrats and royals could afford purple cloth—hence the term *royal purple*. But the true legacy of the Phoenicians is *Uncle John's Bathroom Reader*—and all those other English language books. To catalog their business dealings, Phoenicians developed a simplified alphabet with 22 letters; it's the source of our own alphabet.

In 332 B.C., Phoenicia was conquered by Alexander the Great and never rose again. Crushed murex shells and purple pottery unearthed at Sarepta, Lebanon, are all that remains of their purple dye works. But Lebanese, Libyans, and some Somalians consider themselves descendants of the Phoenicians.

A mysterious ancient Chinese language called Nushu was created and used exclusively by women.

BEFORE ROSWELL

*In 1947, an alleged UFO crash site in Roswell, New Mexico,
fueled curiosity about who or what lives among the stars
(in the universe, not in Beverly Hills). But UFO sightings
predate the Roswell situation by thousands of years.*

POETIC LICENSE TO FLY?

Ancient Hindu scripts make frequent mention of both complex
flying machines and a technologically advanced, nonhuman race
that created them. A lot of people think these ancient documents
are laughably fictional and fantastic, but others aren't so sure. The
ancient Sanskrit poem *Mahabharata* mentions flying discs called
vimanas, or "celestial chariots," that come in a variety of makes
and models, from huge SUV-like affairs for carrying troops and
weapons, to single-person aircraft. According to the ancient poem,
humans weren't allowed to use them—only these divine,
advanced nonhumans.

ASIAN ALIENS

The sun isn't the only thing that's come up in the East. From
Malaysia to Japan, myriad UFO sightings have occurred throughout
Asia. In 1066, a giant pearl was reported to have emerged from a
Chinese lake. It was said to have hovered for a moment, while a
small door opened to reveal a brilliant light, before flying away.

In 1271, south of Yokohama, Japan, a priest was scheduled for
execution. As authorities prepared to behead the man, a bright,
round object appeared in the sky, terrifying everyone. The execution was canceled.

And just a few years ago, Chinese scientists discovered an
ancient, high-altitude pyramid in Qinghai Province; they're now
investigating the possibility that it was an ancient extraterrestrial
observatory!

FRIENDS, ROMANS...AND LITTLE GREEN MEN

From 31 B.C. to A.D. 450, the ancient Romans covered a lot of
ground—and a lot of UFO-prone sky to boot. In 218 B.C. over
Rome, there were reports of glowing lamps, phantom ships, and

shields in the sky. Roman historian Titus Livius (59 B.C.–A.D.17) once reported seeing men in white clothes flittering around in the sky above Rome.

Another Roman claimed to see "a globe of fire" in the sky around 900 B.C. And the Roman scholar Pliny the Elder once observed that "a burning shield scattering sparks ran across the sky at sunset from east to west."

Central Europe has had its share of sightings too. In England, a "fire in the sky, like a burning and revolving wheel, or round barrel of flame," was reported in 1387 in more than one county.

In the 1600s, a long, cylindrical craft was seen flying over Italy, Switzerland, and Scotland. Independently, crowds of people in each of these countries reported the sighting.

AMERICAN PIES IN THE SKIES
As soon as Columbus sailed into American waters UFO sightings may have begun. One night, from the deck of the *Santa Maria*, Columbus saw what he called "a light glimmering at a great distance," which came in and out of sight throughout the night.

Skipping all the way ahead to 1896, a "winged cigar" with a giant headlight on it was spotted over California, spawning a rash of cigar-ship sightings across the country during the next few years.

And in 1897, the *Dallas Morning News* nonchalantly reported that a strange airship downed in Texas was apparently piloted by a man from Mars, whose only documentation was composed of strange and indecipherable hieroglyphics.

ALIENS HAVE A COW
In one especially bizarre before-Roswell American sighting, Alexander Hamilton of Leroy, Kansas, heard a noise amid his cattle on April 19, 1897. He came out of his house, with his son and a friend, to see in the sky what looked like a bizarre, elongated cigar—a football field in length—with a clear cabin underneath. Red ropes dangled low from the cabin, almost touching the ground, and a painfully bright searchlight probed the area. Hamilton claimed to see six "hideous" beings inside the cabin. The ropes snatched up one of his cows, and the craft flew away. While Hamilton was known for telling tall tales, the cow did turn up butchered (and not by a professional) in his field the next day.

Mount Everest's name in Nepal is *Sagarmatha* ("goddess of the sky").

THE MAGIC MAN

Imagine Gandalf from Lord of the Rings crossed with James Bond and you'll have some idea of the man who was John Dee: philosopher, magician—and Elizabethan master spy. Possibly.

For most people in 16th-century Britain, life, as the saying goes, was "nasty, brutish, and short." But not for John Dee (1527–1608). As a mathematician, magician, alchemist, academic, astronomer, and astrologer, this Brit managed to cram a lot into his 81 years.

IT'S ALL GEEK TO ME

The son of a London cloth merchant (who had been one of Henry VIII's tailors), John Dee was born into a fairly privileged position. A bright boy, he was sent to Cambridge University at age 15 to study Greek, Latin, philosophy, geometry, arithmetic, and astronomy.

Dee specialized in mathematics. He also developed an interest in astronomy and astrology. So from an early age Dee displayed these two seemingly conflicting sides of his character: as a scientist, his feet were firmly planted on the ground; as a mystic, he *really* had his head in the clouds. By his early 20s, Dee had traveled across Europe, studying with some of the greatest mathematicians and thinkers of the day. His academic reputation grew quickly and he was offered (but declined) prestigious professorships in Paris and at Oxford.

THE SUM OF ALL FEARS

Up to this point, Dee was living the life of a typical academic, working away in anonymous respectability, writing treatises on math, the stars, the motion of the tides, navigation, and lots of other worthy-but-dull subjects. Then, in 1553, Queen Mary ascended the British throne. Bloody Mary, as she was known, was a devout Catholic bent on overturning the Protestant revolution initiated by her father, Henry VIII. Surprisingly, John Dee found himself on Mary's hit list.

His crime? Calculating. That's right, you could get yourself arrested for being a mathematician back then. According to the

---

In Tibet, Everest is called *Chomolungma* ("mother goddess of the universe").

authorities, studying mathematics was akin to weaving spells and conjuring up spirits. (See? As schoolchildren have suspected since time immemorial, algebra really *is* the work of the devil.) Dee was arrested for calculating in May 1555, and he was held for three months. Although Dee was released without charge, his assets were confiscated, and he was suddenly broke.

It may seem strange, but men like Dee thought there was a supernatural link between math and magic. In the 16th-century mind, the world of spirit really existed, and the way to find it was through scientific and mathematical experimentation.

IN HER MAJESTY'S SECRET SERVICE?
In 1558, Dee's luck changed for the better. Bloody Mary died and was replaced as queen by Elizabeth I. Dee was quickly back in favor. The new queen even asked Dee to use his astrological skills to divine the most auspicious day for her official coronation. Why the dramatic turnabout in Dee's luck? Many writers and historians have argued that Dee acted as a spy for Elizabeth during the reign of her sister, Mary, keeping her informed of who among his academic colleagues was supportive of Mary's regime. It's a hard claim to prove or disprove, but Dee's sudden reversal of fortune does suggest that Elizabeth had something to thank him for. In fact, not only was Dee appointed court astrologer to the queen, but Elizabeth also asked him for private lessons in mathematics. Why any sane person would volunteer for *extra* lessons in math is anyone's guess. But that's what Elizabeth wanted, and it was Dee she singled out to be her personal tutor.

HI MOM! I'M HOME!
Now, as the apple of Elizabeth's eye, Dee was free to continue studying without the thought police cramping his style. He became more and more preoccupied with magic and alchemy as he looked for answers to the mysteries of the universe. In 1566 he moved in with his mom, taking his enormous library of books (the largest in Britain) and his vast collection of scientific instruments with him. After the trials and tribulations of the 1550s, Dee's life settled down, and he was able to continue his studies in peace. He even managed to marry—three times, mind you—and father eight children with his various wives.

THE GRIFTERS

But there was a final twist to come, and in 1582, that twist came in the shape of one Edward Kelley. Kelley (1555–1597) was a medium, or scryer, who claimed he could contact angels and spirits by gazing into a crystal ball. Kelley was also a failed lawyer who had been convicted for fraud, forgery, and counterfeiting—but he forgot to mention that part of his résumé to Dee. Kelley conned Dee into thinking he could help him in his quest to talk to the spirit world, and so an unusual partnership was born.

Together, Kelley and Dee became the Siegfried and Roy of their day. Dee supplied the magical knowledge, while Kelley played the charismatic front man. They claimed they were able to contact angels, especially one particularly talkative divine being called Uriel, and they dubbed their system Enochian Magick, after the biblical character Enoch. They even took their show on the road, touring as far afield as Poland and Bohemia, performing for princes and kings. It was only when Kelley told Dee that Uriel recommended that they indulge in a little wife swapping (Dee's wife was apparently much prettier than Kelley's) that Dee recognized his colleague for the con artist that he was. Their partnership ended in 1589, by which time Kelley had made himself a fortune and earned a knighthood. Dee, on the other hand, hadn't made a penny out of the whole Enochian episode.

SHAKESPEAREAN HERO

Dee's final years were spent in near-poverty and obscurity. He died in 1608, an almost forgotten figure. In recent years, his reputation has been restored, and it is possible to see why his contemporary William Shakespeare, modeled the philosopher-magician character of Prospero in *The Tempest* on John Dee. Dee's breadth of learning was legendary. And his experiments in mathematics, astronomy, and chemistry helped to establish Britain's enviable reputation as a scientific powerhouse. So what if he thought he could talk to angels? If you plunked him down in any number of New Age hotbeds (and hot tubs) in modern-day California, he'd fit right in.

A PROPHET WHO SLEPT HIS WAY TO THE TOP

Did Edgar Cayce really see into the future?
Or was he a huckster and a fraud?

Suddenly, from out of nowhere, on April 18, 1900, a timid, 21-year-old Kentucky photographer lost his voice. The doctors he consulted told him he had paralysis of the vocal cords and would probably never speak again. The young man, who'd long believed he could absorb the contents of books (like his favorite, the Bible) by sleeping on top of them, turned to sleep once more and sought help from hypnotists. Ten months later, the cure worked. His voice returned! Along with something new. Something extra special.

CALLING DR. CAYCE
After the stint with hypnosis, Edgar Cayce (pronounced "Casey") was able to drop into a trance at will. While under, he astounded witnesses with his uncanny ability to diagnose complex medical conditions, using jargon that a layperson couldn't have known. He could even diagnose and recommend treatments—none of which he could remember when he woke from his hypnotic state—for patients hundreds of miles away.

Cayce's exotic abilities caught the attention of the public. Patients started coming from all across the country to meet with the amazing healer; newspapers and magazines trumpeted his successes. The *New York Times* even called him "America's Most Mysterious Man."

THE SLEEPING PROPHET
During the next 43 years, 14,000 people would contact Cayce for readings, the records from most of which are still on file in the archives of the Association for Research and Enlightenment, a Virginia group formed to study Cayce and his mystical powers.

In a 1946 contest in Tokyo, an abacus outperformed an electric calculator.

When he wasn't in a trance, Cayce was a mild-mannered, reclusive type who shunned fame and fortune—in fact, he very often didn't charge for his readings. He would make appointments with faraway patients every day at either 11 a.m. or 3 p.m. He'd spend most of his day fishing or gardening, and at the appointed time, he'd come inside and lie on his couch. He'd place his hands on his abdomen, draw some deep breaths, and relax. When his eyelids fluttered, the reading began; his assistants would provide some details about the subject's life, and Cayce would come up with a diagnosis and recommendation.

But within a few years, Cayce was ranging away from medical problems while in his trances. He began expounding on the nature of reality, and on reincarnation; he talked about the past—telling of lost prehistoric civilizations and the life of Jesus—as well as predicting the future.

NONPROFIT PROPHET

Many things speak for Cayce's truthfulness: the fact that he generally didn't charge for readings, his grasp of medical terminology, and the accuracy of his diagnoses and predictions.

But we know he read a lot of osteopathic literature—describing what today we'd call "naturopathy" or "homeopathy"—which would have taught him a lot about the body. His followers often mention that he seemed to know more about the patient than he could possibly know. But what they fail to point out is that Cayce performed many of his readings on faraway subjects who'd send him letters outlining their conditions, information he could parrot during a reading. And the treatments he recommended—ointments, chiropractic adjustments, natural foods—are of the type that rarely hurt anybody and may help simply because of a placebo effect.

THE PROPHET HAS NO CLOTHES

Cayce had quite a few high-profile failures. He became involved with the Lindbergh kidnapping case (for which he failed to produce any useful information), and with an unsuccessful search for buried treasure. After the digging had been going on for several weeks and nothing was found, Cayce's defenders started claiming—a little hysterically—that there had been treasure there but it had already been dug up. Or perhaps it would be buried there in the future.

Since the mid-18th century, 1.7 million species have been identified and described on earth.

He made numerous predictions about Atlantis (claiming the United States would find an Atlantean death ray in 1958) and world events that just didn't come true. His diagnoses were often screwy too: he recommended oil of smoke for a leg sore, bedbug juice for dropsy, and fumes of apple brandy from a charred keg for tuberculosis.

FINALLY FOUND MR. RIGHT?

But what about the stuff he got right? The oddsmakers say that odds are if you make thousands of predictions and diagnoses in your lifetime, at least some of them will prove true. Put that together with followers who want to believe, and you may have Edgar Cayce's life in a nutshell.

* * * * *

MY STARS!

President Theodore Roosevelt (TR) kept his astrological chart of in his office. Speaking of his horoscope, TR said, "I always keep my weather eye on the opposition of my seventh house moon to my first house Mars." He had his horoscope mounted on a chessboard that always stood on a table in the White House.

I FEEL LIKE A NEW MAN!

David Copperfield is the only living illusionist to receive a star on the Hollywood Walk of Fame (so far). He was born David Kotkin in Metuchen, New Jersey, in 1956.

CHIPS OFF THE OLD BLOCK? PART 1

*If you think your parents gave you a hard time, spare a
thought for the kids of these world leaders.*

I f you've ever wondered what it's like growing up in Stalin's
shadow or whatever happened to Napoleon's son, here are
their (almost always) tragic stories.

RICHARD THE FOURTH?
(Richard Cromwell, son of Oliver Cromwell)

Back in the 1640s, jolly old England was caught up in a messy
civil war between King Charles I and the British parliament over
who really ran the country. By 1649, the issue was settled:
Parliament was the boss. And to prove it, they chopped off
Charles's head.

For the next 10 years, the country was a fun-free zone under
the grim, puritanical military dictatorship of Oliver Cromwell. He
was such a killjoy that he even banned Christmas.

Wake Up, Dick, You're in Charge!

Richard was born in 1626, and after being raised in his father's
puritanical but loving household, he joined the army, where he
managed to avoid seeing any active service—even while the
English Civil War raged around him. In 1649, his run of good luck
continued when he married Dorothy Major, daughter of a wealthy
farmer, and settled down into the idle life of a country squire.

Little was heard of Richard after that, apart from the fact that
his stern father regularly upbraided him for his laziness and over-
spending. So it must have come as a shock when his dad named
him as his successor. Turns out that Oliver, that staunch opponent
of hereditary rule, didn't think that it applied to his *own* family.
When Parliament complained about this, Cromwell—never a big
fan of democracy—closed it down. Cromwell's ministers had little
option but to go along with their revered leader's decision.

Oliver breathed his last disapproving breath on September 3,

The first Girl Scout troop was organized in Savannah, Georgia, on March 12, 1912.

1658, and on the same day Richard Cromwell was proclaimed Lord Protector of the Realm. When Richard took over, the trouble really began. Richard was not cut out for life in the fast lane, and things went downhill fast.

Almost immediately, the army began making waves. To them, Richard was an upstart who traded on his father's name and had no right to rule. A power struggle between Parliament and the army saw Richard pulled this way and that like a rag doll. The London mob, amused by Cromwell's evident lack of brass, took to calling him "Queen Dick." Eventually, the army forced Cromwell to call a new, army-friendly Parliament in spring of 1659. One of the new Parliament's first acts was to call for the Lord Protector's dismissal. Passive to the very end, Queen Dick meekly gave in and resigned in May of that year. Figuring his future career prospects didn't look too good, Cromwell jumped on the next boat to France.

Richard Who?

His father would have been appalled to see what happened next. Within a year the monarchy had been restored, with the flamboyant Charles II (who represented just about everything Oliver Cromwell despised) ascending the throne. As for Richard, he mooched around France and Switzerland for a few years before returning to England in 1680. His rich wife had died while he was in exile, so he was unable to resume his old life as a gentleman farmer: he had run up huge debts in his short time as Lord Protector and was never able to fully pay them off. Back in Britain, he assumed a new name—John Clarke—and paid 10 shillings a week to lodge quietly with an old family friend (this was as much to avoid his many creditors as it was to keep Royalist supporters off his tail). His long life came to an end in 1712. Today, while every English person knows who Oliver Cromwell is, hardly any of them have heard of Richard—or the fact that he was once their ruler!

THE LITTLE CORPORAL'S LITTLE BOY (Napoléon Jr.)

Some sons try to emulate their fathers, but when Daddy is the greatest military mind of his age, things can get tricky. For a start, neighboring countries might object if you try to conquer them, like Daddy did. Especially if your pop was Napoléon.

René Descartes introduced the terms "real number" and "imaginary number" to mathematics.

Napoléon François-Charles-Joseph Bonaparte was born on March 20, 1811, to the emperor Napoléon and his second wife, Archduchess Marie Louise of Austria. At the time, his father was the virtual ruler of Europe. All of France sighed with relief when Napoléon Jr. was born. Here at last was the son and heir Napoléon had been hoping for (part of the reason he divorced his first wife, Josephine, was because she could not bear him a child). But things change. Within the space of four short years, Napoléon was defeated at Waterloo, stripped of power, and sent into exile on Saint Helena, a godforsaken lump of rock in the South Atlantic Ocean, about midway between South America and Africa.

Bird in a Gilded Cage

When Napoléon fell from power, he named Napoléon Jr. as his successor. The countries that had beaten Napoléon said no way, and restored the monarchy that had been kicked out during the French Revolution of 1789. Junior's mother decided he was best off out of it, so she moved back to Vienna to live with her folks (who just happened to be the emperor and empress of Austria). Junior, known as l'Aiglon (the Eaglet), was raised in the Austrian imperial palace, speaking German rather than French as his first language.

As he grew into a teenager, Junior became a popular figure at the Austrian court. He was charming, good-looking, and always well dressed—his ringlets were a particular hit with the ladies. His grandparents doted on him and gave him his own palace and a large staff. The trouble was there was no role for him. Apparently, he had a lively mind and was interested in military history, but there was no way, given who he was, that he would be allowed to join the army.

Family Ties

During his time in Vienna, Junior was supervised closely by Metternich, the politician who ran Austria on behalf of the emperor. Metternich knew that Junior was a powerful symbol to French nationalists: they called him Napoléon II, even though he was never crowned. When he was a child, one of Junior's French nannies tried to kidnap him and return him to France as the

---

The earliest evidence of beer was found in a pottery vessel in western Iran of 3500–3100 B.C.

rightful heir to the crown and savior of the nation. As a result, Junior lived as a virtual prisoner. His short life came to an end in 1832, when he died of tuberculosis, aged just 21. Rumors began right away that he had been done away with, but no proof has been found—yet.

A final twist on the Bonaparte family saga came in 1940, when Adolf Hitler, in a rare moment of generosity, arranged for Junior's remains to be sent back to France from Vienna. Napoléon François-Charles-Joseph Bonaparte now rests under the dome of the Les Invalides mausoleum, next to the father he never really knew.

PAPA DON'T PREACH
(Mussolini's Five Bambini)

Italians are known for their love of family. But in the Mussolini family, love was a rare commodity. Benito Mussolini had five children with his wife Donna Rachele: Edda (1910–1995), Vittorio (1916–1997), Bruno (1919–1941), Romano (born 1927), and Anna Maria (born 1929). Anna Maria, the youngest, has led a blameless life and has managed to keep out of the public eye. The rest have not been so shy and retiring. Vittorio was a high-ranking movie executive in Fascist Italy, and he helped launch the career of director Roberto Rossellini, the man whose affair with Ingrid Bergman scandalized the world in 1949. Bruno was an air force pilot who died while testing an experimental plane in 1941. Romano, in contrast, is a celebrated jazz pianist. He is married to the actress Anna Maria Scicolone, the sister of Sophia Loren. His daughter, Alessandra Mussolini, is a parliamentarian in the Republican Chamber of Deputies of Italy (and a sometime topless model!). And then there is Edda.

Poor Little Rich Girl

Edda Mussolini hit her teenage years just as Daddy became dictator of Italy in 1922. This made dating a little tricky. Not only did her father terrify potential beaux, but Edda herself was a fearsome character. She grew to be a strong-willed, potty-mouthed, chain-smoking, whiskey-drinking gal who did daring things like tearing around town in a sports car and wearing slacks in public. She was no shrinking violet.

The earliest known pictures of witches flying on broomsticks date to about A.D. 1440, in France.

In 1929, she met and fell in love with a dashing Italian diplomat, Galeazzo Ciano. Surprisingly, Mussolini liked the cut of Galeazzo's jib, and in April 1930, Edda and Galeazzo married. A liberated pair, they agreed that theirs would be an open marriage—Galeazzo was a compulsive womanizer, while Edda was said to enjoy the company of "alpine guides and lifeguards." In 1935, Galeazzo was appointed minister of propaganda, and the following year he was made minister of foreign affairs. He kept this position until 1943 when, disillusioned with Mussolini's wartime leadership, he resigned. In 1944, Mussolini took revenge; he had Ciano executed as a traitor—tied to a chair and shot in the back.

Swiss Miss

Soon after, Mussolini was overthrown and murdered by Italian partisans. In the space of a few months, Edda had seen her husband murdered by her father, who was in turn murdered himself. Pregnant and abandoned, Edda disguised herself as a peasant woman and escaped across the Swiss border to a convent. The only thing she was able to take with her was Galeazzo's diary, hidden beneath her skirt. She was later tracked down by Paul Ghali, a journalist for the *Chicago Daily News*, who arranged for the diary to be published.

Edda remained in Switzerland for few years before settling in France, where she wrote her memoirs. In 1995, shortly before her death, she astounded the world by revealing that her mother, the saintly and long-suffering Donna Rachele, had cheated on the philandering Mussolini in the mid-1920s—a daughter's revenge, of sorts, on the man who killed her husband.

* * * * *

If you want to read more about dads and their kids, turn to page 259 for Part II.

According to the U.S. Census Bureau, we spent $856 million to wash our cars in 1982.

ATTACK OF THE KILLER BALLOONS

The secret weapon aimed at the West.

On May 5, 1945, Reverend Archie Mitchell, his wife Elsie, and five children from his Sunday school drove from the tiny southern Oregon town of Bly for a picnic on Gearhart Mountain. While Reverend Mitchell parked the car, his wife and the children explored. They came upon a device the U.S. government knew about but had kept secret. When one of them touched the device, it exploded: Mrs. Mitchell and the five children were killed. The six Oregonians became the only known fatalities on the U.S. mainland from enemy attack during all of World War II.

MADE IN JAPAN

The exploding contraption was a Japanese Fugo balloon bomb, the brainchild of Major General Sueyoshi Kusaba of the Japanese Ninth Army Technical Research Laboratory. The balloons measured 33 feet across and 70 feet long from top to bomb. They were constructed (by Japanese schoolgirls) from bits of a tough paper called *washi*, made from mulberry trees, and glued together with potato paste. The bomb parts were made in a factory—not by schoolgirls.

Filled with hydrogen gas, the payload consisted of 36 sandbags for ballast, four incendiary bombs, and one 33-pound antipersonnel bomb. Launched to rise to 35,000 feet, the balloons were designed to use the prevailing Pacific eastward winds to reach the west coast of North America. As the balloons leaked gas and lost altitude, barometric pressure switches caused the sandbags to drop off and the balloons to rise back to the jet stream. The trip took three to five days. By the time they reached the United States, the balloons, now out of sandbags, were supposed to drop the bombs and then self-destruct. The Japanese hoped the bombs would cause forest fires and panic the American public.

The oldest sandals known were made of sagebrush bark fibers and were about 9,500 years old.

FUGO, FUGO, FUGO!

Between October 1944 and April 1945, Japan launched 9,300 of these balloons. Estimates are that fewer than 500 balloons reached the United States or Canada; the rest fell into the Pacific Ocean.

In November 1944, one balloon was discovered in the ocean off San Pedro, California. In January 1945, a balloon bomb landed in Medford, Oregon, without exploding. At some point, a rancher in Nevada discovered a balloon and used it as a tarp to cover his hay; police later discovered that two bombs were still attached to it.

WHAT BALLOONS?

Most of the balloons either exploded harmlessly or failed to detonate on impact. Approximately 90 of them were recovered in the United States as far east as Michigan. Strict censorship kept their existence out of the newspapers, and those who knew of their presence were sworn to secrecy. It was feared that news of the balloons' arrival would encourage the launching of more balloons. They weren't seen as much of a danger, but the hush-hush handling of the situation worked: the Japanese abandoned the project because they didn't hear of any successes.

But after the Mitchell family tragedy in Oregon, the public was warned. The last balloon bomb was found in Alaska in 1955; its bombs were still capable of exploding. Ironically, on March 10, 1945, one of the last paper balloons descended near Hanford, Washington. The balloon landed on electrical power lines, shutting off the Hanford nuclear reactor for three days. The Hanford reactor, part of the top-secret Manhattan Project, was producing plutonium for the bomb that was dropped on Nagasaki, Japan, five months later.

The Fugo balloon bombs are considered a failure as a weapons system. There were no proven bomb-caused forest fires, and they caused little other damage. Elsie Mitchell and the five children were the tragic exceptions.

The sandals were found in Catlow Cave, in central Oregon.

MADE IN JAPAN

Japanese business was reserved for good old boys until a guy named Honda drove into town.

S oichiro Honda was an unlikely candidate for success. He was born in 1906 in the rural town of Kyomo, Japan. The country's center of commerce and culture was about 150 miles away in Tokyo. Tokyo's businesses, banks, and industries were completely dominated by family controlled conglomerates called *zaibatsu*. After World War II, the powerful zaibatsu were seen as a threat to democracy and outlawed, but the dynasties only reemerged with many of the same old faces and a new name, *keiretsu*. The only way to join the keiretsu club was to be one of the *gakubatsu*—good old boys who attended the right universities and had all the right connections.

But Honda never cared much about university degrees, and he was the son of a blacksmith who repaired bicycles in his father's small shop. Honda could never be a member of his country's industrial aristocracy—so how did he become a force in Japanese business?

GREASE

What Honda had going for him was an inventive mechanical genius and a love of cars that began when he saw his first auto at age eight. As a teenager, Honda was apprenticed to a mechanic in Tokyo, and by the age of 22 the young man was an excellent mechanic who returned home to open his own successful shop.

For a time the restless Honda used up extra energy racing, building, and competing in his own cars. He set a speed record in 1936, but after he suffered injuries in a crash, Honda's wife nixed the sport as too dangerous. So the following year, the mechanic put his energy into starting a company that made piston rings.

Determined to succeed, Honda enrolled in school to gain formal learning on metallurgy and mechanical engineering. But he only paid attention in class when the teacher discussed topics related to piston making, and since Honda considered tests a waste of time, he refused to take them. An eccentric student at best, Honda still managed to learn how to successfully manufacture piston rings. That was only the beginning.

JAPAN'S MOTORCYCLE REBEL

Going up against much bigger companies, Honda began manufacturing motorcycles. His first product was developed soon after World War II when Japan was short on gasoline, and bicycles were in wide use. Honda took surplus engines designed to power military radios and used them to power bicycles instead.

In 1952 Honda Motor Co. brought out the Cub, a small, easily operated motorcycle that produced big sales. Yet because he lacked gakubatsu status, he had trouble employing Japan's top college graduates. Worse, the stodgy Ministry of International Trade and Industry (MITI) made it hard for his company to get permits or loans. Honda fought back by adopting design ideas from the competition, listening to customers, and constantly improving his product. By 1961, Honda motorcycles were the most popular in Japan with sales of 100,000 a month! This was unheard of for someone with no good-old-boy credentials.

But when Honda decided to export his popular motorcycles, MITI discouraged him. Fortunately he ignored the government and introduced his motorcycles into the United States in 1959. To meet the demands of the American consumer (Americans drove faster than the Japanese) Honda reengineered his motorcycles, and by 1963, they were America's top seller.

HIS FIRST FOUR WHEELER

So how did bureaucrats react when Honda came to the MITI with the idea of making cars? You guessed it, they discouraged him again. He was still an outsider; MITI wanted all Japanese carmakers to merge into two major companies under Toyota and Nissan.

Honda brought out a sports car anyway. The S360 made its public debut at the 1962 Tokyo Motor Show. Like his motorcycles, Honda's S360 was small, well-engineered, and popular with consumers.

Yet Honda was still the little guy upstart, and when his expanding auto line was exported to the West, no one paid much attention—except drivers. The small, fuel-saving Honda Civic went on sale in 1972 amid rising gas prices, and Americans

New Zealand was formerly known as the Cook Islands.

snapped them up. By 1989, the Honda Accord was the best-selling car in the huge U.S. auto market.

RINGING THE BELL

Soichiro Honda passed away in 1991, but the upstart's motorcycles and cars can be found everywhere from South Africa to Slovakia. In America alone, Honda Motor Company sold 1.24 million cars in 2002. These days Honda sells more than 11 million products—everything from jet skis to jet airplanes. They sell robots too. Honda's ASIMO model looks like a human, and in 2002 it rang the opening bell at the New York Stock Exchange!

* * * * *

HONDA, A DRIVING AMBITION
Words of Wisdom from Soichiro Honda

"Although I made one mistake after another, I never made the same mistake and I always tried my hardest and succeeded in improving my efforts."

"To me, success can be achieved only through repeated failure and introspection. In fact, success represents 1 percent of your work and results from the 99 percent that is called failure."

RITES OF PASSAGE

For several centuries, Japanese boys coming of age have undergone the elaborate Genpuku ceremony, which represented the time when a member of the samurai class became a full-fledged adult samurai. Historically, this happened between the ages of 12 and 18. Attending females wore ceremonial dress as the boy was honored with his own samurai sword.

Japan's modern equivalent is a national holiday known as Coming of Age Day held annually on January 15. Modern Japanese boys are considered adults when they turn 20, and are then granted the right to legally smoke, vote, and drink.

America's first speeder was arrested in 1899 by a New York policeman riding a bicycle.

A BREED APART

Boning up on man's best friend.

A 12,000-year-old grave in Israel has touching evidence of the long, close relationship between humans and dogs. The grave contains a human skeleton whose hand rests upon the bones of a small puppy. Through the centuries dogs have given people loyalty, aid, and companionship. So what did people do to get such understanding and helpful friends? Well, actually, they created them themselves.

NEVER CRY WOLF

Scientists have discovered 400,000-year-old wolf bones mingled with human bones. But they believe that the man and wolf relationship goes back hundreds of thousands of years before that. Early humans probably first used wolves as food; but wolves would also have been using humans, scavenging through their garbage dumps and over time moving closer and closer to the center of camp and the human's food source—the campfire. After a while, the gentler wolves were accepted by the humans as part of the group.

Wolf packs and early human tribes had a lot in common. They were both willing to follow a leader, cooperate, and work together to protect members of their group. So, a wolf-human cooperation was natural—especially when it came to hunting.

Wolves began to follow humans when they went hunting. Wolves gave off cues when prey was around and humans soon figured out that wolves possessed a superior sense of smell and could detect prey at long distances. Man and wolf began to cooperate and eventually wolves became active participants and true partners with humans in the hunt for food.

AN EVOLVING PUPPY TALE

When selecting a wolf pal, humans naturally favored the most cooperative animals. They associated cooperative behavior with a puppylike appearance in an adult wolf and encouraged those animals to stick around. They also began picking out the most gentle, trainable puppies to raise.

In effect, humans replaced nature's selection process with a man-made one. And after thousands of years of human meddling—about 14,000 years ago—a new animal evolved. Thanks to domestication and their diet, these animals had smaller brains, heads, and teeth than wolves. We call them dogs. As wolves evolved into dogs, they became even more important to humans because of their usefulness and their companionship.

Dogs always had a wide variety of size and body proportions, but about 3,000–4,000 years ago, unable to leave well enough alone, folks tinkered with Mother Nature in earnest to create specialized working and companion dogs. That's when the difference in breeds really began to emerge.

The Romans bred and trained working dogs and lap dogs. As breeding continued, dogs became more and more specialized. Herding dogs were bred to work with livestock. Sporting dogs were bred for bird hunting. Hounds were bred to hunt by scent or by sight. Working dogs were bred to perform many tasks, including herding, hauling, and guarding. Terriers were bred to hunt rodents and other vermin. Toy breeds were bred to be companions and some of those were bred simply to be lap warmers.

DOGS OF WAR

Alexander the Great was said to have helped develop a huge breed, called Molossus, as a battle dog that could knock a man right off a horse. In the 16th century, Spanish conquistadors used kill-trained greyhounds and large mastiff-type dogs against Native Americans to assist in their conquest of the New World.

During the Civil War, dogs were used for sentry duty, to guard prisoners, and to accompany troops as mascots. In World War I, dogs were used to detect enemy forces, carry messages, search battlefields for wounded soldiers, and evacuate wounded soldiers by pulling small ambulance carts. Dogs also cheered up soldiers at the front lines and those wounded in hospitals.

During World War II, the United States really got serious about using dogs to protect its military and military-related property. Scout dogs were used to good advantage in Vietnam; they served double duty as security dogs. Mine-detector dogs and tunnel dogs were both trained during this conflict. Vietnam also saw the development of the tracker dog. Tracker dogs were used to hunt down the enemy.

Susan Butcher won the world's longest dog sled race, the Iditirod, four times.

The modern canine soldier is trained to save lives, not take them. American war dogs help our troops avoid potentially deadly encounters. They work as sentries on sensitive military installation, or lead their handlers to hidden caches of weapons, explosives, and drugs.

COP DOGS
The organized use of dogs in law enforcement for the apprehension of criminals was established in the early 1900s. Working German shepherds became so good at helping law enforcement personnel that they were nicknamed "police dogs." The idea of using dogs for police work was largely brought about by the development and organization of purebred dog clubs. The earliest examples of police dog programs were those in Germany, Belgium, and England.

EXCEEDINGLY WELL BRED
Dogs have been successful as a species because they have adapted well to the needs and desires of humans for loyalty, companionship, and assistance. Dogs and people communicate effectively through voice, body language, and facial expressions, though in many ways dogs are much better at understanding humans than humans are at understanding dogs.

Dogs and humans have a relationship that is based on mutual support. Dogs have great difficulty surviving on their own and a dog's dependence on humans makes it a sensitive pal—cooperative and responsive to its owner's moods. Dogs are wonderful companions, they help people make a living, and they save lives. Man's best friend is even a healer, reducing stress and lowering blood pressure.

Dogs may be mankind's greatest accomplishment—the creation of a superior being. After all, a dog will never turn on you as long as you treat it right. The same can't be said about people.

* * * * *

"Dogs look up to you. Cats look down on you. Give me a pig. He just looks you in the eye and treats you like an equal."
—Winston Churchill

Toto of *Wizard of Oz* fame was a cairn terrier.

PERU'S POOPER SCOOPERS

The next time a pigeon drops a load onto the windshield of your car, spare a thought for the guano miners of Peru's Chincha Islands. They spent their working lives knee-deep in the stuff.

The economies of most countries are founded on things like farming or factories. But that was not the case for Peru, that mountainous South American country just north of Chile. Back in the 1800s, this county's national wealth was based on bird poop!

THE REIGN OF SPAIN

The Spanish explorer Francisco Pizarro arrived in Peru in 1532. After taking a good look around and figuring out that the local Indians would be no match for Spanish firepower, he claimed the country for Spain. In 1533, he did away with Atahuallpa, the Incan king, and formally made Peru a Spanish colony. The Spanish remained in control for the next 300 years. When independence came in 1821, the Peruvians suddenly realized that they had to look out for themselves. One of their main problems was how to make money. Peru wasn't overly blessed with natural resources, but it did have a lot of birds. And where there are birds there's usually a whole lot of bird crap.

WHAT A DUMP!

It's true what they say: birds of a feather really do flock together. And the area where all discerning South American cormorants love to flock to is a group of three unimpressive-looking lumps of Pacific rock just off the coast of Peru called the Chincha Islands. Maybe it's the fishing; these seabirds just love to hang out *en masse* there. And what do cormorants do after they've gorged themselves on the poor, unsuspecting anchovies that swim in the waters thereabouts? Well, they relieve themselves. In fact, they've been doing it there for centuries. So, by the early 1800s, the Chincha Islands were coated in a very deep and very smelly layer of cormorant crud.

The first "Burma Shave" jingles were posted in Minnesota in 1926.

Don't ask who discovered that bird poop, or guano, was an excellent fertilizer, but it's true that few things will help your roses bloom better than a good dollop of cormorant droppings. So, starting in the 1840s, citizens of Peru, under the control of a military strongman called General Castilla, realized that there was white gold in the hills. And that all that waste was too good to, well, waste. The general dished out licenses to the highest bidders (or bribers) to "mine" guano. And he set himself and his cronies up in prime positions to exploit the amazing profits that were expected from guano sales to the United States and Europe.

CHINESE TAKE-OUT

The only problem was, who in his or her right mind would want to spend days working on what are possibly the smelliest islands on Earth, knee-deep in guano, while being dive-bombed by incontinent cormorants? The people of Peru were poor and desperate, but they weren't *that* desperate.

The usual solution to this sort of problem is obvious: oppress your local minority. Castilla tried this, but there just weren't enough natives to go around. Fortunately, one of the important businessmen controlling the guano trade, Domingo Elias, knew where he could get his hands on some really cheap labor: namely, China. The Taiping Rebellion in China was a civil war that drove hundreds of thousands of Chinese out of the country. Many were desperate to leave and would go anywhere: the United States to build the railroads, England to work in sweatshops—or the Chincha Islands to mine guano. The first coolies (from the Hindi word *kuli*, which refers to an unskilled laborer, usually from the Far East, hired for low or subsistence wages) arrived in 1820. Soon, they were probably wishing they'd stayed at home. They were kept in conditions of near slavery and were flogged if they didn't meet their quota of two to five tons of guano—each!—per day. Needless to say, they were paid terrible wages. The only avenues of escape were suicide or opium, both of which were rife on the islands.

CLEANING UP THEIR ACTS

Castilla and his bunch of guano gangsters did very well. During the 1850s, there was so much guano waiting to be shipped out that vessels would commonly have to wait at the dock for 30 to 80 days to load up. Between 1840 and 1875, the value of Peru's exports rose from 6 million pesos to 32 million pesos ($43,351 to $231,226). Unfortunately for the rest of Peru, Castillo and company didn't get around to plowing the profits they made back into the economy. In fact, on the rare occasions they did, the results were disastrous. Again using coolie labor, Peru built over 770 miles of railroads around the country in the 1860s, at a cost much higher than the profits yielded by the guano trade. In just a few years Peru leaped from last to first place as the biggest borrower on the London money markets.

OH, POOP!

By the 1860s, new and cheaper forms of fertilizer were being developed. Guano's big rival was salitre, or nitrate of soda. As most of the salitre trade was conducted through neighboring Chile, Peru began to lose out. Then, in 1866, Spain tried to recapture the Chincha Islands from Peru. Although Peru won that little skirmish, the financial cost of the war was crippling. In 1879, Peru went to war with Chile in an attempt to wrestle control of the growing salitre trade. Peru lost the war in 1881 and was occupied by Chilean soldiers, who went on an orgy of looting and destruction. The Golden Age of Guano was well and truly over.

ENOUGH OF THIS POOP

By the time Peru got back on an even keel in the early 1900s, it had learned not to place all its cormorant eggs in one basket. It diversified into agriculture, copper mining, oil production—in fact, anything that didn't involve guano.

And today? Well, those hungry cormorants are still creating one almighty mess on the Chincha Islands. But, fortunately for all involved, there are no Chinese laborers to clean up after them.

* * * * *

THE OLIVE COMES TO AMERICA

The olive made its debut in the Western Hemisphere in 1560 via Peruvian missionaries. Spanish-speaking travelers first brought olives to Mexico. In 1700, Franciscan missionaries planted olive groves in what is now the state of California. Many of these original groves still exist.

The first U.S. driver's license was issued in Denver, Colorado, in 1906. Cost: $1.00.

A FLY ON THE WALL

If you happen to visit Africa and feel more sleepy than usual, you'd better start worrying!

Since it is only a little sting, a worker in the fields would probably just swat at the pain in annoyance. A few weeks, or months, later he might begin to feel a little run-down. A headache, fever, joint pains; it's probably just a little case of malaria that'll get better soon, right? No. A rash steals across his body, his eyes and hands swell horribly, and he can't seem to get out of bed to work—or to do much of anything. Pretty soon he can't wake up at all. He sleeps the day away. When he wakes, he can barely slur his words out, stumbles around gracelessly, and is prone to fits of rage. Eventually, he falls into a deep coma and dies.

YOU'RE FEELING VERRRRY SLEEEEPY

Though most Westerners haven't even heard of the disease, African sleeping sickness (aka trypanosomiasis) is a disease that affects an estimated 300,000 to 500,000 Africans yearly, mostly in the continent's tropical regions. Transmitted by the bite of tsetse flies carrying the parasite *Trypanosoma brucei*, sleeping sickness exists in two forms. The Western type causes a chronic and sometimes fatal hepatitis-like infection. The Eastern form is the truly brutal, deadly kind: in a few months it can make near zombies out of previously healthy humans and kill them soon after.

AS OLD AS THE HILLS

Sleeping sickness has always existed in Africa. Slave traders (among the first whites to come into contact with Africans) knew the disease well and rejected potential slaves with swollen glands, knowing they were marked for death. The illness was mainly confined to small villages and other rural areas until around 1896, when hundreds began dying from the mysterious sickness in Uganda and the Congo basin.

The root of the problem was colonization. Vast slices of the continent were being claimed by the French, British, Germans, Italians, and Dutch. With the new populations came new cities.

Monaco's principal source of income is from gambling.

The birth of these cities meant the death of natural habitats, and tsetse flies were forced to move to new homes. There they congregated more thickly than before and infected more and more unlucky Ugandans.

By 1900, the disease was in full swing. In some villages, a third of the population had died or was dying; primitive hospitals were set up with thousands of makeshift beds to accommodate the suffering until they died their agonizing deaths. There was little that could be done for victims since the disease had no cure and no one knew its cause.

FLY CATCHER

British scientists began studying the disease and eventually they isolated the parasite that caused the sickness. A breakthrough occurred when Dr. David Bruce recognized a correlation between areas where the disease was epidemic and ones that had large populations of tsetse flies. Now that doctors knew the cause and means of transmission, they tried atoxyl, an arsenic compound, as a treatment. It worked with limited success, but it had the horrible side effect of blindness.

In desperation, the British commissioner of Uganda asked local tribal chiefs to move their people away from the areas of the worst fly infestation. It took a lot of convincing, but they finally agreed. Mass evacuations halted the wildfire-quick spread of sleeping sickness in Uganda by around 1907. But only after about 200,000 people had died.

Since the Ugandan epidemic, more and better drugs have been introduced that help prevent, treat, and sometimes cure the sickness. Africans also learned how to manage the tsetse fly populations that spread the disease using measures such as insecticide.

All the same, the number of reported cases took a sharp spike upward in the 1970s. And the number is still way up from the peaceful period in the 1960s, when the disease was thought to be eradicated. What happened? Some of the fallout from Africa's ongoing political instability has meant a decline in disease control measures such as screening, reporting, insect control, and regular medical oversight for those in danger zones. In 2001 the World Health Organization estimated that from 300,000 to 500,000 people then had the disease.

Shakespeare originated such familiar phrases as *fair play, a foregone conclusion,* and *catch cold.*

HEY, WHO TURNED THE LIGHTS OFF?

Some people would rather refer to it as the Middle Ages, as if that were less judgmental. Truth be told, the much-maligned Dark Ages could have used a good press agent.

The term "Dark Ages" suggests a murky period between the fall of Rome and the Renaissance, when people finally got their acts together. Can't we be more generous to the era that gave us the invention of the rigid horse collar, which revolutionized agriculture? This humble tool gave horses and oxen better purchase into the hard northern European soil so that there'd be more grain for both serfs and livestock.

And there's more. So put aside your moldy rye bread and rancid meat for a moment as we recount some of the bright spots in the Dark Ages.

OH, MY GOTH!

First off, the Dark Ages was the age of Gothic architecture—so labeled because later, when everyone became "enlightened," they didn't care for the leftover buildings and named them after those nasty Nordic tribes who previously overran the Roman Empire. Florentine historian Giorgio Vasari (1511–1574) called them Gothic, implying that those Nordic types swept down and built a slew of ugly buildings—in between lootings and pillagings. He used the term in a derogatory sense, to mean that the buildings were considered ugly or base—not much different than if he named it Caveman-style architecture. (In fact, though, the architecture was created a couple centuries before Mr. Vasari by local Europeans who were doing their best to prop their walls up higher and higher.)

And where would we be without flying buttresses, that most prominent feature of Dark Ages buildings? By reducing a building's excessive exterior to the barest of skeletons, the buttresses allowed for higher walls—and more room for stained glass. Just ask yourself which are more likely to appear in your travel photos: load-bearing stacks of rocks or huge, 800-year-old stained glass windows backlit by the sun?

ARISTOTLING REVELATION!
Saint Thomas Aquinas (1225–1274), one of the principal saints of the Roman Catholic Church, did what he could for his besmirched era. For instance, in an age when Greek philosophy was considered pure heresy due to the precipitous rise of Christianity, St. Thomas was able to dust off old Aristotle and save his texts from the destruction of book burners. A couple of hundred years later, the Renaissance tried to take all the credit. But we know better.

A LONG TIME AGO, IN A UNIVERSITY FAR AWAY...
Even luminaries like Saint Thomas, Chaucer, and Dante can't convince some people that Middle Ages folk weren't a bunch of ignorant oafs. But out of these "dark" times the concept of the university was originated. From the 9th century on, universities sprang up to further train up-and-coming lawyers, doctors, and theologians: Salerno (9th century), Bologna (11th century), Oxford University (12th century), Montpellier (13th century), Salamanca (13th century), Prague (14th century), and Vienna (14th century)—to name a few.

And, luckily for some parents in the Dark Ages, Charlemagne, ruler of the Carolingian Empire (751–987), was kind enough to establish plenty of children's schools across class lines.

DIGGING DEEPER
Maybe the thing that's darkest is our current popular notions about the period. So slap a rigid horse collar on your beast of burden, and plow a little deeper—you'll find the Dark Ages had its shining moments.

* * * * *

KEEPING COWS CONTENTED

Benjamin Franklin tried to talk the French into adopting Daylight Savings Time, but farmers resisted the idea, insisting that cows could not change their habits.

Indy 500 cars do not run on gasoline. Since 1964, they've used methanol, a wood-based alcohol.

TIME OF
THE SEASONING

Taking the history of the world with a grain of salt.

I t's historically linked to industry, political power, and war. It's been a source of great wealth and one of the most desired substances in human history. Yet today, it's plentiful and dirt cheap. What is it? It is, of course, salt.

Early humans soon learned that their bodies needed salt to stay alive. Nobody knows if ancient hunters salted their mastodon meat, since red meat already contains plenty of salt. But after the Ice Age, when people turned to agriculture, they ate less meat and more grains, and had to supplement their diets with salt.

Salt also draws water out of bacteria, so they shrivel and die. Since bacteria causes food to spoil, killing bacteria helped to preserve food. Before refrigeration, salting, brining, or pickling was the only way to keep meat, fish, and vegetables edible for long periods.

Salt was also used for antibiotic and healing purposes. As civilization progressed, salt was used to make everything from glazed pottery to gunpowder. And in ancient Egypt, dead bodies were preserved with salt in the form of natron (baking soda) before being wrapped in strips of linen and sent along to the afterlife.

SALTING IT AWAY
How much was salt worth? Plenty! Ancient Greek traders bartered their slaves for salt. A lazy or rebellious slave was deemed "not worth his salt"—an insult still used today. Our word "salary" dates back to Roman times when soldiers were paid a dispensation, called a *salarium argentum*, so they could buy salt. In Mali, West Africa, salt was once worth its weight in gold. And some cultures dispensed with the middleman and just used salt itself as money.

WE BUILT THIS CITY ON ROCK SALT
Since salt was so valuable, cities and empires grew up around it. Jericho was founded 10,000 years ago as a salt-trading center. Salt profits built the Great Wall of China, and some historians believe

At 200 mph, an Indy driver can cover the length of a football field in less than one second.

that the expansion of the Roman Empire was, in part, a determination to control reliable sources of salt. Some cities, like the Austrian city of Salzburg (which means "city of salt"), still retain a grain of their salty history in their names.

Some places like Austria (which has many outcrops of salt-bearing rocks) were loaded with the stuff, while other areas had to pay a fortune for it. The idea of getting salt cheaply and selling it at a high price inspired trade routes across oceans and deserts.

Salt gave our ancestors freedom to travel—they could keep food fresh and carry it with them over long distances. Travel, in turn, made trade possible, and the need for salt fueled commerce. Much of the exploration around the world has a salty flavor.

Salted fish loomed large in the European diet, so scouting out new fishing beds led, in part, to the exploration of the New World. First the Vikings, then the British, French, and Portuguese fleets fished in the North Atlantic and explored the Americas searching for salt to preserve their catches.

A SALT AND BATTERY

The history of war may seem unsavory, but it does have a salty side. Those devious Hapsburg dukes of the 14th century sold salt to the Swiss—then used the money to make war against them!

Salt, or the lack of it, was also a strategy in the war between Holland and Spain. When the Dutch revolted against Spanish rule in the 16th century, they successfully blockaded Spain's Iberian saltworks—and that gave Spain a shove into bankruptcy, causing her to lose the war.

During the American Civil War, Union generals went after Confederate salt manufacturers, and they refused to allow any salt to make its way South. The lack of salt kept the Confederacy from curing pork for rations. The hunger that Southern troops and their families at home endured was an important factor in the South's defeat.

DEATH, TAXES, AND SALT

Levied in 2200 B.C. by China's emperor Hsia Yu, the world's first tax was on (you guessed it) salt. Chandragupta, who ruled India in 324 B.C., came up with the same idea. The Roman emperors put a tax on salt, and some salt taxes exist in Italy even today.

Charles I wore two shirts to his execution because it was a cold day...

One of the most hated salt taxes was the French tax called the gabelle. As the French kings and their courts sought more money, the gabelle became a notorious example of taxploitation—from 1630 to 1710 the tax increased ten times over.

Eventually, every French citizen older than the age of eight was forced to purchase a weekly minimum amount of salt for a fixed price—forcing some families into starvation since they couldn't afford both salt and food. To nobody's surprise, repeal of the salt tax became a cause célèbre of the French Revolution.

SHAKING THINGS UP

Even in modern times, salt has had power—as Mahatma Gandhi understood. In 1930, the British had a monopoly on the manufacture of salt in colonial India. They taxed salt so highly that millions of Indians suffered.

Gandhi won international sympathy when he led thousands of Indians in a "salt march" to Dandi beach, where they illegally gathered salt mud. Arrests followed, but the British were utimately forced to negotiate. Gandhi's nonviolent movement was launched, helping India eventually win its independence from Britain.

Salt, however, is still fighting to win its independence from pepper.

* * * * *

SALTY TIDBITS

- In *The Last Supper,* Da Vinci painted an overturned saltcellar in front of Judas Iscariot. This was intended to represent bad luck or looming evil.
- There are 30 references to salt in the Bible. The word *salvation* has its origins with covenants, often sealed with salt, in both testaments of the Bible.
- During World War II, the Nazis hid plundered artworks in salt mines.
- The Hotel de Sal Playa in Bolivia, built in 1993, is made entirely of salt. It is located near the Uyuni mine, one of the world's largest salt mines. Its walls, roof, tables, and bar consist of sodium chloride. According to a CNN article, during the rainy season, the hotel's walls are reinforced with additional blocks of salt. Guests are urged not to lick the walls.

BEFORE THEY WERE POETS

You know them as the men and women who smoked, brooded, and set the world on fire with their words. Yet you may not have been aware of their earlier avocations. Take it from Uncle John—don't roll your eyes when the waiter or doorman tells you he'll be a famous poet one day…you just never know.

Poet: Sappho (625 B.C.), lyric poet of ancient Greece
Past: Schoolmistress at an academy for unmarried young women

Poet: Thomas Wyatt (1503–1542), English poet often credited with creating the sonnet
Past: Keeper of Henry VIII's jewels

Poet: John Milton (1608–1674), English poet who wrote the epic poem *Paradise Lost*
Past: Secretary of foreign languages for the English government

Poet: Johann Wolfgang von Goethe (1749–1832), German writer who penned *Faust*
Past: Lawyer

Poet: Ann Yearsley (1753–1806), successful 18th-century English poet
Past: Dairymaid

Poet: Samuel Taylor Coleridge (1772–1834), English lyrical Romantic poet
Past: Soldier, enlisted to escape drug debts incurred while studying at seminary

Poet: John Keats (1795–1821), one of England's flagship Romantic poets
Past: Junior surgeon at a London hospital; spent a lot of time dressing wounds

Poet: Joaquin Miller (1837–1913), American poet who wrote about the West
Past: Gold miner

Maya Angelou was the first black U.S. Poet Laureate.

Poet: Robert Frost (1874–1963), called "America's Premier National Poet" by some
Past: Chicken farmer

Poet: T. S. Eliot (1888–1965), distinguished American Nobel Prize–winning poet
Past: Banker at Lloyd's of London

Poet: Langston Hughes (1902–1967), American Harlem Renaissance poet
Past: Ship's steward

Poet: Ogden Nash (1902–1971), renowned American writer of lighthearted verse
Past: Wrote advertising for streetcars

Poet: Dorothy Parker (1902–1971), famous American poet who wrote for leading publications
Past: Pianist

Poet: John Berryman (1914–1972), Pulitzer Prize–winning American poet
Past: Shakespeare scholar

Poet: Wallace Stevens (1916–1955), Pulitzer Prize–winning American poet
Past: Vice president of an insurance company

Poet: Frank O'Hara (1926–1966), groundbreaking poet of the New York School
Past: Sonar operator for the navy

Poet: Maya Angelou (1928–), poet who wrote the autobiographical novel *I Know Why the Caged Bird Sings*
Past: Streetcar conductor

* * * * *

"You don't have to suffer to be a poet; adolescence is enough suffering for anyone."—John Ciardi

"A true poet does not bother to be poetical. Nor does a nursery gardener scent his roses."—Jean Cocteau

---

The world's most widely spoken language is Mandarin Chinese.

THE OOPS FACTOR

The famous charge of the Light Brigade was a clear case of guys getting in trouble when they're too proud to ask for directions.

Alfred Lord Tennyson's 1855 poem *The Charge of the Light Brigade* immortalizes bravery and glory in defeat—and one of the most famous goofs in military history.

> *Forward the Light Brigade!*
> *Was there a man dismay'd?*
> *Not tho' the soldier knew*
> *Some one had blunder'd:*
> *Their's not to make reply,*
> *Their's not to reason why,*
> *Their's but to do and die:*
> *Into the valley of Death*
> *Rode the six hundred.*

The "six hundred" (the figure is usually put at 673) never should have been in that "valley of Death" in the first place. Oops, they were going the wrong way!

A STORM IN THE PORT

In March 1854, England, France, and Turkey joined forces to keep an overly aggressive Russia from gaining too much power in the Mediterranean. To that end, the British took over the harbor of Balaklava, a Black Sea port on a narrow inlet in the Crimea surrounded by steep hills.

On the morning of October 25, 1854, thousands of Russian troops stormed a lower ridge of the Causeway Heights, two miles north of Balaklava. The Turkish troops stationed on the Causeway held the Russians off as long as they could but finally fled, leaving their cannons behind. The victorious Russians swarmed down the ridge and south toward Balaklava.

THE PREGAME SHOW

The 93rd Highlanders (later famously described as the "thin red line") were outmanned, sometimes more than ten to one, but they

---

The cover for the 1971 Rolling Stones' album *Sticky Fingers* was designed by Andy Warhol.

held back the Russian cavalry. The heavy cavalry, also desperately outnumbered, charged into the Russian troops and drove them back. Balaklava remained in British control. But as the Russians retreated, they weren't pursued, and they reformed in heavy numbers once back on the Causeway.

From a protected position atop the ridge at British headquarters, Commander Lord Raglan could see both the southern and northern valleys that ran from the Causeway. From his perch, Lord Raglan saw the Russian forces preparing to drag away the naval cannons abandoned by the Turks. In the 19th-century "etiquette of war," losing those guns meant defeat. So Raglan issued one of the most controversial orders ever given—and launched a military disaster.

CALL OUT THE CAVALRY

The most famous (or infamous) part of Lord Raglan's order was, "Lord Raglan wishes the cavalry to advance rapidly to the front...Follow the enemy and try to prevent the enemy from carrying away the guns...Immediate." He gave the message to Captain Nolan, who galloped down from British headquarters and delivered the message to the Earl of Lucan, commander of the cavalry.

Lord Lucan was stationed on the plain below, so he couldn't see the Causeway or any guns being carried off. All he saw were Russian gun batteries sitting at the far end of a thin northern valley that ran over a mile between two rows of Russian artilleries positioned on the hills. Attacking those guns would be suicide.

Lucan slowly and carefully reread the order in front of the impatient Nolan, who had been ordered to get action immediately. When Lucan asked Nolan for clarification, the antsy captain yelled, "There are your guns, sir." He threw up a hand in a direction that seemed to indicate the northern valley beyond the Causeway, where the Russian cannons sat.

Fearing disaster, but feeling he had no choice, Lucan rode to Lord Cardigan, the commander of the Light Brigade, and ordered him to go after the Russian guns at the far end of "the valley of death." Cardigan couldn't see any sense to it either, but he was determined to obey the order.

NO, WAIT!

When Captain Nolan saw the brigade ride toward the Russian guns, he galloped toward Lord Cardigan, waving his sword wildly and pointing toward the Causeway Heights. But before he could reach Cardigan or redirect the cavalry (if that was his intention), the Russians fired and Nolan was killed. The suicidal charge began.

Riding as if performing on a parade ground, Cardigan led his men straight into the mouth of booming Russian guns belching fire and smoke, aimed straight at them. Atop the ridge, French general Bosquet saw the brave cavalry keep perfect formation while men continually fell to their deaths and famously observed, "C'est magnifique, mais ce n'est pas la guerre." (It's magnificent, but it's not war.) Yet despite the overwhelming advantage of the Russians, the heroic Light Brigade rode through the valley and disabled the Russian cannons.

But the charge took a terrible toll. Fewer than a third of the 600-plus men who'd charged at the wrong guns made it to roll call the following day. The rest were dead, wounded, or captured. About 500 horses were lost. And the Light Brigade as a fighting force in Crimea was finished.

WHO'S TO BLAME?

Just like Tennyson's poem said, "someone had blundered." Accusations exploded immediately among the lords, who weren't exactly chummy. Lords Lucan and Cardigan were feuding brothers-in-law who'd hated each other for 30 years. Cardigan constantly tried to undercut Lucan's authority over him, and Commander Raglan was often pulled into the feud, angering Lord Lucan by seeming to take Cardigan's side. But not this time.

The furious Raglan accused Lord Cardigan of stupidity. Cardigan blamed the orders given to him by Lord Lucan. Raglan then accused Lucan of ineptness, but Lucan protested that the vague orders he'd been given were easily misunderstood. Lord Lucan blamed Captain Nolan for not clarifying the order correctly. Captain Nolan, of course, was in no position to blame anyone—because he was dead.

There was, in fact, plenty of blame to go around. Commander Raglan had a panoramic view and should have known that Lucan couldn't see the guns or the Russians on the Causeway. Instead, he issued an order that didn't tell Lucan exactly which guns he should capture or where they were.

Captain Nolan was a brilliant cavalry officer. But in this case, instead of helping Lord Lucan understand the orders, Nolan treated him with impatient contempt and sealed the fate of the Light Brigade.

Lord Lucan, as head of the cavalry, was expected to use reconnaissance to learn where his enemy and their guns were. He also might have talked over the problem of the suicidal orders with Cardigan. But because the two were feuding, they spoke as little as possible.

Finally, there was Lord Cardigan, who was hated by his men for arrogance and stupidity. (He'd once court-martialed an officer for drinking wine from a black bottle instead of decanting it.) He cared more about the flash and dash of his unit than its welfare.

BRITAIN IN BLUNDERLAND

During the charge, Cardigan insisted on a drill formation through the northern valley when a rough gallop could have saved lives. The brigadier general rode right up to the guns. But when the Light Brigade attacked the Russian gunners, they did so without the aid of Cardigan. Too aristocratic to fight with Russian rabble, Cardigan left his men and rode out of the valley to lodge a complaint against the now dead Captain Nolan. It was said that he returned to his yacht that night and enjoyed a bath, dinner, and a bottle of champagne.

LET THAT BE A LESSON

The Crimean War gave no glory to its British commanders. After the Crimea, Britain began to make reforms to a military in which officers had been promoted for their wealth and class status, and not for their fighting smarts. One British journalist summed the Crimean up as a war of "lions led by donkeys." That description was never more apt than in the disastrous charge of Britain's Light Brigade.

Roquefort was the favorite cheese of the emperor Charlemagne.

LITTLE THINGS MEAN A LOT

A trip for shoes, a fighting professor who believed in the value of study, a Confederate soldier with a "queer notion." These little things shaped the big battle at Gettysburg. And the course of the Civil War.

Don't sweat the small stuff? That may be good personal advice, but in history, small stuff can be a big deal. One little-known, split-second decision by one Confederate soldier had a powerful influence on the battle at Gettysburg—and maybe even the course of the Civil War.

SHOE SHOPPING
The Confederate Army was winning the war for secession when it marched into Gettysburg, Pennsylvania, looking for shoes. The Union Army had retreated after decisive victories by Confederate general Robert E. Lee, who was now on the offensive, pushing deep into Union territory.

That June 30, 1863, the battle-worn Southern army was hungry for Northern supplies and spoiling for another victory. If General Lee could push through the line of Union troops, he and his men had a clear shot at marching through Washington, D.C., and raising the Confederate flag over the U.S. Capitol.

THE RED STAIN
To stop the Confederate threat, Lincoln had dispatched General George Meade and his men, who caught up with Lee in Pennsylvania. On July 1, two closely matched armies—75,000 troops under a Confederate flag and 88,000 under Union stars and stripes—faced off in the green hills around Gettysburg.

It was July 3 before the battle was over. More than 7,000 of those 163,000 troops were dead. Another 27,000 were wounded. And more than 48,000 were missing in action. Gettysburg was littered with body parts, exploded caissons, and dying horses. Its green hills were stained blood red.

The awful battle horrified both North and South; it also marked the turning point of the Civil War. General Lee never took that march through Washington. The Union line had held—just barely. That Independence Day, President Lincoln knew the country had come through a close call. But even he didn't know how close.

DO OR DIE

By the second day of battle, the Union army was faltering, and Confederates were poised to take a strategic hill, called Little Round Top, on the far left edge of the Union position. Taking the hill would allow the Confederate forces to outflank and circumvent the Union Army line. They could put more of the Union men in their sights, and they would have a clear, undefended path to Washington. To defend the hill, a volunteer militia, the 20th Maine, was sent to take up the southern spur of Little Round Top—with orders to hold the ground or die trying.

The 308 men of the 20th Maine weren't led by a professional military man. Instead, their colonel was a scholar of languages: Joshua Lawrence Chamberlain, a graduate of Bangor Theological Seminary and professor of rhetoric and oratory at Bowdoin College. Chamberlain was on sabbatical and could have been studying in Europe. But he'd chosen to defend his country instead. Some historians believe that it was Chamberlain's scholarship and leadership, combined with the bravery of the men of the 20th, that changed the course of the Civil War.

A STUDIED DEFENSE

The professor believed in learning and had studied everything he could about military strategy. At Gettysburg, in the thick of battle, outnumbered by the 500 Confederate troops of the 15th Alabama, Chamberlain ordered a complicated military maneuver called the "refusal of the line." The action helped the 20th Maine defend against flank attacks. Against all odds, they held their ground.

Confederate colonel Oates would later say that he thought that his men nearly penetrated the Union line five times, but five times the 20th Maine turned them back. As Chamberlain would later write of his troops, "How men held on, each one knows—not I." Historians agree that the men were aided by Chamberlain's leadership. At one point, the center of the Union line opened. Determined to keep the hill, Chamberlain filled that position himself. (Remember that center position; it comes up later.)

But though the volunteers of the 20th managed to hold out, their ammunition was nearly gone. The men were tired; a third of the regiment was dead. The command was to keep control of the hill. Retreat wasn't an option. Yet Chamberlain knew there was no way that the 20th Maine could repel the 15th Alabama again.

LITTLE ROUND TOP WAS A BIG DEAL
So, Chamberlain went on the offensive. And because his unit was running low on bullets, he ordered his men to charge with bayonets. Like a scene in a movie, the 20th Maine, in one long line, swept down the hill with bayonets at the ready. By now, they were only 200 men, but they screamed with a bloodcurdling noise that made them sound like 600. The Confederates, exhausted and suffering horrific casualties of their own, may have believed that they were outnumbered. In any case, they fled.

The 20th Maine, under the brilliant leadership of Colonel Chamberlain, had saved Little Round Top. Because the Union line was so vulnerable there, some U.S. historians give the Battle of Little Round Top credit for saving the day at Gettysburg. Colonel William C. Oates, leader of the 15th Alabama, wrote, "Great events sometimes turn on comparatively small affairs."

SOUTHERN GRACE
And sometimes on even smaller affairs. Remember above when we told you that Chamberlain filled the Union's open center position himself? Years after the war was over, Chamberlain received a letter from a soldier of the 15th Alabama. "Twice in that fight I had your life in my hands," the soldier wrote. Describing Chamberlain's position, he explained:

> You were standing in the open behind the center of your line, full exposed. I knew your rank by your uniform and your action, and I thought it a mighty good thing to put you out of the way. I rested my gun on the rock and took steady aim. I started to pull the trigger, but some queer notion stopped me. Then I got ashamed of my weakness

and went through the same motions again. I had you, perfectly certain. But that same queer something shut right down on me. I couldn't pull the trigger, and gave it up—that is, your life. I am glad of it now, and hope you are.

And, on that fleeting moment, hung the course of U.S. history.

* * * * *

Joshua Chamberlain was awarded a Medal of Honor for his service on Little Round Top. Thirty years after the battle, Chamberlain received a small package in the mail containing the medal. The citation read: "Daring heroism and great tenacity in holding his position on the Little Round Top against repeated assaults."

FORD'S THEATRE

This landmark is best known as the place where President Abraham Lincoln was shot by John Wilkes Booth on April 14, 1865, while attending a performance of the comedy *Our American Cousin*.

Perhaps that ill-fated day would not have happened had theatre proprietor John Thompson Ford heeded the warnings of others when he was told it would be bad luck to convert the former Baptist church he leased in 1861 into a theater. Prior to Lincoln's assassination, the theater was destroyed once by fire. Later, in 1893, part of the theater collapsed (talk about a performance to bring down the house!) injuring 68 people.

After Lincoln's death, the theatre was shut down. Ford's Theatre was reopened in 1968 as a living memorial to Lincoln. The theater is still an operating theater and is currently maintained by the National Park Service, where it has since had better fortune.

The first smoking ban on U.S. airline flights went into effect on April 23, 1988.

SMITHSONIAN
BY THE NUMBERS

You haven't experienced American history until you've experienced the wonders of the Smithsonian Institution. So, just in case you haven't been there lately, allow Uncle John to give you a numerical snapshot of this awesome American must-see.

0

Number of bag lunches you're allowed to take into the Smithsonian. Collectively, there are more than 20 sit-down restaurants among the Smithsonian museums, not counting outdoor courtyard grub.

2

Percentage of the Smithsonian Institution's holdings on display at any given time.

3

Number of one-cent stamps affixed to the first piece of mail flown across the Atlantic, which is housed in the Smithsonian's National Postal Museum.

4.5

Millions of botanical specimens housed by the Smithsonian's National Museum of Natural History; this represents around 8 percent of all plants collected in the United States.

17

Number of museums that make up the Smithsonian. Among others, these include the American Art Museum and its Renwick Gallery, the National Museum of the American Indian, the Freer Gallery of Art and Arthur M. Sackler Gallery (Asian art), the Hirshhorn Museum and Sculpture Garden (modern and contemporary art), and—whew!—the National Museum of Natural History.

The first cafeteria in the U.S. was opened in 1895 in Chicago by Ernest Kimball.

24
Number of 2004 Smithsonian visitors, in millions.

25
The number, in thousands, of Africana books in the institution's Warren M. Robbins Library at the National Museum of African Art.

32
The number of huge, metal buildings dedicated just to restoring and storing aircraft on display at the Smithsonian's National Air and Space Museum and related centers. Smithsonian airplanes include the *Enola Gay*, the Wright 1903 Flyer, the Ryan NYP *Spirit of St. Louis*, the Space Shuttle *Enterprise*, the Lockheed SR-71 Blackbird, and the Concorde.

37.2
Weight, in tons, of a section of Route 66 delivered to the Hall of Transportation in the National Museum of American History for a recent exhibit.

40
Number, in thousands, of three-dimensional objects housed in the Smithsonian's Cooper-Hewitt National Design Museum, including Irish cut glass, Soviet porcelains, and Japanese sword fittings. The museum has more than 250,000 objects—drawing, prints, books, and textiles—all dedicated to the study of design.

45.52
Number of carats in the Hope Diamond at the Smithsonian Institution's National Museum of Natural History. It glows in the dark after exposure to UV rays and is semiconductive, too! If it truly belongs to the people of America to enjoy, Mrs. Uncle John wants to know when it'll be her turn to wear it out to dinner.

75
Number of years after the institution's namesake, James Smithson, died that Smithsonian regent, Alexander Graham Bell, brought Smithson's body from his place of death in Italy to a tomb at the Smithsonian Institution.

The first Chinese laundry in the U.S. opened in 1851 in San Francisco.

100,000
Amount of money, in British pounds sterling, that James Smithson originally willed to the United States upon his death in 1826. This eventually became the financial start of the Smithsonian.

7,635,245
That same willed amount adjusted to reflect 2002 U.S. dollars.

78,000,000
Millions of visitors that the Web site, www.smithsonian.org, hosted in 2004.

143,500,000
Approximate number of objects, works of art, and specimens in the Smithsonian Institution.

* * * * *

HOW TO FIND A BATHROOM

The Smithsonian probably has a lot of bathrooms too. But if you lived in the 1930s, you'd better know how to ask a stranger directions to the nearest facility. A few of the slang words for "bathroom" that came into being way back then.

Bank	Joe
Can	Marble palace
Crystal	Mine
Domus	Old soldiers' home
Egypt	Ruth (a women's toilet)
Honey house	Shot tower
Jake (a men's toilet)	Temple

And our favorite: John.

The first revolving restaurant was The Top of the Needle, in Seattle on May 22, 1961.

LEW WHO?

Given the clues below, can you identify the man in question?

Here are your clues:
- He was the Union's youngest Civil War general, at age 34.
- He was governor of the New Mexico Territory.
- He wrote a best-selling novel that's never been out of print.
- Three movies were made from the book. The first one was a one-reeler made in 1907. The second one, made in 1925, for $3.9 million, was the most expensive silent film ever made. The third film won 11 Oscars, including Best Picture, Best Actor, and Best Director.
- He was the son of a governor.
- He ordered up the posse that killed Billy the Kid.
- He was a judge at the court-martial of Abraham Lincoln's accused assassins.
- He's been portrayed 12 times on film and TV.
- He was U.S. minister to Turkey.
- There's a museum devoted to him in his hometown of Crawfordsville, Indiana.

THE MAN IN QUESTION

Even with all those achievements, most people have pretty much forgotten about the remarkable Lew Wallace (1827–1905), the lawyer-soldier-statesman-novelist who wrote *Ben-Hur: A Tale of the Christ* in 1880. The movie (minus the subtitle) helped make Charlton Heston a superstar. Trivia buffs: Two gold stars if you know Ben-Hur's first name.* One gold star if you knew that he *had* a first name.

MULTITASKING MAN

The versatile Wallace was a busy man. At age 19 he was fighting in the Mexican War (1846–1847). After the war he worked as a newspaper reporter and lawyer; he was admitted to the bar in 1849. Later, he was active in Indiana politics and was elected to the Indiana Senate in 1856. At the outbreak of the Civil War, he became a brigadier general in 1861, and he was a major general by March 1862. He commanded troops at the Battle of Shiloh. He was in command at the Battle of Monocacy (near Frederick, Maryland), which saved Washington, D.C., from the Confederate Army.

When President Andrew Johnson ordered a nine-man military commission to try the conspirators who plotted the assassination of Lincoln, Wallace was one of the nine.

THE KID IN QUESTION

In New Mexico, Wallace's efforts were aimed largely at fighting lawlessness. He signed the death warrant of William Bonney, who became notorious as Billy the Kid. When Bonney escaped from the Lincoln County courthouse, it was Wallace who ordered up the posse that tracked him down to Fort Sumner, where—according to most versions of the story—Sheriff Pat Garrett shot the Kid dead.

A BOOKIE AT HEART

What Wallace liked best was writing. His first book, *The Fair God*, about the Spanish conquest of Mexico, was reasonably popular. He wrote the huge best seller, *Ben-Hur*, while serving as governor of New Mexico, a job he did conscientiously but never really liked. ("I have spent enough time in this place," he wrote in a letter to his wife. "There is nobody here who cares for me, and nobody I care for.") His other books included *The Boyhood of Christ* (1888), *The Prince of India* (1893), *The Wooing of Malkatoon* (1897), and *Lew Wallace: An Autobiography*, published in 1906, a year after his death.

ACTORS WHO PORTRAYED LEW WALLACE

Frank Reicher in *Billy the Kid* (1930)
Berton Churchill in *The Big Stampede* (1932)
Joe King in *Land Beyond the Law* (1937)
Claude Stroud in *I Shot Billy the Kid* (1950)
Robert Barrat in *The Kid from Texas* (1950)
Otis Garth in *The Law vs. Billy the Kid* (1954)
Ralph Moody in *Strange Lady in Town* (1955)
Cameron Mitchell in *The Andersonville Trial* (1970) (TV)
Jason Robards in *Pat Garrett and Billy the Kid* (1973)
Rene Auberjonois in *Longarm* (1988) (TV)
Wilford Brimley in *Billy the Kid* (1989) (TV)
Scott Wilson in *Young Guns II* (1990)

*Ben-Hur's first name was Judah.

RETURN OF THE "RELAX, THIS WON'T HURT A BIT" AWARDS

*While stuck in the dentist's chair, don't bite
the hand that heals you. Instead, be glad you
had a toothache in the 21st century.*

Just when you thought it was safe to open wide, we're back with more of our awards for the most horrific histories in the hideous saga of dentistry.

"MOST PUTRID PAINKILLER" AWARD

This award is definitely not for the ancient Greeks, who probably used opium as a painkiller, both during dental procedures and afterward to treat the pain. No, that sounds quite sensible considering our other contestant.

The winners are the Romans (again!). Romans applied the pickled root of a chrysanthemum to gums to deaden pain. This had a side effect of destroying and loosening the membrane and fibers holding the tooth in place—so you lost the tooth you were trying to fix. Another popular painkilling potion in Roman times combined opium, celandine (a derivative from poppies), and saffron. This sounds like "a good thing," but trust the Romans to go and ruin it by adding ground lizards, bone marrow, and human fat.

Still, they wouldn't get the award if they hadn't used this painkiller: applying pressure to the carotid arteries in the neck, which would slow blood flow and induce unconsciousness. This deadly painkiller often led to *permanent* unconsciousness.

"THIS HURTS ME MORE THAN IT DOES YOU" AWARD

Somehow, toothaches didn't only make the people who had them miserable. They made dentists miserable too. Woeful dentist candidates include the following:

In 1683, Antoni van Leeuwenhoek, a Dutchman, invented the microscope and was horrified when he turned his new invention on the scrapings from teeth. He found so much bacteria that he declared that there was more microscopic life in one human mouth than people living in his country. So did he ever kiss anyone again? We doubt it.

In 1896 (only months after the X-ray was invented by Wilhelm Roentgen in Germany), an American doctor, C. Edmund Kells of New Orleans, built his own machine and began using it to help his patients. He held the film in the mouths of thousands of his patients, exposing his hand to the radiation. The great dentist saved people lots of grief—and teeth. But he lost three fingers to cancer and then his whole hand; his suffering eventually led him to commit suicide.

As much as the great Dr. Kells deserves admiration, our award goes to Horace Wells (1815–1848), an American dentist from Hartford, Connecticut, who discovered the practice of anesthesia in 1844. He administered nitrous oxide (laughing gas) to relieve pain during a procedure. Since Wells was afraid of giving his patients too much gas, in one demonstration, he didn't administer enough anesthesia; his patient awoke to great pain in front of a skeptical crowd.

Onlookers thought Wells was a quack, and as a result, the use of laughing gas fell out of favor for years. Disgraced, Wells sunk into a deep depression. And the man who'd discovered a wonderful use for laughing gas felt so little like laughing himself that he committed suicide at age 33.

"HISTORY'S MOST HORRIBLE DENTIST" AWARD:
The first-known dentist Hesi-Re, an Egyptian who lived around 3000 B.C., was a definite candidate. Hesi-Re was known as "the Chief of the Toothers." He didn't just wield a frightening dentist drill. He drilled in the wrong place. His favorite way to treat a toothache, judging from the skeletons he left behind, was drilling into the jawbone beneath the aching tooth, presumably to relieve pressure.

But it's the Romans (who seem to be on a sweep of dental horrors awards) that win this one. Physician Celsus (about 25 B.C.–A.D. 50) suggested that to treat bleeding gums, a patient should chew unripe pears and let the juice run into the crevices of the teeth. If that didn't work, not to worry, he had another

Colonial Americans considered it unnecessary to bathe more than once every two to three months.

cure—cauterizing the infected gums with a red-hot iron. Bet the patients were just lined up outside his office clamoring to get in.

THE "OH, WHAT THE HECK" AWARD

We had to do it. Give an award for actually making progress in dentistry. So, here goes. Pierre Fauchard (1678–1761), a Frenchman, took the scientific information that Leeuwenhoek discovered with his microscope and applied it to dentistry. As a result, Fauchard is known as the father of modern dentistry. In 1728, he published a book titled *The Surgeon-Dentist,* or *Treatise of the Teeth,* which was the first complete textbook on treating teeth.

Deserving an honorable mention was American dentist Greene Vardiman Black who, in 1858, invented the foot-powered drill, so dentists could use both hands during a procedure. Now there was an idea whose time had come!

* * * * *

AND HE'S...SAFE, SORT OF

On September 21, 1923, Clarence "Climax" Blethen, a 30-year-old Red Sox rookie, took out his false teeth because he thought it made him look older and meaner when he pitched. He put them in his hip pocket, then forgot to put them back in his mouth, so when he slid into second base later in the game, he bit himself in the butt.

JUST THOUGHT YOU'D LIKE TO KNOW

A mosquito has 47 teeth.

The Globe Theatre was built in London in 1599.

WORDSVILLE

Big Band leader Tommy Dorsey coined the word squaresville in the 1940s, but the suffix "ville" reached its pinnacle in the 1950s: "dullsville," "weirdsville," "splitsville," "you-name-itville." When not attaching suffixes, here's what the cool cats of the 1950s were saying.

Ad-lib: To play the field

Big tickle: Something funny

Blow your jets: Get angry

Cast an eyeball: To look

Chariot: A car

Chrome-plated: Dressed up

Classy chassis: A nice body

Cooties: Nonexistent germs

Cube: Someone who's beyond square

Cut the cheese: To fart

Fracture: To amuse in a big way

Iggle: To persuade

Kook: A screwball

Knuckle sandwich: A punch in the face

Large charge: Something that's wonderful

Lumpy: Okay, not great

Made in the shade: Assured of success

Make the scene: To attend an event

Mental case: A weirdo

Nerd: A social outcast

Nowhere: Inferior

Panic: Something that's very funny

Passion pit: A drive-in theater

Punk out: Back down from a fight

Ragtop: A convertible

Real gone: Amazing

Sanitary: Wonderful

Slip: Give, as in "Slip me five"

Subterranean: A hipster

Unreal: Exceptional

Wig out: Go crazy

The first posthumous #1 record in history was Otis Redding's "Dock of the Bay."

GUERRILLA WARFARE PART 4

The Green Berets

U.S. Army Special Forces had its genesis during World War II, when the Office of Strategic Services (OSS) was created. The OSS mission definition was intelligence gathering, support of resistance movements, and sabotage. Toward these ends, the OSS created Jedburgh teams (named after the town in England where they trained) consisting of three men: a leader, an executive officer, and a radio operator. Normally, the radio operator was American, one officer was American, and the other was a member of the French Resistance.

They parachuted into Nazi-occupied France to conduct sabotage and guerrilla warfare, and to lead French guerrilla forces (called the maquis) against the Germans. They provided advice, expertise, and leadership, and they arranged airdrops of arms and ammunition.

THE COLD WAR

It wasn't until 1952 that the Army Special Forces were formed by recruiting former OSS officers (with Jedburgh experience) and veterans from the elite Rangers and Airborne Army units. Captain Aaron Bank was recruited from the OSS and became the first leader of the Special Forces. Headquartered at Ft. Bragg, North Carolina, the unit's mission was "to infiltrate by land, sea, or air deep into enemy-occupied territory and organize the resistance/guerrilla potential."

Candidates were required to speak more than one language. They were trained in at least two of the basic Special Forces skills: intelligence, communications, demolitions, weaponry, and medical aid, as well as how to operate behind enemy lines with little or no outside support. Special Forces units were organized into A teams, consisting of two officers and ten enlisted men.

During the 1950s, the Green Berets carried out plenty of cold war missions, supporting rebels fighting against their Communist

The winner of the first Kentucky Derby was Aristides, ridden by Oliver Lewis, on May 17, 1875.

governments and helping friendly countries battle Communist insurgencies. But they weren't well known outside the military establishment because nearly all of their missions were secret.

The Green Beret headgear was designed by Major Herb Brucker in 1953, based on the berets worn by elite troops in European armies. But the beret wasn't officially authorized army headgear until President John F. Kennedy—a big supporter of elite Special Forces—helped persuade the army to make it so in 1961.

VIETNAM

After WWII, the French reoccupied South Vietnam in an ill-fated attempt to resurrect their prewar empire. The North Vietnamese wanted to reunify their country, so they fought a guerrilla war to convince the French to leave. In 1956, Green Berets were sent to Vietnam to assist the French and train South Vietnamese soldiers in modern warfare and counter-insurgency techniques.

The Green Berets won 17 Medals of Honor, 814 Silver Stars, and more than 13,000 Bronze Stars in the war. They also provided medical care and built schools and hospitals as part of the program to win the "hearts and minds" of the local populace.

A book about their exploits, *The Green Berets*, by journalist Robin Moore, was published in 1962; Green Beret staff sergeant and medic Berry Sadler wrote and recorded the hit song called "The Ballad of the Green Berets" in 1966; and in 1968, John Wayne produced, directed, and starred in a movie called *The Green Berets*.

On November 20, 1970, a rescue mission called the Son Tay Raid was launched to rescue 75 American POWs from a North Vietnamese prison camp about 23 miles (37 km) from Hanoi. The mission was executed brilliantly, and no Green Berets were lost. Unfortunately, no prisoners were rescued, either—the POWs had been moved a couple of days earlier. The raid did help the POWs morale though, because the North Vietnamese decided to move all the POW's to a central facility in Hanoi where they were no longer kept in isolation from their other captured comrades.

After the United States withdrew from Vietnam, budget cuts in the late 1970s forced the army to rethink its dependence on large conventional forces and to consider the use of more elite units. It was thought that in the future, wars could be fought with air power and small units of highly trained men.

John DeLorean was the chief designer of the 1965 Pontiac GTO.

PANAMA

The army put this plan into effect during Operation Just Cause, the invasion of Panama to remove its leader, Manuel Noriega, and stop him from allowing Panama to be used as a way station for drug runners. The invasion and capture of Noriega was carried out entirely by Green Berets, Rangers, and Navy SEALs.

IRAQ I

During the first war against Iraq, Special Forces went into Kuwait early to train resistance forces. Once the air war was launched, Green Berets operated well behind enemy lines, providing intelligence and targeting data to direct air units to hidden and elusive targets, like the Iraqi mobile SCUD missiles.

Before the ground war began, Special Forces were instrumental in clearing lanes through minefields and trenches that blocked invasion routes for U.S. conventional forces. After Kuwait was liberated, Special Forces helped reconstitute the Kuwaiti armed forces.

AFGHANISTAN

The ground war in Afghanistan was fought almost entirely by Special Forces and Rangers leading, or in cooperation with, Afghani forces. The war was over quickly, but as of this writing, terrorist leader Osama Bin Laden has yet to be captured. He's believed to be hiding in the border region between Afghanistan and Pakistan, where the rugged terrain makes military operations difficult to sustain; Special Forces continue to hunt for him there.

IRAQ II

Special Forces spearheaded the invasion of Iraq on March 20, 2003. The war lasted approximately three weeks, but securing the peace has been far more difficult. As of this writing, Special Forces are now training the new Iraqi Army and police force, as well as providing humanitarian aid to the people of Iraq.

ELSEWHERE

The Green Berets' motto is De Oppresso Liber (To Free the Oppressed), and today, Special Forces troops are stationed in trouble spots all over the world, fighting terrorism and training local forces in counterterrorism tactics, techniques, and procedures.

For more, see "Guerrilla Warfare Part 5"—*Delta Force, page 263.*

For more, see "Guerrilla Warfare Part 5"—*Delta Force, page 263.*

New College (now Harvard University) started out in 1636 with nine students and one instructor.

NUCLEAR NIGHTMARES

When we went poking around inside the atom, we released a very powerful and destructive force. Here's a tour of a few now well-known nuclear disasters of the 20th century.

THE RUSSIANS WON'T COOL IT

On September 29, 1957, an explosion occurred at Mayak, a nuclear fuel reprocessing facility in the Ural Mountains near Chelyabinsk, Russia. Desperate to catch up with America's nuclear program, the Russians were none too careful with their cooling systems. When the tank of radioactive waste exploded, it leaked an estimated 20 million Curies of radiation. (A Curie is the degree of radioactivity or radiation producing potential of a given amount of radioactive material. The higher the Curies, the greater the amount of radiation.) Estimates of the number of people exposed to dangerously high levels of radiation range from 124,000 to 270,000. Of these, approximately only 7,500 were evacuated—most too late to avoid exposure to dangerous levels; an area the size of Rhode Island was evacuated until 1974.

A series of lessor accidents occurred before and after this meltdown in addition to a polluted water supply for the area's residents. Some sources report that so much radioactive waste was deliberately pumped into a nearby lake that even today anyone who bathes in its waters for an hour would be stricken with fatal radiation poisoning.

All told, most estimates put the number of inhabitants of the region exposed to radiation at 500,000. The Soviets said nothing about the accident; they didn't even acknowledge it until 1989, three years after Chernobyl.

THE UNITED STATES' NEAR MELTDOWN

America's infamous nuclear accident occurred in 1979, when Pennsylvania's Three Mile Island nuclear power facility came perilously close to exploding. The calamity began on March 28 at

4 a.m., when a water pump feeding the plant's steam-generating system failed. The plant's reactor continued to produce heat, but with no pump to carry it away, temperatures began rising in the reactor. Human error combined with system-wide failures, and Three Mile Island's containment building was flooded with thousands of gallons of steaming-hot radioactive water that immediately started escaping into the atmosphere.

Luckily the reactor didn't explode. If it had, it would have contaminated the entire state of Pennsylvania. Ironically, the accident occurred just 12 days after the opening of the movie *China Syndrome*, a thriller that involved the near-meltdown of a power plant reactor that threatened to destroy "an area the size of Pennsylvania."

AN EXPLOSIVE SITUATION

Operators at the Soviet Chernobyl nuclear power plant near Kiev were only conducting a simple experiment: just how long would a generator keep producing power after a nuclear reactor shut down? They would soon regret their curiosity.

On the afternoon of April 25, 1986, the operators began the experiment on a plant reactor, one of four. In an effort to carry it out, the operators made one mistake after another. By midnight they'd disconnected three different safety systems, each designed to shut the reactor down in case of an emergency. At 1 a.m. on April 26, the disaster occurred—cooling water inside the reactor was so low that the reactor overheated in seconds. Operators immediately activated a 20-second shutdown system, but were too late. Seven seconds later the reactor exploded, blowing the 1,000-ton concrete lid through the roof of the facility.

Flames shot 100 feet into the air while massive doses of radiation—several million times the amount that leaked at Three Mile Island—spread across northeastern Europe from Poland to the Ukraine, and as far north as Norway. The Soviets didn't release any information about the accident until two days later, when Swedish power plant workers detected huge amounts of radiation at their plant. The government released a terse statement claiming the accident was under control.

It's impossible to say how many people were killed by the catastrophe, since radioactive rains and wind washed heavy doses of radiation throughout Ukraine and much of Europe. About 100,0000 people were evacuated in areas of heaviest fallout, and government officials estimate about 30,000 people have died, or will eventually die, from radiation poisoning and radiation-related cancer.

What's really shocking is that Chernobyl's other reactors continued to be used until 2000 (the damaged reactor was covered with a leaking concrete cover, prompting fears of yet another nuclear Armageddon). It was finally shut down due to worldwide pressure and after $370 million in cleanup aid was received from 40 countries worldwide.

* * * * *

PISTOL-PACKIN' WHITE HOUSE MAMA

It's one thing to learn that while he was president, Franklin D. Roosevelt always slept with a pistol under his pillow. But did you know that his wife Eleanor carried a gun as well? She usually had one in her pocketbook and glove compartment.

In his book *Silk and Steel: Women at Arms*, firearms expert R. L. Wilson wrote that Eleanor Roosevelt was "a deadly shot with a handgun."

In 1958, at age 74, she was planning to speak at a civil rights workshop in Monteagle, Tennessee. When the Ku Klux Klan heard about that, they put a $25,000 bounty on her head. The FBI told her about the Klan bounty and warned her that they couldn't protect her. "You can't go," they said.

"I didn't ask for your protection," she told them. "I appreciate the warning. I have a commitment. I'm going."

And she did. At the Nashville airport, she was picked up by a friend, a white woman of 71. Mrs. Roosevelt got into the car, lay a loaded pistol on the front seat, and the two women drove through Klan country to their destination, the Highlander Folk School, a tiny school in the mountains, where the former first lady talked to black students about nonviolent civil disobedience. "She was tough as nails," said historian Geoff Ward.

WHO "NOSE" THE REAL CYRANO DE BERGERAC?

A nosy inquiry into history's famous swashbuckler.

In 1897, in Paris's Théâtre de la Porte-Saint-Martin, young Edmond Rostand waited in white-knuckled suspense to see how the audience would react to his new play. He hadn't had a hit yet, and he'd already been told that his latest effort would probably fail. Those sophisticated Parisians wanted the grit of reality, not historical romance. This was almost the 19th century, why had Rostand bothered about a story set in the 1600s? But he had persisted, inspired by a real-life French soldier. The play was called *Cyrano de Bergerac.*

OPENING NIGHT
In that first performance, Cyrano swept across the stage in lace-trimmed doublets, a flowing cape, and plumed hat. But he was no well-dressed sissy. He was a proud cadet in the Guards of Gascony. Bullies and villains ran from the wicked thrust of his flashing sword. Scoundrels cringed when he mocked them with his quick wit. And he was no slouch in the romantic poetry department either. His words of love inflamed the heart. Everything about the character of Cyrano de Bergerac was larger than life. Especially his gargantuan nose.

HOW ROMANTIC CAN YOU GET?
The heart of Rostand's story was Cyrano's love for his beautiful cousin, Roxane. She, in turn, was infatuated with a handsome cadet named Christian, and she asked Cyrano to help and protect him. Even though Cyrano longed to declare his own love, he did as Roxane asked. He helped Christian, as promised, by writing a series of passionate love letters for the strong, but completely non-verbal, cadet to send to Roxane. Beautiful letters. How could any girl resist? All through the many twists and turns of the plot,

Cyrano stayed a man of his word: loyal to Roxane, to the tongue-tied Christian, and to honor—no matter the cost.

BRAVO! BRAVO!
When the first performance ended, the audience leaped to their feet in a standing ovation. Perhaps no one was more surprised than Rostand himself. Soon *Cyrano de Bergerac* was wildly popular, and Rostand found himself a famous man. The appeal of the play hasn't faded with time. Today, the idealistic Cyrano with his grotesque nose is beloved around the world. So why is the historical figure who inspired the play all but forgotten?

THE REAL STORY
With his ready sword, cape, and plumed hat, Cyrano de Bergerac closely resembled D'Artagnan, the hero of Andre Dumas' famous adventure story, *The Three Musketeers*. The real D'Artagnan was a soldier for Louis XIV, and in fact appears as a character in Rostand's play. A lot of people thought that Cyrano was based on the famous musketeer. But that's because they didn't know about another, less famous, French soldier. Like D'Artagnan, this classy cadet also wielded a dangerous sword and had a witty way with words. The difference was that he also had an oversized nose. His name was Savinien Cyrano de Bergerac.

OH, WHAT A CUTE NOSE—I MEAN BABY!
The real Cyrano—and his nose—were born in 1619 in Paris. He was the son of a nobleman, and though he wasn't rich, he was well educated. An engraving of the adult Cyrano shows him with a nose much too large for his face. He wasn't a handsome hero, just a hero with all the other trimmings.

THE NOSE GROWS UP
At the age of 20, Cyrano enlisted in the king's cadets, serving under Louis XIII. Even among the great swordsmen of the time, he was considered a marvel. He was a demon with the sword and completely fearless. Many of the incidents in Rostand's play came straight from Cyrano's life, including the story of the hero facing down 100 armed men alone. When the real Cyrano learned that a deadly mob lay in wait for one of his friends, he took them on

single-handedly. He killed and wounded so many of the murderous band that the rest were put to flight.

HERE'S TO MEN WITH BIG NOSES!

But was the real Cyrano as smart as the hero of the play? You betcha. After receiving a serious saber wound to his throat, he gave up soldiering and took up writing. His works satirized the conservative ideas and conventions of his time. Among them are two satirical romances about voyages to outer space, and a story about a utopian society that honors men with big noses.

BUT WHAT ABOUT ROXANE?

If Cyrano was a great fighter, a loyal friend, and a brilliant intellectual, what about love? Did the real Cyrano spend his life longing for his cousin? Well, actually, no. He apparently did have a cousin, Magdeleine Robineau, who married a nobleman named Christian, but there isn't much evidence that our hero's heart pounded when Magdeleine was around. All the same, Rostand might have picked up on an unproven, but plausible, story in which Cyrano wrote love poems for an officer friend to send to his wife from the front.

HAPPY ENDING

Edmond Rostand never wrote another play that touched audiences like *Cyrano de Bergerac*. Some critics thought that for the rest of his career, Rostand was overshadowed by his big-nosed creation. Oh, yeah? We personally think he's lucky that cosmetic surgery wasn't available in the 17th century. If Cyrano had had a nose job, both the playwright and generations of audiences would have been deprived of an only slightly fictionalized, truly noble hero who never let his looks overshadow his talent.

* * * * *

"To see what is in front of one's nose needs a constant struggle."
—George Orwell

"If your nose is up in the air, you cannot see where you are going."—Mason Cooley

In Bali, the soul is believed to leave the body after exactly 42 days after death.

THAR SHE BLOWS

Today, reaching for a Kleenex is so reflexive that we don't realize that the handkerchief is a relatively recent invention.

Life used to be so easy. If one saw something to eat, one grabbed it and stuffed it in one's mouth. When nature called, the response was immediate, regardless of where one happened to be. If one's nose was full of mucous, one simply blew it out.

BLOW-BY-BLOW DESCRIPTION
But then, during the Middle Ages, everything began to change. The rise of the nobility led to rigorous rules of propriety, or "court-esy," a way for nobles and courtiers to differentiate themselves from peasants and the common folks.

All of a sudden, everything a man or woman did was prescribed by a set of increasingly complicated rules. People started eating with utensils instead of their hands, their place at table was rigidly defined according to their rank—and bodily functions became taboo. One medieval text goes so far as to advise gentlemen not to spit upon the dinner table, but to do it only under the table or against the wall.

NO LONGER A FIVE-FINGER EXERCISE
Ditto blowing one's nose (into one's hands, where else?) over the dinner table or wiping one's nose on the tablecloth. Later, delicacy dictated that the hand used for nose blowing not be the one used for taking food from the common platter. A nice idea. As time went on, nose blowing became even more regulated: Now etiquette demanded that the nose be blown with only three fingers, rather than with the entire hand. You can see where this is leading.

HERE COME THE HANDY WIPES
Finally, the 15th century—and civilization—arrived. A guide to manners read:

> Any courtois [courtly person] who wishes to blow his nose should beautify himself with a cloth. When he is eating or serving he should not blow through his fingers.

It's believed that the first person to use an actual handkerchief was a fashionable Italian lady who, with too much time on her hands, cut herself a fabric square of pure flax (linen) and embellished it with lace. This created quite a stir among her aristocratic friends (hey, they didn't have TV to occupy their time—they had to find *something* to get excited about).

In that same century, theologian (and astute commentator on human vulgarity) Erasmus of Rotterdam wrote:

> *To blow your nose on your hat or clothing is rustic, and to do so with the arm or elbow befits a tradesman; nor is it much more polite to use the hand if you immediately smear the snot on your garment. It is proper to wipe the nostrils with a handkerchief, and to do this while turning away, if more honorable people are present.*

WHAT A CONCEPT!
The handkerchief seemed like such a good idea, that its use quickly spread throughout Europe. And because they were so expensive, only the very rich had them. In 1594, Henry IV, the king of France, owned five of them. This seemed like an outrageous extravagance. We're not talking plain cotton cloths, here. These handkerchiefs were made of the most expensive fabrics, embellished with fine lace and elaborately embroidered. It was almost a shame to blow your nose in one.

HIP TO BE SQUARE
The Sun King, Louis XIV, was the first person to keep a large supply of them on hand. During his reign, their use became widespread among the nobility.

A few Louises later, Marie Antoinette decided that a square shape for a handkerchief was more esthetically pleasing than a rectangular one. Dutifully, Louis XVI, her hubby, decreed that handkerchiefs throughout the kingdom should only be as wide as they are long. Even after the royal pair lost their heads during the French Revolution, and nearly all institutions collapsed, the square handkerchief concept remained.

HIS & HERS HANKIES
As handkerchiefs became more common, traditions grew up

Pure metaphor: The Underground Railroad wasn't underground and wasn't a railroad.

around them. It was a common ploy of a flirtatious woman to acci-
dentally-on-purpose drop her hankie in front of an eligible man.
He was then honor bound to pick it up and return it—thereby, presumably, giving the woman the opportunity to bat her eyelashes.

The modern man's suit jacket almost always sports a small
pocket on the left breast. It was never intended to hold pens, cigarettes, or a comb. Instead, it was supposed to display the very tip
of a folded handkerchief, usually made of silk and coordinated to
enhance the rest of the outfit.

FIRST GOLF, NOW THIS!

But perhaps the most mind-blowing bit of nose-blowing history
can be found in the National Archives of Scotland, where a five-
page document, dated 1810 to 1815, is devoted entirely to military
instructions on how a soldier on parade should blow his nose.

It suggests that the fourth buttonhole from a soldier's chin be
"significantly enlarged, so as to afford free ingress and egress of the
Nose." A handkerchief is to be hidden behind this buttonhole;
then the soldier only needs to drop his head to perform the nose-
blowing operation.

The document goes on to list the various types of noses: the
Grecian nose, the Roman, the Magazine, the Carbuncle or
Magnum Bonum, the Broccoli, the Sweetbread, the full Battoned,
the Oblique or twisted, the Trunk, the Trumpet, and the
Extinguisher, all of which can be accommodated by the enlarged
buttonhole and the method specified.

4-F, SCOTS STYLE

But, the article further states, proprietors of noses that cannot
easily accommodate the method are unfit for military service:

> The upright, foreshortened, snubbed, or what is vulgarly called the
> Pug Nose is unquestionably the most impracticable for a Soldier.
> The Proprietors of such Noses should therefore be totally excluded
> from every well-regulated Regiment, for they would infallibly dis-
> grace the Corps, and tarnish the Cloth. This category includes the
> Pug, the Tartar, the Snub, the Button, the Button Snub, the Pickled
> Mushroom, the Snout, the Truncated ...the broken Back, the
> Pudding, the Wafer, the Pancake, and the Invisible.

The first victim of the guillotine was a highwayman named Nicolas Pelletier, on April 25, 1792.

KILLER FLU

*Nothing in known history has ever killed so many people
so fast as the influenza virus of 1918.*

D uring ten months in 1918 and 1919, a strain of influenza
killed between 20 and 40 million people, ten times more
than the bubonic plague's toll back in the Middle Ages.
The virus was called "the Spanish flu" because of the millions of
early cases reported there. Worldwide one out of every five people
contracted it; in the United States the figure was one out of every
three people. Check with your grandparents—wherever you're
from, chances are that someone in your family had it and maybe
even died from it.

OVER THERE
In 1918, thousands of young men were crowded into army camps
in the United States and in the trenches of World War I Europe.
A virulent flu outbreak swept through the camps and by year's
end, more American soldiers had died of the flu than had died
fighting in the war during that same period.

That August, a second, deadlier wave of Spanish flu hit.
During one week, a few people sickened and died in three port
cities around the world: Boston, Massachusetts; Freetown in Sierra
Leone, and Brest, France. Within weeks, dozens, hundreds, and
then thousands of people were dead.

ONLY THE STRONG DON'T SURVIVE
Viruses are usually most dangerous to children and the elderly
because their immune systems are either still developing or
declining with age. A bizarre twist to the 1918 pandemic (an epidemic gone global) was that it killed so many healthy, young men
and women—often within hours. Scientists have figured out that
the 1918 bug partially disabled the victims' immune systems, but
exactly how it killed so many so fast remains a secret.

TAKING ITS TOLL
The flu mutated constantly and killed quickly. Stories of horror

and hope abounded. Mothers died, leaving their babies untended. Small children nursed entire families back to health. Families dug their own graves and coffins were reused, either by adding a new body to one already there, or in the case of undertakers, using a coffin in a funeral, then burying the body and using the coffin in another funeral. And this wasn't done secretly; there just weren't enough coffins to go around.

THE BOTTOM LINE
It's estimated that 675,000 Americans died from both influenza and pneumonia in the epidemic; worldwide, the official tally was 21 million. The real total could be double that number or even more for a couple of reasons. In 1918, many parts of the world couldn't accurately keep records or even count dead bodies, and secondly, many people died from heart attacks, diabetes complications, or diseases like bronchitis that may have been caused by the flu.

THE VERY LATEST WORD
In 2004, scientists managed to re-create the DNA of the Spanish flu in a laboratory. Their research proves that the Spanish flu originated with birds, which partially explains its devastating nature. Bird flus have certain features that make them especially deadly to human populations: the way the flu neutralizes antibodies, for instance, or the way the virus binds to host receptors in the body. The virus is still being studied; there are still mysteries to solve before another bird flu hits.

* * * * *

WASHINGTON'S MEN GET NEEDLED

In 1777, General George Washington ordered smallpox vaccinations for the entire Continental Army, and some 3,000 to 4,000 men were inoculated. Smallpox vaccination was still a new and controversial procedure, and few American doctors then believed in it. Washington himself had been a victim of an earlier smallpox infection, and his decision to inoculate his troops probably saved more lives than the total number killed in battle.

Danish biologist Wilhelm Johanssen (1857–1927) coined the term "genes" in 1909.

A PLAIN HISTORY OF THE AMISH

Wherefore come out from among them and be ye separate.

Amish roots go back 500 years to the Protestant Reformation in Europe when a radical group of Swiss Protestants, the Anabaptists, split from other Protestants. *Anabaptist* means "baptized again"; the Anabaptists, who'd been baptized into the Catholic faith as infants, were rebaptized as adults in their new faith.

The Amish are a splinter group of Anabaptists begun by Jakob Amman (hence the name) in 1693. Amman's followers wanted a stricter separation from the world in order to better preserve their identity as a religious community. And they got it.

IT'S NOT EASY BEING AMISH

Swiss and German Anabaptists and Amish were persecuted in Europe. Their belief that infant baptism was invalid because the infant hadn't made the choice to follow Christ was a direct challenge to both Roman Catholicism and Lutheranism: rebaptism was punishable by public execution. Because they believed literally in turning the other cheek and not fighting, they refused military service and, in Germany, were imprisoned for it.

Believers were hunted down, imprisoned, and/or killed. Today, every Amish household has *The Martyrs Mirror*, a book that recounts the atrocities against their ancestors and strengthens their faith.

A MATTER OF LIFE OR DEATH

Given the choice between being burned at the stake, starved to death, mutilated, drowned, tied up in sacks and thrown in the river—or leaving for America, it's not surprising that there are no Amish left in Europe today.

The Amish came from Switzerland, the Alsace region of France, and Germany's Rhine valley as part of a larger migration of German-speaking people. William Penn himself had traveled up the Rhine recruiting colonists to Pennsylvania with the promise of

---

Princeton University statistician John W. Tukey coined the term "software" in 1958.

religious freedom. The first Amish arrived in the colonies in the early 1700s, and more came in the 1800s after they heard about the success of American Amish communities.

THEY MUST BE DOING SOMETHING RIGHT
Now, 150,000 Amish live in 20 U.S. states and in Ontario, Canada; 75 percent live in Ohio, Pennsylvania, and Indiana. The communities are still growing, especially in the last 50 years. The Amish have large families that average seven children—and 80 percent of the offspring remain in the Amish faith.

NO CAN DO
Amish communities don't forbid new technology just because it's new, and not all Amish communities have the same rules as to what's allowed and what isn't. The Amish look at every new innovation from the standpoint of how it will affect the togetherness of their communities and their religious beliefs.

The horse and buggy keep the Amish close to each other and close to the land. Their plain clothes foster humility and group identity rather than individualism. Visiting in person is preferable to using the telephone.

Other rules and traditions that most Amish follow are:

- No televisions, radios, or movies that would bring outside values into the Amish home
- No jewelry, including wedding rings
- No buttons on clothing (At the time this rule was started, buttons on clothes were ornate like jewelry.)
- No musical instruments. Singing is allowed but not solos or singing in harmony, because it encourages pride.
- No flying on airplanes
- No central heating at home
- No wall-to-wall carpeting
- No electricity from public power lines
- No toasters, microwaves, blenders, coffeemakers, or dishwashers (but propane refrigerators are allowed)
- No picture taking or possessing photographs of people
- No makeup; no shaved legs or armpits
- No haircutting at all for women. Men may grow beards after

marriage but are not permitted mustaches (because mustaches were associated with the military).
- No owning or driving cars, but riding in them, when necessary, is okay.
- No life, health, or accident insurance
- No daylight saving time

HECK NO, WE WON'T GO!
Amish beliefs are frequently at odds with Uncle Sam's. Participation in war or violence of any kind is forbidden; the Amish won't take a human life even in self-defense. Although the Amish qualified as conscientious objectors during World War I, they were sent to military camps because the law didn't provide for any other type of service. Some commanding officers tried to bully them into changing their minds, and a lot of them were abused for refusing to take rifle training or wear the army uniform. But during World War II, as conscientious objectors, the Amish were allowed to perform public service as civilians.

SCHOOL'S OUT
There are no Amish doctors, lawyers, veterinarians, or any other occupation that requires higher education. In fact, the last year an Amish child may go to public school is eighth grade because high schools teach science and sex education, have physical education classes requiring gym clothes, and use videos as teaching tools—all of which are objectionable. As technology becomes more pervasive in public schools in all grades, the Amish prefer to use their own schools, which are close to home and employ Amish teachers. Children learn the three Rs along with farming, woodworking, or another Amish trade.

State laws that require children to attend school to age 16 used to pose a problem. In 1972, however, in the case of *Wisconsin v. Yoder*, the U.S. Supreme Court ruled that the right of the Amish to their religious practices was more important than a state's interest in having an educated citizenry.

HOW ABOUT SIGNING THIS PATRIOT ACT?
The Amish usually vote in local elections only. They don't sing the national anthem or recite the Pledge of Allegiance. They don't run

for public office, serve on juries, or file lawsuits to collect debts.

The Amish refuse Social Security, Medicare, and other forms of governmental assistance. They believe that they should care for each other voluntarily.

JUST PLAIN RADICAL

In 1955, when the government extended Social Security taxes to include the self-employed (such as farmers), many Amish refused to pay—even after the IRS confiscated their farms and farming equipment. In 1965, Amish lobbying resulted in an exemption. Later, Amish employers got an exemption from contributing to Social Security for their Amish employees. The exemption applies to any religious group that opposes Social Security and which provides for their own elderly—an exemption that applies only to the Amish.

HOW THE AMISH HALF LIVES

Despite modernization—or maybe because of it—the Amish are thriving. The four million tourists who visit Lancaster County, Pennsylvania, every year to see Amish life up close bring in a cool $30,000 (about 24,787 euros) for every Amish resident of the county.

The traffic, of course, interferes with buggy travel, and tourism is an intrusion. But the Amish have adapted by selling wood products, quilts, and traditional foods to the visitors. Where farms have become too expensive to buy and farm income too low, Amish men work in factories. In Indiana, many Amish men work building recreational vehicles and mobile homes. The Amish have made the adaptations necessary to maintain their core principles and their way of life.

It's ironic—but somehow comforting—that in the 21st century of computers and space travel, there are more Amish people in more Amish communities than there were in the so-called horse-and-buggy days.

* * * * *

"An Amish woman told me, 'Making a batch of vegetable soup, it's not right for the carrot to say I taste better than the peas, or the pea to say I taste better than the cabbage. It takes all the vegetables to make a good soup!'"—Sue Bender, *Plain and Simple Wisdom*

The Diadochi were generals of Alexander the Great who sought power after his death.

WHERE ARE THEY NOW?

The Goths

Dear Uncle John,

I thought that Goths were an ancient people who fought with Rome. But when I went to a wedding of two Goths last Sunday, the groom wore a skull mask and the bride wore black. Were they really Goths?

Confused

Dear Confused,

The Goths of early Europe were a tall, fair-haired people who probably came from Scandinavia. They were nomadic and wandered around northeastern Europe for several centuries before settling near the Black Sea. The Romans regarded the fierce Goths—who were still mainly in the hunter-gatherer stage—as rude, frightening barbarians. The Goths felt the same way about the Huns, who'd driven them out of Romania and terrified them in battle. In 300 B.C., a group of Goths sought Roman protection. They received protection and land in exchange for service in the Roman army.

The Goths were a freedom-loving people who soon resented Roman attempts to exploit them. They rebelled and got their revenge at the Battle of Adrianople, where they defeated the Roman army and gained increasing power within the empire. In A.D. 410, a young Gothic general in the Roman army named Alaric led another Goth rebellion. But this time the Goths went straight through the gates of Rome where they sacked the Eternal City (and the heart of the empire) for three days.

Though the Goths hastened the fall of the Roman Empire, they preserved its art and culture in their kingdoms until they also fell from power. In the eighth century, Goths disappeared from history as a separate people and were assimilated into the peoples of modern France and Germany—where you can still find them.

As for that Goth wedding, the couple's attire probably had less to do with the ancient Goths than with the term "Gothic," which by medieval times had come to mean anything crude and barbaric.

The Maltese alphabet contains 29 letters but does not contain the Latin letter y.

HOLLYWOOD REWRITES HISTORY: *GLADIATOR*

*A disclaimer at the end of the credits says that the story is
"based on historical fact [but] the story itself is fictional."
We've still got a few bones to pick.*

The Rewrite: The Roman soldiers wear red tunics under their armor.
The Facts: Dyed clothing was reserved for the elite; Roman soldiers would have worn undyed tunics.

The Rewrite: In the battle against Germania, the Roman soldiers stay behind their shields with their *pila* (heavy javelins) pointed against the enemy—as the Germans approach, the soldiers don't throw the javelins. Then, when the Germans are upon them, they break rank.
The Facts: The formation was correct. But the Roman soldiers would have thrown their javelins as the Germans approached and then would have lunged with their swords while staying under cover of their shields. The formation would never have collapsed the way it did, especially against barbarians who were far better at hand-to-hand combat than the soldiers.

The Rewrite: A sign at the battle scene is marked Praetoria XIV.
The Facts: The year was A.D. 180. The subtractive form of Roman numerals (using *IV* for 4, *IX* for 9, and so on) was used only as an alternative form at the time; Praetoria IIII would most likely have been used on official signs and banners.

The Rewrite: After the Romans win the battle, Maximus (Russell Crowe) shouts, "*Roma victor!*"
The Facts: *Roma* is feminine, so *victor* should have been feminine, too: Maximus should have yelled, *Roma victrix!*

The Rewrite: Marcus Aurelius (Richard Harris) shows Maximus a sword with his own name spelled as MARCUS AURELIUS.
The Facts: The Latin alphabet used *V* to stand for *U, V,* and *W.* The inscription should have read MARCVS AVRELIVS. The letters *U* and *W* were added to the alphabet during the Middle Ages.

The Rewrite: There are several points in the film that show horses with stirrups (even a horse that had been pulling a chariot turns out to have them).
The Facts: Either way, the Europeans didn't use stirrups (a Chinese invention) until the Middle Ages.

The Rewrite: An injured Maximus, now a slave and gladiator-in-training, is carried in a cart drawn by horses.
The Facts: Horses were not used as draft animals, certainly not to carry slaves; instead asses, mules, and oxen were deployed.

The Rewrite: Maximus has a tattoo of the symbol of Rome on his upper arm: SPQR, which stands for *Senatus Populusque Romanus* (the Senate and the people of Rome).
The Facts: A Roman would never wear a tattoo; only barbarians wore them.

The Rewrite: In Rome, Proximo shows Maximus the sword that symbolizes his freedom; it reads "Proximo."
The Facts: *Proximo* on the sword means "*to* Proximus." So Proximo really should have been called Proximus—along with Maximus, Commodus, Gracchus, and all the other guys.

The Rewrite: Before his true identity is revealed, Maximus is nicknamed "the Spaniard."
The Facts: There was no Spain at the time; if they thought he was from the area that is now Spain, they would have called him "the Iberian."

The Rewrite: Groups of gladiators are pitted against each other both in North Africa and Rome.
The Facts: Even small-time gladiators were too valuable an asset to risk their deaths, especially to entertain a few hundred

non-Romans. A gladiator's death could mean financial ruin for his owner. A successful gladiator in Rome would be as valuable (and as wealthy and popular) as an NBA or NFL star today; his life would only rarely be put in danger.

The Rewrite: The streets of Rome look as if they're covered with sand.
The Facts: The streets of Rome were paved with stones.

The Rewrite: The very top of the Coliseum is ringed with flags on poles.
The Facts: The poles were not flagpoles: they held pulleys that were part of a mechanism that rolled a covering over the arena to protect spectators from the sun.

The Rewrite: There are flyers everywhere, advertising GLADIATORES VIOLENTIA.
The Facts: For one thing, the Romans used handwritten scrolls that were much too expensive to have been handed out on the street or in the arena. If something were to be publicized, it would have been written directly on the walls or announced by a town crier. Also, the term *gladiatores violentia* is meaningless in any language, including Latin.

The Rewrite: An assassin puts a red striped snake into a senator's bed.
The Facts: The snake is a scarlet ring snake, native to the Americas, and it is not poisonous.

Possible Rewrite: The spectators use the thumbs-up sign for a gladiator they favor and signaled thumbs down for those they want to see killed. Regardless of what movie reviewers (and the rest of the world) think, historians have never been able to pin down which gesture stands for what. The only documentation refers to turning the thumb—without saying which way.

Mickey Marcus is the only person buried at West Point who died fighting under a foreign flag.

CHIPS OFF THE OLD BLOCK? PART 2

For Part 1 of this story see page 195.

HAPPY FAMILIES, SOVIET-STYLE (Stalin's kids)

The Soviet dictator Stalin may have been the Father of the Nation, but he wasn't much of a father to his own kids: one committed suicide, one drank himself to death, and the third defected to the West the first chance she got. Well, when your pa is a paranoid psychopath, what do you expect?

Bathroom Breakdown

The eldest Djugashvili child (*Stalin* was a pseudonym adopted by Joseph Djugashvili before the 1917 revolution) was Yakov. He was born to Stalin's first wife, Ekaterina, who died when Yakov was still a child. Stalin was never close to his first-born, and following Yakov's unsuccessful suicide attempt in the 1920s, Stalin came to despise his "weakling" son. When the Soviet Union went to war with Germany in 1941, Yakov was called up—and quickly captured. When the Germans offered to exchange Yakov for a high-ranking Nazi prisoner of war, Joseph Stalin refused. His reply was "There are no prisoners of war; there are only traitors." Gee, thanks, Dad.

What happened next is shrouded in mystery. In one version (tailor-made for the Bathroom Readers' Hysterical Society), Yakov was mercilessly taunted by fellow British POWs over his, shall we say, poor potty training. They were constantly complaining about the mess he made in the stalls. One day in 1943, legend has it, the teasing got too much, and Yakov flung himself onto the electrified fence surrounding the camp. More recently, U.S. intelligence papers have been released that claim he was shot while trying to escape from the camp. Either way, it was definitely not a dignified end.

Flying into Trouble

Stalin tried a little harder with his second son, Vasily. He was the product of Stalin's second marriage, to Nadezhda Alliluyeva, who committed suicide in 1932. Vasily was sent into the military, and

---

He assisted Israel in its 1948 War of Independence.

although he wasn't overly blessed with brains, his father made him an air force general. He even made it onto the cover of *Time* magazine in 1951, looking heroic while posing against a Soviet jet plane. But, behind the military bearing, Vasily was just as emotionally damaged as his mother and his half brother, Yakov.

Vasily's way of forgetting that his father was possibly the most evil man on Earth was to turn to drink. When he was placed under psychiatric care, a doctor wrote to Stalin to tell him his son was suicidal. It took Dad 33 months to reply. When Stalin died in 1953, Vasily's problems only got worse. The new regime had it in for the Stalins. They falsely accused Vasily of making anti-Soviet statements and of financial abuses. The poor guy was sentenced to eight years in prison in 1955; he died shortly after his release in 1962.

Runaway Bride

Svetlana, Stalin's only daughter, fared slightly better than Vasily. Born in 1926, she had her first run-in with Pops when she was just 16. She'd fallen in love with Alexei Kapler, a Jewish filmmaker. Stalin, a notorious anti-Semite, went crazy when he found out; the boyfriend was packed off to a Siberian labor camp, where he died. The following year, Svetlana, now a student at Moscow University, announced she was in love with Jewish fellow student Grigori Mozorov. This time, Stalin grudgingly allowed the couple to marry. They had a son, Joseph, in 1945, and they divorced two years later.

In 1949, Sveltana married Yuri Zhdanov, the son of Stalin's right-hand man, Andrei Zhdanov. But this marriage, possibly undertaken to please Stalin, was dissolved shortly afterward. Following her father's death, Svetlana adopted her mother's maiden name of Alliluyeva (which means "hallelujah!") and worked quietly as a teacher and translator in Moscow. In 1964, she married Brajesh Singh, an Indian who was a Communist and a resident of Moscow. When Singh returned to India, Svetlana wasn't allowed to go with him. When he died in 1966, she was allowed to visit his remains in India—and while she was there, Svetlana took the opportunity to defect.

Svetlana eventually settled in the United States where, in 1970, she married architect William Wesley Peters and began calling herself Lana Peters. Inevitably, this liaison also ended in

---

The geology of the Grand Canyon area includes more than 40 identified rock layers.

divorce. During her time in exile, Svetlana wrote several books denouncing the Soviet regime—and her father. At last sighting, Svetlana was living in a retirement home in the United Kingdom, no doubt reflecting on her long and eventful life.

VOODOO CHILD (Baby Doc Duvalier)

Most of the kids we've come across so far have mercifully failed to follow in their fathers' footsteps. Unfortunately for the people of Haiti, there was one son who almost outdid the father in the crazy-as-a-loon stakes.

What's Up, Doc?

François "Papa Doc" Duvalier was not your typical head of state. For a start, the man who ruled the Caribbean state of Haiti from 1957 to 1971 was a voodoo priest. He also had his own private army, the Tontons Macoutes, which, according to one estimate, disposed of 30,000 of Papa Doc's subjects during his reign. When he died in 1971 (and, surprisingly, failed to rise zombielike from the grave), Haitians breathed a sigh of relief—until they found out that Papa Doc's 19-year-old son, Jean-Claude "Baby Doc" Duvalier, was taking over the family butcher's business.

If anything, Baby Doc was worse than his father. For a start, he was more interested in motorbikes than politics and would race his souped-up hogs around the palace gardens for fun, as hapless gardeners leaped out of the way. When he did apply his mind to affairs of state, it was usually to work out the best way of embezzling the country's oil and agriculture revenues. While Baby Doc was plundering the national cash register, Haiti was becoming one of the world's poorest countries.

French Leave

In 1986, following a rigged election (Baby Doc got 99 percent of the vote), the people of Haiti decided enough was enough. They took to the streets—well, many of them already lived on the streets anyway—and Jean-Claude fled for his life. He eventually pitched up in France—which let him in but refused to grant him asylum. He was, in effect, a sort of semi-illegal alien.

Despite arriving in France with half of his country's national wealth stashed away, Baby Doc managed to eventually lose it all.

Dallas District Attorney Henry Wade never lost a case until *Roe v. Wade*.

In one police raid on a villa in which he and his shopaholic wife were staying, a notebook was recovered detailing recent spending: $168,000 on clothes at Givenchy, $270,000 on jewelry, $9,752 on two Hermes kid-sized horse saddles, and $68,000 on an antique clock.

A Bad Debt Always Follows You
When his money ran out in the early 1990s, so did Baby Doc. He was last spotted in public hurriedly leaving a hotel in the French Riviera resort of Mougins in 1995. He did not pay his bill. He is believed to still be living in France and occasionally gives interviews (via his lawyer) in which he reflects nostalgically on his time in charge of Haiti. In 2002, he announced he wanted to return to Haiti and stand for president. When asked what he did wrong in the past, he answered, "Perhaps I was too tolerant." Indifferent is more like it.

* * * * *

THANKS, POP!

J. Paul Getty III, the grandson of oil billionaire J. Paul Getty, was kidnapped as a teenager in 1973 by the Italian Red Brigades, who demanded a $3.2 million ransom. When the family balked at paying, the kidnappers cut off the boy's right ear and sent it to a Rome newspaper. The family then paid a $1 million ransom and Jean Paul III was released after being held hostage for five months.

* * * * *

A PLANFUL PATER

"I must study politics and war that my sons may have liberty to study mathematics and philosophy. My sons ought to study mathematics and philosophy, geography, natural history, naval architecture, navigation, commerce and agriculture in order to give their children a right to study painting, poetry, music, architecture, statuary, tapestry, and porcelain."—John Adams

Most "tin cans" are actually made mostly of steel, with a thin layer of tin to prevent corrosion.

GUERRILLA WARFARE PART 5

Delta Force

D elta Force was formed in 1977 by the legendary Special Forces commando Colonel Charles "Chargin' Charlie" Beckwith, in response to terrorist activities in the 1970s. The unit was modeled after the British SAS (Special Air Service), one of the most elite special forces units in the world. Delta Force is a counterterrorist unit specializing in hostage rescue and reconnaissance, equipped with the most advanced weaponry and equipment available in the U.S. special ops arsenal.

Delta Force "operators" are recruited from the U.S. Army, mainly from the Green Berets and Rangers. The exact composition and strength of Delta Force is a closely guarded secret. For years, the existence of Delta Force was officially denied—though it was known that the unit took part in the failed attempt to rescue American hostages in Iran in 1979.

The unit conducted successful hostage rescue operations during the invasions of Grenada (1983) and Panama (1989), and participated in the first Iraq war (1991), although the full extent of what they did there has not been revealed. What is known is that Delta operators provided security for senior U.S. officers and officials, including General Norman Schwarzkopf, and took part in the hunt for SCUD missile launchers inside Iraq.

BLACK HAWK DOWN

In 1994, UN relief efforts in Somalia were being hampered by local warlords. UN troops were sent to protect the humanitarian workers, among them a group of Pakistani troops who were ambushed and killed. So Army Rangers and Delta Force launched a mission to capture the most powerful warlord—General Mohammed Farrah Adid—and several of his lieutenants. But during the mission two Black Hawk helicopters were shot down. The mission then changed to rescuing the crews from the downed choppers.

Two Delta snipers circling above in a helicopter volunteered to defend one of the crash sites that was about to be overrun by Somali gunmen. They knew it was probably a suicide mission, but they agreed to be dropped off at the crash site because they could see that at least one of the American soldiers there was still alive. They held off hundreds of Somali gunmen until they were overrun and killed. They saved the life of the chopper pilot, Michael Durant, who was captured by the gunmen and later released. The snipers, Master Sergeant Gary Ivan Gordon and Sergeant First Class Randall D. Shughart, were each awarded the Medal of Honor posthumously for their extraordinary heroism.

By the time the Rangers and Delta Force operators arrived at the crash areas and set up defensive perimeters, they were surrounded by hostile natives and under near-constant attack. They were trapped in the city overnight and suffered heavy casualties. But the next morning, a relief force arrived, led by the 10th Infantry Division, and they managed to fight their way out, along what became known as the Mogadishu Mile.

AFGHANISTAN AND THE INVASION OF IRAQ

Before the war in Afghanistan began in 2002, Delta operators were sent to the major cities and contested areas in the north to do reconnaissance. During and after the war, Delta Force searched for the leaders of the Taliban and Al Qaeda, including Mullah Omar and Osama bin Laden.

Just before the second Iraq war in early 2003, Delta Force operators entered Baghdad and established a network of informants, while also eavesdropping on and sabotaging Iraqi communications lines. During the invasion, they searched for senior Iraqi officials and weapons of mass destruction. After the capture of Saddam Airport (now Baghdad International Airport), Delta Force set up a secret Battlefield Interrogation Facility for insurgents and suspected terrorists; it went under investigation by the Pentagon inspector general's office for allegations of torture and other prisoner abuses.

For more in the series, see "Guerrilla Warfare Part 6"—Navy SEALS—on page 291.

ALL THAT JAZZ

*Today, jazz is an American institution, but at the turn of
the 20th century, it was known as the devil's music—
immoral and dangerous. See how much you know about
jazz's journey from the underground to uptown.*

1. Roving jazz bands on the streets of 1920s New Orleans would
   challenge each other to public duels for the prize of:
   a. "Le toit est sur le feu"—a crown of purple and yellow flowers
   b. A kiss on the hand from every unmarried lady in the crowd
   c. Spare change
   d. Nightclub attendance
   e. Sunday "morning after" breakfast at the loser's expense

2. Which types of music helped create jazz?
   a. African American slave songs
   b. Blues
   c. Ragtime
   d. Marching band tunes
   e. All of 'em, baby

3. Which one of these cities is *not* considered a major birthplace
   of jazz?
   a. New Orleans, Louisiana
   b. New York, New York
   c. Chicago, Illinois
   d. Memphis, Tennessee
   e. Kansas City, Missouri

4. Technically speaking, what was so melodically different about
   jazz when it came out?
   a. The audience influenced what the band was playing
   b. It was improvisational; not played precisely from sheet music
   c. It drew listeners from all races, regions, and socioeconomic
      backgrounds
   d. It was polyrhythmic, employing contrasting rhythms in each
      tune
   e. All of 'em, baby

The catchphrase "Kowabunga!" was popularized by the NBC program *Howdy Doody.*

5. In 1926, the *Saturday Evening Post* ran an advertisement for:
   a. Jazz-resistant fedoras, to protect you from "immoral thoughts"
   b. Jazz-proof furniture
   c. Antijazz protest signs warning of a jazz-induced apocalypse
   d. "It's Never Jazz Time in the House of the Lord" pocket watches
   e. Cecil B. DeMille's Thou Shalt Not Jazz rally

6. Match these jazz geniuses with their mellifluous melodies:
   1. Count Basie   a. "So What"
   2. Miles Davis   b. "Rockit"
   3. John Coltrane   c. "'Round Midnight"
   4. Thelonious Monk   d. "One O'Clock Jump"
   5. Herbie Hancock   e. "A Love Supreme"

7. During the Roaring Twenties, jazz music was *not* popularly associated with:
   a. Seedy, smoky cabarets
   b. Lazy nonconformists
   c. Urban and industrial society
   d. The goatee
   e. Dancing

8. Many talented New Orleans–based jazz musicians—such as Louis Armstrong, Jelly Roll Morton, and Albert Glenny—made a decent living at times playing in:
   a. Hotels
   b. Cruise ship lounges
   c. Houses of ill repute
   d. Government buildings
   e. The street

9. Which of these is not a real form of contemporary jazz?
   a. Tap jazz
   b. Hard bop
   c. Fusion
   d. Free jazz
   e. Cool jazz

For answers, see page 481.

A HAIR-RAISING STORY

*Most of us use stuff in and on our hair to
make it look better. But what's the history of all these
contraptions and concoctions?*

DYE JOBS

Men and women have been altering the color of their hair since
ancient times. Early Babylonians powdered their hair with fine
gold dust, yellow pollen, or yellow flour. Roman women in the
first century A.D. went for dark, shiny locks, so they colored their
hair with dyes made from boiled walnuts and leeks.

Up until the 1900s, those who wanted to change the shade of
their hair used herbs and natural dyes. All that changed in 1907
when French chemist Eugene Schueller developed the first synthetic hair dye. He called it "Aureole" and sold it through his
newly created company with a name that carried an automatic
disclaimer: the French Harmless Hair Dye Company. The product
didn't sell well at first. But one year later, people were warming up
to the product, and Eugene changed the name of his company to
the shorter, snappier-sounding L'Oreal.

During the 1950s, hair dyeing was considered something only
cheap and flashy women did. That is, until the Clairol company
started a campaign to promote the product as something a *respectable*
woman would use. All their early advertisements featured a child,
which suggested that the model with the colored hair was a mother
and, therefore, an honorable woman. Today, 75 percent of American
women have dyed their hair at one point or another in their lives.

HAIRPINS

Bone hairpins worn during the Roman era served a double purpose. They held a woman's hair in place, but they also concealed
poison in their hollowed-out centers. Some historians think that
Cleopatra—who loved her jeweled, ivory hairpins—might have
used this style of pin to conceal the poison she used to kill herself
unless she used an asp instead.

Fritz the Cat was the first X-rated animated feature.

But hairpins were used for centuries before Cleopatra, the Romans, or the Greeks. Ancient tribes, like primitive tribes today, used animal spines and thistle thorns to hold their hair in place. The early Asians used iron, bronze, gold, silver, or bone hairpins.

The use of hairpins increased during the 17th century because wigs were the look of the day. Wig wearers of both sexes had to pin their real hair tightly so their wigs would fit well. Soon hairpins were referred to as bobbing pins (as in bobbed hair). A hundred years later, the English shortened the name to bobby pins. The two-prong, lacquered-steel bobby pins we use today began being mass-produced during the 19th century and were introduced to America in 1916—so handy for the post-World War I "bobbed" hairstyles.

THE HAIR DRYER

Ancient kings and queens probably had slaves to fan their hair dry, but everyone else had to let theirs air-dry. Until, that is, the idea of blowing hair dry was posed in vacuum cleaner ads in the 1920s. What could be easier than plugging the hose into the hot-air exhaust after you'd cleaned the house with your new Pneumatic Cleaner?

The first hand-held, electric hair dryer had to wait for the invention of a smaller, lighter motor. A German inventor, whose name is lost to history, created his version in the 1920s: a relatively huge appliance made from a nickel-covered electric heater placed on an asbestos board, with a compact version of a vacuum cleaner motor. A brown, wooden handle made it possible for women to lift this new product of beauty—and dry their hair while toning their biceps.

By the early 1930s, hair dryers began to look a little more like modern-day appliances. The handle was still wood, but now it was painted black, to match the color of the hair dryer. The introduction of a plastic motor and fan switch made the dryer lighter, but it was still much heavier than modern ones. (In fact, the hair dryer was the first domestic electrical appliance to use plastics.) Some of the fancier dryers included built-in mirrors and deodorizers.

The rigid hood-type hair dryer, like the ones used in beauty salons, didn't come along until the 1950s. Ditto the soft plastic head bag dryer, which was connected to a motor and fan that could be slung over a woman's shoulder like a purse.

People who collect thimbles are known as digitabulists.

But it wasn't until the late 1960s that the hand held dryer took off. Know why? Because all of a sudden, *men* had to deal with the angst of drying and styling long hair. Now—long hair or not, used every day or never—just about every home in America has one.

STYLING AND CURLING

Thousands of years ago, the Malagasy people, of what is now called Madagascar, stiffened their hair with a mixture of honey and animal fat. Around 500 B.C., West Africans used clay as a setting gel and sticks as curlers. In 1500 B.C., Assyrian slaves fire-heated iron bars to curl the hair of kings, warriors, and noble-women. We've come a long way since then. Take a look.

1759: American Enoch Noyes created the first commercially sold combs. He made them out of flattened animal horns.

1789: Ivory combs were created and sold by Andrew Lord. He cut each of the comb's teeth with a handsaw.

1905: Charles Nestle invented the first machine that created temporary waves for hair.

1928: African American inventor Majorie Joyner (who worked for Madame Walker) patented the first permanent-wave machine. (For Madame Walker's story, see *Uncle John's Bathroom Reader Plunges into Great Lives*.)

1930: African American inventor Solomon Harper created thermostatically controlled hair curlers.

1943: Lyle David Goodhue and W. N. Sullivan developed a small aerosol can pressurized by a liquefied gas, which made the use of hairspray possible. In the 1950s, Robert H. Abplanal invented the first pump spray bottle.

1972: The hair crimper was created by Geri Cusenza.

1980: The curling iron was patented by Theora Stephens.

HATS OFF TO MUSTAFA KEMAL!

A nation can be defined by many things–its history,
its food, its culture. But how many can be summed up
by its choice of headgear?

L et's talk Turkey—the country, not the bird. It's a land steeped
in history. Constantinople was in Turkey, so was Byzantium—
in fact, they're the same place, and today that place is known
as Istanbul. Then there's Troy. You thought it was in Greece, right?
Wrong—it's in Turkey too! With a culture stretching back at least
3,000 years, there was nothing the Turks liked better than a bit of
tradition. That is, until Mustafa Kemal came along.

TURKISH DELIGHT
Turkey had been ruled for hundreds of years by the Ottoman dynasty,
which fulfilled every Western cliché of the Near East: it was ruled by
a sultan and everyone wore turbans, followed Islam, and lived in
plump-cushioned, harem-filled, incense-smelling splendor. In 1826,
Sultan Mahmud II introduced the fez. This small, conical hat, made
of purple or scarlet felt and topped with a tassel, replaced the turban.
But other than that, nothing had changed for centuries.

LEFTOVER TURKEY
The Ottomans had once governed an enormous empire that covered the entire Middle East and most of North Africa; it stretched
into Greece and Yugoslavia in Europe. But by the turn of the 20th
century, the Ottoman Empire was on the verge of collapse. When
World War I broke out, the Ottomans backed the wrong side. So,
in 1918, the old empire was carved up by the victors: the United
States, Britain, and France. All the Ottomans were left with was
Turkey.

THE YOUNG TURKS
Some young Turkish army officers, called the Young Turks (yes,
that's where the term comes from), led by a young colonel called

Mustafa Kemal, felt that the time had come to drag Turkey into the modern age. First, they defeated the American, British, and French troops that had been occupying Turkey since the end of World War I. After that, they beat back an invading Greek army. They then turned on their own sultan, Mehmed VI. On November 1, 1922, the sultan was forced to stand down; he immediately went into exile on the Italian Riviera resort of San Remo.

GENTLEMEN MUST PLEASE REMOVE THEIR HATS

On October 29, 1923, the Republic of Turkey was proclaimed. The Ottomans were banished forever, and Kemal was inaugurated as Turkey's first president. Kemal was desperate to Westernize his country. Islam was abolished as the national religion, and Turkey became a secular state; people were made to adopt surnames, which they had never used before; and women were given the vote. But far more controversial than any of these already earth-shattering events was Kemal's decision to ban the fez!

HEADGEAR HOO-HA

The fez hadn't been a Turkish innovation. It had originated in the Moroccan city of Fez (hence the name) and spread throughout the Middle East. Ironically, when Sultan Mahmud II introduced it, he'd seen the fez as a badge of modernity. Now, almost 100 years later, Mustafa Kemal wanted to abolish it for being a symbol of Turkey's backwardness! It turns out that, as a young diplomatic delegate to a conference in Paris, a be-fezzed Kemal had been mocked by a French officer who asked him, "Why do you wear that ridiculous thing?" It was something Kemal never forgot.

TAKE MY HAT—PLEASE!

On August 30, 1925, Kemal made the most radical decision of his career by passing a bill outlawing the fez. "We had to throw off the fez," he said, "which sat upon our head as an emblem of ignorance, fanaticism, and hatred of progress and civilization." Kemal set off on a junket to enforce his new law, first visiting Kastamonu, the most conservative backwater his advisors could locate for him in all Turkey. The locals were naturally delighted to see their beloved leader. They were less happy to see what he had on his head—a rather natty and distinctly un-fezlike fedora, à la Humphrey Bogart.

Worse still, Kemal kept taking his hat off—in public! Peasant women swooned at each glimpse of the hitherto unseen presidential forehead; grown men wept at the sight of Kemal's naked locks blowing in the breeze. Boos were heard. A rumble of discontent spread through the crowd. Kemal's visit to Kastamonu was a public relations disaster.

Following the botched launch of Kemal's very own "Just Say No" campaign, things went from bad to worse. All those found wearing fezzes were sentenced to a minimum three months' imprisonment. Some overly zealous local governors took things even further: Women were barred from wearing veils in one region; men were ordered to shave off their beards in another. Fueled by stories like these, the pro-fez faction took to the streets. Mass demonstrations took place in major cities. Posters insulting Kemal went up, and threats were made against local officials. Riots broke out. Martial law was declared, and troops were sent into the most militant areas. Nineteen people were quickly executed for wearing fezzes, while hundreds more were sentenced to hard labor.

FEZZING AND FIGHTING
But the lure of the fez proved irresistible. In 1930, a special unit of Turkish fez-busting federal police raided a warehouse in the northwestern city of Bursa. Inside, they found more than 100 crates packed with contraband fezzes, which they cracked open with axes, Eliot Ness–style.

More bizarrely, Kemal's fez ban even provoked a coup attempt in 1930. Extremist fez freedom fighters in the towns of Omelette, Manisir, and Balikisir tried to stage an uprising against Kemal. The supposed revolution was ruthlessly put down; 28 conspirators were executed and 200 more jailed.

PUTTING A CAP ON THINGS
In time, the pro-fez movement died down and Turkish men got used to wearing other types of hats—especially after Western hatmakers flooded the Turkish market with all manner of cheap head wear. Soon panamas, derbies, and even top hats were commonly seen on the streets of Istanbul and other Turkish cities. By the 1940s, Kemal's work was done: the fez was virtually extinct. But Turkey was a far less colorful place for it.

CORN: THE A-MAIZING STORY

*Skunk odor remover, plastic bags, birdcage liner,
disposable plates and eating utensils, car tires, and the fuel
to run the car—what do these products have in common?
All of them come from corn or corn derivatives.*

THE CORN OF PLENTY
Less than 15 percent of the world's corn production (including popcorn) is intended for human stomachs. Eighty-five percent of the annual corn crop is used for animal feed, starch, sugar, oil, alcohol—more than 3,500-plus products.

MAIZE AS MYTH
Corn—or maize, as it's more commonly known outside North America—was not only the dietary staple of the Mayan, Aztec, and other native peoples of Central America and Mexico, but also an important element in their creation myths and rituals. The Mayan people, for example, believed that the first men were made out of mud, after which the gods improved on the model; the next batch was made out of wood. Finally, their First Mother mixed human blood with ground maize to fashion "the living flesh," the perfect man, (who was, of course, Mayan).

SOMETHING TO CHEW ON
Maize is one of the few crops that had to be domesticated in order to provide food. Originally, the plant was just another wild grass, a great nosh for birds but not something the average human forager would consider worth chewing. Then the realization dawned that corn might be edible. Some archaeologists think a perceptive hunter noticed undigested kernels in animal dung. Hunters would understand that if animals could eat corn it wasn't poisonous.

NORTHERN EXPOSURE
Years before Columbus showed up, northern natives were hip to maize. The practice of growing corn took centuries to creep

northward. As it did, growers made changes to accommodate the different growing seasons. By the time maize reached New England and the Great Lakes regions of the United States, the locals had figured out how to shorten the growing season to coincide with the shorter summer.

Maize was as important to the natives of the north as it had been to the Mayan people. During the transition of cultures from hunter-forager to farmer, new creation myths developed around the staple crops. The Penobscot tribe of New England believed maize had been brought by a crow. For this reason, they permitted crows to raid their fields but chased off other birds. Other tribes believed the Great Spirit had provided maize as a gift of thanks. Seeding and harvest times were occasions for great festivals and important ceremonies. Besides its obvious value as provender for local folks, maize was good PR for local shamans; it was such a hardy crop that a shaman could "predict" a good output year after year.

Early in post-Columbus years, Europeans recognized the value of maize. And, in quick time, the Spanish, Portuguese, and English had spread its cultivation throughout their known world.

MORE KERNELS TO THE COB

The first corncobs provided only eight or ten kernels and one cob per plant in early Mayan days. The kernels were tough and only palatable when ground to powder and made into bread—a lot of work for not much reward. Now, a plant can produce four cobs of 1,800 kernels apiece. As a crop, maize ranks in world production with wheat and rice; of the three, maize is the most versatile.

Popcorn, in case you were wondering, is actually the original domesticated type, called *reventador*. It accounts for less than 1 percent of commercial corn, something Orville Redenbacher's would probably like to see change.

INEVITABLY, A "CORNY" JOKE

As for "corny" jokes, there's an explanation for them, too. The corny joke is an American invention, a punny joke included in corn seed catalogs during the late 19th and early 20th centuries to lighten up the reading. The jokes were so terrible that they established a category all their own: the corn catalog joke, which was eventually shortened to just plain corny.

GOD OF THE DANCE

What drove Nijinsky over the edge? That thin line between genius and insanity? Those two years in prison camp? Or maybe it was his marriage to that bisexual Hungarian noblewoman.

Vaslav Nijinsky was one of the greatest dancers of the 20th century and, some say, the greatest male dancer ever. His spark of madness may have enhanced his genius, but his career lasted only 12 years before the madness took over.

ALL IN THE FAMILY

Nijinsky was born in St. Petersburg in 1890 into a dancing family. Both his parents and his sister, Bronislava Nijinska, were dancers. His talents were obvious from an early age. By the time he graduated from the Imperial School of Dance, he was being called the Eighth Wonder of the World.

But he was as difficult a student as he was brilliant. He had trouble getting along with others and could be, at times, wild or withdrawn. The only time he seemed happy was while he was dancing.

WHO SAYS WHITE BOYS CAN'T JUMP?

Nijinsky became famous in Russia while still a teenager, but his career went international when he joined a tour of Russian ballet and music bound for Paris. That touring company became the Ballets Russes, and Nijinsky was its male star. He had a gift for creating characters, and a unique, androgynous stage presence (think early David Bowie). His slender upper body was as graceful as any ballerina's was, but his powerful legs gave him the ability to leap to amazing heights and seemingly pause in midair. Paris loved him. Before the end of his first season, Nijinsky was an international star—and a universal sex symbol.

But his genius wasn't confined to leaping: Nijinsky was also a choreographer decades ahead of his time. When his short, erotic ballet *Afternoon of a Faun* premiered in Paris in 1912, it caused a sensation and played to packed houses. A year later, his choreog-

---

The colorful Sri Lanka Junglefowl is part of the family from which our modern chickens derive.

raphy for a *Rite of Spring* caused a riot in the theater. (See "A Riot of Spring" on page 366 for more details on that incident.)

The Ballets Russes broke with traditional ballet in every way: dance styles, costumes, music, plots, and stage settings. It influenced theater, music, fashion, and even interior decor. Nijinsky's ballets caused a revolution in dance.

DANCING ON THE EDGE

Nijinsky had a dramatic personality both on and off stage. For years, his lover, Serge Diaghilev, the impresario behind the company, supported his career with the Ballets Russes. That open secret aside, his sexual adventures were many. The dancer Ida Rubenstein asked him to father a child with her; he declined. In 1912, Romola Pulszky, a bisexual Hungarian noblewoman, saw him and decided she was going to marry him. She pursued him relentlessly, even going to the trouble of studying ballet herself to get close to him. They married in March 1913.

Neither his affair with Diaghilev nor his marriage was happy. Nijinsky always needed someone to organize his life for him, but he resented feeling controlled. He had a quick, occasionally violent temper and suffered periods of black depression, which only got worse after he was interred for two years in a prison camp (because he was a Russian and unlucky enough to be in Austria-Hungary when World War I broke out). He was released in 1916.

Many things have been blamed for the failure of Nijinsky's mental state: his rift with Diaghilev, who was both a lover and a father figure to him; his stormy marriage; even the marriage of his sister Bronislava (who may have been the only person who really understood him). He was diagnosed with various conditions over the years—neurasthenia, depression, catatonia, and schizophrenia. But the diagnosis hardly matters, because there were no effective treatments for any of those disorders at the time. Nijinsky was never able to work seriously again. He gave his final public performance in 1917, when was just 27 years old.

NIJINSKY HAS LEFT THE BUILDING

Legends began to grow around Nijinsky as soon as he retired. The continuing popularity of the Ballets Russes kept his reputation alive. Nijinsky's sister Bronislava had a long career as a choreogra-

William James Sidis, a child prodigy, entered Harvard University at the age of 11 in 1909.

pher and teacher and helped perpetuate his revolutionary ballets.

Romola helped things along by publishing an unreliable biography in the 1930s to help pay her husband's medical bills (he lived until 1950). Soon Nijinsky-the-genius-madman was more famous than Nijinsky-the-dancer had ever been. People who'd never seen a ballet knew all about him from reading magazines or seeing films about his life.

Nijinsky's name is still a byword for the glamour and sexiness of the Ballets Russes, but his writings show him confused and obsessed with his past, his dances, his roles, his relationships, and the title he had been given years before by ecstatic journalists: God of the Dance.

* * * * *

WHAT SET THEM APART

The word *teenage* wasn't new, but when the media latched on to teenagers as a distinct group in the 1940s, the beginning was near: think Archie and Veronica, sweater sets, and crew cuts. But teenagers were still a tame bunch, still tied to the old ways. Even if they dressed differently, they liked the same music as their parents—can you imagine?

It wasn't until rock and roll burst on the scene in the mid-1950s—specifically "Rock Around the Clock" by Bill Haley and the Comets—that the generation gap really expanded. The new musical genre, mostly performed at first by blues singers and country western bands, horrified the adult world. Frank Sinatra said, "The music is sung, played, and written for the most part by cretinous goons and the lyrics are sly, lewd, and dirty." Yeah! Then came Elvis, *American Bandstand*, and James Dean in *Rebel Without a Cause*.

The teenager was officially born.

EAR PIERCING

*Whether your voice is sultry or squeaky, there's a bar waiting
somewhere where you can be the next golden-throated idol.*

You've seen these setups—popular music plays from a
machine that looks like a big-screen television. Amateur
singers pick up the microphone, supply the vocals, and bask
in their 15 minutes of fame. Karaoke is a combination of two
Japanese words. The word *karrapo* translates as "empty." The word
okusutura means "orchestra." Shortened for convenience, the
phrase became *kara-oke*, or empty orchestra.

It all started when a bar owner in Japan learned that the
singer he hired for the night couldn't make the gig. Not wanting
to leave the guests sitting around peeling the labels off of their
Sapporo bottles, the manager, Daisuke Inoue, hooked a tape player
and some microphones up to his stereo for his patrons to sing
along to. They took turns performing center stage, and soon the
lack of a *scheduled* performer became a plus. Beer was swilled.
Songs were sung. A good time was had by all.

WARBLING WONDERS

Inoue packaged the concept for sale to other bars and got rich—
so his city, Kobe, Japan, is typically credited with being the birthplace of karaoke. In 1977, an engineer from Pioneer Electronics
saw Inoue's setup and created a video disc that both played the
music and rolled the lyrics on a TV screen. Since Inoue never got
that piece of paper called a patent, karaoke was a free-for-all as
the fad caught on and spread to other countries.

In the 1980s, karaoke became *the* way to entertain business
associates in Japan. Entepreneurs designed special rooms, called
"karaoke boxes," so as not to disturb the neighbors. Experts
estimate that there are more than 100,000 karaoke rooms in
Japan alone. If you're one of those purists who covers your ears
when your soused coworkers warble "Like a Virgin" at the
Christmas party, our condolences. You may never be safe in
Japanese bars again!

THAT STINKING FEELING: PART I

Now that the Hundred Years' War was finally over, people were ready to tackle a more malodorous problem.

As they conquered their way through Europe, the Romans left behind a number of souvenirs, like the (still-standing) aqueducts that used to bring water to homes and businesses. But the Romans also established a system of sewers to dispose of, well, you know. The sewers consisted of a network of underground pipes that ran beneath houses and streets, and terminated at the nearest body of water. In fact, the word *sewer* derives from the English *seaward*.

In medieval London, all sewers led to the river Thames. The Thames, of course, was also where drinking water came from. And where laundry was washed.

FLUSH WITH SUCCESS

So, just how did townspeople of the Middle Ages conduct their "business"? All homes had chamber pots, which were the preferred conveniences, particularly at night and in bad weather. In the morning, the contents were simply thrown out the window into the street. "Rakers," or street cleaners, regularly swept the waste into the sewers, and from there to the river. The more fastidious citizens had privies and latrines, usually shared by several households. The rich, of course, had servants to empty chamber pots out the window.

In rural areas, outhouses continued to be used well into modern times. Outside the capital, it was in monasteries that many advances in hygiene and sanitation were first developed. Although monks reputedly reject worldly conveniences, the relatively large numbers of monks sharing communal living quarters created a need for efficient disposal of human waste.

Most monasteries were situated near large bodies of water, and they employed a system of latrines that were periodically flushed by water under pressure from large, elevated cisterns. Unlike aver-

Her Bobbs-Merrill editor suggested changing it to *The Fountainhead.*

age citizens, monks didn't use chamber pots. Only the very sick were exempt from the need to walk to the latrines, regardless of weather. There's even strong evidence that monks used thin, linen rags as primitive toilet paper.

A ROYAL FLUSH
Castles, both in and out of London, weren't much different from monasteries—except that their noble inhabitants demanded more creature comforts. Walk to the latrines in the cold night air? Not on your life. They used chamber pots in a pinch, but much preferred private toilets. These were similar in design to the monastic latrines, but they were often built into the castle walls—usually near a fireplace for cozy comfort.

Since castle walls were usually several feet thick, it was no problem to carve out a small space, called a *garderobe*, (French for "clothes closet"), perfectly situated near milady or milord's bedchamber. As in monasteries, these were periodically flushed by gravity's pull on the castle's drainage system.

LOOK OUT BELOW!
Ever stop to admire the serene, romantic look of the moat surrounding medieval castles? Well, here's a dose of reality. Aside from their value as protection against enemies, moats also served a far more utilitarian function: the disposal of household waste. In castles that didn't enjoy the luxury of flushing drains, privies were often cantilevered out over the moat.

YOUR TAX MONEY AT WORK
The city of London generously provided public latrines, conveniently situated near the Thames. In a lot of cases, the need for pipes was eliminated by simply building the privies on bridges. This greatly facilitated "dumping" into the river. As a result, navigating the Thames was a real challenge, especially when sailing under a bridge.

People who lived too far away from the water used cesspits, big holes in the ground that stored the waste until they could be cleaned out, usually at night. The contents were then dumped (you guessed it) into the river.

HUMAN INGENUITY

People sometimes went to great lengths to save a little money. Paul Newman's book *Daily Life in the Middle Ages* recounts the story of one ingenious Londoner, who came up with a way to avoid the expense of building a proper cesspit. Instead, he ran a pipe from his privy to his neighbor's cellar. The neighbor may have been particularly clueless, because the plan seems to have worked for quite a while. The neighbor only caught on when sewage completely filled the cellar and began seeping into his first-floor rooms. Predictably, the hapless neighbor sued. And it's through the record of that lawsuit that we know of it today.

DO ALL ROADS LEAD TO ROME?

To offset the expense of maintaining public toilets, city governments turned to a commercial practice known since Roman times. Urine was collected from latrines and sold to wool manufacturers. Urine, it seems, contains ammonia, which is used to remove some of the natural oils in unprocessed fleece. Urine was also used in the tanning of leather.

EDWARD III TO THE RESCUE

By the middle of the 14th century, London was a mess. The air was foul and the river flowed with sewage. Clothes washed in river water retained the odor of cesspools. Rats were thriving in the filth, and the plague was resurfacing.

King Edward III, fresh from the Hundred Years' War, turned his attention to the problem of the stench. He issued a proclamation specifically forbidding the dumping of "rubbish, earth, gravel, or dung from dwellings or stables" into the Thames. Instead, it was to be carted away by "dungboats" and disposed of outside the city.

It didn't take long for old habits to resurface. Two years after his decree, the king wrote the mayor of London, complaining that the streets of London were foul with human feces thrown from houses.

There were no significant advances in sanitation until the 19th century. Things had to get much worse before they got better.

* * * * *

To find out what happened next, see "That Stinking Feeling: Part II" on page 299.

...was rejected by the first six English publishers she submitted it to.

FLOWER POWER

Can you name the flowers we're sniffing around for?

1. In the family Asteraceae, this pretty flower originated in Mexico's high-elevation region and was brought to Europe by the Spanish. It's named after Andrew Dahl, a Swedish botanist.
2. Classified in the genus *Bellis*, this dandy flower was often worn in the hair of hippies in the flower-power era. Victorian maids used to pick its petals off one at a time, musing, "He loves me…He loves me not."
3. This tall flower was known in Tudor England as a larkspur because it looked like the claws of a lark. But its common name came from the ancient Greeks, who thought the flower sort of looked like a dolphin.
4. Also called grenadine, this originally Mediterranean flower was selected in 1907 by a Philadelphia woman as the official flower of Mother's Day.
5. Its scientific name is *Cichorium intybus*, and it served as a popular substitute for coffee during the American Civil War.
6. In 1532, Spanish explorer Francisco Pizaro reported having seen the Incas worshiping this flower.
7. One of the oldest cultivated plants on the planet, this flower dates back to Asia Minor during the second millennium B.C. It comes in Madonna, Turk's Cap, and Easter varieties.
8. This flower's name is the Greek word for "testicle" because of the shape of the plant's root tubers.
9. This pretty plant was thought to ward off evil, and old-time Europeans brought a sprig of it into the house during cold winter so that good fairies would have a place to play. This was the birth of the Christmas wreath tradition.
10. In the 8th century A.D. when this flower appeared in Japan, the people were immediately smitten, adopting it as the emperor's official crest. The Japanese word for this flower is *kiku* and the word for crest is *mon*, creating the word *kikumon*—not to be confused with Kikkoman, the soy sauce.

Answers
1. Dahlia 2. Daisy 3. Delphinium 4. Carnation 5. Chicory 6. Sunflower 7. Lily 8. Orchid 9. Holly 10. Chrysanthemum

---

Jacopo Peri's *Dafne*, composed in 1594, was the first Italian opera.

A NOBEL EXPERIMENT

How Dr. Frederick Banting took the serendipitous road to success.

In 1920, Dr. Frederick Banting was facing ruin. A farmer's son with a medical degree, he'd come to London, Ontario, Canada, in hopes of establishing a small practice. Unfortunately, his waiting room was usually empty. He worried that he'd never make his way in medicine. Failure weighed heavily. He would always remember "the awfulness, the loneliness and the financial worries that were associated with London."

NOTABLE NOTES
To make some badly needed income, Fred became a part-time assistant to Professor Miller, a physiologist. Late one night, after helping prepare a lecture on diabetes for Miller's students, Banting stayed up reading a medical journal article about the islets of Langerhans, (which are located inside your pancreas). This would put most of us in snoozeville, but it had the opposite effect on the doctor. Soon he was jotting down notes for an experiment.

EXPLORING THE ISLANDS
Diabetes was fatal back in those days. Diabetic patients had too much sugar in their blood and urine; the high blood sugar caused exhaustion and a rapid weight loss ending in death. Fred wasn't alone, of course, in mulling over possible cures. The disease had been discovered in ancient Egypt, so by 1920, researchers had known about it for a while. And one thing they knew was that people with diabetes needed a hormone secreted by the islets of Langerhans.

The hormone seemed to keep blood sugar balanced in healthy people. Scientists wanted to extract it from animals and try giving it to diabetics, but so far, they'd had little success. They'd also tried feeding diabetics fresh animal pancreas (ugh!), but that hadn't helped.

It was Banting's idea that digestive enzymes in the pancreas were destroying the hormone. So if he could extract the hormone directly from the islets of Langerhans and keep it isolated from

---

John Henry was the first thoroughbred to win a million-dollar race, in 1981.

those pancreatic enzymes, the hormone might control diabetics' deadly symptoms.

DOG DAYS OF SUMMER

Banting wanted to extract the hormone from healthy dogs and use it to restore a diabetic dog's health—a bold thought for someone who wasn't even a trained scientific researcher. And when Banting took his idea to Professor John Macleod, a physiologist and researcher at the University of Toronto, the prof was unimpressed with the doctor's lack of qualifications. Macleod pretty much told Banting to get lost.

But Banting believed in his idea and pestered Macleod until the professor finally agreed to give him laboratory space for eight weeks, ten dogs to experiment on, and a student assistant named Charles Best. No salary, though; Fred had to borrow money and sell his car. Never mind. He and Charlie scrounged meals and went to work.

In the summer of 1921, while the illustrious Professor Macleod vacationed in his native Scotland, Banting and Best rushed to isolate and extract the hormone. (Banting would later name it "insulin," from the Latin for "island.") First, they removed the pancreas from one dog to make her diabetic. On July 30, Banting injected the insulin into the diabetic dog and...a miracle! The sick dog recovered before their eyes. They kept the dog alive and relatively healthy with more injections. Banting and Best were overjoyed—and then Macleod came back from Europe.

STRIKING A BLOW FOR SCIENCE

Macleod insisted on more experimentation, but he quickly realized the value of Banting and Best's work. By the end of 1921, papers were published announcing Banting's discovery. But there were problems: the insulin that saved the diabetic dog wasn't pure enough or reliable enough to use on humans, and it caused harmful side effects.

Fred and Charlie's lack of experience was slowing things down. So Professor Macleod brought in Dr. James Bertram Collip, a distinguished biochemist, to purify the extracts of insulin.

Soon Collip and Macleod were running the experimental show. Fred began to feel sidelined on the most important project

---

The lyrics of a 1909 song called "Uncle Josh in Society" had the first use of the term *jazz*.

of his life. Known for his hot temper, Fred already had plenty of trouble working with Macleod. But his relationship with Collip was worse.

Collip, who'd agreed to share all information with Banting and Best, decided *not* to tell them how he refined the insulin. (Speculation is that he intended to keep the process for his own profit.) So, Banting slugged him! News of the fight got out, and a cartoon of the day showed Fred sitting on Collip and choking him. The caption read: "The Discovery of Insulin."

THAT'S SIR FRED TO YOU

After the fight, Banting and Best worked separately from Macleod and Collip for a time but eventually agreed to cooperate. Fred, the farmer's son, realized that the pancreas of slaughtered cows could provide a steady supply of insulin. Collip purified the cattle insulin for human use. For about sixty years after Banting's discovery, diabetics were kept alive through injections of purified insulin obtained from cattle and pigs. In 1982, the U.S. Food and Drug Administration approved the first synthetic insulin, humulin.

In 1922, less than a year after Banting's experiments began, the group gave a dying diabetic teenager named Leonard Thompson injections of insulin. Leonard, who weighed 64 pounds, immediately started gaining weight and grew stronger. Leonard's life was saved; many more lives would be saved because of this breakthrough.

In 1923, Dr. Frederick Banting and Professor James Macleod were co-recipients of the Nobel Prize for Medicine. Banting voluntarily shared his prize money with Charlie Best, as did Macleod with Collip. Dr. Banting went on to many other honors, including knighthood.

And though he never forgot his hard times and struggles, Sir Frederick eventually had another take on them. He said in 1940, "Had I not failed in my one year at London, I might never have started my research work."

* * * * *

BOY GENIUS

In his search for a way to waterproof fibers inexpensively, 25-year-old Thomas Alva Edison invented waxed paper.

TEATIME

Like a lot of other great things, tea was discovered by accident.

Chinese legend says that Emperor Shen Nung sampled the first cup of tea in 2737 B.C. The emperor, a pretty smart guy to begin with, thought that water should always be boiled before drinking. During one of his travels, he and his caravan stopped to rest. As his faithful servant boiled water underneath a tree, some leaves fell into the pot. The water turned a dark color and so intrigued the emperor that he took a swig. Shen Nung gave the new brew a thumbs up, and tea took China by storm.

HAVE A LITTLE TEA WITH YOUR T'ANG

The English word "tea" is from early Chinese dialect names for "tea," like *tchai*, *cha*, and *tay*. Tea became China's national drink during the T'ang dynasty (A.D. 618–907). Around A.D. 780, Chinese author Lu Yu wrote *Ch'a Ching*, a three-volume opus about everything from the cultivation to the preparation of tea.

ZEN AND THE ART OF TEA BREWING

Buddhist monks took tea to Japan, but the Japanese didn't take a permanent interest in the drink until A.D. 1191, when the leader of the Zen Buddhists, Yeisai, brought seeds from a tea plant to Japan and wrote a book about tea. But he went one step further when he "healed" an ailing shogun with a cup of the brew. In a clever marketing move, Yeisai then presented the shogun with a copy of his book. Once he had the shogun's royal seal of approval, Yeisai's book became an instant best seller.

WORTH ITS WEIGHT IN TEA

The Portuguese opened the first trade route to the Far East and transported tea back to Lisbon—where it was distributed by Dutch ships to the Baltic countries, France, and the Nether-lands. Eventually, in the early 1600s, the Dutch set up their own trade route and started importing tea themselves. Because it was so scarce, tea was incredibly expensive at first. But as more tea was imported, the price went down; tea went from

---

The first Ironman Triathlon was held on Oahu, Hawaii, in 1978.

being an aristocratic drink to a common brew enjoyed by rich and poor alike.

HEY, WE WANT SOME TOO!
The Dutch brought tea to their recently established colony, New Amsterdam (later rechristened New York), and head colonist Peter Stuyvesant started brewing it around 1650.

IT'S OFFICIALLY TEATIME
It may be hard to believe, but England was the last to jump on the tea wagon. Britain's East India Company brought minimal amounts of tea back from the Orient during the early half of the 17th century. It took a while before the drink caught on, but after 1650, tea was served at coffeehouses throughout the country. In 1660, King Charles II imposed a tax on tea. Nine years later, the crown outlawed tea imported from Holland and awarded the East India Company their very own tea monopoly. By 1700, tea was all the rage in Great Britain. And it's still pretty popular, from what we hear.

A TEA PARTY
In 1767 the British passed the Townsend Acts, new taxes on goods shipped to the colonies from Britain, including a tax on tea. Outraged, the colonists refused to drink English tea.

The whole matter came to a head on December 16, 1773, when some radical colonists held a little tea party in Boston— which led to the American Revolution.

ICE IS NICE
In 1904, tea took a different twist: That year, at the St. Louis World's Fair, a vendor named Richard Blechynden set up a concession to turn people on to his India tea. But the hot summer weather left him with few takers. In a stroke of genius, Blechynden stuck some ice into glasses, poured his steaming hot tea over it, and offered *that* to customers. They loved it and came back for more.

IT'S IN THE BAG
Four years later, New York tea merchant Thomas Sullivan wanted to send out small samples of tea to potential and established

---

Adam de la Halle wrote the first operetta, *Le Jeu de la Fuillee*, in A.D. 1262.

customers, so he packaged them in little silk bags. Nearly everyone responded positively. But they were disappointed that their tea orders arrived in bulk instead of in those cute, little bags. Sullivan switched from silk to gauze, and the tea bag business was on its way.

TEATIME TODAY
Even 20 years ago, at least in America, Earl Grey (a black tea flavored with bergamot or lavender oil) was considered exotic: The selection of teas was restricted mostly to brands like Lipton, Salada, or Red Rose—all in tea bag form. Today, all three brands are owned by one huge food conglomerate: Unilever.

But that's okay, because the world's second-most-consumed beverage—the first being water—is now available in so many forms and flavors that it would take you years of teatimes to try them all. Your choices range from black tea (which accounts for 75 percent of world trade), to green tea, to combos of the two (like oolong), to all the scads of variously flavored herbal teas.

And attention, health nuts! Black tea is just as effective as green tea for curing and preventing serious illnesses like heart disease and cancer; it also helps control cholesterol and even prevents tooth decay. So, do yourself a favor: instead of (or besides) that next double half-caf latte, treat yourself to a nice cup of tea.

* * * * *

"Love and scandal are the best sweeteners of tea."—Henry Fielding, *Love in Several Masques*

"Tea is drunk to forget the din of the world."—T'ien Yiheng

"If you are cold, tea will warm you. If you are too heated, it will cool you. If you are depressed, it will cheer you. If you are excited, it will calm you."—Gladstone, 1865

"Tea to the English is really a picnic indoors."—Alice Walker

"Tea does our fancy aid,
Repress those vapours which the head invade
And keeps that palace of the soul serene."
—Edmund Waller, *Of Tea*

TEMPEST OVER A TEA PARTY

The Boston Tea Party—every schoolchild learns the story.
On December 16, 1773, Boston patriots disguised as Indians
boarded ships in Boston Harbor and dumped the tea overboard.
Test your knowledge of the tea party that brewed a revolution.

1. The British imposed a tax on tea in the American colonies:
   a) to raise money to pay off the British national debt
   b) to pay off the debt, and to bail out the East India Company, Britain's largest company
   c) to pay off the debt, to bailout the East India Company, and on principle.

2. The colonists hated the tea tax because:
   a) the tax was so high that tea would have become unaffordable for most people.
   b) coffee and cocoa were untaxed, a move seen as discriminatory to tea drinkers.
   c) of the principle of the thing.

3. The 150 men who took part in the Boston Tea Party disguised themselves as Native Americans. What they *didn't* do was:
   a) wear rags, old shawls, and red caps.
   b) smear ashes or burnt cork on their faces.
   c) smear reddish makeup on their faces and wear feathered war bonnets.

4. When the Boston men took over the three ships and began throwing the tea overboard:
   a) the British sailors fought them fiercely.
   b) the ships were set ablaze.
   c) some of the British sailors helped them.

5. The tea that was dumped into the harbor:
   a) sank to the bottom in heavy, wooden chests.
   b) poisoned the fish.
   c) piled up like large haystacks in the shallow harbor.

Jacob Shallus, the calligrapher of the U.S. Constitution, was paid $30 for his work

6. Samuel Adams, leader of the Sons of Liberty and one of the chief instigators of the Boston Tea Party, had once worked as a:
   a) tax collector.
   b) tea merchant.
   c) lawyer.

7. At today's prices, the approximate value of the tossed tea was:
   a) $10,000 (8115 euros).
   b) $100,000 (81,153 euros).
   c) $1,000,000 (811,525 euros).

8. The type of tea hurled into the harbor was:
   a) Earl Grey.
   b) Darjeeling.
   c) Oolong.

9. The men who participated in the Boston Tea Party:
   a) had all their assets confiscated to pay for the damage.
   b) were tarred and feathered.
   c) went unpunished.

10. When Ben Franklin learned of the Boston Tea Party:
    a) he offered to pay for the damages out of his personal fortune.
    b) he invented a substitute tea made from grape leaves.
    c) he wrote a new edition of *Poor Richard's Almanac* titled *In Praise of the Destruction of the Tyrant's Tea*.

For the answers see page 482.

* * * * *

"Great love affairs start with Champagne and end with tisane."
—Honoré de Balzac

"Remember the tea kettle—it is always up to its neck in hot water, yet it still sings!"—Author Unknown

"You can never get a cup of tea large enough or a book long enough to suit me."—C.S. Lewis

Montréal in Canada is the second-largest French-speaking city in the world.

GUERRILLA WARFARE
PART 6
Navy SEALs

The SEALs—whose name is an acronym for **SE**a, **A**ir, **L**and—conduct special operations alone or in small groups; they're experts in weapons, tactics, demolition, martial arts, and hand-to-hand combat. The first SEAL units were authorized by President Kennedy in 1962, as the navy's counterpart to the army's Green Berets. But Navy SEALs trace their heritage back to the elite frogmen of World War II, who were called Amphibious Scouts and Raiders and Underwater Demolition Teams (UDTs).

During WWII, the navy needed personnel to perform reconnaissance on areas where amphibious assaults were planned, so they recruited divers from Naval Construction Battalions (the Seabees) and gave them advanced training in reconnaissance and demolition. The frogmen scouted beaches and cleared the approaches of mines and obstacles prior to the amphibious landings in Africa and Europe and during the island-hopping campaigns in the Pacific theater. During the Korean War, the frogmen attacked railroad bridges and tunnels along the Korean coastline, and cleared mines and obstacles before the amphibious assault at Inchon, Korea's second-largest port.

VIETNAM
Once the first SEAL teams were created, they were sent to Vietnam as advisors, instructing the South Vietnamese Navy in underwater demolitions and maritime special operations. Later, the navy maintained eight platoons of SEALs that patrolled rivers, destroyed obstacles and bunkers, snatched prisoners, and eliminated low-ranking Vietcong officers and Communist cadre leaders). With a kill ratio of 200 to 1 in Vietnam, the enemy was justly afraid of the SEALs and put a bounty on their heads, calling them "men with green faces" because of their camouflage makeup.

GRENADA
SEAL teams provided beach reconnaissance for the invasion of Grenada in 1983. During the invasion, they assaulted the airfield and set up radar beacons to guide the aircraft carrying airborne Ranger battalions. They also captured the Radio Free Grenada transmitting station so that the enemy (the Grenadan Army and a few Cuban soldiers) couldn't use it to rally their forces. SEALs also carried out an assault on the governor general's mansion and rescued Governor General Paul Scoon, who was being held there under house arrest.

PANAMA
In the invasion of Panama in 1989, SEAL teams were assigned two small, but important, missions designed to prevent the escape of the dictator Manuel Noriega by disabling his boat and Lear jet. The mission to disable the boat went as planned, but the assault on Patilla Airfield to disable the plane ran into fierce resistance. Four SEALs were killed and eight were wounded during the mission.

IRAQ
During both Iraq wars, the SEALs carried out a number of missions, most of which are still classified. It is known that SEALs were involved in the rescue of navy pilots, in mine-clearing operations, and in the capture of ships and oil platforms.

SOMALIA
In 1994, SEAL teams provided beach reconnaissance for the marine landing in Somalia during the UN peacekeeping mission. And at least one SEAL member participated in the failed attempt to capture the warlord General Mohammed Farrah Adid.

AFGHANISTAN
During the war in Afghanistan in 2002, SEAL teams discovered an extensive network of tunnels in eastern Afghanistan that contained nearly a million pounds (450,000 kg) of ammunition and equipment. Today, SEAL teams are still involved in the hunt for members of the Taliban government and the Al Qaeda leadership.

Minnesota is the only state with the source of three main river systems...

* * * * *

SEAL TRAINING

SEAL training is conducted at the Naval Amphibious Base located in Coronado, California. The six-month basic training course is mentally and physically demanding and is designed to test the individual's stamina, leadership, and ability to work as part of a team. During the 18-week advanced training period, SEALs are instructed in airborne assaults, counter-terrorism, small-unit tactics, long-distance reconnaissance, supply interdiction and raids.

FAMOUS SEALS

Rudy Boesch became famous after his appearance on TV's first *Survivor* series; he subsequently appeared on *Survivor All Stars*. He joined the Navy in 1945 and volunteered for the Amphibious Scouts and Raiders. Later he completed Underwater Demolition Team training in 1951. In 1962, he was one of the first men selected to join the original SEAL team. Rudy retired from the Navy in 1990, after 45 years of distinguished service.

Jessie "the Body" Ventura, former professional wrestler, actor, and governor of Minnesota, served as a Navy SEAL in Vietnam.

Former Nebraska Senator Bob Kerrey lead a SEAL team in Vietnam that was nicknamed "Kerrey's Raiders." He was awarded the Medal of Honor, "for conspicuous gallantry and intrepidity at the risk of his life above and beyond the call of duty." Kerrey led an assault on an enemy headquarters and was severely injured when a grenade landed at his feet. Though bleeding profusely and suffering great pain, he led his men in the assault, called in fire support on the radio, and directed the evacuation of the prisoners that were captured.

SEUSS ON THE LOOSE

Theodor Geisel had a lot to thank his mother for:
his love of children's stories, his interest in rhymes—
and the name he's most recognized by.

Henrietta Seuss Geisel was a big woman: six feet tall and 200 pounds. She was also an accomplished high diver (it's true). But what we care most about is that she was a mother who read bedtime stories to her son, Theodor.

THE DR. GETS HIS DEGREE
At Dartmouth College in the 1920s, young Theodor was banned from extracurricular activities for throwing parties in his room. He needed a pseudonym if he was going to write for the undergrad newspaper. So he took the pen name Seuss, which is correctly pronounced something like "zoice," but which everyone read as "soose." He graduated from Dartmouth and went to Oxford, but he didn't stay long. When he got back—without the doctor of philosophy degree that his father had wanted for him—he added the *Dr.* to his pen name.

WHERE'S THE FLIT?
Once back in the United States, he started freelancing. He wrote and cartooned for all the popular magazines of the day—*Vanity Fair, Life,* the *Saturday Evening Post*—but it was an advertising job that made him nationally famous. The slogan he wrote for an insecticide, "Quick, Henry, the Flit!" became a catch-phrase of the 1930s. He wrote his first children's book on the side; *And to Think That I Saw It on Mulberry Street* was published in 1937—after 27 publishers had rejected it.

THE WAR EFFORT
He did a lot of political cartooning and writing in the 1940s. Most of his work attacked Hitler and Mussolini. But some of it also depicted Japanese Americans as traitors. He illustrated war posters and wrote propaganda films; he and his first wife, Helen, won an Oscar for Best Documentary in 1948 for *Design for Death*, about how a police state fosters war.

The oldest capital city in the U.S. is New Mexico's Santa Fe (1609–10).

HAPPY DAYS ARE HERE AGAIN
After the war, he turned to lighter subjects, winning another Oscar for the animated Best Short Subject, *Gerald McBoing-Boing*, about a little boy who only spoke in sounds. The movie spawned more McBoing-Boing shorts and a popular TV show in the 1950s.

THE RIGHT PLACE AT THE RIGHT TIME
Meanwhile, Geisel had cranked out more Dr. Seuss books, from *The 500 Hats of Bartholomew Cubbins*, published in 1938, to 1954's *Horton Hatches the Egg* (both of which had hidden political and social commentaries). Writer John Hersey (*A Bell for Adano*) was so impressed with Geisel's work that in 1954 he published a piece in *Life* magazine that lambasted children's reading primers and mentioned the Seuss books as a possible remedy.

The best-seller *Why Johnny Can't Read* came out that same year, arguing forcibly against the middle-class tedium of the non-adventures of Dick and Jane. According to author Rudolph Franz Flesch, phonics was the way to go; American first and second graders couldn't read because there wasn't a single book on the market that they could read by themselves. The ingredients for a revolution were converging, and unbeknownst to him, Dr. Seuss was at the center of it.

RHYMING SCHEME
The man who made Geisel/Seuss a literary star was William Spaulding, director of the education division at the Houghton Mifflin publishing house. Spaulding challenged Geisel to write him a book that "a first grader can't put down." He gave the writer a list of about 300 words and told him to make a book out of them.

Seuss added a few words and sat back to look at the list. In his own words, the task looked "impossible and ridiculous." Just as he was about to give up on the idea, his eyes fell on two words: *cat* and *hat*.

AND THAT IS NOT ALL
The Cat in the Hat is 1,702 words long, but, because of repetition, uses only 220 words in all. Written in the inimitable Seuss meter, it pretty much wiped the floor with Dick and Jane. It was

published in 1957, at the peak of the baby boom, and within a few weeks was selling at a rate of about 12,000 copies a month.

Random House publisher, Bennett Cerf, acquired the textbook rights from Houghton Mifflin and, inspired by the success of *The Cat in the Hat*, started a division called Beginner Books. In 1960, Cerf bet Geisel $50 that he couldn't write a book using only 50 words. The result was *Green Eggs and Ham*. Forty-nine of the words had only one syllable; the 50th was *anywhere*. This book is the most successful of all the Dr. Seuss books. Reportedly, though Cerf never paid up. But by then, $50 wasn't going to make or break the career of the famous Dr. Seuss.

* * * * *

THEM'S FIGHTING WORDS

Born in New Jersey and raised in Brooklyn, author Norman Mailer didn't take any lip from anyone. Educated at Harvard, in Boston, and the Sorbonne, in Paris, he originally studied to be an engineer but his talent for writing took over. His first book *The Naked and the Dead* made him an instant celebrity. Over the course of Mailer's life, his body of work became a pillar of contemporary American literature.

But in the 1990s, critics worldwide bashed his novel *Harlot's Ghost*. One review in particular got on Mailer's nerves—John Simon's in the *New York Times Book Review*. Simon called *Harlot's Ghost* an "arbitrary, lopsided, lumpy novel that outstays its welcome." Mailer, by then well into his 60s, flew into a rage (as he was known to do). He went to the *New York Times* and demanded to be allowed a printed response in the paper. Amazingly, they gave it to him. In a fiery retort, Mailer challenged Simon to a fistfight in front of the building to defend his honor. Simon didn't show.

The first known club for nudists, *Freilichtpark*, was opened near Hamburg, Germany, in 1903.

SHAOLIN SMACK DOWN

Seems there was a time in ancient China when you could tell a monk, "Go out there and break a leg!"

Martial arts meant to ancient China what the six-shooter meant to the Wild, Wild West. If someone tried to break into your house or mug you, you fought him with kung fu, using the traditional tools: fists, knives, swords, or sticks. Back then, there was no 911 to call, so you called on your trusty kung fu Fist of Death.

MACHO MONK MEDITATION

"Kung fu" is a collective term for any traditional fighting art that comes from China; it means "work time," because it takes a long while to learn the skills of the art. The Chinese may have been practicing kung fu as early as the Han dynasty (206 B.C.–A.D. 220), though they've refined it throughout the centuries. The mother of all Asian martial arts, kung fu includes punching, kicking, throwing, and locking and breaking of joints and limbs—ouch!

Popular legend has it that the Chinese Buddhist Shaolin temple was the birthplace of kung fu. Tales are told of a Buddhist monk named Ta Mo who brought both Buddhism and martial arts to China from India. He began using the Shaolin temple as a kung fu school in A.D. 506, the first date that can be corroborated. According to the stories, in between meditations and prayers, the Shaolin monks cranked out superhuman fighting machines

Other historians have a different view of Shaolin. In ancient China, if you were a wanted criminal, you could run to the temple and seek refuge. Hiding in Shaolin temples were tough street fighters, who used kung fu as a method of self-defense—and warfare. Since kung fu could also be practiced to improve health and bring spiritual enlightenment, the Shaolin monks were experts in it too. (Nothing like breaking a few bones to raise your consciousness!) With all those fighters under one roof, Shaolin wasn't a school as much as a martial arts clubhouse. Both crooks and

Germany's Wilhelm Wundt (1832-1920) was the first person to call himself a psychologist.

monks practiced diligently, and their moves probably made those of the Worldwide Wrestling Federation look like patty-cake.

FU FIGHTERS MONKEY AROUND
Kung fu flourished. Skilled kung fu fighters became wealthy as knight-errant bodyguards and bandits. Fathers passed their knowledge to their sons. The best kung fu teachers grew famous, with huge schools that challenged one another publicly.

From all this kung foolery came hundreds of fighting styles. Some mimicked animal movements like Monkey, Tiger, or Praying Mantis. Others carried names such as White Eyebrow or Supreme Ultimate Boxing (Tai Chi). From the Long Fist style to the Eight Directions style, there was much debate—and smack down—over which method was best.

Over centuries, kung fu spread from China to other parts of Asia, where aspects of it inspired other fighting arts in Japan (karate), Korea (tae kwon do), and Thailand (Thai kickboxing).

A REVOLTING SETBACK
Kung fu kicked butt right up until the Communist revolution of 1948. The totalitarian Communist government felt that citizens who had personal fighting power could get uppity. So kung fu schools and Buddhist temples were burned. Masters and monks were murdered. Important martial arts documents and relics were destroyed. Kung fu was crushed, and its teachers and students fled to other countries. Kung fu masters opened schools on every continent and shared their skills with non-Chinese. Those schools—along with movie stars like Bruce Lee, Jackie Chan, and Jet Li—got folks worldwide hyped on Chinese martial arts.

FU FIGHTS ON
Sensing a tourism opportunity, the Communist Chinese relented. They rebuilt the temples around the nation and reinstated a new generation of flashy fighting monks. Fist-flying fans flock to China to train—and the government is happy to oblige them. But it's still illegal to dedicate a building strictly to the study of fighting. If you want to teach or learn kung fu in China, you have to do it out in the open, where everyone can see what you're learning. Guess they don't want kung fu as a "secret" weapon.

The most famous recipe in *The Alice B. Toklas Cookbook* (1954) was for "Hashisch Fudge."

THAT STINKING FEELING: PART II

Victorian England is famous for its prudery and its reluctance to talk about bodily functions. But 1858 was known as The Year of the Great Stink in London. They had to start talking! (Part I is on page 279.)

A s awful as hygiene had been in medieval London, it was nothing compared to the state of sanitation in the 19th century. Despite various efforts at sanitary reform, Londoners kept reverting to their old habits. You'd have thought city dwellers would have learned their lesson about public health and sanitation—but you'd be wrong. For five centuries, things went from bad to worse.

FLUSH WITH OPTIMISM
In 1810 a new invention, the flush toilet, was introduced. Of course, only the rich could afford them; and while they may have considered themselves better off with their new status symbols, they really weren't. The newfangled flush toilets still dumped into the same sewers and still polluted the same water. As it turns out, the rich were no different than you or me—at least when it came to breathing.

WHAT'S THAT SMELL?
In 19th-century England, people flocked to the cities to take advantage of the Industrial Revolution (in which they themselves would be taken advantage of, but that's another story). The sewers hadn't been much improved since Roman times, when they were first built. By mid-century, two and a half million people were producing bodily waste. The city had taken on a decidedly odoriferous quality, and the river Thames had grown darker and ranker than ever.

The summer of 1858 was unusually warm, and of course, the heat intensified the effect. Without air conditioning, windows of houses and businesses had to stay open, so there was no escape. The stench had become so powerful that Parliament had to close down.

The ingredients were a mixture of fruit, nuts, spices and "canibus sativa" [sic], or marijuana.

EEEUUWW!

People hadn't yet caught on to the germ theory of disease. They thought all sicknesses were caused by "bad air," so they didn't pay much attention to what they put in their mouths. Drinking water still came from the Thames, often just downstream of where the sewers let out. Eight glasses of water a day was a recipe for disaster.

IT'S ENOUGH TO MAKE YOU SICK

Disease was rampant. Cholera and typhoid fever, both directly related to polluted water, were epidemic. And with so many people suffering from diarrhea, the sewer system was even more taxed. It got so bad that waste would seep back into houses through cracks in the floors and walls. People were dying at a rate close to that of the plague. By 1858, The Year of the Great Stink, 30,000 Londoners had died as a result of three cholera epidemics alone.

A MAN WITH A PLAN

An engineer, Sir Joseph Bazalgette, had a vision. He proposed a system of interlocking underground sewers, complete with pumping stations and holding tanks. Government officials, who'd previously ignored him, realized that something had to be done. They gave the go-ahead, and 82 miles (132 km) of sewers were built.

HOW IT ALL CAME OUT

The new sewers reversed the pollution in the Thames. Fish made their way back to the river, the air became breathable, and illness declined. Today, the Thames is considered one of the cleanest bodies of water in all Europe, and Bazalgette's sewers, now nearly 150 years old, are still in use.

* * * * *

SMELL THIS AND CALL ME IN THE MORNING

Aromatherapy is one of the oldest types of medicine on the planet. The oldest known book of aromatic medicines is the Chinese *Pen Ts'ao* (2700–3000 B.C.), listing over 200 herbal and aromatic medicines.

Access to essential incenses and oils was oftentimes limited to kings, spiritual leaders, and healers because they were so expensive. But doctors would frequently "smoke" their patients by wafting burning oils and herbs recommended for specific ailments into the patients' faces—or allow the patient to simply inhale the fragrance.

The wheel and the plow were invented in the early third millennium B.C.

A HUN-NYMOON IN VENICE

When life hands you lemons, make gondolas!

Ah, Venice—one of the most beautiful cities in the world. No roads filled with cars or trucks mar the scene—just motorboats and gondolas that honeymooners love to smooch in. Who could have been responsible for such a gorgeous, romantic place? Try skull-collecting barbarians and the likes of Attila the Hun.

THEY'RE RUINING THE NEIGHBORHOOD

Flash back to A.D. 451–452 when Attila was busily expanding his kingdom into Europe. He and the half a million men he'd pulled together did their invading on horseback, heading toward Rome. On their way there, they devastated what is now France and northern Italy. His technique was to burn, rape, pillage, and totally terrorize the people he conquered. As the Huns rode into northern Italy, fields of crops, peasant dwellings, and cities such as Aquileia and Padua were destroyed. Refugees fled their burning homes and searched desperately for safety. But where to go?

IT CAME FROM ON TOP OF THE SWAMP

Flash back to about 2,000 years ago, when fishermen began living on the hundred-plus islands at the mouth of the Adriatic Sea. Lagoons separated the islands from the mainland, and canals or narrow waterways divided island from island.

The marshy, muddy islands were so low in the water that a lot of the land was lost in high tide. Few people had even tried to settle there, and for hundreds of years the islands remained the lonely domain of a few fishermen. But in the fifth century, with the fires set by the Huns smoldering behind them, mainlanders suddenly found swamps and marshes attractive. The new lagoon lovers fled to the islands and built cottages on rafts, which were in turn set on posts driven into the mud and sand. A description of the lagoon residences was written by Cassiodorus,

---

When the chief of an early Indian group died, his horse was buried alive with him.

a Roman author and statesman who described the Venetians as living like seabirds: "There lie your houses like seabirds' nests, half on sea and half on land."

WATER, WATER EVERYWHERE
When Attila finally withdrew, some folks could hardly wait to kick the marsh mud from their shoes and return to the mainland. But other refugees stayed on the islands, and in 452, the same year as the Hun withdrawal, Venice was officially founded.

The Venetians made the best of their watery world. To get around, they built boats and kept them tied to their doors, the way their mainland neighbors kept horses in their barns. They fished in the open ocean for food. They dried seawater to make salt, a valuable commodity to trade with the mainlanders. And in 466, the islands formed a council of their own representatives to govern their affairs.

THERE THEY GO AGAIN
Despite the progress, people didn't flock to the lagoon until the sixth century. In about 573, another horde struck. This time the invaders were Lombards, from northwestern Germany. They were led by King Alboin, the kind of guy you never wanted to meet in a dark forest. He had murdered his wife's father, then kept the skull as a drinking mug.

The refugees were rich and poor, from the cities and from the countryside. This time, they had a good idea of where they wanted to go: the inhospitable islands of Venice. Isolated by water, the islands were easier to defend from armies like Alboin's, who were skilled horsemen but not skilled navigators.

The Catholic bishop of Altino (the most important city in that area at that time) made his way to the Venetian island of Torcello to escape the barbarians—and brought a large part of the city's population with him. As the Lombards overran Italy and made it their own, real estate (or wet estates) around the lagoon experienced a definite boom.

A STAKE IN VENICE
Gradually, peace returned. But by now, the refugees wanted to stay in Venice, where the maritime communities and the salt industry

were thriving. They put down roots—or rather stakes in the mud. Venetian maritime businesses and the salt trade made them wealthy. The city became a republic and elected its first ruler, the doge, in 697.

Wealth and trade made Venice a great European power, the Queen of the Adriatic. The city became a cosmopolitan center of learning and fashion. The pilings on the lagoons became the sites of palaces, cathedrals, and elegant villas built of waterproof stone. In 814, construction began on the Palazzo Ducale in what would become the renowned St. Mark's Square—"the finest drawing room in Europe," according to Napoléon. (He neglected to add that most drawing rooms don't have quite as many pigeons.)

FROM REFUGE TO RICHES
The Republic of Venice was the most long-lived in history, lasting more than 1,000 years until Napoléon finally conquered it in 1797. With more than 400 bridges, almost 200 canals, and stunning baroque and Gothic architecture, Venice evolved from a refuge from terror to one of the most admired cities in the world. Take that, Attila!

* * * * *

NAPOLÉON COMPLEX

Les Invalides in Paris, France, was begun in 1671 and designed by Libéral Bruant during the reign of King Louis XIV. Les Invalides, as King Louis envisioned it, was originally intended to be a home for as many as 6,000 army veterans. It does in fact still house a small number of veterans (living ones, that is!). But now it is famous as the mausoleum of French Emperor Napoléon I (1769–1821).

In the center of the current configuration of the complex, behind a large courtyard called the Cour d'Honneur, are the church of Saint Louis, also known as the Soldiers Church, and its royal chapel, the Dôme des Invalides, designed by French architect Jules Hardouin-Mansart between 1678 and 1708. The Dôme is 351 feet high and is laid out in the form of a Greek cross. Napoléon's massive tomb is inside the Dôme. It is built of red porphyry marble with a green granite base, and it was completed in 1861. It is surrounded by 12 sculptures representing Napoléon's military victories. Napoléon feared he would be remembered only for the battle of Waterloo—his one colossal failure—but thanks in part to this mausoleum, folks tend to focus on the positive.

WHERE ARE THEY NOW?

The Huns

Dear Uncle John,
What can you tell me about those ancient tough guys, the Huns?
Macho Hun-admirer

Dear Macho Hun-admirer,
Europeans called the Huns and their ruler Atilla, "the Scourge of God," but they were more likely nomads of Turkish stock who were driven out of China and were looking for new worlds to conquer. The Huns rode onto the European scene in A.D. 370. They were such fierce warriors and so talented at fighting on horseback that they developed a demonic reputation among the terrified citizenry. Rumors flew that the Huns were devils that drank blood. Though this was a myth, meeting the Huns was no picnic. Attila boasted, "Where my horse has trodden, no grass grows."

The Huns had already settled in Hungary and Transylvania when, in 445, Attila came to power after murdering his brother. Under Attila, armies of Huns united to capture nearly half of Europe and prepared to go after the Roman Empire. Some historians claim that Pope Leo I held a meeting with Attila and so impressed the barbarian that Attila spared Rome, but most scholars believe that the Hun king had simply turned his conquering eye in other directions.

Hun rule ended suddenly in bloodshed—though not blood spilled in battle. Hun power ended with Attila's bleeding nose! In 453, Attila married for the umpteenth time (he had many brides and sons). On his wedding night with young bride Ildico, Attila lay in their bedchamber, passed out, drunk. In that state, the feared warrior had a nosebleed and choked to death on his own blood.

With Attila gone, his sons squabbled over his empire. No longer united, the Hun "hordes" retreated from conquered lands and regrouped in southeastern Europe. They eventually turned to more peaceful pursuits, and their descendants today can be found in Bulgaria, Romania, Turkey, and Hungary.

That famous Dodge City marshal was born Wyatt Berry Stapp Earp.

THE GATES OF PARADISE

The road to hell may be paved with good intentions, but the gates to paradise are cast in bronze!

The Italian Renaissance (beginning in the early 15th century and continuing into the 16th) was a time of artistic superheroes whose talents and egos spurred them to tackle monumental tasks that could take a lifetime to complete. The city of Florence was at the heart of this cultural revolution, and the Baptistry doors competition may have been the opening salvo.

ROOM WITH A VIEW

Florence is an embarrassment of artistic riches. It was home to the Medici, the greatest art patrons of all time; they and their employees, such as Michelangelo and Leonardo da Vinci, left their marks all over the city.

The Santa Maria del Fiori cathedral is dedicated to St. John the Baptist, Florence's patron saint. And right next door to it is perhaps the most important building in the life of the city: the octagon-shaped Baptistry, which, until recently, was the place that all citizens of Florence were baptized.

Built before the Renaissance, between 1059–1150, the Baptistry is an example of Tuscan Romanesque architecture. The Arte del Calimala, the wool merchants' guild (the wealthiest of the many guilds then and very influential in civic matters) was responsible for maintaining and beautifying the building.

HEY, IS THERE A DRAFT IN HERE?

To enhance the beauty of the Baptistry—and its own reputation— the Arte del Calimala set out to acquire three sets of huge, bronze entrance doors in bas-relief (a sculpture executed on, and attached to, a flat surface). In 1330, artist Andrea Pisano was hired to create the first set for the south side. Pisano finished his doors in 1336; but in 1348, an economic crash and the outbreak of the Black Death forestalled plans for the other two sets of doors.

Crooner Bing Crosby's first group, in 1925, was called Two Boys and a Piano.

THE CONTEST

It wasn't until 1400 that the guild started looking for an artist to complete the two remaining sets. Seven artists (all Tuscans) were asked to compete, among them were Filippo Brunelleschi and Lorenzo Ghiberti. Ghiberti was only about 20 years old at the time and trained as a painter—he hadn't even done much sculpture at this point. Brunelleschi and the other artists were already famous for their work, and each one of them was certain he would win.

The artists were each asked to cast a panel in bronze. Judges from Florence's elite would pick the best, and the winner would complete the two remaining sets of doors. The subject matter was to be the very dramatic biblical story of Abraham and Isaac. Isaac was Abraham's only son, born to him and his wife Sarah in their very old age—a precious child. To test Abraham's faith, God commanded that Abraham sacrifice Isaac. But at the last minute, God sent an angel to spare the boy and told Abraham to sacrifice a ram instead.

Each artist spent almost two years crafting the best panel he could. It soon came down to two artists: Brunelleschi and Ghiberti. (And theirs are the only two panels to survive to this day.)

AND THE WINNER IS...

Ghiberti's entry won unanimously, and it isn't hard to tell why: his artistry is fluid and graceful, and the figures seem poised to leap from the panel. Brunelleschi's panel is flat and lifeless by comparison; his figures seem contorted and out of scale (a donkey in the foreground seems smaller than Abraham). It also probably didn't hurt Ghiberti's chances in the competition that he used a different casting technique. Brunelleschi's panel was solid bronze, and Ghiberti's was hollow. The Arte del Calimala probably at least *considered* the cost savings that Ghiberti's technique would afford them.

After winning the commission, Ghiberti and his workshop (including, for a while, his student Donatello, who would become even more famous than Ghiberti), worked on the doors for a backbreaking 21 years, until 1424. Renaissance superstar and fellow Florentine Michelangelo said the doors were worthy of being called "the gates of paradise."

RENAISSANCE MAN OR EGOMANIAC?

So how did Ghiberti react to being the victor of the high-profile, hotly contested competition? He gloated. In his memoirs *Commentarii*, he wrote:

> To me the honor was conceded universally and with no exception. To all it seemed that I had at that time surpassed the others without exception, as was recognized by a great council and an investigation of learned men...The testimonial of the victory was given in my favor by all, the consuls...and the entire merchants guild, which has charge of the church.

That's not the end of Ghiberti's immodesty. He actually added his own portrait into the third set of doors, intermingled with the portraits of the prophets and prophetesses of the New Testament. The self-portrait is in the form of a medallion. If you ever get a chance to visit the doors, look for the sculpture of a bald man sticking his head out of what looks like a porthole. And across both doors, just above eye level, Ghiberti applied his conspicuous signature.

SOUR GRAPES OR SAVING GRACE?

How did Brunelleschi react to being the loser of the competition? He pouted—at least at first. In 1403, after he lost, he was so insulted—and more than a little bit annoyed—that he swore off art and sculpture altogether and dedicated himself solely to architecture. It's a good thing for Florence that he did. The Cathedral of Florence was missing a dome, and he was the only one who could figure out how to finish it. Earlier architects had built a massive building that they envisioned being topped off with a classical dome. But the size and scope of the building created an engineering nightmare as to how to raise a dome large enough to cover the opening without it being so heavy that it might squash the building underneath it.

Brunelleschi solved the problem with an ingenious design innovation. He created a system of two domes, one inside the other. The lower dome gives support to the upper one, thus allowing it to appear hollow from inside the cathedral. The Duomo, as it's known, was the largest dome built since Rome's Pantheon and the highest ever to be built at that time.

LET THEM EAT LE BIG MAC

A history of fast food—mostly American and mostly McDonald's—around the world…

Belgium
Belgium is the original home of the french fry, and specialty french-fry shops, called *friteries*, abound—which makes American "French" fries a tough sell. Regardless, McDonald's has been ensconced there since 1978, and you'll see the occasional Domino's Pizza or Pizza Hut. (The locals favor ham, mushrooms, and tomato slices on their pies.) But most Belgians prefer their own food: fast food makes up less than 5 percent of all food sales in the country.

Brazil
McDonald's arrived in 1979, and Dunkin' Donuts came in 1982. Today, McDonald's is Brazil's single largest private employer.

China
The first American fast-food restaurant in China was KFC (then Kentucky Fried Chicken) in 1987. Five years later, thousands of people waited in line for hours when the first McDonald's opened in Beijing. Today, KFC has more than 1,000 restaurants in China because they tailor menus to local tastes, serving dishes such as the notably non-Kentuckian rice, spinach, and tomato porridge. China is also where McDonald's little giveaway toys are made.

England
The dynamic duo of McDonald's and Burger King swooped in as the first-fast food purveyors, in 1974 and 1977, respectively. Since fish and chips is a dish native to England, Yankee food is just a variation on a centuries-old theme. In the 1950s, British started their own burger joint called Wimpy's. Today, the British eat more fast food than any other western Europeans, hosting more than 1,000 McDonald's restaurants, 700 Burger Kings, and 270 Domino's Pizzas (ham and pineapple is the favorite).

Before striking it rich as a writer of westerns, Zane Grey had a dentistry practice.

France

Many French find the idea of fast food repulsive; but American burger chains have been a fixture in Paris since the 1970s. A fellow named Jose Bove became an instant celebrity when he bulldozed a McDonald's into bite-size pieces near his home in Millau in 2000. But American fast food is a hit with Americanized French youth, who call it McDo, for short.

Germany

During the 1970s, America launched a burger blitzkrieg—tapping into a ready market of young adults raised learning English in a post-WWII climate. Today, McDonald's is the largest restaurant company in Germany.

Guam

The northern Pacific island of Guam had the first international Taco Bell in the late 1970s. At last count, the bite-size paradise had six Taco Bells, thirteen Subway sandwich shops, five Burger Kings, five KFCs, seven McDonald's, five Pizza Huts, two Sbarro restaurants, and two Denny's. It also has the world's largest Kmart (with a Little Caesars—pizza! pizza!—inside).

Hong Kong

The region is elbow-to-elbow people, and most houses are too small to entertain guests in. So eating out at restaurants is popular, and American food is trendy. The locals weren't used to standing in line to get to a cash register, so McDonald's hired women to yell at customers who got out of line.

India

In the early 1990s, KFC was on a worldwide roll—and wanted to strut its stuff in India too. But its timing was bad. It plunked down big bucks and marketed heavily just as a nationalist political party was inciting a backlash against foreign companies. The locals protested, and KFC all but pulled out. McDonald's and Pizza Hut came in successfully when the climate improved a few years later. Today, Maharaja Macs and Masala Pizzas are gaining popularity.

"Perry Mason" author Erle Stanley Gardner had a stint as a professional boxer.

Iraq
Any day now.

Italy
Sure, all the usual suspects swarmed in during the 1970s. But in 1986, an Italian named Carlo Petrini created the Slow Food Movement encouraging people to chuck the burgers for a long, enjoyable meal.

Japan
McDonald's paved the burger path to Japan and opened its first restaurant in 1971. Its Bi-gu Ma-ku (Big Mac) is hugely popular. Japan is now home to more than 3,800 McDonald's restaurants. Its store on the world's busiest street, the Ginza of Tokyo, serves an average of 641,857 customers daily!

Kuwait
Three years after U.S. troops pulled out after Operation Desert Storm, McDonald's pulled in. On opening day, the drive-through line was 7 miles (11 km) long. There are more than 50 McDonald's in Kuwait today.

Russia
Getting burgers into the land of borscht took 14 years of negotiation. The first one opened in 1990. Today, Russia has more than 100 McDonald's, as well as some KFCs and Pizza Huts. Recently, Papa John's Pizza got in the mix, hitting the onetime Soviets with its To Russia with Love pizza: mashed potatoes, bacon, onions, and garlic butter sauce.

Sweden
The Swedish McDonald's serve nothing but organic food in edible or degradable packaging. And in 2002, the first McDonald's drive-through window for snowmobiles was opened in Piteaa, Sweden.

Switzerland
Geneva, Switzerland, welcomed the first McDonald's in 1976. The menu today offers sandwiches like the Fish Mac, McCroissant, and

Sigmund Freud was known as "The Clock Man" because he lived his life to such a tight timetable.

the Vegi Mac. And Zurich has the first ever McDonald's hotel—complete with golden arches headboards. Pizza Hut has set up shop too, and they deliver.

Tahiti

In his book *Fast Food Nation*, Eric Schlosser notes that in 1986, the Tahiti Tourism Board ran a promotion that showed a picture of Tahiti's breathtaking natural beauty along with the words: "Sorry, no McDonald's." Not only was it true, but it was also fitting for a French annex with an emphasis on the slow life. Alas, one opened in the capital, Papeete, about 10 years later.

* * * * *

YOU TELL 'EM, AMERICANUS!

Like it did with Australia, the British government sent convicts to America—not to be the first colonists, but to be servants of the colonists who'd already arrived. After a series of inevitable crimes from shoplifting to vicious murders, Benjamin Franklin published an article in the *Pennsylvania Gazette* on May 9, 1751.

Under the headline, "On the Transportation of Felons to the Colonies," Franklin put forth a brilliant and sarcastic idea. Why didn't America, in return, transport its rattlesnakes to Britain?

In the Spring of the Year, when they first creep out of their Holes, they are feeble, heavy, slow, and easily taken; and if a small Bounty were allow'd per Head, some Thousands might be collected annually, and transported to Britain. There I would propose to have them carefully distributed in St. James's Park, in the Spring-Gardens and other Places of Pleasure about London; in the Gardens of all the Nobility and Gentry throughout the Nation; but particularly in the Gardens of the Prime Ministers, the Lords of Trade and Members of Parliament; for to them we are most particularly obliged. Rattle-Snakes seem the most suitable Returns for the Human Serpents sent by our Mother Country. In this, however, as in every other branch of trade, she will have the Advantage of us. She will reap equal Benefits without equal Risque of the Inconveniencies and Dangers. For the Rattle-Snake gives Warning before he attempts his Mischief; which the Convict does not. I am

Yours, &c.
AMERICANUS

Alexander, King of Greece (1917–1920), died at age 27 from the bite of a pet monkey.

WHERE ARE THEY NOW?

The Maya

Dear Uncle John,

I've always liked a good mystery. I want to know about those people called the mysterious Maya.

Mystery fan

Dear Mystery Fan,

The Maya created a great civilization in Central America stretching across present-day southern Mexico, Guatemala, northern Belize, and western Honduras. At the high point of their culture, they lived in flourishing cities that included elaborately decorated stone pyramids that served as temples, palaces, and observatories. The Maya were accomplished astronomers and had a solar year of 365 days, just like we do. They were excellent mathematicians and engineers who designed a water storage system of reservoirs, canals, and cisterns. And they were a literate people who had their own form of writing.

But—ever so mysteriously—in A.D. 950 this cultured people abandoned the massive pyramids of their southern cities to the overgrowth of rain forests and tropical jungles. They never rose to prominence again. When archaeologists rediscovered the Mayan ruins in the 1850s, the big mystery was...what happened?

For more than a century, scholars argued various theories. In the 1990s, scientists from the University of Florida (examining sediment in Lake Chichancanab on the Yucatán Peninsula for evidence of climate change), discovered that the Mayan collapse coincided with the region's driest time in 7,000 years. A terrible drought probably caused people to abandon their cities.

Today, the Maya number about six million people with large groups found in Mexico, Guatemala, and Belize. Many Mayan communities still preserve some of their ancient, "mysterious" heritage—especially the Lancandon of the Chiapas rain forest in Mexico, who it's believed, still practice a form of the Mayan religion.

Emile Zola, the French novelist (*Nana*), died of carbon monoxide poisoning from a defective flue.

THE SAINT THAT AIN'T

The patron saint of death...

L ooking for a patron saint? You shouldn't have much trouble finding one. The 1956 edition of *Butler's Lives of the Saints* contains 2,565 named saints. You can find a patron saint for button makers, dairymaids, and pastry chefs; for gravediggers, grocers, and grandfathers; for fugitives, jugglers, and truck drivers— not to mention hundreds of other specific purposes. So it is passing strange that in Mexico, the world's second-biggest Catholic country, the favorite saint for more than a few people is a figure known as La Santa Muerte, or Saint Death.

UNDERCOVER SAINT
We hasten to add that Saint Death is not one of your canonized saints. You won't find this particular saint in *Butler's* or on any official list. The Catholic Church not only doesn't acknowledge his (or her, or its) existence but is downright opposed to the worship of this character. Indeed, Catholic Church officials consider Saint Death "an evil figure, a grisly embodiment of satanic purposes."

GENDER CONFUSION
About that gender problem? It's all part of La Santa Muerte's mystique. People personify the saint as either he or she without any apparent rationale except their own perception. Saint Death is sometimes shown as a man dressed as the Grim Reaper and sometimes as a woman in a long white satin gown and wearing a golden crown.

THE BROTHERS GRIM
In a shop in Ojinaga, in Chihuahua, Mexico, figures of Saint Death come in three colors—white, black, and red—and which one you buy depends on what you're praying for. The figures look exactly alike, except for their color. The statues are of a robed Grim Reaper on a pedestal, with a skull for a head, holding a set

---

The jazz musician Cab Calloway (1907–94) is credited with coining the word "jitterbug."

of balance scales. Sometimes, instead of scales, the statue may carry the more familiar scythe. You'd buy the white one if you're looking for a cure or for luck. The black one is for protection and vengeance. The red one is for love spells.

CULT-URE CLASH
The church's disapproving attitude doesn't seem to register on Saint Death's petitioners. The saint is worshiped by thugs, criminals, and drug dealers, but also by everyday folk who invoke the saint for protection and for the recovery of health, stolen items, or even kidnapped family members.

Santa Muerte seems to appeal especially to the poor and downtrodden, perhaps because this saint is so tolerant. "When you go to church you get told off," one man said as he stood before a shrine to Santa Muerte. "But she does not discriminate. Here nobody cares who you are or what you do." At the shrine, offerings to Saint Death include roses, tequila, chocolates, colored candles, and cigarettes.

Some view Santa Muerte as a figure of black magic, yet others consider him/her as a Catholic saint worthy of worship. "In some parts of Mexico," writes author Amy Welborn, who's written several books on religion and Catholic saints, "she is becoming a rival in popular affection to the Virgin of Guadeloupe, the manifestation of the Virgin Mary that is the reigning symbol of Mexican national identity."

DEAD FROM THE START
Where did Saint Death come from? Anthropologists date the origin of the cult to the Spanish conquest that brought Christianity into contact with Aztecs who worshipped death figures such as Mictlantecutli. In pre-Columbian times deities like Coatlicue and Xipe Totec were often portrayed in skeletal form. Others say that Saint Death's origins are a mix of Roman Catholicism, voodoo, and Santeria, a religion in which African deities are identified with Catholic saints. It all seems to fit comfortably with the tradition of Mexico's popular Day of the Dead holiday, in which people picnic on tombs, eat candy skulls and coffins, and decorate their homes with paper streamers depicting skeletons—embracing death as a part of life.

HORSEPOWER

One of our historians, Uncle Ed (we've never seen him, but we send him five bales of hay every month), claims that history books have neglected the most important animal in Western history. To prove his case, he's agreed to answer questions on the subject. And his answers come straight from the horse's mouth.

Dear Uncle Ed,

How did people and horses get together in the first place?

Old Nellie

Dear Nellie,

Man's first relationship with horses wasn't too promising—at least from the horses' viewpoint. About 20,000 years ago, Cro-Magnon man went after horses for food. In Salutre, France, a prehistoric valley is filled with the bones of some 10,000 horses that were run over a cliff by Cro-Magnon hunters. It took tens of thousands of years for folks to finally figure out that horses were more than good eatin'.

The Eurasians from the Ukrainian steppes are believed to have been the first to tame and ride the horse, about 6,000 years ago. The evidence? Six thousand-year-old horse teeth that show signs of bit wear. So people have been on riding horses at least that long. It makes my back ache just to think about it.

Dear Uncle Ed,

An old teacher of mine, (who's been put out to pasture) used to say that in history, the cart came before the horse. Do you think he'd been eating too much loco weed?

A. Neighsayer

Dear A. Neighsayer,
Your teacher is right. The Sumerians engineered rollers and wheels for their plows and sledges and made them into carts; they were pulled by oxen and donkeys, not horses. Around 3000 B.C., horses were brought to Mesopotamia from the Ukraine and hitched to

In Egyptian mythology, a person possessed six souls, three of the body and three of the mind.

carts in four-horse teams. Like modern carmakers, the Sumerian cart makers adapted the design of their vehicles to take superior horsepower into account. And chariots were born. Once horses were hitched to chariots, the early world was never the same.

Dear Uncle Ed,

I disagree with the idea that horses are the most important animals in history. Dogs have served as burglar alarms for thousands of years now. Plus, they fetch pipes, slippers, and newspapers. What did horses ever bring anybody?

Chow Hound

Dear Chow Hound,

You're barking up the wrong tree. Horses brought mankind mobility. And more.

Once chariots were invented, they changed the way war was fought. A general with foot soldiers was lucky if his troops could cover a few miles at 15 miles per hour (24 km per hour). Wearing armor, or carrying a heavy spear, a soldier's speed was even slower. But put a soldier in a chariot and the speed for long distances could jump to nearly 45 miles per hour (72 km per hour). Nations with armies of horse-drawn chariots could arrive quickly at the door of the enemy, attack and plunder, and then make a quick retreat—and live to fight another day.

People with horses, like those early horse-owning tribes in the steppes, were richer than their horseless neighbors. Nations fared even better: they conquered their horseless neighbors. Take the Middle Kingdom pharaohs of ancient Egypt. The pharaohs lost their lands to a Semitic people called Hyksos ("rulers of desert uplands") because the Hyksos army overwhelmed them with new-fangled chariots pulled by strange animals—called horses.

Under Hyksos rule, Egyptians gradually took up horsemanship for themselves. After mastering the use of horses and chariots, the Egyptians not only took their country back, but they created an imperial Egyptian empire across Palestine and Syria. Other ancient peoples—like the Hittites, Macedonians, and Persians— caught on to the same idea, using horsepower to expand their empires. The race for power and glory in ancient history was a horse race! Put that in your pipe and slippers.

Dear Uncle Ed,

I come from a long line of cavalry fighters. My great-great-great grand-father was even called Man o' War! To settle a few family arguments, could you tell us which general in history made the best use of horses? How long did the cavalry remain important in world affairs? And when was the last great cavalry battle?

Hay Dude

Dear Hay Dude,

It seems a tough choice to pick just one great general, since so many of the best and brightest relied on the cavalry: Alexander the Great and Attila the Hun are up there with the best. But Genghis Khan, that brutal Mongol general, had every one of his men mounted on a horse. He also had spare horses carrying supplies and equipment for long campaigns, which gave him a mobile army superior to any of his day and allowed him to make lightning-fast raids. Genghis Khan's hordes conquered most of Russia, Asia, and parts of Europe. In one generation, he came to rule the world's largest empire.

Horses gave armies a "mobile arm." The cavalry helped generals spy out enemy positions and charge any breach of infantry lines. Because the cavalry was so important—from Napoléon's time to World War I—commanders and senior officers were usually taken from the cavalry.

In 1920, the last great cavalry skirmish took place between the USSR and Poland at theVistula River; the Poles won. But the horses won too: they retired from much of warfare—to let tanks, trucks, and humans take the brunt of modern firepower.

* * * * *

For "More Horsepower," see page 385.

For "More Horsepower," see page 385.

In 1714, the favorite nonalcoholic drink of early American colonists was chocolate.

THE KNIGHTS TEMPLAR: PART I

*Start with nine very determined knights and a couple of
sacred oaths. Add a jealous and vindictive king, a puppet pope,
a mysterious wagon train, and a medieval "celebrity roast,"
and you get the amazing—and sometimes bizarre—story of
the warrior-monks known as the Knights Templar.*

A t the end of the First Crusade (1095–1099), the Christian armies of Europe had succeeded in wresting control of the Holy Land and the holy city of Jerusalem from the Muslims. But very soon afterward, the Muslims started winning battles and regaining some of their lands, which made traveling to the Holy Land from Europe a perilous undertaking for pilgrims and nonpilgrims alike.

In 1118, nine knights, concerned for the welfare of the Christian pilgrims, bound themselves together in the creation of a knightly order of warrior-monks called the Knights Templar. The order's full name—the Poor Knights of Christ and the Temple of Solomon—was a reference to the Temple of King Solomon in Jerusalem, where the Templars were stationed when they first took their vows. They vowed to consecrate their swords and their very lives to the defense of the Christian faith, and to live humbly and simply according to the monkish dictates of poverty, chastity, and humility.

THE PRICE OF ADMISSION

Candidates seeking to join the Knights Templar had to prove that they came from noble families or that their father was a knight. Potential Templars also had to be at least 21, unmarried, and free from all obligations, including debt. Eventually, the competition for admission was so great that candidates had to pay a very high fee to get in, making it increasingly difficult for anyone but the well-heeled (mostly noblemen) to apply. In addition to fully armed knights, there were originally three other categories of Templars: the sergeants, who formed the light cavalry; the farmers, entrusted with the administration of the Knights Templar's affairs; and the chaplains, charged with ministering to the spiritual needs of the order. Another of their vows was to swear complete and utter obedience to their boss, the grand master (who answered only to the pope).

MONKS WITH MUSCLE
The Templar knights were the shock troops of the Crusader forces. They rarely wielded the largest force in any particular battle. But the effectiveness of medieval armies was usually determined not by numerical superiority, but by training and equipment. Weight of armor, rigor of discipline, and sophistication of battle tactics (all of which the Templars had on their side, and their opponents, for the most part, didn't) proved to be as decisive as firepower would be later.

When the Templars went into battle—a mere dozen fully armed knights, charging on heavy horses—they would function like 20th-century tanks, easily scattering a force of 200 or 300 Saracens (the Crusaders' name for Muslim soldiers). A massed charge of 100 mounted knights could crush 3,000 adversaries.

NO RETREAT, NO NOTHING
When taken prisoner, the Templars (if they were lucky) were told they might be allowed to live—on the condition that they renounce their faith. At the siege of Safed, in Palestine in 1264, ninety Templars met their death in battle; 80 others were taken prisoner and told their lives would be spared if they denied Christ. They refused and were executed. This fidelity to the faith, although very admirable, cost the Templars dearly. Overall, it's been estimated that in less than two centuries, almost 20,000 Templars—knights and sergeants—perished in war. This death toll could also be attributed to one of their most solemn vows: when in battle, no matter what the odds, they swore not to retreat.

AND THEY WERE WELL MANORED TOO
Remember those other vows the Templars swore? To live like monks and obey the vows of poverty and humility? Apparently, someone needed to remind them. Within a few decades of their

founding, the Knights Templar had become—perhaps with the exception of the Papacy—the most powerful, most prestigious, most apparently unshakable institution of its age. And the foundation of this tremendous power and influence was money.

From 1128 (a mere decade after the organization's founding) onward, the order began expanding at an extraordinary pace, taking in not just new members recruited from the noblest houses of Europe, but also huge donations of money, property, and arms. Because they were under the pope's protection—and were themselves designated the protectors of the Christian faith—kings, princes, and church officials were, shall we say, obliged to give freely.

Within another year or so, the Knights Templar owned vast tracts of land in France, England, Scotland, Spain, and Portugal. Another decade passed, and their possessions extended to Italy, Austria, Germany, and Hungary, and as far east as Egypt and Constantinople (modern-day Istanbul), as well as Palestine. By the late 12th century, their European possessions alone numbered more than 7,000 estates. These were mostly manors, farms, churches, monasteries, and castles—all of which generated considerable revenue.

MONKS WITH MUSCLE AND MONEY...

Since the Templars had so many well-fortified castles scattered throughout Europe (more than 800 of them, at one point), these were logical places for noblemen to deposit their wealth when they went on crusades to the Holy Land. A nobleman would naturally take only the ablest men and would have to leave his treasury only lightly guarded. So the Templar castles became a natural place to leave money—especially since they were populated by warrior-monks who'd sworn a vow of poverty.

Being the good businessmen they were, the Templars even gave the noblemen a letter or draft with a secret code that could only be recognized by Templars—sort of like the personal identification number you get with a bank card. They could then present the letter and code to any Templar castle along the way and withdraw gold in coins that were used in that particular area. So the Templars became the de facto bankers of Europe.

...AND TAX-EXEMPT STATUS

The order was exempt from all taxes, as well as tolls on roads, bridges, and rivers. The Templars could offer sanctuary, like any church of the day, or convene their own courts to try local cases. They ran their own markets and fairs, pocketing most of the proceeds. Their many commercial activities included the operation of farms, vineyards, and mines. At the peak of their power, the Templars handled much, if not most, of the available capital in all of Western Europe. They also lent money and collected interest (a practice expressly forbidden under church law) on a massive scale. The English monarchs, for example, were chronically in debt to the Templars.

A RISING STAR

Let's introduce an actual Knight Templar. Jacques de Molay was one of the real up-and-comers of the Templar organization in the 13th century. Born in France in the duchy of Burgundy to a noble but poor family, he joined the Templars in 1265 at age 21. Like those before him, Jacques had most likely joined the Templars in hopes of doing glorious battle with the enemies of Christendom (he did see some action in Syria). But the fame-and-fortune bit may have also served as a motivator.

UP THE ORGANIZATION

On his way up the ladder of Templar success, he was named English master of the temple (the head Templar in England). By 1291, de Molay had moved from England to the island of Cyprus, which, more than 100 years earlier, Richard the Lion-hearted had sold to the Knights Templar (and you didn't even know he owned Cyprus, did you?).

Jacques de Molay was elevated to the office of 23rd grand master of the Knights Templar sometime in the 1290s. He stayed in Cyprus until fate put him on a collision course with the evil and powerful king who wanted to destroy him—and the Knights Templar.

* * * * *

Find out what fate has in store for Grand Master Jacques de Molay in Part II on page 375.

PARALLEL HISTORY

*How some important historic events might have played
out differently if just one letter had been changed.*

WATERLOG, 1815
The real reason that Napoléon was defeated: his army got bogged
down trying to cross a river in Belgium.

THE NORMAL CONQUEST, 1066
You've seen it before: your average, everyday overthrow of
England by a bastard son of a duke.

**THE STOLE AGE,
c. 2,000,000 YEARS AGO–c. 4,000 YEARS AGO**
The period of human history during which people learned to make
wraps out of small, furry creatures.

THE CIVIC WAR, 1861–1865
Conflict between northern and southern Japanese subcompact
carmakers.

THE DARN AGES, 5TH–14TH CENTURIES
Era during which everyone was sort of displeased.

THE HUNDRED SEARS' WAR, 14TH–15TH CENTURIES
Long-term conflict among chain store outlets in Europe.

THE IDEA OF MARCH, 44 B.C.
What Julius Caesar couldn't conceive of—until it was too late.

THE LONDON GLITZ, 1940s
Fashion trend (beaded jackets, gold lamé *everything*) adopted by
Londoners as a way to keep up their spirits in those dark, damp,
underground bomb shelters.

THE BATTLE OF THE BUDGE, 1944–1945
World War II event that gained the Allies a teensy bit of territory.

THE WARS OF THE NOSES, LATE 15TH CENTURY
Cosmetic surgery was just coming into vogue when this violent rivalry between two families of plastic surgeons broke out.

THE GOLF RUSH, 1840s
In which thousands of hopefuls packed up and moved to California, where they could play their favorite sport all year-round.

THE LINCOLN-DOUGLAS REBATES, 1858
Public meetings between two Senate hopefuls from Illinois; held in the good old days when you could get your money back if you weren't satisfied.

THE SALEM PITCH TRIALS, 1692
In which 20 people were executed during the first telemarketing tryouts.

THE LONE MARCH, 1934–1935
Communist leader Mao Zedong couldn't talk anyone into going with him on his trek to northwestern China, so he did it all by himself.

THE TREATS OF VERSAILLES, 1919
Celebration ending World War I for which the Germans had to bring all the desserts.

* * * * *

MORE MISNOMERS

The famous Apache leader Geronimo was called Goyathlay ("one who yawns") by his tribe. Mexican soldiers named him "Geronimo"—Spanish for "Jerome."

Martin Luther King Jr. was christened Michael Luther King Jr. in 1929. Five years later, his father, Michael King Sr. returned from a trip to Europe and changed his and his son's name in honor of the 16th-century German church reformer, Martin Luther.

Ralph Lauren, that epitome of classic fashion, was born Ralph Lifshitz in the then not-so-fashionable Bronx in 1939.

WHEN HENRY MET DAVID

The 19th century was a golden age for explorers.
Here's the story of two of the best.

"Dr. Livingstone, I presume." These were the words uttered by Henry Stanley on that famous day in 1871 when he finally tracked down "missing" Victorian explorer Dr. David Livingstone on the shores of Lake Tanganyika. But what about the man who said them? Who was Henry Morton Stanley exactly, and why was he looking for Livingstone in the first place?

DOING THE CONTINENTAL

In the 19th century, Europe and America didn't know a whole lot about Africa. They knew *where* it was, but they didn't know what was in it. So, from the early 1800s on, inquisitive European adventurers started heading for the so-called Dark Continent. They quickly discovered two important facts: that Africa was very rich in natural resources, and that the primitively armed native tribesmen were no match for Western firepower. Africa was there for the taking.

By the 1870s, the Scramble for Africa (as the opportunistic invasion was called) was well under way. Britain led the field, quickly snapping up huge slabs of real estate in southern, central, and eastern parts of Africa. After which, a second wave of explorers descended on the continent. Their aim was not to grab as much land as possible but to explore and map Africa scientifically—and to convert the heathen Africans to Christianity.

CHINA OR...AFRICA OR BUST

David Livingstone personified this new type of explorer. Born into a poor but pious Scottish family in 1813, Livingstone, through a combination of hard work and faith, raised himself out of poverty to earn a medical degree at the University of Glasgow. His initial aim was to practice and preach in China, but this plan was ruined when Britain went to war with China in 1839. He decided to spread the "good word" in Africa instead. Arriving in Cape Town in 1841, Livingstone eagerly set off inland—and found that a growing interest in exploration soon matched his desire for finding converts.

THEY CALL ME THE WANDERER
When Livingstone became the first European to cross the entire width of southern Africa—discovering and naming Victoria Falls on the way—he became a national hero back in Britain and a celebrity in the United States. His book *Missionary Travels and Researches in South Africa* (1857) was a best seller. In the mid-1860s, he developed an ambitious plan to discover the source of the Nile River. The plan captured the national imagination. Livingstone was given a triumphant send-off from Britain in late 1865—and promptly vanished.

PAGING DR. LIVINGSTONE!
For four long years little or no word was heard from the famous explorer. In the United States, James Gordon Bennett, proprietor of the *New York Herald*, decided in 1871 that the time had come to track down the misguided missionary (and boost his paper's circulation figures with a good, old-fashioned human-interest story). His star reporter, Henry Morton Stanley, was dispatched to Africa to find Livingstone.

POOR LITTLE KID
Stanley had traveled a long way on his rise to journalistic fame. He was born John Rowlands in Wales in 1841, and he spent his childhood in a workhouse (also known as a poorhouse, the 19th-century alternative to living on the streets). In 1859, he set sail for America, finding a job as a cabin boy on a ship bound for New Orleans. In America, he was taken under the wing of a successful merchant named Henry Stanley, who virtually adopted the boy. John Rowlands, in honor of his benefactor, took Henry Stanley's first and last names.

JOHNNY REB REBELS
Now an American, young Stanley joined the Confederate Army when the Civil War broke out. Captured at the Battle of Shiloh, he proved he was a born survivor by switching sides and joining

---

Joel Chandler Harris's home near Atlanta, Georgia, was called Snapbean Farm.

the Union cause. After the war, he took up journalism, working as a foreign correspondent in Egypt, Russia, Persia, and India. So when the call came to head off to Africa, Stanley was more than ready.

PLEASED TO MEET YOU

In March 1871, Stanley arrived in Zanzibar on central Africa's east coast with a virtual army of guides, porters, troops, and hangers-on (2,000 in all). The group ruthlessly crushed any resistance from local tribes that they met along the way and plowed on into the interior. On November 10, 1871, Stanley finally tracked down his quarry at the village of Ujiji, on the shores of Lake Tanganyika (in modern-day Tanzania).

It was a historic moment as the young reporter strode toward the scholarly Scottish explorer, offering Livingstone his hand and uttering the phrase for which he's gone down in history. However, Livingstone seemed a little bit bemused by all the fanfare: he wasn't even aware that he was "lost"! He'd just been exploring some of Africa's deepest, darkest corners and hadn't been able to get word back home as to his whereabouts. *He* knew where he was.

Not letting the facts stand in the way of a good story, Stanley wrote the incident up for his newspaper's readers in the most heroic light possible (and followed it up in 1872 with the best seller, modestly titled *How I Found Livingstone*).

WHATEVER BECAME OF...?

Livingstone wasn't expecting a visit from Stanley, but he was sure glad to see him. Supplies were running low, and Livingstone was suffering from dysentery. Stanley offered much-needed provisions, and the two became fast friends while Livingstone convalesced. After this, their paths diverged radically. Livingstone set off again on his (unsuccessful) hunt to find the source of the Nile, and he died from another bout of dysentery just over a year later.

Stanley, on the other hand, fared much better. Having caught the exploration bug, in 1877 he successfully navigated the 1,864-mile (3,000-km) Congo River, opening it up as a vital waterway into Africa. Never one to miss a trick, Stanley

---

The first U.S. skyscraper was the Home Insurance Co. Building of Chicago, in 1885.

recounted this journey in yet another blockbuster, *Through the Dark Continent*. Many more explorations (and books) followed, as did fame and fortune. In the early 1890s, Stanley decided to return to his native Britain, where he married, became a member of Parliament, and in 1899, was knighted by Queen Victoria. When he died in 1904, Stanley was a pillar of the British establishment—a far cry indeed from the poor, Welsh workhouse boy he had once been.

* * * * *

ORVILLE AND WILBUR, GET IN LINE!

Everyone knows about the Wright brothers' historic flight at Kitty Hawk, North Carolina, on December 17, 1903. Just how historic was it? Three others actually achieved self-propelled manned flight in heavier-than-air machines, as opposed to glider flights and balloons, before the Wright Brothers:

1. 1894: American-born machine-gun inventor Hiram S. Maxim (1840–1916), then in England, built a multiwing aircraft operated by steam engines that briefly rose into the air carrying a crew of three.

2. Late 1902: Texas minister/mechanic Burrell Cannon (1848–1922) built, and a "Mister Stamps" flew, the *Ezekiel Airship*, in Pittsburg, Texas. It was airborne only briefly, but it flew.

3. August 14, 1901: Gustave Whitehead, at Fairfield, Connecticut, flew about half a mile in a single-engine, two-propeller monoplane.

So why do the Wright brothers get the credit? Partly because of prejudice of the times (Whitehead, for instance, was a German immigrant) and mostly because the Wrights were the first to document their achievement—they had the photographs, witnesses, and publicity.

It had 10 floors, and two more were added later.

HEY, YOUR FLY IS CLOSED!

How the zipper made that long trip to the front of your pants.

In the late 19th century, Whitcomb L. Judson, a Chicago mechanical engineer, got tired of the time he spent each morning fastening his shoes. Life would be so much easier if he could create a fastening system to replace the cumbersome buttons and hooks that were used on all fashionable footwear of the era.

So he invented the Clasp-Locker, a metal slider that joined two chains of alternating hook and eye locks. It took two years to get a patent for it, but once he did, Judson presented his baby at the prestigious Chicago World's Fair of 1893.

A FAIR-TO-POOR RECEPTION

He sat in his booth every day during the fair's six-month run. Millions flocked to the event of the century, but poor Judson sold only a few Clasp-Lockers.

The general public thought his invention was silly. And maybe they were right. It didn't really work very well; it had the tendency to pop open. It rusted too quickly, and it was expensive because each one had to be hand manufactured.

PERSISTENCE DOESN'T PAY OFF

Judson kept working on it. And in 1904, he partnered with a couple of friends and formed the Automatic Hook and Eye Company, which later became the Universal Fastener Company. In 1905, Judson came up with a new hookless fastener called the C-Curity. Clothing manufacturers still weren't interested because it would cost too much to change manufacturing methods.

Judson died in 1909, thinking his invention was a failure. And it could have been—if it weren't for the persistence of one of his employees.

PERSISTENCE DOES PAY OFF

Canadian electrical engineer Gideon Sundback took it upon himself to improve Judson's design. In 1913, he produced the practical,

---

Thomas Moore of Brookville, Maryland, coined the term "refrigerator" in 1803.

affordable fastener we use today. (He also invented machines to make the parts so they wouldn't need to be handmade.)

Sundback still had a hard time convincing manufacturers to use the new gadget. But in 1917, a money-belt maker saw the potential in the strange hookless fastener. He bought a bunch of them to use on his button-free money belts. Sales of the fasteners surged when a tobacco pouch entrepreneur decided to market string-free tobacco pouches. Called the Locktite Tobacco Pouch, the item was promoted using the motto, "Keeps Tobacco Right. No Strings—No Buttons."

OH, MY GALOSH!
By now garment manufacturers were taking notice of the product they'd rejected years earlier. In 1918, the fasteners were used on flying suits, and in 1921, B. F. Goodrich Company ordered 170,000 fasteners for the galoshes it manufactured. One story is that during the promoting and demonstrating of said galoshes, an enthusiastic marketing man declared, "Zip, it's open! Zip, it's closed!" From that day forward the sliding fasteners became known as zippers. Other stories say it was Goodrich himself who coined the name.

GOODBYE TO BUTTONS
A sales campaign for children's clothing in 1930 praised zippers as promoting self-reliance in young children by making it possible for them to dress themselves. Fashion designer Elsa Schiaparelli used them as whimsical decorations on the clothes she created for her 1935 collection.

THE ZIPPER COMES HOME
But the zipper finally beat the button once and for all in 1937, in the "Battle of the Fly," when French fashion designers installed zippers in men's trousers. *Esquire* magazine declared the zipper the "Newest Tailoring Idea for Men" and among the zippered fly's many virtues was that it would eliminate "the Possibility of Unintentional and Embarrassing Disarray."

Obviously, the new zippered trouser owners hadn't had time yet to discover the experience of forgetting to zip up.

The first U.S. medical diploma was granted by Yale University in 1729.

WHERE ARE THEY NOW?

The Celts

Dear Uncle John,

I bleached my hair and got some blue tattoos for an original look, but my wife says the Celts already invented my style. Is this true?

Blue-in-the-Face

Dear Blue-in-the-Face,
As Romans fought to conquer Europe (France, Holland, Austria, Switzerland, and Britain), they battled tribes of Celts. The Celts were successful farmers, artisans, and ironworkers with a rich oral culture, history, legal systems, and spirituality.

Romans found the Celtic swordplay plenty scary, as they did the Celtic custom of using their enemies' heads to decorate the front door. But the Romans seemed most disturbed by the Celts appearance. Celtic farmers grew an herb of the mustard family called woad; warriors used woad to make blue body paint and tattoos so they'd appear fierce to their enemies.

Roman historian Diodorus wrote about the Celts, "Their aspect is terrifying...They are very tall in stature, with rippling muscles under clear white skin. Their hair is blond, but not naturally so: they bleach it, to this day, artificially, washing it in lime and combing it back from their foreheads. They look like wood demons."

Warring was a Celtic obsession. Better to die young in battle rather than peacefully in old age. Unfortunately for the Celtic tribes, their love of fighting included feuding among themselves. The Romans conquered their lands, and only in Ireland and northern Britain did the Celtic way of life survive.

Today, only six nations and regions—Ireland, Wales, Scotland, Cornwall, the Isle of Man, and Brittany—are still in touch with their Celtic heritage. But Celtic culture still makes its mark. The Celtic belief that there are healing spirits in trees encourages us to "knock on wood." And millions enjoy Celtic music (Scottish bagpipes are one example) and Celtic dance (*Lord of the Dance* and *Riverdance* attest to that).

The first law school in the U.S. was the Litchfield Law School in Connecticut.

WORST IMPRESSIONS

*For the sailors of the British Navy, the romantic life
of adventure on the high seas had some definite lows,
usually starting with enlistment.*

B ack in England during the rules of Elizabeth I, Charles I,
and Oliver Cromwell, the term *press gang* didn't refer to
newspaper reporters or dry cleaners. Press gang described
hard-nosed toughs recruited by the Royal Navy in English seaports
to persuade local men, by any means, to "take the king's shilling,"
which was a euphemism for enlisting on the Admiralty's ships—
like it or not.

DOWN TO THE SEA IN SHIPS
During Elizabethan days, merry olde England wasn't all that merry.
Not only was England losing out to Spain and Holland in the
great colonialist land grab, but also the Spanish king, Phillip II,
decided to invade England. To that end, he put together a large
armada of ships. Its first objective was to crush the English fleet, a
motley assemblage of termite-ridden tubs and hulks, former pirate
ships, and big, clumsy merchant ships.

THAT DOES IT!
England had spent most of its early history being invaded—by the
Norse, the Normans, the Romans—just about anybody with a
boat and a sharp sword. Well, the Brits had had enough. They
beat back the Spanish Armada, and then they went on a ship-
building binge. About the same time, flush with victory, the
English royals decided Britannia should rule the waves. At which
point, they discovered that they were suddenly very big on ships—
but very short on sailors.

AH, THE SEAFARING LIFE
Trusting to nationalistic ardor, the navy sought volunteers, the
origination of "taking the king's shilling," payment in advance for
enlistment. "Thanks, but no thanks," was the response. So the
navy tried conscription (the draft), based on the population of

---

Its graduates have included Aaron Burr, Horace Mann, and Noah Webster.

each county. It worked during years of poor crops and high unemployment, but when the crops were good and jobs were plentiful, the quotas always fell short. (It should also be mentioned that the counties used conscription as a way to foist their thieves, scofflaws, laggards, drunkards, and sundry other scoundrels on the Admiralty and army. After a time even that supply thinned.)

Despite all this, Britannia did come to rule the waves. But it didn't stop the other great nations of Europe—quite the opposite, in fact. Napoléon, for one, went on the march, which meant the need for more ships, and more warm bodies to man them, for England.

But the image of the Royal Navy had been tarnished. Service wasn't seen as a noble career for potential officers anymore (officer commissions often being purchased in order to shuffle off second sons who had no hope of inheriting the family estate). No remotely respectable fellow wanted to take up seafaring with the navy, knowing they'd have to crew with England's human dregs.

The Royal Navy had a reputation for having more ways to punish a sailor than to keep him happy. Add to that the fact that the food was bad, the pay was worse, and life expectancy was lower than a pub crawler's in a London slum.

Of course, in seaports like London, Spithead, Liverpool, and Plymouth, too long at the pub could also be hazardous. Every port had a press gang and each had a quota. If the "gangers" failed to meet their quota, they could end up pressed themselves. During time of war, which seemed to be most of the time, the Royal Navy wasn't too picky.

OFF LIMITS

Not everyone was prey to the gangers though. The English lords and pooh-bahs of the realm weren't about to have the best of their blood reduced to cannon fodder. Along with these connected people, indispensable harbor pilots, ferry captains, and inshore ships' officers were exempted, saved by a written Protection document, which they had to carry at all times.

Of course, you could buy forged Protection papers. Or, if you weren't the kind of guy who thought ahead, the gangers would accept cash.

The first telephone book ever issued contained only 50 names.

S.O.S.

In a lot of ports, citizens set up early warning systems. When the press gang went prowling, a clamor went up, signaled by bell ringing, for instance. Local men immediately knew they had to find deep cellars, high attics, and dark closets to hide in. This mostly occurred when a "hot press" was ordered, which meant that Protections were temporarily rescinded by a desperate Admiralty.

As a last resort, luckless captives could sometimes be bought back from the gangers, but those occasions were rare. More likely were violent clashes, near-riots on the streets when the gangers snagged a local favorite son. Informal underground railways developed to spirit men inland—free to many, at a price to others.

During the Napoléonic Wars (1803–1815), the Admiralty stumbled on a surefire source of recruits—of exchanged prisoners of war. This worked well for everyone except the returned POWs, most of whom believed they'd already done enough for king and country. Once the citizenry realized what the Admiralty was doing, they took action to protect the returning prisoners. On one occasion, as navy ships waited at anchor to take on 300 newly pressed POWs, locals conspired to land them upriver from the harbor and rush them into hiding in the countryside.

Generally, Englishmen—especially those living inland—accepted the notion of press gangs. But the brazen Admiralty took the business a step further when they decided they could waylay ships of other nations on the high seas and help themselves to *their* crew members.

They restricted their pickings to British citizens, of which there were many because merchant ships paid salaries that were three or four times as much as the Royal Navy paid. Instructed not to strip a ship of its crew so as to endanger it, the navy managed to exchange their troublemakers and scruffs for seasoned sailors.

THIS MEANS WAR!

The British got into the habit of stopping American ships; this was not a smooth move, as it turned out. Politics and economics put an end to it. The British habit of high-seas impressment of American sailors—particularly in a single incident in 1807, that of

---

The lollipop was named by George Smith after a popular racehorse, Lolly Pop, in 1908.

impressing four sailors from the USS *Chesapeake*, two of whom were American-born—resulted in the War of 1812.

To the eventual relief of everyone, except a few hidebound old admirals ruminating over cigars and brandies in cloistered London gentlemen's clubs, the press gangs were retired by 1850.

These days, the Royal Navy attracts its recruits the modern way: through advertisements, photos of fun-filled activities and events, and mottoes like "Anything's possible with a career in the Royal Navy." A far cry from the old days.

* * * * *

WHICH WAY IS UP?

In the first *Uncle John's Bathroom Reader Plunges Into History* we rightly credited the Chinese with the invention of the compass. But it wasn't invented so that some explorer could find his way through uncharted territory; it was invented to be used in the art of feng shui (pronounced "fung shway").

The Chinese believe that chi, the invisible energy of life, flows through the earth the way blood flows through the veins of the human body. They use feng shui when designing a building and deciding which direction it should face on its site so that it will attract the most chi.

It wasn't until later that Chinese sailors adapted the compass for navigation at sea. Arab traders brought the compass to Western Europe in the 13th century, just in time for the European explorers to leave the coastlines they'd been hugging and start navigating toward unknown and out-of-sight land.

WHAT A PAINE IN THE NECK

Thomas Paine was a writer, agitator, Anglo-American revolutionary, and professional troublemaker. They certainly don't make 'em like him any more—and that's a pity.

T om Paine's life was pretty exciting, to say the least. He was a central figure in both the American War of Independence and the French Revolution. During Paine's event-filled 72 years, he took on the British government and army, the French king, and anyone else he considered an opponent of liberty. Though Paine was entirely self-taught, his works—*Common Sense*, *The Rights of Man*, and *The Age of Reason*, to name just a few—probably did more to advance the cause of democracy than those of any other modern writer.

REBEL WITHOUT A CAUSE

Born in England in 1737, Tom Paine was poor and badly educated. He grew into a cranky young man, unable to hold down either a regular job or a relationship. By his mid-20s, Paine had held and lost a string of positions and had been married twice.

Paine's life was at a low ebb when, in his late 30s, he found work as a customs officer. Customs men were held in low esteem (even the smugglers they were hired to capture were more popular). The work paid little and was thankless—so Paine decided to do something about it. He had a passion for self-improvement and was constantly reading books on science, politics, and philosophy. Inspired by his reading, Paine organized his coworkers into a protest group to agitate for better conditions. He also wrote the first of his many political tracts, *The Case of the Officers of the Excise*. But Paine's attempt at a workers' revolt failed, and he was fired.

SAVED BY THE BEN

That was when things started to look up. Paine moved to London and, while there, got to know Benjamin Franklin (both men attended meetings of the same scientific society). Franklin

---

...farmers were required by law to mark all of their pigs.

recognized Paine as a man of spirit and energy, and so recommended that Paine head for America, where his ornery nature would fit right in. Franklin even wrote Paine some letters of introduction. It was Paine's good luck to arrive in America just when the colonies' simmering squabbles with the mother country were coming to the boil. As someone who already had a grudge against His Majesty's government, Paine wasted no time in joining the fray. In late 1774, he found a job with the *Pennsylvania Magazine* and set about writing article after article denouncing what he saw as the inequality, injustice, and corruption around him. Aged 37, Thomas Paine had a new lease of life.

LET'S GET RADICAL

Up to that time, the main gripe between the British government and the American colonists was about why America's settlers should pay taxes to the British government when they were not allowed any representation in the British parliament ("no taxation without representation," as the saying goes). But as far as Paine was concerned, Americans shouldn't be negotiating for representation in the British Parliament—they should be demanding independence from Britain itself. Thomas Paine's pioneering role in passionately and powerfully arguing for America's independence should never be underestimated. On January 10, 1776, Paine published *Common Sense*, a 50-page pamphlet that laid out the case for American independence in no uncertain terms. It was an immediate sensation, with 500,000 copies sold. *Common Sense* heavily influenced Thomas Jefferson's writing of the Declaration of Independence, published on July 4, 1776, just six months later.

KEEP UP THE GOOD WORK

But after having written the script for the American Revolution, Paine found that his services were no longer required. He was given a number of minor political posts by the Continental Congress during the war, but just to keep him out of the way. Wealthy, politically ambitious Brahmins like John Jay and John Adams were not prepared to give a loose cannon like Paine any responsibility. Instead, Paine was encouraged to continue his verbal assaults on the hated British. Between 1776 and 1783, Paine reeled off 16 pamphlets designed to boost the war effort. They were called the *Crisis Papers*. The first of these, which begins with the famous line "These are the times that try men's souls," so inspired George Washington that he ordered it read aloud to the troops during their darkest days at Valley Forge.

THE $64,000 ANSWER
At the end of the war, Paine found himself famous but poor. Although his pamphlets had sold hundreds of thousands of copies, Paine accepted no royalties from them, insisting instead that the price of each pamphlet be kept low enough for ordinary folk to afford. To alleviate Paine's poverty, his supporters in Congress put forward a bill offering financial assistance to the hero of the revolution. But the Brahmins blocked the bill. In the end, the State of Pennsylvania came to Paine's rescue by offering him a sum of £500 (which would translate to about $64,000 in today's U.S. currency). New York State also pitched in, donating a farm for him in New Rochelle, now a suburb of New York City.

RIGHTS PLACE, RIGHTS TIME
So, having sort of single-handedly launched the American War of Independence, Paine turned his attention to Europe. Once again his timing was perfect: Paine arrived just after the outbreak of the French Revolution of 1789. When, in 1791, the British politician Edmund Burke wrote *Reflections on the Revolution in France*, attacking the uprising, Paine hit back with *The Rights of Man*.

PAINE SEES LONDON...
Paine's book was an immediate sensation, and has since been recognized as an all-time classic of political writing. It has sold more than 500,000 copies and was the best-selling book of the entire 18th century. The book didn't just defend the French Revolution, it attacked the monarchy, undemocratic governments, the rich, the powerful, and pretty much anyone else Paine saw as responsible for the misery around him—in Britain as much as in France.

He then laid out his own plans for an alternative government, with policies including pensions for the poor, free education, and lots of other radical ideas. The British government was horrified by all this radical theorizing: Paine was declared a traitor and a warrant was issued for his arrest. Memorial coins were created with

Paine's face on them, so that British aristocrats could set them into heels of their boots and grind Paine's face into the dust each time they went for a walk!

PAINE SEES FRANCE...
But Paine had already fled. The French, recognizing a kindred spirit, had elected Paine to a seat in their revolutionary government, the National Convention. However, as in America, Paine managed to tick off his revolutionary colleagues. When the National Convention voted to execute the ousted king, Louis XVI, Paine was among those who protested. At this time the revolutionary government was under the control of Maximilien Robespierre, a hard-line radical prone to chopping off the heads of anyone who got in his way. Paine was imprisoned in 1793, threatened with execution, and held captive until Robespierre's fall from power the following year. On his release, Paine published the *Age of Reason*, an attack on organized religion and his last great work.

PAINE GETS KICKED IN THE PANTS
Paine hung out in France until 1802, just to make sure the revolution was safe. (It wasn't. By this time, Napoléon had seized power and set up a military dictatorship.) Fed up with infighting among the French, Paine returned to America. But when he got there he wasn't welcome any more. America was no longer Britain's rebellious younger sibling, but a grown-up power in her own right. Professional revolutionaries like Paine were unwanted in a country looking for a period of peace and quiet. Outgoing president John Adams branded Paine as "that insolent Blasphemer of things sacred and transcendent, Libeler of all that is good." If that weren't bad enough, Adams went on to describe Paine as "a mongrel between pig and puppy, begotten by a wild boar on a bitch wolf."

NOT SUCH A BAD GUY AFTER ALL
Rejected by the country he helped to create, Paine turned to drink. He died penniless in 1809 in New York City. His obituary in the *New York Citizen* claimed, "He had lived long, did some good and much harm," which just goes to show how much history had been rewritten even during Paine's own lifetime. It was only in the mid-20th century that Paine's rehabilitation began.

Cleveland, Ohio, chocolate maker Clarence Crane invented Life Savers in 1912.

On May 18, 1953, a bust of Paine was unveiled in the New York University Hall of Fame, and since then, his reputation as a fighter for freedom and justice has been gradually restored, piece by piece.

SOME LAST WORDS

Thomas Paine was a writer of power and passion whose life-long quest was to make the world a better place. His words—such as these—are as relevant now as ever:

> When it shall be said in any country in the world, my poor are happy; neither ignorance nor distress is to be found among them; my jails are empty of prisoners; my streets of beggars; the aged are not in want; the taxes are not oppressive...When these things can be said, then may that country boast its constitution and its government.

* * * * *

OH, RIGHT, THE SKY IS FALLING!

President Thomas Jefferson was a scientist as well as a statesman. He studied and classified fossils, experimented with new varieties of grain, and was constantly making scientific measurements and observations with sophisticated instruments he kept at Monticello. But even Jefferson's faith in science had its limits. He refused to believe, for instance, that meteorites fall from the sky. When he heard that two Yale professors had reported a meteorite fall at Weston, Connecticut, on December 14, 1807, Jefferson is reported to have said, "I would rather believe that two Yankee professors would lie than that stones fall from the sky."

The first Life Savers flavor was Pep-O-Mint.

A PRETTIER PAUL REVERE

Move over, Paul, this teenaged heroine is tired of being overlooked.
Listen my children and you shall hear
Of the midnight ride of... Sybil Ludington?

Okay Longfellow's verses really celebrate the midnight ride of America's Revolutionary War hero, Paul Revere. But Sybil Ludington was only 16 years old during the Revolutionary War, when she completed a heroic ride that was just as important and dangerous.

PICKLED REDCOATS AND BURNING BEEF
Sybil was the oldest daughter of Colonel Henry Ludington. On April 26, 1777, the Colonel's New York militiamen had recently come home to their farm to do their spring planting. The teenager was also at home that evening in Frederiksburg (now Ludingtonville), New York, helping her mom to put her seven younger sisters and brothers to bed—a heroic task in itself.

That evening a patriot rode up to the Ludington home, bringing word that 2,000 British soldiers, led by General William Tyron (who was also the colonial governor of New York) had launched a surprise attack on Danbury, Connecticut. The British soldiers were looting and burning Continental Army supplies and ammunition, and everything from thousands of barrels of beef and pork to thousands of shoes and stockings were either being stolen or going up in smoke. Meanwhile the redcoats were also getting drunk on any alcohol they could find, and even their general was having trouble maintaining order.

WITH A STICK AND A STAR
After delivering his message, the rider collapsed in exhaustion which left the Colonel with a problem. His men were needed to help rescue Danbury, but they were at home on their farms. Who would take the message to them and warn the patriot homes and villages that Redcoats were burning and looting? Sybil bravely agreed to take on the job even though April 26 was a moonless,

---

Nabisco made 16 billion Oreo cookies in 1995 at its Chicago cookie and cracker factory.

rainy night, and the roads were narrow, muddy, and rutted by cartwheels and animal tracks.

Holding a stick she used both for prodding her horse, Star, and for knocking on militiamen's doors, Sybil set out. Riding over unmarked roads, Sybil went from Carmel to Mahopac, then on to Kent Cliffs and Farmer's Mills. She reached home again at dawn the next day. Some 400 men responded to her summons and gathered just in time to help Ludington and General Wooster drive the drunken redcoats back to their ships in Long Island Sound.

Sybil died in 1839, Today a statue on the shore of Lake Gleneida in Carmel, New York, honors the teenager and her daring, successful ride.

* * * * *

FRIENDS TO THE END—AND THANKS FOR THE TEA!

The world could take a lesson from England and Portugal, two countries that have never been at war with each other. In 1386 they signed the Treaty of Windsor, a nonaggression pact still in effect today and, thus, the longest surviving alliance in the world.

The alliance was strengthened by the royal marriage in 1387 between Philippa of Lancaster, the daughter of John of Gaunt, Duke of Lancaster, and João I of Portugal. The couple's youngest son was Henrique, known as Prince Henry the Navigator, whose sea voyages led to a golden age of exploration for Portugal. Christopher Columbus learned to navigate at the school established by Henry.

Another royal wedding between the two countries occurred nearly 300 years later in 1662, when Charles II married the Infanta Catherine of Braganza, who made tea drinking fashionable in England by introducing it to the royal court. The custom does seem to have caught on; the British now drink 185 million cups of tea every day.

Actor Lon Chaney was the son of deaf-mute parents, and thus learned early to pantomime.

THE MONA LISA CAPER

*How could a thief walk into the Louvre in Paris and,
within 20 minutes, walk out of the museum with the
world's most famous painting? For one thing, security was
practically nonexistent; for another, it wasn't the world's
most famous painting until after it was stolen.*

August 21, 1911. Louis Beroud, a painter, busily set up his easel in the Salon Carré, one of the Louvre's more than 200 rooms, directly facing the spot where the *Mona Lisa* usually smiled out at her admirers. Beroud had painted copies of *La Gioconda* plenty of times before. But this time he planned to set up his own model next to the painting and paint the two together, with his model using the *Mona Lisa*'s protective glass case as a mirror. Beroud was looking back and forth between his equipment and the glass case, when suddenly he froze. There was an empty space where the *Mona Lisa* should have been.

When he asked a guard where the painting was, he was told that it was in the photography room, where copies were made. Beroud waited three hours for the painting's return, but eventually, his patience gave out. He asked the guard to go and see what was taking so long. When the guard returned after a few minutes, he had to admit to Beroud that the painting was nowhere to be found.

A DISPOSAL PROBLEM

What would an art thief do with the painting? At the time, it was worth about $5 million (4 million euros)—today, it's priceless). But to whom would the thief sell it? Even if a buyer were willing to spend that much, the painting was too high profile to be passed along the art-theft network. It would be too easily traced, which meant that the perpetrators would be too easily caught.

Theories abounded in France; some thought it was an elaborate practical joke, while others thought it was a political ploy by

For over 400 years, pirates were hanged at Execution Dock on the north bank of the Thames.

the Germans to humiliate the French. Some accounts of the theft say that local Paris artists—Pablo Picasso, among them—were brought in for questioning. The city could not believe that such a treasure was gone forever.

OVERNIGHT SENSATION
In truth, the Louvre housed many treasures. But the theft transformed this particular one from valuable painting to icon. The *Mona Lisa* was now a cottage industry: Posters, postcards, mugs, pamphlets, nightclubs, silent movies, and magazine and newspaper articles featured her image. If T-shirts had been the fashion, her face would have graced every one of them. And behaviorists find it especially peculiar that after the theft, record crowds swarmed into the Louvre to gaze at the empty space where the *Mona Lisa* had once hung. Most of these visitors had never even seen the original. Why did people go to a museum to see a work of art that wasn't there?

TURNING THE PLACE UPSIDE DOWN
It took a week for the museum to be searched completely. All that turned up was the painting's empty gilt frame, found at the top of a staircase that the thief must have used as his escape route. The 38 x 21-inch (97 x 53-cm) wood panel that the *Mona Lisa* had been painted on was gone. Months passed, then years, and still no sign of her.

A LETTER FROM LEONARD
November 29, 1913. A wealthy Italian art dealer, Alfredo Geri, received a letter from a Leonard Vincenzo. In the letter, Leonard offered to return the *Mona Lisa* to Italy, her home country—for a fee. Geri thought Leonard might be a crackpot, but he was intrigued enough to set up a meeting in Florence. There, in a hotel room, Leonard, a short, dark-haired, mustachioed Italian who'd been living and working in Paris at the time of the theft, reached under the bed and retrieved an object wrapped in red silk. He uncovered it and showed it to Geri and Giovanni Poggi, the director of Florence's Uffizi Gallery. Poggi verified its authenticity: it was the *Mona Lisa*.

Today a pub called The Captain Kidd overlooks the original site of the gallows.

ARREST THAT MAN!

While the painting hung temporarily in the Uffizi before being returned to Paris, Leonard was picked up by the police. His real name, he said, was Vincenzo Peruggia. He described the caper to the police. He'd entered the Louvre the morning of the theft dressed in a painter's white smock and had gone straight for the girl of his dreams. No one else was in the Salon Carré that morning, so Peruggia simply removed the painting from the four wall hooks and concealed it, frame and all, under his smock. When he got to the staircase, he removed the painting from its frame, tucked the *Mona Lisa* back under his smock, and walked out. The whole thing took about 20 minutes.

THE PATRIOT?

In court, Peruggia said he'd stolen the painting for purely patriotic reasons: because she belonged in Italy—she had, after all, been painted by Leonardo da Vinci—and because he wanted to take vengeance on Napoléon for his various Italian conquests.

But during the trial, prosecutors brought up Peruggia's criminal past. He had a prior record: an arrest in France for attempted robbery and illegal possession of firearms. What's more, Peruggia's diary was filled with the names of art dealers and collectors in the United States and Italy: names like J. P. Morgan, Andrew Carnegie…and Alfredo Geri, the art dealer who had helped bring him to justice.

ALL ROADS LEAD TO PARIS

Peruggia was sentenced to one year and 15 days; he served seven months. He eventually moved back to Paris and opened a hardware store. In true Italian style, when he died in 1927 he still thought of himself as one of Italy's greatest patriots.

The *Mona Lisa* has been safely back at the Louvre since her recovery. Today, she smiles out—from her nearly impregnable, climate-controlled, bulletproof glass case—at more than five million admirers a year.

In London, by about 1700, "frigate" was naval slang for "a woman"—specifically "a shady lady."

THE PLUNDERING POLITICIAN

Boss Tweed was possibly the most corrupt politician in U.S. history. Here's how he got into office and how the good guys brought him down.

The Society of Saint Tammany, founded in 1789 in New York City, is named for Tamanend, a chief of the Delaware tribe. It started out as a patriotic and charitable organization, created by tradesmen who weren't allowed to join the more exclusive clubs that the wealthy belonged to. As wave after wave of new immigrants arrived in New York City during the 1800s, Tammany gave them a helping hand with food, shelter, and jobs.

Meanwhile, the Tammany politicians were building an enormous base of support by organizing immigrants into a voting bloc. By the time Boss Tweed came along, the society had evolved into a well-oiled political machine that was known as Tammany Hall after its headquarters (aka its "wigwam") on East 14th Street.

SAY HELLO TO THE BOSS

William Marcy "Boss" Tweed was born in 1823 on the Lower East Side of New York City, an immigrant neighborhood that was the traditional starting point for new arrivals in the United States. Tweed never talked about his ethnic background—probably because it served his political interests to keep it ambiguous.

After public school, Tweed became an apprentice chair maker. Later he became a bookkeeper and a volunteer fireman, because the fire department was a traditional gateway into politics. Before you know it, Tweed was captain of his local fire company—and was busily building a power base in Tammany—and then in the Democratic Party, which got him elected as a city alderman in 1851.

THE MAN BEHIND THE MACHINE

Once he'd worked his way to the top of Tammany, becoming its grand sachem, Tweed bribed officials and openly bought votes to put his cronies into nearly every elected and appointed office in the city and the state. New York City became completely controlled by the Tweed Ring.

He used his influence with state politicians to pass legislation that shifted power away from the state and toward New York City. He finagled the passage of the New York City charter in 1870, which gave him and his associates the final say concerning all city expenditures. New projects (buildings, parks, sewers, docks, street improvements) provided plenty of opportunity for graft—especially for Tweed himself after he started his own companies and made sure the city did business with them.

GANGS OF NEW YORK
Tweed shrewdly exploited the turf wars between Irish, Scottish, and Dutch gangs. He used them to eliminate or intimidate people, and to round up voters on election day and force them to vote the way he wanted them to. He used an elaborate system of bribes to control judges, the police, and other officials, and he bought favorable coverage in the press.

THE PRESS APPLIES SOME PRESSURE
Tweed seemed unstoppable, until one lowly county bookkeeper, unhappy with his cut of the graft, handed over some incriminating documents to the *New York Times*. The *Times* published a series of articles about huge cost overruns in the construction of the Tweed Courthouse, which was supposed to cost only $500,000 (407,000 euros) but ended up costing the city $13 million (10.5 million euros). Thomas Nast, the political cartoonist for *Harper's Weekly*, created scathing cartoons depicting Tweed as thief, a convict, and an enormous glutton.

Tweed tried to bribe Nast and the publisher of the *Times* to leave him alone, but they turned him down. Reform groups and disaffected Democrats demanded that he be held accountable.

SPY VS. SPY VS. SPY
Prosecutor Samuel J. Tilden traced money directly from contractors to Tweed's bank account; but when Tweed was brought to trial, the case resulted in a hung jury. Tilden was sure that Tweed had bribed the jurors. So when he retried the case, he assigned one police officer to guard each member of the jury, another police officer to

watch the first one, and a private detective to watch both of them. Tweed was found guilty of failing to audit claims against the city, and he was convicted on charges of forgery and larceny.

YOU'RE NOT THE BOSS OF ME
The ex-Boss was sentenced to 12 years in jail, but that was later reduced to one year. When he was released, the city sued him for $6 million (5 million euros). Tweed was jailed again, but he was allowed to visit his family every day, accompanied by a guard. During one of those visits, he managed to escape.

CARTOON CHARACTER
Tweed fled to Cuba and then to Spain, where he was working as a common seaman on a ship when someone recognized him from one of those Thomas Nast cartoons. He was sent back to his jail cell in New York. Very ill in his final months, he wanted to die at home instead of in jail. He offered to reveal everything he knew about Tammany Hall in exchange for a parole. But his offer was rejected and he died in jail in 1878.

BUT THE TAMMANY LINGERS ON
Samuel J. Tilden's reputation as a reformer launched his political career. He was elected governor of New York and nearly won the U.S. presidency in 1876. In fact, Tilden won the popular vote that year, but lost by electoral votes to Rutherford B. Hayes. Tammany Hall continued to control much of New York City politics till the 1920s, and it was still influential in local politics into the 1960s. But when civil service reforms eliminated patronage and welfare became a function of government instead of social clubs, average people didn't need organizations like Tammany Hall anymore. As its membership declined, so did its political influence.

The club finally disbanded in the 1960s; today the "wigwam" is the home of the much more respectable New York Film Academy. As of 2002, the Tweed Courthouse became home to the New York City Board of Education.

* * * * *

Talking about Nast's cartoons, Boss Tweed once said, "Let's stop them damn pictures. I don't care so much what the papers write about— my constituents can't read—but damn it, they can see pictures."

RAGE AGAINST THE MACHINE

If someone hates technology, we call him or her a Luddite.
Why? It's a hangover from a 19th-century group of
machine-smashing rebels.

I t all started with the weavers. For centuries, the weavers and
lace makers of Nottingham, England, were some of the most
respected artisans in the world. But the invention of the power
loom and other machines, which produced fabric much more
quickly and cheaply than the hand-weavers, put them out of business. Just to survive, a lot of them started working for miserly
wages at the factories that produced the cheap and inferior cloth
they hated. But they simmered with rage at the factory owners
who appropriated their life's work—and the machines that helped
them do it.

WHOOPS!
All of a sudden, factory looms started to break down. At first, just
a couple. Then a few more. When asked what had happened, the
workers would just shrug and attribute the damage to the mythical
Ned Ludd. In fact, the disgruntled ex-weavers were already meeting in private to plot their revenge. In the early months of 1811,
they began sending menacing letters, signed by General Ned
Ludd, to Nottingham factory owners, warning of dire conse-
quences if factory conditions and wages didn't improve. Some of
the bolder Luddites showed up in person to make their demands.
Intimidated, most factory owners complied. Those who didn't
found their expensive machines smashed, by the dozens, in after-
hours Luddite attacks.

THE POWDER KEG IGNITES
The rebellion leaked to nearby British regions. The first Luddites
had been strictly nonviolent, venting their anger only on the
hated machines. But in Yorkshire, the owner of Rawfolds Mill,
aware of worker unrest at his factory, had prepared for an attack

---

The full name of the *Simpsons* character Krusty the Klown is Herschel Schmoeckel Krustofski.

on April 11, 1812, by hiring private guards. Two men were killed in the clash. Seven days later, the Luddites killed a mill owner in the region, William Horsfall.

The violence didn't end there. On April 20, an angry mob of thousands attacked Burton's Mill in Manchester. Like the Rawfolds mill owner, Burton knew trouble was coming and had hired private guards who fired on the crowd and killed three men. The furious Luddites dispersed, returning the following day and burning down Burton's house. In clashes with the military (who rushed into the fray) and Burton's guards, a total of 10 men were killed.

THE UPRISING COOLS DOWN
A police crackdown ensued. Scores of leaders and rank-and-file Luddites were arrested and tried for their crimes. A lot of men were hanged; others were imprisoned or exiled to Australia, which put an effective end to the immediate uprising. There were further sporadic outbreaks of violence, but by 1817 the Luddite movement ceased to be active in Britain.

Of course, the Luddites were right all along: the hated machines were making their jobs obsolete. These days, only a tiny fraction of the world's cloth is made by hand. And machines make almost every article that is found in the modern home, from shoes to electronics to furniture.

* * * * *

AN ELECTRIC CHAIR THRONE
Menelik II, was the emperor of Ethiopia from 1889 until 1913. News of a successful new means of dispatching criminals reached him when he learned that in New York, criminals were being executed with a modern device known as an "electric chair." Eager to modernize, the emperor ordered three of the new execution devices. It wasn't until the chairs arrived and were unpacked that the emperor realized that the chairs were useless for killing anyone since his country lacked electricity. Menelik tossed two of the chairs, but frugally recycled the third by converting it into his throne.

The Simpsons cartoonist Matt Groening's name rhymes with "raining."

PUBLISHED IN PRISON

*Bad food. Uncomfortable furniture. It doesn't seem
inspiring, but writers worldwide have somehow gone from bunk
mate to best seller just by spilling a little ink in the clink.*

ADOLF HITLER

This jailbird jotted down the first draft of his manifesto, *Mein
Kampf*, while sitting in the hoosegow. He was there after his failed
Beer Hall putsch, where he tried to overthrow the government by
attending a business luncheon at a beer hall that featured several
government members as its guests of honor. He messed it up and
ended up hiding in a friend's attic, talking about suicide, for three
days until he was arrested.

His self-centered and logically flawed rant of propaganda
started as a pamphlet. But then grew to book length, as the
angry, little man rambled on and on about everything from his
childhood to something almost resembling economic theory—
but without the valid conclusions. The book was a huge flop
that was openly mocked.

Unfortunately, the creep was released from jail, which gave
him the opportunity to act on his misguided guidebook.

MARQUIS DE SADE

Born in 1740 of minor French nobility, Donatien-Alphonse-
François de Sade grew up to be not only a disaster at dinner parties but also a man with serious mental and legal problems. He
regularly attacked women, and sometimes men, for purposes of
perversity unprecedented in 18th-century France.

A promising soldier with the world at his feet, his bizarre
and insatiable appetite for kinky brutality was often masked by a
façade of charm, eloquence, and education. So it took the authorities a while to catch on to the depths of his criminality. But his
behavior only got worse, and he eventually earned himself a 13-
year sentence in the Bastille. There he wrote his first books, with
fun-filled titles: *The 120 Days of Sodom* and *Misfortunes of Virtue*.
He wrote them under a pen name to shield himself from the
inevitable uproar about their content.

The Beatles original name was Johnny and the Moondogs.

His writings were filled with such ahead-of-its-time (and ours) obscenity that those who owned his books kept them hidden away under lock and key. While no rational person has defended his personal behavior, his literature has remained a study in the underbelly of human nature for psychologists, sociologists, and criminal behaviorists.

CERVANTES

Miguel de Cervantes was born in Spain in 1547, the son of a doctor and minor nobleman. He went to college and then into the military, where—listen to this—he ended up being sold into slavery in Algiers for five years. When he got out, he took a number of odd jobs, including that of tax collector. He was eventually inspired to write.

He wrote a romance, *Galatea*, a play about Christian slaves in Algiers (hey, he'd done the research), and some other plays and poetry. Writing brought him big-time joy, but puny paychecks; he couldn't quit his day job. And to make matters worse, he was imprisoned for irregularities at his tax-collecting job. While locked up, Cervantes came up with the concept for the novel *Don Quixote*. When he got out, he went to work.

After publication, it wasn't just popular—it helped shape the development of European prose fiction. Though it didn't make him wealthy, it finally rewarded him with a decent wage for writing full-time. In addition, Cervantes achieved world fame and had his work translated into every modern language on the planet.

SIR THOMAS MALORY

Thomas Malory was born in 1420 England, that's for sure. And most, but not all, historians say he was from Warwickshire and inherited a large estate from his father, after fighting at the Siege of Calais in France. He eventually became embroiled in local politics, holding the office of member of Parliament for Warwickshire. He was either a lousy politician or a guy who just couldn't say no to trouble; he was in and out of jail most of his life for everything from burglary to adultery to robbing a church. Eventually, he served a lifetime stint for his involvement in Cook's Conspiracy of 1468 (an unfortunate legal squabble resulting from royal politics).

For a University of Maine magazine, Stephen King wrote a column called "King's Garbage Truck."

But before he died, Malory wrote the literary masterpiece *Le Morte D'Arthur*, the most revered tale of King Arthur ever penned. As opposed to the story of his life as a jailbird, this tale, of eight interwoven stories, was chock-full of chivalry and honor—the definitive Arthurian work. It was the only story he'd ever written: a whopping epic composed of 21 books and hundreds of chapters— all written before the widespread use of the printing press.

VOLTAIRE

Considered France's greatest writer, Voltaire (née François-Marie Arouet) was born in 1694, the son of an office clerk. He attended a Jesuit college and then moved on to a job his father had arranged for him at a law firm. But his true love was writing, which horrified his father who said (like any intelligent person would) something like, "You'll starve, you fool!"

One day, Voltaire insulted a local government official and was imprisoned. While in the Big House (the Bastille again), with nary a legal brief in sight, he wrote his first play, *Oedipe*. For him, the process was heaven. When he was released 11 months later, the play was staged and well received. It would turn out to be the first of 56 that he wrote. He went on to write insightful, revolutionary work in every genre and to achieve a lifetime of vast fame and fortune.

* * * * *

"IS THIS THE PERSON TO WHOM I AM SPEAKING?"

Most people have an image of early telephone operators as women, but the first operators were teenage boys and men. Unfortunately, the boys often tended to be rude and quarrelsome, so young women were hired instead, in the belief that they would be naturally more polite. The first female telephone operator was Miss Emma Nutt, who began working for the Telephone Dispatch Company exchange in Boston, Massachusetts, on September 1, 1878, for three dollars a day. She remained in the job for 33 years.

PINBALL'S RISE AND FALL

The invention of the pinball machine rolled out a new era of good times, violence, pop art, and obsession. More than 50 years later, the United States is the only country still making them. And their glittering past assures them a bright future.

The first sign of a pinball-like game on the world radar was the French game of bagatelle. Usually enjoyed by nobility, this game featured a long, wooden cabinet with a series of holes and pins that was navigated using a metal ball and cue stick. It was a popular parlor game in the late 1700s, and when the French came to the United States to help in the Revolution, they brought a little lounge sophistication to the backwater colonies. The game didn't become hugely popular, but it beat the existing American parlor game of complaining about taxes.

WIFFLE BALL'S DARK SIDE

The coin-operated pinball machine was born in Ohio during the Great Depression. Jobs were scarce, money was tight, and people needed cheap entertainment. So a company in Youngstown, Ohio, invented a coin-operated bagatelle in 1931 called Whiffle Ball. These countertop machines were designed to be played in bars, pool halls, and bowling alleys. There were no flappers on the side to keep the ball going; you popped your ball up and your score was determined by whatever it hit on the way down. But people couldn't get enough; these were fun. And besides—with no job, what else was there to do?

The craze caught on, and the competing Baffle Ball machine followed quickly. The hugely popular Ballyhoo game appeared in 1932 (the birth of the still profitable Bally arcade game company). Machines often paid for themselves in less than a week. Bar and restaurants owners even offered prizes, free games, or tickets for high scores.

GAME OR SKILL?

Is luck the reason you keep losing your quarters, or do you just stink? This seemingly rhetorical question became a legal matter of some consequence once pinball grew in popularity. Remember those prizes they gave away? Well, if indeed pinball were a game of chance, then its payers were gambling—a serious legal prohibition in several states. The machines also had PR problems. Their location in seedy venues and the productivity lost to such a frivolous and wasteful pursuit found many vocal opponents among mothers, teachers, and religious leaders. The debate came to a head in 1941, when New York's mayor banned payout pinball machines—and personally smashed a number of them with a huge sledgehammer. They weren't legalized again until the 1970s, when a pinball expert wheeled one into a courtroom and proved that it was a game of skill.

PINBALL'S GOLDEN AGE

The golden age of pinball was between 1948 and 1958. By then, they had assumed their present-day form with flappers, bumpers, and legs. But they had a distinctive look. Their legs were wooden, and they had wooden side rails. And all the possible scores were listed on the back glass, with a light bulb backlighting *your* score. But the back glass was more than a scorekeeper—it was a showstopper. Hand-painted and carefully crafted, the back glass held backlit images of monsters, ladies in distress, tuxedoed gamblers, and even—during WWII—Adolf Hitler (with a target on his face). The back glass became itself a work of art, one a player could interact with. Just sitting there, pinball machines had aesthetic value.

POP ART CULTURE

In the 1960s, what with free love and all manner of psychedelia, pinball was no longer the latest and greatest entertainment craze. But its popularity continued, with new designs and innovations coming out monthly. For the next 25 years, whenever a popular movie came out, there was a pinball machine to match. They became more reliable, with solid-state electronics. There were talking pinball machines, machines with little drop-down targets, and even little magnets to save balls.

The word "dream" didn't come to mean "sleep-images" until the 13th century.

More than games, these were true popular art—innovating themselves through new artists just enough to never go out of fashion. New overwhelming lights, bells, and whistles could create a hypnotic, Vegas-like effect. The 1969 song *Pinball Wizard* by The Who, and its accompanying movie starring Elton John, were testaments to the machines' cult following. Guitarist Joe Perry, from the band Aerosmith, noted in a video called *The History of the Pinball Machine*, "Sometimes just before I walk on stage if there's a pinball machine back there, I'll play it because it clears my mind out; it centers me—it's almost like a Zen thing."

BIGGER, BETTER VIDEO GAMES

With everything from *Space Invaders* in the 1980s to today's virtual reality golf, it's no wonder that pinball machines aren't as popular as they used to be. And while they don't take center stage in pop culture any more, they still bring in billions of bucks at U.S. arcades and various hangouts nationwide. They may just live on forever. Pinball machine collecting is a huge craze right now; you can pick one up for around $500 (416 euros). And while you can turn a profit on them, people seem more interested in buying them for the nostalgic value—picking up that old talking Gorgon that was in the pizza shop of their childhood. Kids seem drawn to them as if by magic. And as collectors age, collectable machines simply move up a decade. So it's OK that they're no longer cutting-edge entertainment; that shiny, metal ball just keeps coming back.

* * * * *

THE REAL THING

The popular Charles "Kid" McCoy boxed his way to success at the end of the 19th century. His technique? To feign illness before bouts or spread the word to the media that he'd been neglecting his training. Then, when fight night came around, to the surprise of the press and his opponents, McCoy was usually fit and ready to fight. Thus, reporters started asking, "Is this the real McCoy?"

In Old English it originally meant "joy," "noise," or "music."

A TOUGH JOB

The yakuza gangsters of Japan are plenty mean.
And they could be hiring you.

Despite the way they are often portrayed in movies like *The Godfather* and TV shows such as *The Sopranos*, not all gangsters are Italian. Crime is an equal opportunity employer. If the yakuza of Japan were hiring, their ads might look something like this:

WANTED: ENTHUSIASTIC SELF-STARTER!

F/T or P/T:	Full-time, especially late at night in seedy neighborhoods
Reports to:	The traditional yakuza boss, known as the *oyabun*
Education:	Street smarts
Salary:	Commensurate with ruthlessness
Benefits:	Might let you live

THE YAKUZA: ABOUT US

In the 16th century, with no more wars to keep them employed, lots of samurai had to turn to crime to make a decent living. We, the yakuza, are their descendants organized into crime families. Our name comes from the worst possible score in an old Japanese card game called *hanfuda*. *Hanfuda* was our blackjack, and if you were dealt a sequence of 8-9-3, too bad, you lost. *Ya Ku Sa* is the old Japanese way to say 8-9-3 or *yakuza*. We were those who turned to crime after feeling we'd been dealt a losing hand.

THE IDEAL CANDIDATE

In the last five centuries, our business enterprises have included smuggling, blackmail, extortion, loan-sharking, gambling, infiltrating labor unions, and running massage parlors and prostitution. Do you fit in?

As a new yakuza, you'll report to lots of bosses within our strict hierarchy. The ideal candidate will understand our dealings that take place in the gray area between legitimate deals and

---

Geoffrey Chaucer was the first person interred in Westminster Abbey's "Poets' Corner."

blatant crimes. The ideal candidate will also be good at a *jiageya*, a sideline we developed during the Japanese real estate boom in the 1980s. When a real estate developer wanted to buy up all the land in a certain area, we "convinced" current residents to get the heck out. Are you good enough at vandalism and assault to succeed in *jiageya*?

The ideal employee will also help out *sokaiya*. Sokaiya buy shares of stock so they can get into a shareholders' meeting and blackmail the managers. Sokayiya threaten to reveal damaging company secrets (usually made up) for profit. Does this sound like you?

JOB ETHICS AND RESPONSIBILITIES
Should we bring you on board, you'll have to follow these rules:
1. Don't mess with your coworkers' wives and kids.
2. Don't use drugs (it's OK to sell them, though).
3. Don't hold back any of your profit from the bosses—we take most of your money.
4. Do what we tell you.
5. If you're caught, you're on your own.
6. Keep your business a secret, and don't run to the cops—even if we try to kill you.

You also must be willing to travel. In the 1960s, we branched out from Japan to our Asian neighbors such as Korea, China, the Philippines, and Thailand. We are also now in France, South America, and the United States. In Los Angeles, we've been running gambling and other operations since before WWI.

ON-THE-JOB TRAINING
Employees make mistakes. We understand and will train you with our practice of *yubitsume*, slicing off pieces of your finger. Every time you mess up, one of your superiors can demand that you cut a piece of your little finger off at the joint, wrap it ceremoniously in a scarf, and present it to him as a gift. We bet you'll learn fast.

THE COMPANY UNIFORM
Our mandatory uniform has been around since the 3rd century. A simple suit is fine. But underneath that suit, you'll have to get a major tattoo, covering the flesh of your body in dragons, writing,

The other 21 interred there include Charles Dickens and Alfred, Lord Tennyson.

colors, and designs. The only flesh-colored flesh showing will be on your hands, feet, and face.

The good news is that modern tattooing is quick, with only moderate pain. The bad news is that if you get your full-body tattoo the modern way, your superiors will think you're a softy. To get ahead as a traditional yakuza, you'll need to follow the tradition of being painfully stabbed with bamboo thousands of times until the color enters the skin. Needles are for wimps—like the Sopranos!

GROWTH OPPORTUNITIES

You'll become part of our still-growing organization that brings in around $11 billion (9 billion euros) annually. And you will inherit the heritage of Japan's criminal class. Officials estimated that by the mid-20th century there were more than 150,000 of us going strong. If you're a master of threats, extortion, violence, and general rottenness, we'll take you straight to the top!

* * * * *

OTHER JAPANESE ICONS

Icon	In 2005 it will have been around for:
Yu-Gi-Oh	9 years
Hello Kitty	31 years
Sony Corporation	59 years
Sumo	1,285 years
Sushi	1,405 years
The chopstick	3,797 years
Lacquer	5,001 years
Sake	6,805 years

MAKING THEIR MARK

So you think your tattoo is cool and the latest thing?
Sorry, but tattooing has been the coolest, latest thing for
thousands of years. How much do you know about
ancient cool dudes, dudettes, and their tattoos?

1. In 1991, two hikers discovered a tattooed, freeze-dried body in
   the Alps. The man, nicknamed Otzi Iceman, is thought to have
   lived in 3300 B.C. He was covered with almost 60 tattoos.
   These tattoos depicted:
   a. a mastodon
   b. a cross on the inside of the left knee and parallel lines on
      the ankle
   c. a spear

2. Archaeologists have discovered engraved clay figurines suggesting that people in Japan tattooed themselves as early as
   5000 B.C. Literature from the Yayoi period (A.D. 250 to 300
   B.C.) showed Japanese men with tattoos on their faces to keep
   evil forces away. These tattoos were of:
   a. snakes
   b. bonsai trees
   c. Japanese characters that translate into "I love you, Mom."

3. Tattooed mummies, carbon-dated from 2000 B.C., were
   found in Egypt. Paintings of men and women in Egyptian art
   show images that probably represent tattooing on both sexes,
   but only female mummies have been discovered with tattoos.
   The lines and dot patterns found on these mummies are
   thought to honor:
   a. their grandmothers
   b. their mothers
   c. female deities

4. In 55 and 54 B.C., Julius Caesar came to conquer these people
   with a Roman army. He reported that the barbarians dyed
   themselves blue; lots of historians believe that he had seen

Before the advent of Christianity, *wicces* (witches) were shamans—spiritual advisers and healers.

folks with blue tattoos. No, it wasn't the Smurfs—but who
were they?
a. ancient Celts
b. ancient Greeks
c. ancient Greenlanders

5. European sailors were the first Caucasian people to be exposed
to South American and South Pacific natives. The Spanish
sailors who first saw South American natives thought the devil
possessed the natives because they imprinted themselves with
images of:
a. flames
b. pitchforks
c. demons

6. Native Americans probably practiced a form of tattooing for
centuries before Jesuit priests made the first record of the
practice during the 17th century. The Osage people were only
entitled to tattoos after success in war or other great deeds.
One Osage man who had never fought in battle was punished
after he tattooed himself, to impress his sweetheart, with a:
a. tomahawk
b. peace pipe
c. heart with her name inside

7. In 1841, an American sailor deserted his whaling ship in the
South Pacific to live with the inhabitants of the Marquesas
Islands, whose bodies and faces were tattooed with geometrical
designs. Many readers first learned about tattooing from this
sailor's novels—including *Moby Dick*—based on his experiences. This sailor-author was:
a. Nathaniel Hawthorne
b. Herman Melville
c. Barnacle Bill

8. Tattooing temporarily became more acceptable in England
when the aristocracy decided it was a status symbol—because
it was expensive and time-consuming. In 1862, Edward VII,

when he was the British Prince of Wales, went to Jerusalem and got tattooed with a:
a. crown
b. scepter
c. cross

9. In this culture, women traditionally stitched animal skins. From ancient times, elderly women were also expert tattoo artists, who were said to be "stitching the human skin." They are:
a. Chinese
b. Eskimo
c. Aztec

10. These ancient people are famous for inventions, but they didn't invent many tattoos. They disapproved of tattooing except as a punishment. They are:
a. the Chinese
b. Eskimos
c. the Aztec

Answers
1(b); 2(a); 3(c); 4(a); 5(c); 6(a); 7b); 8(c); 9(b); 10(a)

* * * * *

"Tattoos are like marriage: it's a lifelong commitment, it hurts like hell, and the color fades over time." —Terri Guillemets

"Show me a man with a tattoo and I'll show you a man with an interesting past."—Jack London

"Women, don't get a tattoo. That butterfly looks great on your breast when you're twenty or thirty, but when you get to seventy, it stretches into a condor."—Billy Elmer

"The world is divided into two kinds of people: those who have tattoos, and those who are afraid of people with tattoos."
—Author Unknown

The *quinceañera* is a young Latina woman's celebration of her 15th birthday.

NOBODY HELPED

*It's called the Genovese Syndrome, the phenomenon
of a crime being witnessed by numerous people
who don't try to stop it or call for help.*

itty Genovese got home from work very late. As a bar
manager, she had to close and clean up before she could
head home to her Queens, New York, apartment. Usually
her late hours were no problem. But on March 13, 1964, when
the 28-year-old, 105-pound (48 kg) Genovese parked her car at
3 a.m., there was someone waiting for her. As Kitty began to walk
toward her home, the man waylaid and stabbed her.

A CRY FOR HELP
She shrieked in terror, "Oh, my God, he stabbed me! Please help
me!" Genovese's neighbors in the snug apartment complex, many
of whom knew her, turned on their lights and opened their apartment windows. One male neighbor shouted from his window,
"Leave that girl alone!" Kitty's attacker left. She began staggering
to her apartment, bleeding from several stab wounds, while her
neighbors shut their windows and turned off their lights. Kitty no
doubt thought the worst was over. But her attacker returned and
stabbed her again. "I'm dying!" she screamed. Her neighbors threw
open their windows again, but nobody came out to help. Kitty's
attacker got into a car and drove away.

Kitty crawled into the vestibule of an apartment house and
lay there bleeding for several minutes. At this point she might still
have lived. But once again her assailant returned. He cut off her
underpants and bra, sexually assaulted her, and took the $49 (40
euros) from her wallet before stabbing her one last, fatal time. It
was not until 3:50 a.m., a full 50 minutes after the attack began,
that a neighbor called police. Two minutes later, police arrived to
find Kitty's body.

NOT MY PROBLEM
Police questioned Genovese's neighbors and discovered that at
least 38 people had witnessed the killer attacking Genovese, yet

---

As a boy, Julius Caesar learned several languages, including Hebrew and Gallic dialects.

no one had tried to intervene. Only one had called the police—after Kitty was already dead.

The public reacted with horror and mystification. Why on earth would 38 people, who could easily and safely have picked up the phone and helped, ignore a dying woman's calls of distress? The story caused deep rumbles in the psyche of Americans who were shocked and frightened by the specter of their own dark sides—and the ultimate in big-city alienation. Would they, in the same situation, have helped?

The neighbors offered numerous excuses for their behavior. They hadn't wanted to get involved, they said. They could see that others were witnessing the crime—surely *those* people were calling the police. Some claimed they feared for their own safety; others worried that their English wasn't up to the job of making a phone call. One heartless soul merely said, "I was tired." Another alleged that she didn't want to interfere in what she thought was a "lover's quarrel."

Police admitted that there was no law forcing witnesses to call for help. So the crime that the neighbors were guilty of, if any, was a moral one.

SOME CONSOLATION

The murderer was caught less than a week later. He readily admitted to killing Kitty Genovese, as well as two other local women, claiming he had an "uncontrollable urge to kill." In June 1964, 29-year-old Winston Moseley was found guilty, and he remains in state prison to this day.

But Kitty Genovese has not been forgotten. The case has lived on in plays and TV dramas—it even spawned a whole new branch of psychology. When experts refer to the Genovese syndrome, they're theorizing that the neighbors' failure to act was due to "diffusion of responsibility"—there were so many people watching the crime that no one person felt they had any personal responsibility, because they were sure that someone *else* would do something. The case is still taught in every Psych 101 class in the country. Which is not much of a consolation for poor Kitty.

"Caesar" means "hairy." This branch of the family was known for having fine heads of hair.

POKERS, DRAWN

You'd think that two big-time philosophers would fight it out with words not with fireplace pokers. You'd think.

At a meeting of the Moral Science Club at Cambridge University in October 1946, the guest speaker was Karl Popper, the author of *The Open Society and Its Enemies*. Popper began his lecture by taking issue with the invitation to the meeting, which asked him to give a paper that stated a philosophical puzzle. The chairman of the club—and the most famous living philosopher at that time—Ludwig Wittgenstein, believed that all questions of philosophy were just puzzles. Popper believed that there were real problems in philosophy that were more than puzzles. In his lecture, Popper said that the invitation he'd received was in itself argumentative.

SHOWDOWN

Wittgenstein stood up to make his case, punctuating his points by gesturing aggressively at Popper with a fireplace poker. Popper interrupted him and fired off examples of real philosophical problems, including the question of how we should choose moral rules. Wittgenstein retorted, "Give an example of a moral rule."

Popper responded, "Not to threaten visiting lecturers with pokers."

Enraged, Wittgenstein stormed out of the room, slamming the door.

RAISING THE STAKES

That's the way Popper tells it in his memoirs. But after it was told and retold, the story became slightly distorted, like what happens in the game of Telephone: Popper got a letter soon after the incident asking if he and Wittgenstein had really been dueling with fireplace pokers.

ALL BETS ARE OFF

The whole thing may not seem important to you—but it was legendary enough to attract the attention of two journalists, David Edmonds and John Eidinow, who actually wrote a book called

---

The white rose (*Rosa alba*) was the symbol of the House of York during the "War of the Roses."

Wittgenstein's Poker: The Story of a Ten-Minute Argument Between Two Great Philosophers. In it, they say the story that Popper's comeback caused Wittgenstein to storm out is almost certainly not true. They find it more likely that Popper thought of it after Wittgenstein had already left, just like we all think of that perfect comeback—minutes, or days, after the fact. Bummer. But it's still a cool story, even if that's all it is.

* * * * *

BIG BULLY

To hector someone is "to intimidate or harass [them] in a blustering way." The word derives from the name of the chief Trojan warrior and prince of Troy (as played by Eric Bana in the 2004 movie *Troy*—who also played the title role in 2003's *Hulk*).

DONNYBROOK ACRES

"Donnybrook," meaning "a knock-down, drag-out free-for-all," comes from the wild and woolly Donnybrook Fair in County Dublin, Ireland. The first fair was held in 1204, but over the centuries it became an excuse for so many violent brawls and general debauchery that even the earthy Irish thought it was getting out of hand. In 1885, the fair was discontinued. Today, Donnybrook is a peaceful suburb of Dublin

The "White Rose" was also the name of an anti-Nazi resistance movement in Nazi Germany.

THE RIOT OF SPRING

The Rite of Spring was such a spectacle at its Paris
premiere that the audience went completely bonkers.

It was an unseasonably hot and humid spring night in Paris on
May 29, 1913. Well-dressed members of the upper class mingled with chic bohemians on their way into the Théâtre des
Champs-Elysées for an evening of music. On the program was the
premiere of a ballet by Igor Stravinsky and Vaslav Nijinsky called
The Rite of Spring—in French, *Le Sacre du Printemps*. It promised
to be enthralling: Stravinsky was considered one of the greatest
composers alive, and Nijinsky was notorious for his daring choreo-
graphy. Most of the see-and-be-seen audience members came
expecting to see lavish costumes and elegant dancing, accompanied by lush, late Romantic music. They were to be disappointed.
Or maybe "appalled" is a better word.

THE BIG NIGHT
After lulling the audience into a false sense of security with an
innocuous opener, the orchestra started the overture, after which
the curtain rose to show, as Stravinsky himself later described it, a
"group of knock-kneed and long-braided Lolitas jumping up and
down." Nijinsky had instructed the dancers to jump heavily and
flat-footed, in contrast with the usual light, graceful ballet leaps.
Stravinsky's music had strong, pounding accents on repeated, dis-
sonant chords. The overall effect was jarring for an audience
expecting flowers, birds, and sunshine. Instead, they got savagery.
   Speaking of which, the second act of the ballet portrayed a
ritual sacrifice. In the story, the young woman chosen to be the
sacrificial victim dances herself to death.

THE BIG FIGHT
The crowd was scandalized. A few audience members started
laughing and catcalling. Discouraged, Stravinsky left the audience
area and went backstage. Supporters of the music yelled back, and
pandemonium broke loose. The proponents and opponents of the
piece attacked each other with fists and canes, or spat in each

In Sweden, male customers of prostitutes are known as "torskar," which means "cod."

other's faces. In one box, a lady slapped a young man who was hissing in the next box. A countess shouted to the crowd in general, "This is the first time in my sixty years that anyone has dared to make fun of me!"—and stormed out.

Meanwhile, the performers gamely tried to keep going while chaos reigned around them. The dancers could no longer hear the music, so Nijinsky stood backstage shouting numerical cues to them. Stravinsky had to restrain Nijinsky from running onstage "and creating a scandal." (Too late, Igor.) The head of the Ballets Russes ran backstage to order the lights turned on and off to try to distract the rioters. Nothing worked. The only thing that quieted the audience, like the lull in the eye of a hurricane, was when the sacrificial victim performed her death dance.

THE MORNING AFTER

Reviews in the Paris papers in the next few days alternated between denouncing the performance and condescending toward the unruly audience; a few called it the "Massacre du Printemps." All the reviewers agreed that the audience had behaved abominably, even though many thought the piece was *just* as abominable.

There's an irony in this story. The divided audience may have lost control of themselves in a fight over whether the piece was worth listening to, but the actions of both groups—those for it and against it—were just as primitive as the rite being depicted onstage.

To read more about Nijinsky, see "God of the Dance," page 275.

To read more about Nijinsky, see "God of the Dance," page 275.

* * * * *

SOMETIMES THEY FEEL LIKE A NUT...

"People like eccentrics. Therefore they will leave me alone, saying that I am a 'mad clown.'"—Nijinsky

Ex-president Theodore Roosevelt coined the phrase "lunatic fringe" in 1913. He was referring to some of his own too-zealous supporters. "Every reform movement has a lunatic fringe," he said in his autobiography.

Torsk is also slang for "loser."

ANOTHER BLOOMING QUIZ!

Travel around the world to share our rosy view of history!

1. A rose fossil that is at least 40 million years old was discovered.
   That makes the rose at least 30 million years older than the first
   human on Earth. The rose fossil was discovered in this state:
   a. Florida
   b. Colorado
   c. Hawaii

2. Five thousand years ago, people in this philosopher's homeland
   were among the first to grow roses in gardens. This famous
   philosopher is said to have had 600 books on how to grow roses.
   He was:
   a. Greek philosopher Plato
   b. Roman philosopher Cicero
   c. Chinese philosopher Confucius.

3. In this ancient country, roses have been found buried in tombs
   with the dead:
   a. Egypt
   b. Persia
   c. Cyprus

4. A rose bush said to be 1,000 years old can be found at the
   Hildsheim Cathedral in this country:
   a. Italy
   b. Poland
   c. Germany

5. Rose wine, made from rose petals, is one of the oldest wines
   around, dating back to this ancient, spirited people:
   a. the French
   b. the Maya
   c. the Persians

13 is considered a lucky number in China because its ideogram means "must be alive."

6. Roses were a symbol of fertility to these ancient peoples. Their famous goddess gave the flower its name. And their poetess Sappho called the rose "the Queen of Flowers." These rosy folks and their goddess were the:
a. Egyptians and their goddess Isis
b. Greeks and their goddess Aphrodite
c. Romans and their goddess Juno

7. Roses flooded this civilization like spam in your inbox. The people used rose petals as carpeting in their houses and as an addition to their bathwater. They ate roses as snacks, threw them like confetti at parties and festivals, and used them to make perfume. These people were:
a. Aztecs
b. Vikings
c. Romans

8. In the Middle Ages, healers valued a type of rose that they called the Apothecary Rose for its medicinal properties. They used rose hips and petals to cure sore throats and skin rashes, and to help digestion. But the Apothecary Rose is believed to date all the way back to these great gardeners:
a. Aztecs
b. Persians
c. Egyptians

9. In this rose-loving nation, the flower played a role in the War of the Roses. In 1200, two different factions—the House of York and the House of Lancaster—vied for control over the nation. Seizing on King Edward's adaptation of the rose as his official symbol, York used a white rose and Lancaster a red rose as their respective insignias. In the civil war that followed, the red roses (and the Lancasters) won the day. This nation was:
a. France
b. Italy
c. England

The Navajo is the largest Native American tribe in the United States.

10. This famously romantic nation was no slouch when it came to roses either. The empress had a collection that included more than 250 varieties. She was:
   a. France's empress Josephine
   b. Austria's empress Maria Theresa
   c. Russia's empress Maria-Feodorovna.

Answers

1(b); 2(c); 3(a); 4(a); 5(c); 6(a); 7(c); 8(b); 9(c); 10(a)

* * * * *

PAYBACK TIME

Known as the "Father of Botany," the Swedish botanist Carl Linnaeus laid the groundwork in the 18th century for taxonomical classifications of living organisms: you know, the Latin genus, class, order, and all that stuff you learned in school. It was all based on his discovery that plants were sexual beings. His *Systema Naturae* made a big splash when published and promoted. But he did have his detractors. The most outspoken was J. E. Siegesbeck—a big-shot botanist who wrote an article slamming Linnaeus in 1737 and basically calling him a joke. Linnaeus would not forget this critical slap in the face. In fact, he exacted a critic-revenge only the Father of Botany could pull off: naming a small, ugly and useless European weed Siegesbeckia.

San Francisco's Golden Gate Park is 174 acres larger than New York's Central Park.

OFFICE ETYMOLOGY

The origins of the words and phrases you hear while you're standing around the water cooler and the copier and the soda machine and the smoking area...Hey! Get back to work!

Boss
This word came from the Dutch word *baas*, meaning "master." But early Americans didn't like using master—it was too aristocratic to survive as a general term. So they started using "baas" in the late 18th century. It caught on (against the objections of some word snobs) and eventually became "boss."

Cubicle
Dating back to the 1400s, this word stemmed from the Latin *cubiculum*, meaning "sleeping area" (completely apropos). It became obsolete after the 16th century, but it was revived in the 19th century as a word for "dormitory sleeping compartment." Its use as any partitioned space didn't surface until the 1920s.

Getting Fired
The phrase "fired out," meaning to throw out or eject someone from a place, was first used in 1871. When the "out" was dropped a few years later, the phrase was narrowed to mean "dismissal of an employee." There's a consensus among etymologists that both "fired" and "fired out" refer to the firing of a gun.

Learning the Ropes
Before an old-time apprentice sailor could really help out on a big ship, he had to learn which ropes had what effect on which sails. Before he did, he wasn't much use to anyone. After he "learned the ropes," he could finally hoist the right mast—and avoid being flogged.

Logging On
This phrase's predecessor was "logging in" (sometimes still used interchangeably). Back when mainframe computer operators used to go on shifts, they'd have to write everything they did in a paper

---

Band-Aid is the trademarked name for the 1920 invention belonging to Earle Dickson.

log, beginning when they arrived. So when you log on to a computer today, you're signing in.

Memorandum
From the Latin word meaning "to be remembered," it was originally a word written at the top of a note. But by 1542, it became the word for the note itself.

Rank and File
This phrase that refers to an organization's mass of low-ranking peons has military origins: soldiers in formation marched side by side (rank) and one behind the other (file). Its first known usage was in 1598. Later, it became generalized to mean common soldiers and then further generalized to refer to common people.

Suit
The word dates back to the 1200s, to the funky English-French word *siwte*, referring to the uniform worn by the royal court's stable servants. It came to mean a more general set of clothes to be worn together in the 14th century. As a derisive term for a businessman, it dates from 1979, possibly from the hippie term for an FBI agent, circa the late 1960s. The term "empty suit," meaning a person of small intellect or personality, evolved in the 1980s.

Teamwork
The original Middle English meaning of *team* was applied to a group of draft animals yoked together. Around 1828, someone thought of combining the word "team" with the word "work"—probably hoping to spur sluggish workers into action. So "teamwork" really means working like one of many beasts of burden. Depressing, huh?

* * * * *

THE SKINNY ON SKIN CREAM

In 1914, Baltimore pharmacist George Bunting invented a skin cream he named Dr. Bunting's Sunburn Remedy. He changed the name to Noxzema after a customer swore that the cream had "knocked out his eczema."

Thor Bjørklund, a Norwegian, invented the cheese slicer in 1925.

TENNIS, ANYONE?

At first, tennis was the sport of kings. Common folk didn't know a tennis ball from a matzo ball. But its noble days were numbered as the masses reached out to snatch up match, game, and set.

Tennis wasn't always the game we know and love. Starting as Royal Tennis or Real Tennis, it was invented by French monks around the 11th or 12th centuries. They would knock a cork ball around the monastery using their hands; they batted it to each other over a net made of rope or hit it off of the courtyard wall. Some say that the name "tennis" came from the monks yelling, "*Tenez!*" (A French way to say, "take that!")

Other countries might also have claim to the game. There are theories that Egyptians named the game after their city Tinnis. Greek and Roman literature mentions a sport played with ball and paddle. But since it was the French who played it—first with a glove and, eventually, with a racquet to protect their stinging palms—most historians accept tennis as a French gift to the world.

DUMB AND DUMBER

Regardless of its pedigree, aristocrats loved tennis. By the year 1200, there were almost 2,000 tennis courts in France alone. It became such a distraction that the pope tried to ban it, as did Louis IV. Maybe that wasn't such a bad idea, considering royal stamina and brainpower. In the 14th century, Louis X supposedly died of a chill immediately after a game. About a century later, Charles VIII expired after bashing his head on the door frame that opened on to his tennis court. (Ouch!)

But there was no stopping the game. By the 16th century, players used a racquet strung with sheep gut to bat custom-made balls of hair or cork covered in cloth. Soon, every self-respecting noble worth his castle had an expensive, indoor tennis court. Even Henry VIII took up the game—and watching him puff around the court must have been a royally entertaining sight.

A CLASSY GAME

In 1870, tennis moved outdoors. Lawn tennis gave the aristocracy

Around the time of the Three Kingdoms period (A.D. 220–265), China's name for Japan was Wa.

the benefits of fresh air and a new use for their parklike grounds. Then, Charles Goodyear (of Goodyear Tire fame) devised a way to vulcanize rubber. And more Victorians discovered that they were part of a growing middle class with some precious leisure time. These two discoveries changed the game of tennis forever.

Vulcanized rubber brought the world the modern, bouncy tennis ball. In 1873, seizing on the new bouncy ball and general concepts of Royal Tennis, Major Walter C. Wingfield devised a more accessible game. You needed a racquet, a net, a white tennis outfit, and one of those new balls. No castle was required.

The new sport wasn't perfect. Players disliked the first courts (which were shaped like a giant hourglass: narrow at the net and wide on the ends). But eventually, the courts became rectangular, and tennis competed with croquet as a popular lawn game. Middle-class Victorians in white tennis duds volleyed from Dover to Durham.

FOR LOVE AND MONEY

The new tennis became popular everywhere. The game grew most quickly in the former English colonies, particularly in the United States. Throughout the decades, tennis kept its aristocratic (some say stuffy) image. But that began to change by the mid-20th century, as minorities and women went after prize money and endorsement dollars at tournaments such as Wimbledon or the U.S. Open. These days, the sport really is tennis (for) anyone.

* * * * *

- The word "service" originates from the fact that royalty ordered their servants to place the ball into play.

- The score love means you have zero points. That score is said to have come from the French word *oeuf*, or "egg." The oval shape of the egg is the same shape as a zero.

THE KNIGHTS TEMPLAR: PART II

*When we last left Jacques de Molay, he was minding
his own business, doing his Grand Masterly thing on Cyprus.
Little did he know that he was on a collision course
with a fate worse than death. (Part I is on page 318.)*

The knights had some very powerful enemies, notably King Philip IV of France and Pope Clement V. Philip was enormously ambitious both for himself and for his country, and had little compunction about crushing anyone or anything that stood in his way. (His nickname, "Philip the Fair," referred to his good looks—he was tall and handsome, with long blonde hair and blue eyes—and not his political modus operandi.)

PHILIP THE UNFAIR
He'd already engineered the kidnapping and murder of one pope, Boniface VIII, and is widely believed to have orchestrated the death, probably by poison, of another (Benedict XI). By 1305 he'd installed his own puppet pope, Clement V, on the papal throne, which had been moved to Avignon, France (it's a long story). Anyway, with the pope in his pocket, the French king had the latitude he needed to move against the organization whose wealth and power he coveted: the Knights Templar. (In addition to greed, the king had a personal grudge against the knights. He'd asked to be received into the order as an honorary Templar—the kind of status previously conferred on Richard the Lionhearted—and had been insultingly refused.)

The official reason for Philip's displeasure with the Knights Templar was that they were a bunch of heretics who indulged in a variety of "perversions" at their secret ceremonies. The Templars, it was alleged, worshipped demonic powers. They were accused of infanticide, and if that wasn't bad enough, of engaging in "obscene kissing" at their initiation ceremonies.

What *really* happened at these ceremonies? This much is known: When a new knight was admitted to the order, the secret proceedings began with the candidate answering a long series of questions

---

...by German geographer Ferdinand von Richtofen in the 18th century.

designed to determine whether he was truly ready to swear complete obedience to the Templars. If the candidate passed this test, he was admitted. The white mantle of the order (a loose, sleeveless cloak) stamped with the red cross of the Crusaders was placed by the master over the neck of the candidate. Then the master kissed the new entrant on the mouth. To end the ceremony, the master delivered a lengthy sermon on the duties of every Templar.

THE OLD "SATANIC RITUALS" CHARGE
One charge leveled against the Templars stands out as the most bizarre and improbable. These soldiers of Christ, who had fought and laid down their lives for Christendom by the thousands, were accused of ritually denying Christ and of trampling and spitting on the cross. These charges, like most of the aforementioned accusations, were in all likelihood fabricated. No matter. With this laundry list of charges and the blessing of the pope, Philip the Fair planned a secret operation designed to strike a swift and lethal blow to the Templars' organization. Philip and Clement V summoned Jacques de Molay to France—supposedly to discuss a new crusade to retake the Holy Land—in the autumn of 1307.

FRIDAY THE 13TH: THE PREQUEL
In a dawn raid on Friday, October 13, 1307, Philip's forces captured and arrested de Molay and many of his brethren in Paris and throughout France, apparently without a hint of struggle or protest. There has never been a definitive explanation of why the Templars, who were reputed to be such fierce warriors on the battlefield, went into captivity so meekly.

A lot of evidence suggests that de Molay and his men had been tipped off in advance of the supposedly supersecret raids. Although exact numbers are impossible to come by, many knights apparently remained at large—as did the entire Templar fleet of ships, which appeared to have vanished, along with whatever it may have been carrying (probably most of the Templars' loot).

Another possible clue lies in the story of a number of wagons, rumored to be loaded with Templar treasure, which was seen leaving Paris a week before the mass arrests. Some believe that the unlucky ones such as de Molay were willing to stay behind to face whatever fate had in store in order to help protect whatever was in those wagons. Speaking of luck: the superstition that Friday the 13th is a day of misfortune is believed to stem from Philip's raids against the Knights Templar on that date.

PARIS WHEN IT SIZZLES

Philip had no actual proof of his accusations—because Templar meetings and initiations were held in the highest secrecy—so he had to resort to torture in order to get the confessions he wanted. Seventy-two Templars in France eventually "confessed" to the aforementioned perversions and heresies against the church, but 54 of them later recanted. Philip declared that the 54 were heretics and had them burned at the stake.

A COALITION OF ONE

Philip's efforts to badger other European leaders into joining him in his persecution of the Templars met with limited success.

In Lorraine, which today is in France but was part of Germany at the time, the reigning duke supported the Templars; a few were tried and quickly exonerated. Most Templars simply shaved their beards, dressed like civilians, and melted away into the local populace—who, significantly enough, did not betray them.

In the rest of Germany, the Templars defied their would-be judges, appearing in court fully armed. Thoroughly intimidated, the judges promptly pronounced them innocent.

In both Germany and Spain, whole new orders were created as a refuge for fugitive Templars.

In Scotland Robert Bruce was getting ready to fight the English and he needed all the help he could get; it's rumored that he ignored the papal order to arrest the Templars and welcomed them into his army.

In Portugal, the Templars were cleared by an inquiry and simply modified their name, becoming the Knights of Christ. (Vasco de Gama, the Portuguese sea captain and explorer who commanded the first fleet to reach India from Europe in the late 1490s, was a Knight of Christ.)

GOOD KNIGHT, JACQUES

After his arrest on that morning in October 1307, de Molay spent nearly seven years in prison. Pope Clement officially abolished the

Knights Templar in March 1312, after which most of the knights still being held were released, but de Molay wasn't so lucky. Even though he confessed to denying Christ and trampling on the Holy Cross, he steadfastly denounced any accusations that his order's initiation ritual consisted of homosexual practices. On March 18, 1314, de Molay was paraded before the populace to publicly confess his and his order's sins. But he refused to play ball. Instead, he withdrew his earlier confessions and said that the only crime he was guilty of was lying about his so-called sins in order to end the torture to which he was subjected. Understandably, this did not sit well with either Philip or the pope.

A CURSE ON YOUR MAISON
After this disappointing performance (to Philip, that is), the French king had Grand Master de Molay roasted slowly on a spit over burning coals. Scholars have claimed that, as de Molay burned in agony, he cordially invited both King Philip and Pope Clement to meet him before God within one year. Sure enough, both died within a year of de Molay's death. Whether de Molay actually made this statement will forever remain a mystery. As will the question of that scheduled meeting in heaven.

THE MYTH LIVES ON
Jacques de Molay's death in 1314 signaled the end of the Knights Templar as a formal—and formidable—organization. But in the centuries that followed their mystique only seemed to intensify; it's even speculated that the Templars traveled to North America before Columbus. In any case, the surviving Templars were no doubt peeved at Philip and Clement for their treachery, so their navy declared guerrilla war on all French ships. The naval battle flag of the Templars is familiar to everyone even today. After all, who hasn't seen a black flag with a white skull and crossbones?

* * * * *

PUTTING DA VINCI TO THE TEST
In his best-seller, *The Da Vinci Code*, author Dan Brown fingers the "Machiavellian" Pope Clement V (and his "ingeniously planned sting operation") as chiefly responsible for engineering and carrying out the arrest and torture/murder of the Templars in 1307.

But most—if not all—historians agree that it was Philip who was responsible for crushing the Templars. It was his royal officials who did the arresting in 1307, and it was the local Inquisitorial courts in France who had the Templars burned at the stake. Few of them suffered death elsewhere.

Clement, a weak and sickly Frenchman who was manipulated by his king, had no one in Rome burned at the stake, as stated in *The Da Vinci Code*. In fact, historians say that, as far as can be determined, Clement never set foot in Rome during his papacy. (Clement was the first pope to reign from Avignon—exactly where King Philip wanted him.) So when one of Brown's characters says, "Many of [the Templars] were burned at the stake and tossed unceremoniously into the Tiber River," he's only half right—burned, yes, Tiber, no.

WHAT WOULD YOU DO IF YOU WERE ROYALTY?

- King Ptolemy IV of ancient Egypt liked to build enormous ships. The largest needed 4,000 oarsmen and was 420 feet long and 57 feet wide. Too big to maneuver, these immense ships were useless.

- Charlemagne, the Frankish Emperor (A.D. 742–814) tried to learn to write but never mastered the skill.

- Akbar, third Mogul emperor of India, reigned from 1556 to 1605. He cultivated rare plants, crossbred birds, and learned to play the pipe organ, which he imported from the West. Most importantly, he tried to decrease friction between India's Islamic, Hindu, and Buddhist cultures by producing beautifully illustrated histories of each religion to encourage understanding.

- Henry VIII, famous for wedding six wives, had a passion for music. He composed masses (which are now lost) and ballads. It's rumored, though not confirmed, that he wrote the ballad "Greensleeves."

- Queen Elizabeth (1533–1603) wrote poetry and enjoyed dancing, archery, hunting, and tennis.

- Louis XIV, the Sun King (1638–1715), performed in 30 ballets.

Its capital is Amsterdam, and the seat of government is The Hague.

THE THIRD LEG

We're talking walking sticks. They've served a lot of purposes through history—as necessities, accessories, and symbols of rank.

Shepherds and foot travelers carried walking sticks since forever. In ancient Egypt, the common folk used staffs rarely longer than three feet (one meter), often with a peg on the side to carry a bag or a bottle. The rulers carried staffs too, but they were much longer (three to six feet or one to three meters long) and more elaborate. And they didn't have a peg because kings didn't carry their own belongings.

European rulers didn't start carrying fancy walking sticks to symbolize royal power until the Middle Ages. Most kings carried two: one symbolizing royal power and the other symbolizing justice. In the sixth century, the top church officials carried ceremonial staffs with crooked handles as a sign of prestige and to symbolically draw believers to them with the hook.

Between A.D. 1000 and 1600, European gentlemen carried a sword when formally dressed. But in the early 1600s, the sword was replaced by the walking stick as a symbol of gentility. Also around this time, walking sticks became known as canes because they were often made out of bamboo. The name stuck, even when walking sticks went back to being created from wood in the late 17th century.

A British gentleman of the 1700s had to follow strict rules regarding his walking stick. It was considered a privilege to be allowed to carry one, and all English men had to buy a license. In the license, they promised not to wave the stick in the air, hang it from a button, or carry it under an arm. It appears that the government wanted to make sure true English gentlemen didn't break any fashion rules—or accidentally use their walking sticks as weapons.

Today, walking sticks are no longer a fashion statement or a symbol of class. Some people use them for hiking, but most cane users have health problems and need their "walking sticks" for additional support when standing.

THE LONGEST MILE

Yonge Street, the longest street in the world,
is especially long on dreams and schemes.

The world's longest street begins on the Toronto, Ontario, Canada, waterfront. From there it stretches 1,178.3 miles (1896 km), eventually ending in Canada's mosquito-ridden, blackfly-infested northern wilderness at a town called Rainy River. Along the way, travelers can encounter everything from a belligerent bull moose to a few Starbucks.

1793

John Graves Simcoe got the street going. At the time he was Upper Canada's British-appointed governor. When Upper Canada's capital was established at Toronto (then an army garrison town known as York), Simcoe decided local improvements were in order.

For one thing, Canadian fur traders needed an overland route to western Canada's furs. Mostly Simcoe wanted to bypass those feisty, newly independent Americans, who nominally controlled the traditional route through Lakes Ontario and Erie. A road north, connecting to Lake Huron, was Simcoe's solution.

Simcoe couldn't afford to build a road to anywhere, but once he started swapping land grants for road building, he soon had himself 30 or 40 miles (between 48 and 64 km) of really bad road studded with rocks and tree stumps. It climbed steep hills and made its way through deep valleys, swamps, and virgin forests so thick the Amazon jungle would seem like a freeway. Simcoe named it Yonge Street in honor of a British secretary of war (whom he may have secretly disliked).

The few blocks inside Toronto were mostly a muddy route that the wooden sidewalks sank into with regularity. Farther out of town, some sections were so poor that wagons had to be dismantled and dragged along piece by piece. Conestoga wagons were popular because they floated across creeks and flooded areas. (Bridges? Don't be silly.)

1814

By now Yonge Street had made it 80 miles (129 km) from the shore of Lake Ontario to Georgian Bay, which led into Lake Huron. Work on the road had been pushed forward by the War of 1812. Using it as a supply route, the British planned to build ships on Lake Huron and thus assert control on the upper Great Lakes. Unfortunately, the war ended too soon for the strategy to work.

1817–1850

Meanwhile, back in York, early risers could have witnessed Canada's last official duel, conducted on a Yonge Street lot between two "gentlemen," Messrs. Ridout and Jarvis. Looking to get an edge, Ridout shot before the count was completed. Jarvis then used his shot to snuff out any further potential for ungentle-manly conduct from Ridout. The coroner's report said that Jarvis had been "seduced by the instigation of the Devil," and a jury found him guilty of murder.

On a slightly less interesting note, 1817 also saw the intro-duction of parking restrictions on Yonge Street, the first in North America.

1820

William Lyon Mackenzie (remember that name) arrived in York and started publishing a newspaper, the *Colonial Advocate*.

1825

Mackenzie's newspaper reported on the journey of Sir John Franklin and his full-blown expedition up the length of Yonge Street en route to find the Northwest Passage. Some wag com-mented that if Franklin could make it safely up Yonge Street, find-ing the passage would be child's play.

1833–1835

Twelve and a half miles (20 km) of Yonge Street were macadamized, quite a sensation at the time.

In 1834, York became Toronto, and Mackenzie became Toronto's first mayor. After one term, he was tossed out by voters. He didn't take the loss lightly, railing long and loud in his newspa-per and in the bars and back rooms of the city.

The first wax figure made by Marie Tussaud was of Jean Jacques Rousseau, in 1778.

1837

Thinking himself the George Washington of Canada, William Lyon Mackenzie fomented a rebellion against England, the loss of which he blamed on the sorry condition of Yonge Street—apparently forgetting he had attempted his silly business in the dead of a Canadian winter when sensible Canadians hunkered near their home fires.

1850

While traffic continued to flow bumpily along Yonge Street, political deal makers and dreamers still worked the street's bars and back rooms. An 1850 survey found one bar for every mile (1.6 km) of Yonge Street, 80 in total. That enabled a lot of scheming.

1861–1900

Toronto's first public transit made its appearance in 1861: horse-drawn street trams. (The horses were confined to the barns when public transit was electrified in 1890.)

Officially, Yonge Street didn't progress an inch from 1861 to 1900. But rail lines had crept north, bringing homesteaders, lumberjacks, and prospectors; and unofficially, a wagon trail was being tramped down alongside the rail lines. By the turn of the century, this traffic had added another 60 miles (97 km) to the street and road builders were agitating to go another 40 miles (64 km) to North Bay, despite the terrain being mostly swamp and rock. Toronto financiers and government representatives were not impressed. Until…

1900–1926

This was one of Yonge Street's biggest boom times. Settlements were popping up around lumber camps. Pulp and paper interests established huge paper mills in the north. But most important of all, north beyond North Bay, gold was discovered, plus silver, nickel, and copper. Soon the street would host the largest gold lodes in the world.

In the space of a few years, the 40 miles (64 km) to North Bay was completed. After that came a 200-mile (322 km) leap to Iroquois Falls, then Kapuskasing another 100 miles (161 km) and, finally, westward to Thunder Bay—another 380 miles (612 km) finished in 1926.

Madame Tussaud established her first wax exhibition in London's Baker Street in 1835.

Yonge Street had opened up the riches of Ontario's north. In all, the street now stretched 896 miles (1,442 km). From Toronto, the street ran north to Cochrane, then due west following the rail line to the head of Lake Superior.

1948
Canada's government declared its intention to construct a Trans-Canada highway. Much of Ontario's portion was already built—it was Yonge Street!

1949–1954
An idea hatched way back in 1910 came to fruition: Yonge Street was to have a subway, the first in all of Canada. Four and a half miles (7.2 km) of Yonge Street were transformed into a gulch, track was laid, the gulch covered over, and Canada's first subway was officially opened.

1965
The last extension of 280 miles (451 km) was officially opened when the ribbon was cut on a 3.5-mile (5.6-km) causeway that hooked up Rainy River, Ontario—host to the annual Canadian bass fishing championships—to downtown Toronto.

The town of Rainy River is just across the Minnesota border, which is a little ironic. The street that was started to get away from the Americans ends only a few miles from an international bridge to the United States.

* * * * *

CANE YOU TOP THIS?

- The French philosopher Voltaire owned 80 canes. His contemporary, the writer and philosopher Jean Jacques Rousseau, had 40.

- Marie Antoinette, known for carrying a shepherd's-crook, helped make canes fashionable in late 18th century France.

- According to a *Wall Street Journal* article, King Tutankhamen, Henry III, Louis XIII, Napoleon, Frederick the Great, and George Washington all collected canes.

Suspected of royalist sympathies, Madame Tussaud was scheduled to die on the guillotine.

MORE HORSE POWER

Uncle Ed has more answers—straight from the horse's mouth.

Dear Uncle Ed,

Okay, okay, horses were a big deal in wars. I may have even bunked with a few. But what about in peacetime? Why do they get all the good press?

Francis T. Mule

Dear Francis,

For good reason. People who wanted to deliver mail, for instance, found it faster to deliver it on the horse hoof—like the Chinese who invented the idea during the Shang dynasty in 1300 B.C. The Pony Express in 1860 proved that rugged riders and their mounts could successfully deliver mail from St. Joseph, Missouri, to Sacramento, California. Horses and riders kept communications open summer and winter. The mail took ten days in summer, and twelve to sixteen in winter to travel nearly 2000 miles.

It wasn't just mail that traveled by horse. Knowledge did too. The great civilizations of the ancient Americas—the Inca, Maya, and Aztecs—didn't have horses to spread their knowledge or their culture. So most of America's other native peoples had no clue about the progress in math, and astronomy that these civilizations had made—they were still in the hunter-gatherer stage of development when the Europeans arrived. All for lack of horses.

In the Middle Ages in Europe, powerful horses bred to carry knights in armor also pulled plows and carried loads for farmers, stone masons and foresters. Small villages could create wealth by sending their products overland and they could stay in contact with a modernizing world.

Through the next two centuries horses ruled the worlds of transportation and commerce. Well into the 1900s workhorses continued to haul everything from canal barges to public stage-coaches to milk carts. When English engineer James Watt needed a term to measure how much work was done by a steam engine, what was the phrase he used? Horse power, of course.

She was spared because of her talent in wax work.

So, Francis, if you want to get somewhere—literally and figuratively—get a horse!

Dear Uncle Ed,

Why is thoroughbred horse racing called "the Sport of Kings?" I've never seen one at the track. And I go a lot.

M. T. Pockets

Dear M. T.,

The Crusaders brought Arabian stallions back to England where they were bred with Irish and English mares. To prove the value of their horses, their owners began to race them. Eventually the descendants of three of those stallions from the Mideast and North Africa (Byerly Turk, Darley Arabian, and Godolphin Barb) became the only ones allowed to compete in "thoroughbred" racing. And those rules still hold today.

Because horses cost a bundle to feed and house, only the wealthy bred and raced them. But it was King Charles II who made racing "the sport of kings." He didn't just like to watch the races at Newmarket; he liked to compete in them too. Thanks to his support, public races mushroomed up across England, and by 1790, horseracing was England's first regulated sport.

Dear Uncle Ed,

Are you related to the talking horse on the TV sitcom, Mister Ed? And do you know how they got him to talk?

Just Curious

Dear Just Nosey,

Serious historians don't indulge in trivia. But in the interests of explaining that even in television history, horses did their part, I will tell you that I have a famous nephew, who did much historical reading between shots. He gave the following report: Word on the *Mister Ed* set was that his trainer fed him a wad of a sticky, peanut butter–type substance, which he'd then eat and which would make his lips wriggle.

Only ocean fish are used raw in sushi; freshwater fish, which may harbor parasites, are cooked.

Dear Uncle Ed,

Do you think horses will ever make history again, now that machines have taken their place?

Ima Hoarse

Dear Ima,

Machines can't replace the horse completely. Horses loom too large in the cultural heritage in America's western states, for example, horses and cowboys created a way of life that still inspires songs, poetry, and my favorite Clint Eastwood movies. (Also see the above info on *Mister Ed.*)

Today, horses are used mainly for recreation, companionship, and even therapy. But as pollution and oil shortage problems grow, some farmers are returning to the use of draft horses as an organic way to work the land. Stay tuned—for the next few centuries any-way—to discover where horses go from here.

* * * * *

IS BIGGER BETTER?

In its heyday, Rome believed in growth. At its height (around A.D. 200–250), the territory held by the Roman Empire was close to the size of the United States today. The population was over 100 million with the city of Rome at one million.

Julius Caesar, for one, wasn't satisfied. He wanted more Romans, so he punished childless wives by forbidding them to ride in litters or to wear jewelry. At the same time he had to deal with the problems of governing a densely populated city. Traffic, for example, could be a nightmare, so Caesar banned all wheeled vehicles in Rome during the daylight hours.

Roman invaders in 52 B.C. called the city Lutetia, meaning "marshy place." It is now called Paris.

OVERNIGHT SUCCESS

When Arthur Heineman put up a billboard announcing the construction of the first motel, amateur proofreaders alerted him to a mistake on his sign. There was an M where there should have been an H. There was no such thing as a motel. At least not yet.

On a postcard from the 1930s, the Milestone Mo-Tel was billed as the "Most Delightful and Complete Motorist's Hotel in the World...Complete Hotel Services in Fireproof Bungalows."

YES, THE CAR CAN STAY TOO

In 1925, architect Arthur Heineman came up with a brilliant idea for housing tourists who usually drove all day and stayed in "auto camps" at night because hotels were too pricey or too far off the highway. Cars were a relatively new luxury for the middle-class American, as was the idea of driving hundreds of miles at a time.

Heineman coined the word "Mo-Tel," meaning "motor hotel," which soon became just plain "motel."

He planned a chain stretching from Seattle, Washington, to San Diego, California, and chose the outskirts of San Luis Obispo, California, for his first site because it was halfway between San Francisco and Los Angeles. The property, which would house up to 160 guests, was built in Spanish-mission style, complete with bell tower. It cost $80,000 (66,000 euros) to construct.

For $1.25 (1 euro) a night, guests could snooze in a clean, comfortable, two-room bungalow with a kitchen and a private, adjoining garage. All units faced a common courtyard, complete with a swimming pool and picnic areas.

Alas, the Depression dashed Heineman's dreams of a motel chain. Then, after World War II, travel across the United States dramatically increased with the development of the interstate highway system and better-built roads. Cheap lodging popped up everywhere. By the 1950s, the motel was an American institution. Eventually, these less attractive and less expensive alternatives eroded Milestone's business. Today, a boarded-up portion of the original motel still stands, just off Highway 101.

A smaller version of the Statue of Liberty stands on the river Seine, in Paris.

THE PREPOSTEROUS PLATE OF BRASS

A Berkeley professor gets punked—1930s-style.

In 1936, a pheasant hunter discovered a metal plate near San Quentin State Prison, which overlooks San Francisco Bay. When he cleaned it up a bit, he noticed some writing on it which, if authentic, made the plate an incredible historic artifact. The plate appeared to have been left there in 1579 by Sir Francis Drake; engraved on it was the explorer's claim of having found the land he called Nova Albion for "Herr Majestie Queen Elizabeth." Finally, here was the proof that some historians had been waiting for.

The discovery set off a fierce debate. But for those who were only too willing to believe in its authenticity, it held the answer as to where and when Drake and his ship, the *Golden Hinde*, had first landed on American soil.

The believers had the upper hand: the marker, dubbed Drake's Plate, became a part of American history. It was a centerpiece of the 1939–1940 Golden Gate International Exposition, and photographs of it appeared in textbooks and popular magazines. To most everybody, it seemed to be the real thing.

BERKELEY GOES BERSERKELEY

As the story unfolded behind the scenes, it turned out that the perpetrators of this hoax weren't interested in convincing the world of Drake's landing. Their target was one particular man— the most prominent among the true believers: a Berkeley history professor named Herbert E. Bolton. Fascinated by a legend about Drake posting a brass plate to mark his entry into California, Bolton used to tell his students to be on the lookout for it when in Marin County (home of San Quentin), which faces the city of San Francisco across the Golden Gate strait. The discovery of the plate was a dream come true for Bolton, who was also director of Berkeley's Bancroft Library from 1920 to 1940. Before anyone had a chance to tip Bolton off, he announced the discovery to the world and ensconced the plate in the library.

It was given to the French people in 1889 by the American community in Paris.

THE PLOT

Besides being a member of the California Historical Society, Bolton was a Clamper, that is, a member of E Clampus Vitus, a playful fraternity of Western history buffs that was originally founded to poke fun at stuffy secret societies like the Freemasons. The Clampers were well known for spoofing each other, especially on historical matters; the distinguished Professor Bolton's preoccupation with Drake's landing made him a tempting target.

But when a story circulated that the plate was a phony, planted in a hoax perpetrated by the Clampers, instead of taking credit for it and everyone having a good chuckle, the society categorically denied having anything to do with Drake's "plate of brasse." They even went so far as to publish their own report on it: *Ye Preposterous Booke of Brasse*.

THE PLOTTERS

Researchers now point the finger at a band of respectable gentlemen of the day—only one of whom was known to have been a Clamper.

The instigator: G. Ezra Dane, a prominent member of the Clampers and of the California Historical Society.

The designer: George Haviland Barron, curator of California history at the de Young Museum in San Francisco until 1933 and a leading member of the California Historical Society. He borrowed most of the text from *The World Encompassed by Sir Francis Drake*, a detailed account of Drake's voyage that was first published in 1628.

The engraver: George C. Clark, an inventor, art critic, appraiser, and friend of Barron's, designed the layout for the plate and chiseled the lettering.

The aiders and abettors: Also fingered were Lorenz Noll, an art dealer and restorer; and Albert Dressler, a dealer in Western artifacts.

THE AGING PROCESS

The scientists who later investigated the brass plate noted that the text had to have been carved with a chisel and that the letters' raised edges were hammered down. They found evidence that the plate had been heated over a wood fire to create a dark patina; hammered once more; darkened more with dirt, ash, and possibly more chemicals; then possibly subjected to fire once again; and buried for a time.

SINCERELY YOURS, THE CLAMPERS

What should have given away the prank was the fluorescent initials ECV—the signature of E Clampus Vitus—applied to the back of the plate. But Bolton ignored this dead giveaway; he unquestioningly supported the plate's authenticity. The inside joke, intended to be resolved with a good laugh over a dinner table, had escaped the plotters' control.

And it wasn't just Bolton they'd taken in. The president of the California Historical Society, along with other society officers and members, donated $3,500 (2,900 euros) to buy the plate for the library. The historical society's directors, who authorized publications about the plate, were also fooled.

Because the tricksters and most of the hoaxed all belonged to the same small world of California history enthusiasts, it made a public confession very difficult after the fact. The tricksters tried to warn Bolton indirectly, but he was too thrilled with his discovery to notice the warnings.

FESSING UP

Three of the tricksters—Dane, Barron, and Clark—died in the early 1940s, freeing up Lorenz Noll to confess the real story to the Clampers and at least one well-respected honcho at the California Historical Society.

After Professor Bolton died in 1953, Noll started telling the truth to a wider circle. But the facts didn't reach the right ears until the mid-1970s, when the director of the Bancroft Library (where the plate still resided) commissioned a new study in anticipation of the quadricentennial of Drake's landing.

ANALYZE THIS

In 1977, two Berkeley lab scientists—who had started with the expectation that the plate was authentic—began their research. They immediately began seeing things that made them suspicious: the thickness of the plate was too consistent for something that would have been hammered out, drilling into the plate turned up no corroded metal, and a too-high level of zinc (which hadn't

Going into the catacombs has been illegal since November 2, 1955.

been yet been identified in the 16th century) suggested that the brass was a mixture of high-purity copper and zinc, which would not have been available at the time. The plate was most probably manufactured between the last half of the 19th century and the early part of the 20th.

Finally, the connection was made; attention was turned back to Lorenz Noll's story. An article on this final chapter of the hoax was published in the *UCBerkeley News* in February 2003.

A MAN WHO LEFT HIS MARK, IF NOT HIS PLATE

Californians are mostly optimists so you can still find historians there who think the hoax had a positive impact; they point out the increased public awareness of the state's explorer-era history and a wide range of related historical research.

The fake plate is still on display at the Bancroft Library. No one's quite given up hope that the real thing may still be out there—possibly lying deep beneath the water, rocks, and sand of Drake's Bay, and will be discovered someday.

Even if it isn't, Sir Francis Drake left his figurative mark on Marin County: from the aforementioned Drake's Bay to Drake's Landing Office Park; from Sir Francis Drake Boulevard, which runs from the neighborhood around San Quentin all the way to the Pacific Ocean, to Sir Francis Drake High School (Go, Pirates!).

* * * * *

E CLAMPUS VITUS FAQ:

What does *E Clampus Vitus* mean?
No one knows.

What is the purpose of the society?
Depending on whom you ask, it's either a historical drinking society or a drinking historical society. The debate continues.

What are the society's objectives?
Members swear to take care of disabled miners, widows, and orphans—but especially the widows.

Who is the governing authority of the Clampers?
All members are officers and all officers are of equal indignity.

The name Montparnasse stems from the "Mount Parnassus" of Greek mythology.

HOLLYWOOD REWRITES HISTORY: *ROBIN HOOD: PRINCE OF THIEVES*

Just as it was meant to be: long on action, short on authenticity—all taking place in 1194, at the end of the Third Crusade. Let's have a look...

The Rewrite: The sheriff of Nottingham (Alan Rickman) orders his two maids to see him later that evening: "You...10:30 tonight. You, 10:45. Bring a friend."
The Facts: Obviously all in good fun, but the minute hand on a clock wasn't invented until 1577.

The Rewrite: Will Scarlett (Christian Slater) uses the "F word." (Not only that, he says, "F— me!"—a fairly recent usage of the cuss word.)
The Facts: The first recorded use of the word was in 1503 (most probably from the Old German "to strike or penetrate").

The Rewrite: The sheriff uses the term "turncoat" when referring to Will Scarlett.
The Facts: "Turncoat" is usually thought to have originated in the Revolutionary War, referring to British soldiers who turned their red coats inside out when they joined the American side. The term is actually older than that: it was first recorded in 1557, describing Saxons who wore coats that were blue on one side and white the other. When a Saxon wished to be thought a French supporter, he wore the white outside; otherwise, the outside color was blue.

The Rewrite: When Mortianna the witch (Geraldine McEwan) tells the sheriff to recruit the Celts to help him battle Robin and the gang, he answers, "Hired thugs?"

It was given to the Paris neighborhood by students who recited poetry there.

The Facts: One of the earliest authenticated mentions of thugs (from the Hindi *thag,* Sanskrit *sthaga,* meaning "thief" or "rogue") is found in *History of Firuz Shah,* dated about 1356. The "thugees," as they were known, were a well-organized confederacy of assassins who worshipped Kali, the goddess of death and destruction. They traveled in gangs throughout India for several hundred years, until the British wiped them out in the 19th century.

The Rewrite: King Richard the Lion-hearted (played by a 60-ish Sean Connery) turns up at the wedding of Robin (Kevin Costner) and Marian (Mary Elizabeth Mastrantonio).
The Facts: The real King Richard I was 37 years old when he returned from the Third Crusade in 1194.

Possible Rewrite: Azeem the Moor (Morgan Freeman) uses both a telescope and blasting powder.
The Facts: These may not be anachronisms. The medieval Muslims were far more sophisticated than the Europeans of the time. The Western world believes that the telescope was invented in 1608, but because a great amount of Arab scholarship was lost or destroyed during and shortly after the Crusades, who are we to say that Azeem wasn't the proud possessor of a Middle Eastern version of a telescope?

As for gunpowder, it was invented in China in the ninth century and spread to Europe during warfare, though most people think Marco Polo brought it back from the Orient. We can't say for sure that Azeem didn't come across some of it before his fictitious trip to England.

WHEN CONGRESSMEN ATTACK

Think today's politicians play rough? In 1856, a U.S.
representative attacked a U.S. senator in the Senate chamber.
Not with scathing rhetoric or sly innuendo. With a cane.

T hings got pretty uncivil between the North and the South
in the years leading up to the Civil War. The main hot-
button topic was—you guessed it—slavery. The North
wanted it outlawed in newly acquired territories in the West
before they were settled, developed, and added to the Union as
states; the South hated the idea of federal regulation of slavery.
Twice, after a lot of heated debate, Congress managed to work
out compromises that kept the peace (only temporarily, as it
turned out). One of these agreements, the Missouri Compromise,
outlawed slavery above the latitude of 36° 30' in most of the
Louisiana Purchase.

COMPROMISE, SHMOMPROMISE
In 1854, Congress passed the Kansas-Nebraska Act. The act created two new territories, Kansas and Nebraska, from land acquired
in the Louisiana Purchase. These territories were north of the 36°
30' latitude line, and therefore were supposed to be free from slavery. But the Kansas-Nebraska Act explicitly repealed the Missouri
Compromise. It opened the Kansas and Nebraska territories to
slavery under the doctrine of "popular sovereignty," meaning that
settlers in the territories could decide for themselves about slavery.
    The act was sponsored by an Illinois senator named Stephen
A. Douglas, who was tired of watching Southern congressmen
block legislation for railroad construction and other development
in the slavery-free zones of the West. He figured this bill would
make the South happy and speed up Western development, which
would make everyone happy. Shows how much he knew.

OUCH, MY MIDWEST IS BLEEDING
The Kansas-Nebraska Act's nullification of the Missouri
Compromise enraged abolitionists and angered most Northerners.

There were six jurors from each side of the Nile River.

To make matters worse, the act's "popular sovereignty" clause resulted in a rush of both proslavery and antislavery settlers into Kansas as each faction tried to gain a majority in the state. This led to years of violent clashes and riots within the state, which came to be known as "Bleeding Kansas." So instead of helping calm the bitterly divided nation, the Kansas-Nebraska Act pushed the United States closer to war. Thanks a bunch, Stephen A. Douglas.

IF YOU CAN'T SAY ANYTHING NICE...

The antislavery faction in Congress was led by Massachusetts senator Charles Sumner. A staunch abolitionist, Sumner opposed any accommodation with slavery and was outraged by the passage of the Kansas-Nebraska Act. Sumner was a radical guy—he crusaded for prison reform, world peace, and in 1849 unsuccessfully fought to integrate public schools in Boston. He was also a noted orator, famous for long, grandiloquent speeches laced with classical allusions and no-holds-barred attacks on his opponents.

On May 19, 1856, Sumner took the Senate floor to denounce the Kansas-Nebraska Act with an incendiary harangue delivered over two days. Sumner called the act a "crime against Kansas" and "the rape of a virgin territory." He made a point of attacking, by name, several supporters of the act, including a senator from South Carolina named Andrew Butler. Sumner accused Butler of taking a mistress "polluted in the sight of the world," that is, "the harlot, Slavery." (Such language!) He also described Butler as speaking "with incoherent phrases" during the recent debates and accused him of spitting on the representative and the people of Kansas. Some listeners thought that Sumner was making fun of the way the elderly Butler, a stroke victim, spoke. If that wasn't bad enough, Sumner also made a few nasty cracks about South Carolina. Bad move!

THAT'S NOT WHAT'S MEANT BY "MAJORITY WHIP"

Butler wasn't present for the speech, but a South Carolina representative named Preston Brooks, who happened to be Senator Butler's nephew, heard the oration. A traditional Southern gentleman, he decided that Sumner should be thrashed for besmirching the honor of his state and his kinsman.

On May 22, Brooks entered the Senate chamber after the

Senate had adjourned for the day and approached Sumner, who was seated at his desk. He accused Sumner of libeling South Carolina and Senator Butler, and then struck him with his walking stick, a gold-headed gutta-percha cane. Sumner, disoriented by the first blow and trapped by his desk, tried to escape but couldn't. Brooks continued to beat him until the cane shattered. Sumner was unconscious before stunned onlookers could come to his rescue (some claimed that Southern senators failed to intervene on purpose).

SOUTHERN COMFORT

The incident, unsurprisingly, didn't ease the tension between North and South. Abolitionists hailed Sumner as a near-martyr, and many Northerners felt the attack was proof of the brutal and degenerate culture of the slaveholding South.

In Southern states, however, Brooks' actions were applauded. He reportedly received hundreds of canes from admirers—including one inscribed "Hit him again"—to replace the one he'd broken on Sumner's head. The House of Representatives tried to expel him, but Southern representatives defeated the vote. Brooks resigned anyway, after giving a speech in the House of Representatives defending his actions, and was immediately reelected to the same seat by South Carolina voters. He eventually had to pay a $300 fine for the assault.

THE AFTERMATH

The incident would be kind of funny if it weren't for the fact that Sumner was seriously injured. It took him three years to recover from the beating and return to the Senate. (Southerners accused him of exaggerating his injuries.) Massachusetts voters reelected him during his convalescence, leaving his empty chair in the Senate as a silent reproach to the South. When Sumner returned to work in 1860, the first speech he delivered was a four-hour-long address titled "The Barbarism of Slavery." He didn't have to fear any more run-ins with Preston Brooks, who had died after a sudden illness in 1857. After the Civil War ended, Sumner was a leader of the Radical Republicans, a faction of the Republican Party that fought for civil rights for freed slaves. The Radical Republicans also favored dealing strictly with the defeated South, which is perfectly understandable in Sumner's case. He died in 1874.

Dante's *Divine Comedy* established Tuscan dialect as the basis of modern Italian language.

"MY NAME IS BILL…"

"…and I'm an alcoholic." Bill Wilson founded Alcoholics Anonymous and developed the 12-step program that's helped millions of people to overcome their addictions.

Bill Wilson stood in the lobby of the Mayflower Hotel in New York City, listening to the laughter and glasses clinking in the hotel bar. His mind raced and his heart pounded as he fought to resist the lure. Then he remembered that helping others was one way to help himself, and he resolved to find another alcoholic whom he could help. He left the hotel. After a series of frantic phone calls, he found another alcoholic, named Dr. Robert Smith, who agreed to meet with him. A month later, Smith took his last drink. Bill W. and Bob S. became the founders of what would later become known as Alcoholics Anonymous.

DROWNING IN BOOZE

Bill Wilson had his first drink while in the army during World War I. "I had found the elixir of life," he recalled. After the war, he married Lois Burnham and went to work on Wall Street. He lost all of his money in the stock market crash of 1929, but he continued to trade stocks and managed to earn a modest living. His heavy drinking, however, was slowly taking its toll.

Eventually, alcohol completely took over his life, and by 1933, he hit bottom. Bill and Lois were living in her parents' home in Brooklyn; she was working in a department store, while he spent his days and nights in a near-constant alcoholic stupor.

THE SECRET TO BILL'S SUCCESS

In 1934, an old drinking buddy who'd managed to give up his boozing ways and stay sober visited Bill. His secret? A belief that God would help him overcome his addiction to alcohol. When Bill said he wasn't a member of any organized religion, his buddy said, "Why don't you choose your own conception of God?" That made it almost easy: Bill understood that "it was only a matter of being willing to believe in a power greater than myself."

THANK GOD!

Bill had a spiritual awakening. As he later recounted, "God had done for me what I could not do for myself." Determined to get better, he checked into a hospital and underwent the state-of-the-art treatment at that time for alcoholics: the barbiturate and belladonna cure, also known as "purge and puke."

"While I lay in the hospital, the thought came that there were thousands of hopeless alcoholics who might be glad to have what had been so freely given me. Perhaps I could help some of them. They in turn might work with others." Bill then came to understand how helping others would be essential to his recovery.

CLEAN AND SOBER

After his release, Bill managed to stay sober, but he returned to the hospital frequently to help other alcoholics undergoing detox. It was during this time that he faced his moment of truth at the Mayflower Hotel and began his association with Dr. Smith. Soon they were holding meetings for recovering alcoholics so that they could support their group and welcome others who were looking for help.

ONE STEP AT A TIME

By the time the group had about 100 members, Bill began to write down his philosophy as a series of principles for remaining sober. He eventually published them in a book called *Alcoholics Anonymous*, which also became the name of the organization that he and Dr. Smith founded. That book is now known as *The Big Book*.

In it, Bill wrote that the key to sobriety was a change of heart. He defined 12 steps to recovery that included an admission that one is powerless over the addiction, a belief in a higher power, restitution for the wrongs one has committed, and service to others.

MR. ANONYMOUS

Bill didn't want anyone to profit from his or her association with A.A., and he believed that one way to avoid that was for members to keep their identities a secret. Also, A.A. members are not required to donate money, and no contribution over $1,000 is accepted. Bill himself never took a salary for his work or accepted any financial gifts.

The Cherokee name for themselves is Aniyunwiya.

As the membership of A.A. grew, he acted as the public spokesman, but he never revealed his identity. Bill testified before the U.S. Senate in 1969, but he would only allow himself to be photographed from behind. He wouldn't allow himself to be photographed at all—even from behind—for a *Time* magazine cover.

BILL'S OTHER VICES

Though Bill Wilson's contributions to the understanding of alcoholism and recovery are legendary, he was not a saint. He was an unrepentant womanizer after A.A. became famous; many women were attracted to him because of his celebrity within the organization. He would troll A.A. meetings for young women and offer them private "counseling." His wife, Lois, mostly ignored his infidelities.

He was also blind to the ill effects that smoking had on his health—until it was too late. Near the end of his life, he was suffering from advanced emphysema. But he was so addicted to tobacco that he'd turn off the oxygen he needed to help him breathe so that he could have a cigarette. He died in Miami in 1971.

STEP UP AND HELP YOURSELF

Alcoholics Anonymous has more than two million members in over 150 countries today. Because of its success, the American Medical Association officially recognized alcoholism as a disease (instead of a failure of willpower) in 1956. After Wilson died, Lois founded Al-Anon and Alateen as support groups for spouses and children of alcoholics.

Bill Wilson's 12-step program spawned other recovery organizations like Narcotics Anonymous, Overeaters Anonymous, Sexaholics Anonymous, Gamblers Anonymous, Debtors Anonymous, Smokers Anonymous, and Workaholics Anonymous. But so far, no Bathroom Readers Anonymous.

A SEEDY HISTORY

*The fourth Earl of Sandwich had a great concept
and Dagwood Bumstead perfected it, but it took
Charles Saunders to hold it all together.*

Ignoring his PhD in chemistry, Canadian Charles E. Saunders took up a career as a classical pianist instead. He advertised concerts, recitals, and music instruction. But, in Toronto, Ontario, Canada, in the 19th century, demand for his music was as flat as the Earth before Christopher Columbus rounded it off.

Between gigs, Charles loved to munch on well-constructed sandwiches, His dislike of bread that fell apart at first bite led him to a virtuoso performance, a performance that had nothing to do with music—and just a little bit with chemistry.

MAKING BREAD

It finally became clear to everyone—even Charles—that he wasn't going to make any bread (so to speak) playing piano. So, the young man dusted off his chemistry degree and went to work for Sir William Saunders. Sir William was a famous agriculture researcher who'd made his mark crossbreeding seeds to develop new strains of berries, grains, and vegetables. He was also Charlie's dad.

Charlie had spent plenty of summers helping his father do agricultural research. Now, he threw himself into the family profession, during which he would soon make bread in earnest.

UNSETTLING TROUBLES ON THE PRAIRIES

In 1886, Sir William was named director of Canada's spanking new experimental farms—five in all—set up primarily due to his earlier successes at crossbreeding seed. One of the goals of the experimental farms was to develop a wheat seed strain that could withstand harsh prairie climates.

At that time, the Canadian government, worried that the United States might want to push its borders above the 49th parallel, was eager to settle its prairies with loyal Canadian citizens. But farmers on the prairies were desperate for good wheat with a short sowing season because they often lost their entire crops to

---

In 1966, purist British fans booed Bob Dylan when he used an electric guitar for the first time.

the early, hard frosts. Some settlers were leaving the prairies because they couldn't make a living.

Sir William had traveled throughout the world gathering wheat seeds that Charles started mixing as early as 1892. In 1893, fiddling about in his greenhouse, Charles crossbred seed provided by farmers in Ukraine and India. His new strain grew faster than the wheat popular at that time, and the yield was impressive. But would the wheat, once it became flour, make a bread up to Charles's high (sandwich) standards?

CHEWING ON THE PROBLEM

Charles was still on the project in 1903 when Dad made him the Dominion Cerealist. To Charles, this simply meant he could spend his days building a better sandwich. One habit he had learned in all those chemistry classes was to "test, test, test." Charles developed the famous Saunders's gluten test, gluten being the material that provides bread dough with its elasticity and holds the bread slice together. The Saunders's test didn't require a lab; our Charles could pluck a kernel in the field, chew it, and instantly know its gluten quality. If it were a good chew, he reasoned it should make good bread.

He didn't hand off the grain to the local miller or the flour to the local baker either. Charles did the milling and baking himself—and the tasting too. After years of experimentation, he was finally satisfied.

GIVING THE WORLD ITS DAILY BREAD

In 1910, the seed, named Marquis wheat, was distributed to Canadian prairie farmers for spring planting. It was a huge success. By 1920, 90 percent of more than 17 million acres (7 million hectares) of wheat grown in North American prairies was Marquis. Three times in the course of that decade, a farmer who'd entered his Marquis wheat in the New York Land Show won a $1,000 (812 euros) prize for the best hard spring wheat grown anywhere in the world.

Canadian wheat produced such a "baking-friendly" (make that "sandwich-friendly") flour that markets sprang up for the crop. Canadian prairie farmers, thanks to Marquis wheat, grew

The first sponsored fundraising "walk" inside a prison occurred in an Oregon prison in 1988.

prosperous filling the breadbasket of the world. And even now, many years since Charles's death in 1937, the Marquis strain still courses through the pedigree of most wheat.

HERO SANDWICH

And what was our hero's reaction? He was probably gratified by awards that included a knighthood in 1934. But he may have been even happier to know that all his patient work ultimately created a sturdy sandwich.

* * * * *

PHILIPPE THE ORIGINAL

The next time you're in France, don't ask for a French dip sandwich because they won't know what you're talking about and the waiter might be rude to you. It's happened.

Instead, come back with us to 1918 Los Angeles, to a delicatessen and sandwich shop where French immigrant Philippe Mathieu was making a sandwich for a local cop. Oops! Mathieu accidentally dropped the French roll for the sandwich into the pan juices, but before he could replace it, the cop said he'd eat it anyway, as is. The next day, the cop was back with some friends who all wanted their French rolls *au jus* too.

Almost 100 years later, the restaurant called Philippe the Original, is still going strong and is a huge favorite of baseball fans, since it's less than a mile away from Dodger Stadium.

The prisoners were raising money for organ transplants and walked 3,400 miles.

THE STORY OF BUTTER

A jug of wine, a loaf of bread...and butter! Yum.

Butter is the most concentrated form of milk, the result of churning milk until the butterfat separates from the buttermilk. Once it's semisolid (and salt is usually added), it's formed into blocks, wrapped in paper, and shipped to your local supermarket.

WHERE'D YOU GET THIS BUTTER?

Herodotus, a Greek researcher and storyteller of the fifth century B.C., talks about coming across a creamy, rich substance made from mare's milk that sounds an awful lot like butter. He credits it to the Scythians, who controlled most of the land from the Danube east in his day. Pliny, a first-century Roman officer and encyclopedist, wrote that butter, in fact, came from the ancient Germans.

ENOUGH ROOM TO SWING A GOAT

Still, the earliest known process of making butter is credited to the Syrians and Arabs. They'd skin a goat, sew the skin up—leaving only one foreleg open where the cream was poured in—and then hang the whole contraption from tent poles and swing it until its contents changed from cream to butter. Let's not go *there* for lunch.

I CAN'T BELIEVE IT'S BUTTER

All ancient accounts describe it as a sweet, oily cream—not the chilled, firm Land O'Lakes we're used to. Once this gooey version was introduced into Roman culture, it was used as a base to make perfumes, bath oils, and body salves. It was also given to elephants and teething children as a medicine. And the ancient Burgundians (a Germanic tribe) used it as hair conditioner.

By the end of the 19th century, butter was everywhere. It was exported and imported in firkins, tightly sealed white oak barrels that kept it perfectly fresh for months without refrigeration. In 1889, vegetable parchment paper began to be used to line one-pound boxes of butter. By 1909, butter was being mass-produced by machines in creameries, creating the product we know and love (and try not to eat if we're dieting) today.

In late June, a phenomenon known as "white nights" can be seen in parts of Russia.

TYPHOID MARY, QUITE CONTRARY

No doubt you've heard lurid stories of the alpha patient who stalked early 20th-century New York, spreading deadly typhoid fever wherever she went. Here's the truth of the matter.

The summer of 1906 was a bad one in New York City. A typhoid fever epidemic was raging. In New York State alone that year there were 3,000 diagnosed cases, leading to 600 deaths. So banker Charles Henry Warren, hoping to escape to the country with his family and avoid the panic in the city, leased a summer home from a George Thompson in Long Island, hired a staff of servants, and settled down for an idyllic vacation. But it was not to be.

GUESS WHAT'S COMING FOR DINNER

On August 27, one of Warren's daughters fell ill with typhoid fever, followed quickly by Mrs. Warren, three staff members, and another Warren child—6 out of the 11 in the house. The house's owners, aware that typhoid typically spread through water or food sources, decided to investigate just what had happened.

The Thompsons hired George Soper, an engineer who had some experience with typhoid outbreaks. Soper began investigating the Warren's cook, a Mary Mallon, who had been hired for the summer and who had left their employ shortly after the outbreak. When Soper looked at her employment history, he discovered that Mallon had been working as a cook for wealthy families since she had emigrated from Ireland in 1883 at age 15. Since 1900, Soper discovered, Mallon had worked seven different jobs at which a total of 22 people had contracted typhoid fever. One young girl even died from the disease.

YOU, SIR, ARE NO GENTLEMAN!

All of which led Soper to strongly suspect that Mary Mallon was a carrier of the typhoid bacillus (*Salmonella typhi*). He tracked Mallon down in March 1907, where she was working as a cook for yet another family. Mary was intimidated by the strange man who tried to convince her that she was carrying a deadly disease—and who wanted her to provide blood, urine, and stool samples. She threatened Soper with a carving fork and ran away.

Soper retaliated by visiting her house with five police officers, a health department official, and an ambulance. After a five-hour search, the men found her in a closet, whereupon she was dragged out, kicking and screaming, and taken to the hospital.

THE DOCS MUST BE CRAZY

The doctors found the typhoid bacillus in her stool, but Mary, healthy as a horse since the day she was born, refused to believe anything was wrong with her. She knew all about typhoid fever, and those who had it got sick and died. Surely the fact that she wasn't sick meant they were wrong about her transmitting the disease. Typhoid wasn't well understood at the time, even by doctors. They were just beginning to discover that some carriers of typhoid never got sick themselves, but instead lived with the bacterium in their bodies, passing it along to those who came into contact with infected fecal matter (usually caused by cooks who used the bathroom and then prepared food without washing up).

EMPLOYEES MUST WASH THEIR HANDS

Afraid that Mallon would continue cooking—and not washing her hands properly—officials held her in solitary confinement in a cottage on isolated North Brother Island (next to the notorious Rikers Island) for three long years. Meanwhile, the news media had a field day tarring the reputation of the woman they branded Typhoid Mary in their sensationalist stories, calling her "the most dangerous woman in America." One typical cartoon depicted Mary cooking at the stove with a pan full of grisly human skulls.

COOKED? BOOKED

In 1910, health officials decided Mary could go free, provided she agreed to never again work as a cook, to inform the health department if she changed addresses, and to show up regularly for typhoid screening.

She eventually broke all three promises. Finding it hard to make ends meet as a laundress, Mallon assumed a pseudonym and resumed work as a cook. In 1915, five years after her release, the Sloane Maternity Hospital in Manhattan suffered a typhoid fever outbreak. Twenty-five people became ill, and two of them died. An investigation turned up the fact that the recently hired cook, "Mrs. Brown," was in fact Mary Mallon.

MENACE TO SOCIETY

The public was outraged that Mallon could have knowingly caused pain and death. Surely by taking a pseudonym she knew she was doing something wrong. Perhaps she was even a murderess. Mallon spent 23 years of her life imprisoned on North Brother Island until her death in 1932.

Mary was responsible for somewhere from 33 to 63 cases of typhoid fever, and three deaths. To this day the term "Typhoid Mary" refers to a person who carries a contagious illness or is the center from which anything undesirable spreads. Despite being only one of many individuals identified as healthy typhoid carriers, Mary has gone down in history as a pestilent spreader of disease.

If only her parents had taught her how to wash her hands.

* * * * *

MEDICAL MIRACLES?

Doctors didn't always say "take two aspirin and call me in the morning." Historically they often used treatments that were far more interesting:

- In ancient Egypt infections were treated with moldy bread. (Today, antibiotics like penicillin are developed from mold.)
- In about A.D. 75, Chinese physician Hua T'o developed an anesthesia that was a mixture of hemp and strong wine. It was called ma fei san.
- In the 1600s, the plague was treated with live pullets. The bird's tail feathers were pulled and the bird was placed on the patient's infected sores. When the bird became infected and died, it was replaced with another. The "live pullet treatment" was believed to draw the poisons out of the patient.
- Is ketchup a vegetable or a medicine? In the United States in the 1830s it was sold with some success as a medicine called Dr. Mile's Compound Extract of Tomato.

In 1823, Charles Macintosh patented the waterproof cloth he was to use in making raincoats.

PUUUUUSH!

*Throughout history, fathers have had little, or nothing, to do
with the birth of their children; in fact, in some cultures fathers
were (and still are) forbidden in the birthing area altogether.
Here's what's been going on behind closed doors, boys.*

The earliest births on record were attended by midwives, at
least according to the Bible (in Genesis and Exodus).
Throughout both centuries, midwives from all cultures
handed down their knowledge to apprentices. The profession of
midwifery (pronounced mid-WIFF-ery) continued without any
major changes through both the Dark Ages and Middle Ages.

THEY'RE COMING TO AMERICA
There's a record of Parisian midwives having to pass a licensing
exam as early as 1560, but most other European practitioners went
unregulated. The English brand of midwifery came to colonial
America in the person of Brigit Lee Fuller. She attended three
plucky *Mayflower* passengers who were in their last trimesters
when the ship left port.

LIE DOWN AND MAYBE IT'LL GO AWAY
From the dawn of time, women had been squatting or sitting
upright to give birth. But all that changed when the doctor
attending Madame de Montespan, mistress of Louis XIV, placed
her on her back during labor—so that the king could watch from
behind a curtain. And so it became the fashion for women to give
birth lying down.

Now that the expectant mother couldn't help as much in
the birthing process, forceps were invented to pull the baby out.
Childbirth became more difficult for the mother—but more convenient for the doctor.

JUST SAY NO TO DRUGS
Christian tradition of the time was based on the biblical teaching
that women should bring forth children in pain. (Pain was Eve's

punishment for having tempted Adam, having gotten pregnant in the first place, and having being thrown out of the Garden of Eden—and so on.)

In non-Christian cultures, things were handled differently. The ancient Chinese used opiates during childbirth. Persian literature mentions wine (even though it doesn't help much). Various concoctions including hemp, poppy, and hemlock were applied, swallowed, or inhaled by heathens and pagans all over the world—and were even being sneaked to women in labor in the dark corners of Christian Europe. In 1591, a woman in England was convicted of receiving a certain unnamed medicine to help relieve labor pain. She was found guilty of witchcraft, chained to a stake, and burned to death.

WE ARE DEFINITELY NOT AMUSED

And so it remained for a few hundred years. It took a queen (and a queen who had scads of children) to change things. When Queen Victoria lay down on her birthing bed in 1853 to have her second child, she demanded chloroform to dull the pain. She wasn't going to go through *that* again. Lucky for her—and women everywhere—ether and chloroform had been introduced as pain relievers just a few years earlier.

The first woman in the United States to be anesthetized in childbirth was Fanny Longfellow, the wife of poet Henry Wadsworth Longfellow. She called it "the greatest blessing of this age." A storm of controversy erupted over its use, but reason and results eventually won out. Obstetric anesthesia had the added effect of reducing mortality rates for both mother and infant.

Which paved the way for all sorts of pain-relief treatments, including spinal anesthesia for instrument (that is, forceps) delivery in Germany in 1901, followed by the first epidural block in 1909.

IT'S ONLY NATURAL

Natural (drug-free and mommy-participating) childbirth came back into fashion in the United States in the 1960s, and women could finally get off their backs and join the process. Their partners and/or helpers were encouraged to join in.

The movement paved the way for the return of the midwife. She, poor thing, had been forced out of the profession by the

The Eiffel Tower, now a beloved symbol, was once lambasted by critics as ugly or unsafe, or both.

diploma-waving medical establishment starting in the early 20th century. That was around the same time that those serious, injection-type drugs came into use, and women, at least the ones who could afford it, started having their babies in hospitals.

The vast majority of American women (something like 99 percent) still have their babies in hospitals—and U.S. midwives are back in business, but only in a small way. Even though more than 70 percent of European births are attended by midwives today, only 10 percent of doctor-dependent American mommies choose midwives to deliver their babies.

* * * * *

PINK OR BLUE?

Modern medicine has given us the option of knowing what color paint to buy for the nursery ahead of time. Here's how it was handled before the wonders of ultrasound.

- Hungarian Gypsies tied a gold ring on a string and suspended it over the mother's belly. If the ring swung in a circle, it was a girl. If it went back and forth, it was a boy.

- Ancient Egyptians thought that a baby carried low was a boy; Bedouins thought a baby carried high meant the same.

- Sri Lankans believed that if the mother looked very pretty, she was carrying a girl.

- Many cultures have left-right beliefs in predicting the baby's gender. If a baby kicks on the right side of the mother's abdomen, it's a boy. If the mother walks with her right foot first most of the time, it's a boy. The Nepalese believe that if the baby sits on the right side, it's a son.

- Hippocrates believed that a brighter left eye and a bigger left breast meant a daughter.

YOGA STRETCHES WESTWARD

Yoga's roots reach back thousands of years to India, where doing it made you not just one who could twist yourself like a shoelace, but also one with the universe!

Modern yoga isn't a religion; it's a system of mind and body exercise. But it does have spiritual roots, dating back at least 3,500 years to the early Aryan people of India and their practice of Brahmanism (a predecessor of Hinduism, based on sacrifice). Its purpose was to enlighten the practitioner, making him one with the universe. Over the centuries, many interpretations of how to make this happen have sprung up.

VIVA LAS VEDAS
One variant, around the ninth or 10th centuries, was called "hatha" yoga. Hatha (*ha* meaning "sun" and *tha* meaning "moon") implies a bringing together of opposites. Hatha yoga's underlying concept is that it takes a lot of strength to bring together the mind and body. Of all the branches of yoga today, hatha is the most popular in the West. It was meant to transform the body into something divine: free of disease, ageless, and, some say, even with magical powers like levitation. To get these benefits takes the practice of special postures, or asanas.

TRANSCENDING TEATIME
Alexander the Great's conquest of India in 327 B.C. was probably the first recorded Western exposure to yoga practices. Centuries later, during the British colonial period, a group of Englishmen formed a club and called it the Asiatic Society of Bengal. Its mission was to conduct an intensive study of Indian culture and history. They read, analyzed, and interpreted a number of important historical yoga doctrines in English. Soon after, American writer-philosophers Henry David Thoreau and Ralph Waldo Emerson also took an interest in some of these early books on the practice.

REAL INDIAN IN THE LAND OF LINCOLN

The first yoga master to visit the United States was Swami Vivekananda, who gave a speech in Chicago in 1893. Even then, Chicago was a convention town: Vivekananda gave his speech at something called the Parliament of Religions. The crowd was mesmerized: After hearing his thoughts on spirituality and the connection between the world's people, they gave him a standing ovation. The swami opened a yoga school in New York City in 1899, and the practice grew quickly there—until the U.S. government imposed a restriction on Indian immigration in 1924.

Since the yoga masters couldn't come to America, Americans went to the masters. Hundreds of Americans studied in India, and a lot of them wrote books about the experience. By the time World War II was wrapping up, yoga books were everywhere. But it still wasn't the big time.

A YOGI IN YOUR LIVING ROOM

Then, in 1961, New Yorker Richard Hittleman, who'd sold millions of books on yoga, became the first person to teach it on television—on a PBS show called *Yoga for Health*—as a nonreligious exercise. TV, baby! With the maturation of television and the open-mindedness of the time, the early 1960s witnessed an American yoga explosion. In 1965, the restriction on Indian immigration was finally repealed and teachers poured into the country.

EVERY BODY'S DOING IT

Prenatal yoga. Tantric yoga. Bikram yoga, which ideally is performed in rooms heated to 105°F (40.5°C). In fact, around 18 million Americans will hit the floor today for their daily dose of yogic action, including celebrities like Jerry Seinfeld, Charlie Sheen, Jamie Lee Curtis, Madonna, Kareem Abdul-Jabbar, Melissa Etheridge, Christy Turlington, Nicolas Cage, and Sting.

* * * * *

Yogi Berra got his nickname from Bobby Hofman, a childhood friend. While watching a movie about an Indian snake charmer, Bobby noted that Lawrence (Yogi) had a striking resemblance to the Hindu gentleman—and the name stuck.

A BUMP ON THE HEAD

Argentine writer Jorge Luis Borges bumped his head on an open window one day. This is how it changed his life.

On Christmas Eve 1938, up-and-coming Argentinean poet and reviewer Jorge Luis Borges was up and coming on a staircase, and he didn't notice a freshly painted window hanging open over the stairway.

Borges smacked his head on the open window so badly that pieces of glass embedded themselves in his head and the cuts required stitches. Because the wound wasn't properly disinfected, Borges ran a temperature of 105°F (41°C) and was rushed to the hospital, delirious and hovering close to death. After two weeks of hallucinations such as imagining animals in the room, the fever abated and Borges was lucid again.

During his convalescence, Borges worried that the head injury would affect his mental abilities. He was too afraid to try to write a poem or review, his usual gigs. He'd never written any stories before, so it seemed like it might be the thing to try first—if he failed, it might not mean that his writing career was over. So he wrote a story called "Pierre Menard, Author of the Quixote" about a 20th-century writer who wants to rewrite the story of Don Quixote. Menand researches the author, Miguel de Cervantes, so well that he comes to understand the author's mind completely—and writes the exact same book (or at least significant sections of it), word for word.

Borges submitted the story to a magazine and was so anxious about it that he called the editor the very next morning to ask him what he thought of it. The editor said that he had never seen anything like it, and published it in the next issue.

The head injury, ironically, turned out to be one of the best things that ever happened to Borges. And who knows? The hallucinations he had when he was delirious may have given him a jump start, too—that first story showed him to be a master of alternate realities. From then on, writing short stories became the focus of his work, and he since won piles of literary awards. Today, only decades after his death, he's remembered as one of the all-time great short-story writers.

Rationing didn't end in Britain until 1954, nearly nine years after the end of World War II.

SOMEONE'S DERIVATIVE

Calculus involves the study of limits. By the time they were done arguing about who had invented it, Isaac Newton and G. W. Leibniz had probably both reached their limit as well.

S cience has seen a number of simultaneous discoveries. Michael Faraday and Joseph Henry independently discovered electromagnetic induction. Charles Darwin and Alfred Russel Wallace both hit upon the idea of natural selection. None of these coincidences, however, snowballed into an argument as ugly as the one that developed between Isaac Newton and Gottfried Wilhelm Leibniz over the invention of calculus.

THE ROOTS OF THE PROBLEM

Newton didn't like to publish. He was one of the most innovative thinkers of his day, making breakthroughs in physics and mathematics that inspired vast new fields of study, but he never felt his work was quite ready to go to the printer—he always wanted to make changes or write another draft. Because of his hesitation, he didn't get any of his work on calculus into print until 1704. Leibniz, a leading philosopher and mathematician, beat him to the punch by publishing a brief summary in the Leipzig periodical *Acta Eruditorum* in October 1684.

However, Newton had planted a few clues about his pioneering work in calculus. Starting in 1676, he circulated unfinished papers privately among his friends that hinted at calculus concepts. Two letters about calculus topics even went to Leibniz that year. But his first public hint was in his greatest work published in his lifetime, *Principia Mathematica* (1687), when Newton tossed in a theorem about differentiation, one of the basic operations of calculus.

In fact, in a note on this theorem, Newton revealed a secret message from one of his letters to Leibniz. In this letter, Newton had concealed the meaning of a sentence by jumbling all of its letters. The secret message was "Given any equation involving flowing quantities, to find the fluxions, and vice-versa." When Newton wrote the letter, he had wanted to establish proof that he had discovered a fundamental theorem of calculus, but he didn't want Leibniz to know it, so he scrambled all the letters of it together. That way, he could point to it later for proof, but Leibniz couldn't steal it.

Never mind that no one knew what "fluxions" were, since Newton had invented the word. Also never mind that Leibniz couldn't read the message because the letters were all out of order. Newton's point was that he had staked a claim to the concepts in 1676, even though the secret message didn't really communicate anything to Leibniz...or anyone else.

THE TROUBLE MULTIPLIES
At first, Newton and Leibniz were both inclined to give the other credit for being an independent discoverer. It was their friends who really turned them against each other. It started in 1696 when a friend of Leibniz published a challenge problem that required calculus in the Leipzig *Acta* hoping that Newton wouldn't be able to solve it, thus proving that Newton had stolen calculus from Leibniz. Newton, of course, solved the problem easily, as did Leibniz. But Leibniz, who was a careless worker, wrote an article about the problem that seemed (to Newton's friends) to imply that Leibniz had invented calculus and that Newton was Leibniz's student.

DO YOU COPY?
A friend of Newton's then angrily wrote an analysis of the challenge problem in which he indirectly accused Leibniz of plagiarism:

> *As to whether Leibniz, [calculus's] second inventor, borrowed anything from him, I prefer to let those judge who have seen Newton's letters and other manuscript papers, not myself.*

This referred to the letter Newton sent Leibniz with the inscrutable jumbled message—apparently the idea was that Leibniz could have both unscrambled it (not likely) and gleaned its meaning (even less likely).

After this episode, the controversy cooled until Leibniz wrote a review of two of Newton's works in 1705. In it, he compared

Newton and himself to two other mathematicians. Leibniz probably just meant to say that he and Newton, like this other pair, had combined their ideas to come up with greater ideas. Another friend of Newton, however, pointed out that the analogy could be interpreted a different way: one of the two mathematicians Leibniz mentioned had probably plagiarized the other. Was Leibniz trying to say the same about himself and Newton?

COUNT ME IN!
Soon, this friend published a paper in which he cut right to the chase. He stated that Newton was the inventor "beyond any shadow of doubt" and that Leibniz had published it "having changed the name and symbolism." This was too much for Leibniz. He wrote, enraged, to the Royal Society of London demanding an apology. Instead of an apology, he got a counterattack: a letter spelling out all of the claims against Leibniz in greater detail. Leibniz fired back another letter of protest.

The Royal Society's response this time was to appoint a committee to investigate the matter. Unluckily for Leibniz, Newton (who was by now convinced that Leibniz stole calculus from him) was the president of the Royal Society at the time. Newton was not officially a member of the committee, but the report came out suspiciously strongly in his favor. Rather more suspiciously, the report was written in his handwriting. It stated firmly that Newton had been the first discoverer of calculus, and that Leibniz had plagiarized it.

For Leibniz and his friends, this was the last straw. They accumulated more evidence against Newton and published a leaflet making their own case. It was published anonymously (the author was given as a "leading mathematician"), but the question of who wrote it didn't remain open very long. Now both Newton and Leibniz believed unshakably that the other was a dirty rotten thief.

CAN'T WE ALL JUST GET ALONG?
From there, the argument deteriorated into petty personal attacks and rehashings of the evidence already published. Even after Leibniz died the squabble continued. It wasn't definitively established for the historical record that Newton and Leibniz were actually coinventors of calculus until the 20th century. We now

know for certain that Newton came up with the basics of calculus in 1665–66 and Leibniz in 1675–76, before any communication between the two of them.

SUMMING UP

The final reckoning offers a nice compromise in the dispute. Newton was certainly the first one to hit upon the main ideas of calculus, beating Leibniz to it by about ten years. Leibniz, though, in being first to publish, received the honor of having his notation become the standard for the field—most of his symbols are still used today. And ironically, they both became known for all time as coinventors of calculus precisely from the notoriety of the dispute itself.

* * * * *

CAMPAIGN COMEDY

George Smathers sure knew how to sling the mud. In 1950, while running against Claude Pepper for the U.S. Senate in Florida, Smathers conducted one of the most creative name-calling campaigns in political history. He pulled out all the stops in his campaign speeches, at one point even stooping to calling Pepper "a known extrovert."

He had no compunctions about casting aspersions on Pepper's family, either. Smathers said his opponent's sister was "a thespian" and his brother "a practicing homo sapiens."

Furthermore, charged Smathers, Pepper attended college and "openly matriculated." And before Pepper was married, said Smathers, he "engaged in celibacy."

Needless to say, Smathers won the election, and he deserved to for his satirical smear campaign worthy of *Saturday Night Live*.

Actually, Smathers later denied making those speeches, but how can you trust a guy who was rumored to believe in homeostasis?

A CYMBAL
OF SUCCESS

*From the sultans to the Beatles, the Zildjian family
gets a bang out of business.*

Cymbals are used by Buddhist monks to enhance meditation, by drummers to keep time, and by belly dancers to accompany their graceful gyrations. These instruments are manufactured in Massachusetts by the oldest family business in America—and one of the oldest continuously operating businesses in history.

The story starts in Constantinople (now Istanbul), Turkey, in 1623. An Armenian alchemist, Avendis I, developed a secret formula for a metal alloy that made cymbals sound better with a more resounding ring. The Ottoman sultan Murad IV was so impressed that he gave Avendis the Turkish moniker *Zildjian*, meaning "cymbal smith."

THE BIG BANG

Cymbals probably originated in Asia, but the Ottoman Empire introduced them to Europe, in the 17th century when Turkish soldiers marched to Vienna, Austria. Musical bands accompanied the Janissary (a specially trained Turkish militia). These Janissary bands were loud enough to inspire their own troops—and terrify their enemies. The Janissary played the big drum (Kuvruk-Kos), the drum (Tomruk-Davil), and the cymbal (Ceng-Zil), forerunners of the modern drum kit.

As classical European composers incorporated Janissary cymbals, they discovered Zildjian. Hector Berlioz and Richard Wagner asked orchestras to use Zildjian cymbals when their works were played.

THE CYMBALS CRASH

In the early 1900s, hard times brought the Zildjian family to the United States. Though Avedis (he'd dropped the "n") Zildjian III was ready for a new enterprise, his wife convinced him that Zildjian was like a dynasty and should be continued.

Paul Bunyan's cook was named Hot Biscuit Slim.

The Zildjians' first factory opened in Quincy, Massachusetts, in 1929. The timing was awful; people were less interested in the crash of cymbals than the crash of the stock market. The Great Depression made instruments a tough sell.

But Avedis was an innovator, and when the famous swing drummer, Gene Krupa, needed a thinner cymbal, Avedis was his man. Zildjian's various styles of cymbals—thin splash, ride, crash, hi-hat, and sizzle—were soon used in all types of percussion ensembles. The company was on its way.

STARR POWER

Throughout the decades, the family business hit high and low notes. In the 1940s, the United States entered World War II, and the family made cymbals for the military. Since the War Production Board had restricted copper and tin, both crucial metals in the Zildjian alloy, the company might have closed down—but thank goodness for military bands.

Then in 1964, a British musical invasion rocked the United States: a group called the Beatles appeared on *Ed Sullivan*'s TV show. Beatles' drummer Ringo Starr used Zildjian cymbals and demand for the brand exploded. By 1976, Avedis was able to pass a very lucrative company on to his oldest son, Armand.

A new problem arose in the early 1980s, when Armand's brother Robert quit the family's business to found a rival company in Canada. But the Zildjians remained a staple of the American music biz. Armand (a drummer who kept a set of left-handed drums in his office) saw cymbal making as an art. He loved and perfected the Zildjian sound. And he worked closely with musicians (who said he treated them like family).

CYMBAL MINDED

As the company innovated its way into the future, one link with the past never changed—the alloy formula of 1623. For more than 380 years it has remained a family secret, traditionally passed down from father to eldest Zildjian son. But these days, the eldest Zildjian son is a daughter; no, make that two daughters. Craigie Zildjian runs the company, while her sister Debbie is vice president of human resources, the first woman to oversee the melting room—and the secret formula.

The term "encyclopedia" came into use during the 16th century.

MOVE OVER BABE RUTH

Josh Gibson is up at bat.

Statistics don't always tell the whole story. Record books say that Barry Bonds holds the home run record of 73 in a single season, making him the greatest single season slugger of all time. Not to take anything away from Bonds. He did surpass the single season records of players like Babe Ruth (59 homers), Roger Maris (61), and Mark McGwire (70). But these greats are only part of baseball's story. They're all overshadowed by a legendary player who'll never make the major league record books.

In 1936, Josh Gibson is credited with hitting a whopping 84 home runs. In 17 seasons he's believed to have hit 800 home runs. Sadly, Gibson's stats have never been officially verified. They've also stood alone—unsurpassed for over 60 years.

But if you've never heard of Josh Gibson, maybe the greatest slugger who ever lived, it's not because you've been hiding under a rock. It's because Gibson made his home run records playing for the Pittsburgh Crawfords—in the Negro League.

AN EXCLUDED CLUB

Gibson was born in 1911, when America and Major League Baseball were segregated. All of his life, Gibson's race kept him out of the majors. He set his records and created legends—as well as a few tall tales—playing for the Homestead Grays and the Pittsburgh Crawfords. Two of the most successful teams in the Negro League.

Just because they couldn't play in major ball clubs, African American players weren't about to give up on baseball. They started their own teams and eventually formed their own leagues with All-Star games and World Series. They also did a lot of barnstorming—playing in exhibition games sometimes against white players.

The Negro Leagues attracted audiences as big as 30,000 to 40,000 fans. But few of today's baseball mavens know much about them or their players. Statistics and records were sketchy, and

---

As early as 200 B.C. the Romans had directions for how to grow asparagus.

their games weren't written up in the national press. Besides, after baseball was integrated, black players and fans switched their attention to the majors. Gradually the Negro Leagues faded from the American sports scene, all but forgotten.

But Hall of Famers like Leroy "Satchel" Paige, Hank Aaron, Roy Campanella, and Willie Mays got their start in black ball clubs. They might have played in worse conditions for less pay than white players, but plenty of Negro League athletes were giants of baseball. Like Josh Gibson.

CAPITALIZING ON BLACK BASEBALL

When Gibson was 11, his family left Georgia and moved to Pittsburgh where his dad got work in the steel mills. Young Josh was more interested in learning that Pittsburgh was the capital of black baseball. By the time he was a teenager, the athletic Gibson was winning medals in swimming, and impressing spectators when he came up at bat in amateur ball games.

Six foot two, over 200 pounds, and massive as a wall, Gibson swung a longer, heavier bat than his team mates. He was exceptionally strong with a sharp eye for the ball and fast reflexes. And he could always seem to find the ball no matter how it was pitched.

Stories grew up around him even as a teenager. One story goes that the 18-year-old Gibson was recruited to his first pro team, the Homestead Grays, when he was watching them play a night game in Pittsburgh. The lighting was so bad that the catcher injured his finger, and Gibson was recruited from the stands. However he got there, Gibson became their explosive power hitter and star attraction before he went on to play for the Pittsburgh Crawfords. The legends about the Black Babe Ruth were only beginning.

THE POWER AND THE GLORY

The King of Sock led the Negro Leagues in batting at least four times. All his teammates had stories about Gibson-powered balls that went over a fence or over the scoreboard in centerfield— leaving people shaking their heads in disbelief. They told of games being stopped in mid-inning so the home team could measure how far Gibson had hit the ball this time. The mayor of Monessen, Pennsylvania, is said to have used a tape measure to prove that

---

Run DMC was the first rap group to perform on TV's "American Bandstand."

Gibson had hit the ball 512 feet. The *Sporting News* reported that he hit the longest home run ever seen in Yankee Stadium—580 feet.

As he barnstormed around the country, staying in rundown, segregated hotels, without access to decent restaurants, Gibson and his teammates won plenty of games against white teams. The King of Sock reportedly never made fewer than 60 home runs a season, and scoring huge hits off a famous, white pitcher named Dizzy Dean, Gibson's fame spread well beyond the Negro League.

The *New York Daily News* hinted that it was time for the major leagues to consider him. Some teams seemed close to signing him, but never did. Hall of Fame pitcher Walter Johnson summed the situation up, "There is a catcher that any big league club would like to buy...He hits the ball a mile. And he catches so easy he might as well be in a rocking chair. Too bad this Josh Gibson is a colored fellow."

The majors loss was a gain for integrated and baseball-loving countries. The mighty Josh Gibson was sought after and played in Canada, Mexico, Cuba, and Venezuela. In Puerto Rico he was voted most valuable player three times. Toward the end of his career Gibson made a salary rivaling that of some white major leaguers, though he never earned anything to close to the salary of the major league stars like Joe Di Maggio or Lou Gherig—men he might have equaled or surpassed.

Satchel Paige who played in both the Negro League and the majors said simply that Gibson was the "best hitter who ever lived."

GOING GOING GONE

As charmed as his life was on the baseball diamond, Gibson's personal life was always troubled. He was only 18 when he made it to the pros, but that same year, the newlywed ball player lost his wife who died in childbirth. A very private man, Gibson never spoke much about the tragedy, but some in his family said he was never the same.

It could have been personal tragedy, the pressures of constant travel and the aches and pains that came with a catcher's job. Maybe it was just temptations of the baseball high life, but Gibson drank heavily and neglected his health. He died of a stroke in 1947. He was only 35.

Jim Crow in baseball was at least partly to blame for Gibson's death. According to his friends, it had broken the young man's spirit and his heart. Three months after Gibson's death, Jackie Robinson joined the Brooklyn Dodgers to break the color line and open the door to black players in major league baseball.

In 1972, years after his death, the baseball Hall of Fame finally honored Josh Gibson, the slugging king of the Negro League.

* * * * *

THE NEGRO LEAGUE'S GRAND OLD MAN

The Negro League gave baseball one of its greatest pitchers—and shrewdest showmen, Leroy "Satchel" Paige. Playing his first pro games in 1924, Paige (who got the nickname "Satchel," working as a young baggage porter in Mobile, Alabama) pitched for the Mobile Tigers, the Philadelphia Crawfords, and the Kansas City Monarchs. He won games and drew huge crowds with fastballs that he nick-named "the trouble ball" or "the two-hump blooper." His most famous was the hesitation pitch that he stopped in midthrow.

In exhibition games, Paige opposed legendary pitcher Dizzy Dean in six exhibitions games and won four. Heavy hitter Joe DiMaggio called Satchel, "the best I've ever faced, and the fastest."

Paige was about 42 (no one has pinned down his exact birth date) when he finally got the Major League break he'd deserved for 25 years. Signing on with the Cleveland Indians in 1948, he was derided as the "oldest rookie" ever. But Paige famously coun-tered: "Age is a question of mind over matter. If you don't mind, it doesn't matter." He proceeded to silence his critics by drawing huge crowds and helping the Indians finish first in the American League to win a pennant.

At the age of 59, playing for the Kansas City Athletics, Satchel became the oldest athlete to pitch in the major leagues. With typical flair, he sat in a rocking chair in the bullpen encour-aging a nurse to rub liniment on his arm before he got up to pitch three scoreless innings. During Satchel's long career he was almost as famous for his quips as he was for his pitching. His most famous quote? "Don't look back. Something might be gaining on you."

Brazil/Paraguay's Itaipú Dam is the largest hydroelectric complex in the world.

QUEEN ISABELLA

*Everybody thinks Queen Isabella was so great,
financing Christopher Columbus's voyage and all.
But there's a darker side to her story.*

When Isabella came to power in 1479, the Spanish region was at war with itself, a bunch of tiny kingdoms jockeying for position. By the end of her reign Spain was united and becoming a global power. But it wasn't all good.

FIGHTING HER WAY TO THE TOP

Princess Isabella was the daughter of King John II of Castile, but she was a long way down on the royal ladder. For one thing, there was a little problem called the Sallic Law that prevented any woman from ascending the Castilian throne. But when her two brothers died off (one under suspicious circumstances) Isabella stepped up to the plate.

She'd already secretly married Ferdinand of Aragon; their first task was to unite his Aragon and her Castile under their absolute rule. The queen kept the nobles firmly under her thumb and chose royal officials who were university-educated. A student and a great reader, Isabella created a government based on brains rather than birth.

PUTTING SPAIN ON THE MAP

With the domestic home front in hand, the royals looked south where Granada was still ruled by the Islamic Moors. Under the banner of a Christian Crusade, the armies of Ferdinand and Isabella took Granada from the Moors in 1492. The country of Spain was united. Isabella was now free to make the shrewdest of all her decisions.

The wars had cost a fortune; the royal treasury was nearly broke—meanwhile neighbor Portugal was making heaps of money in the African gold trade. So Isabella decided to send Christopher Columbus on his westward search for a sea route to India and Asia.

It's a myth that Isabella hocked her jewels, but she did work hard to get Columbus off the ground—and into the ocean. Two of his ships were from Palos, a city that owed a debt to the crown.

Public executions in colonial America were attended by thousands, including women and children.

Isabella wound up as the wealthy queen of the New World; when Isabella wished Columbus Godspeed, she launched not only his voyage, but the expansion of the Spanish Empire.

IMAGE IS EVERYTHING

Still, it wasn't always easy at the top. Isabella was the only woman ruler in a macho 15th century. Her enemies were quick to use her gender (don't forget that Sallic law) against her. So the savvy queen was careful about her image and always portrayed herself as a pious, subservient female. In 1496, a papal bull proclaimed Isabella "la Catolica" (The Catholic) in honor of her services to the church. Some historians think Isabella was truly religious, but others feel that she projected the image because it made it tougher for her enemies to slander a saint. Either way, her mission was to make Spain a completely Catholic nation.

A VERY BUSY YEAR

When Isabella came to power, the region of Spain was the most diverse in Europe, home to three coexisting religions: Christianity, Islam, and Judaism. Isabella and Ferdinand knew it would be easier to unite and rule a country of one faith. So, seeking religious unity—and maybe some much-needed property and funds—the monarchs put Moors and Jews on notice.

In 1492, the same year that Granada fell and Columbus set sail, Isabella and Ferdinand commanded that all Jews who wouldn't convert to Christianity be expelled from Spain. Ten years later Moorish Muslims suffered the same fate as the crown confiscated the property of the fleeing Jews and Moors.

Those Jews and Muslims who did convert to Christianity, *los conversos*, weren't let off all that easy either. Isabella also initiated the infamous Spanish Inquisition to punish conversos who might still secretly practice their former religion. Trials were held and those who couldn't prove they were true Christians were sometimes tortured. "Proved" heretics not only lost their property, they could be executed in an *auto de fe* where they were burned at the stake. Even the pope, Sixtus IV, tried to stop the Inquisition, pegging it as a cruel scheme that "brought disgust" because it harmed the innocent and grabbed riches instead of saving souls—but Isabella ignored His Holiness.

In 1790 Thomas Halford, found guilty of stealing 3 lbs. of potatoes was sentenced to 2,000 lashes.

THE BOTTOM LINE

By the end of her reign she'd managed to unite Spain and make it a global power. By the time her grandson Charles was born in 1500, he was heir to an empire that included Spain, the Netherlands, Luxembourg, Sardinia, Sicily, Naples, South America, and the West Indies. She'd supported a Spanish golden age in painting, music, theater, and literature, and founded schools, collected works of art, and was a patron for artists and scholars.

But the Inquisition remains a huge splash of red ink across Isabella's balance sheet. After her death, the Inquisition spread across Spain and her colonies. It grew from investigating conversos to persecuting Protestants and finally anyone seen as an enemy to the church or crown. For all her smarts, Isabella made free thinking a crime, chilling the progress of science and enlightenment in Spain. And it didn't help matters when she expelled and killed so many of her most successful subjects. That loss was a big factor in the collapse of Spain's economy in the 16th century—bringing the country's Golden Age to a close.

* * * * *

INVESTING FOR THE LONG TERM?

Isabella and Ferdinand invested about $6,000 in Columbus's first voyage. From her colonies Spain took in a return of about $1,750,000 in gold. That return came in over a century—so it averaged out to $17,500 a year—almost a 300 percent return per annum.

The philosopher and author Eric Hoffer (*The True Believer*) was entirely self-educated.

THE REAL M*A*S*H

You've seen the antics and heroics of the 4077th on the big screen and TV. But do you know about the real Mobile Army Surgical Hospital and its history of heroism?

After WWII, the Army Nurse Corps was in bad shape. In the 1950s, the United States was all about prosperity and personal achievement. Medical students wanted to land jobs where they could specialize—and bring home the big bucks. Nobody wanted to be stuck in a noble-but-nowhere role of keeping soldiers alive. And then along came the Korean War. The U.S. government passed the Doctors Draft Act, calling in the markers of the many who'd taken Uncle Sam up on a free education in exchange for potential military service.

MEDS ON THE MOVE

Korea ushered in a whole new way of mending soldiers. In the first World War, most of the fighting was done from the trenches, so hospitals were set up far from the action in the rear. Teams of ambulances would haul the wounded from the front lines. In World War II, the fighting moved around a lot more, so a group of vehicles was set up closer to the front lines to handle emergencies and prep soldiers for the ride back to the rear hospital.

When Korea rolled around, the army came up with an improved version of their front-line aid trucks: a complete mobile hospital. Composed entirely of tents, the Mobile Army Surgical Hospital (MASH) was a fully functional surgical facility right there at the front lines, a whole hospital that could pack itself into its own trucks and move with just 24 hours notice. Soldiers could get immediate care early—in the vital stages of injury—and then be shipped back to the rear for longer-term care. When the fighting moved, the MASH moved with it.

HOSTILE WORKING CONDITIONS...LITERALLY

With their whole hospital right at the front lines, medical teams could hear the explosions and gunfire, see the smoke, and watch the enemy planes approach. Doctors were like Plains Indians,

He lived for some years as a tramp, then worked as a dishwasher and longshoreman.

migrating from place to place—serving an endless stream of patients. And every part of the hospital was a tent: living quarters, operating room, Xray room, offices, nurses' station, scrubbing room. The odd tin building popped up here and there, but the whole MASH unit was pretty much a tent city.

Drafted MASH doctors weren't trained soldiers or military medics. They had no combat experience and weren't really versed in military culture and customs. And none of them were experienced in the types of trauma that would roll through the door—er, flap—during their tour of duty. The longest tour possible for a MASH doc was only a year or so, but in that year, they'd perform more emergency surgeries than in a whole lifetime of civilian service. The painfully understaffed crew snatched an hour of sleep here or there, but their operating hours included "whenever there was fighting." And there was nonstop fighting between 1950 and 1953.

NONE OF THE COMFORTS OF HOME
Even experienced military medics had never been in a hospital like the Korean MASH unit. At any given time, all of their patients might have to be loaded up and moved. The Korean climate ranged from zero to 100°F (37.7°C), and the tents provided no warmth in the cold and no relief from the heat. The bathroom—heaven help us—was basically a simple trench. Flies the size of pennies swarmed in the summer. And rats overran the perimeters. Add that to the constant smells and sounds of gun battles, often just yards away, and you had a whole new level of stress for docs and nurses.

GRACE UNDER FIRE
The working conditions forced MASH doctors to be creative, and they made some serious innovations along the way. For example, in the old days patients would be moved from a stretcher to an ambulance to a surgical table to a bed—lots of moving around of some very sick folks. But MASH units, pressed for time and equipment, performed surgery and let patients rest on the same stretchers they'd come in on. The need for mobility led to the practice of early ambulatory—making recovering patients move around as soon as possible to promote blood circulation. And doctors also made big strides in blood-loss shock and vascular surgery.

John Hancock, first signer of the Declaration of Independence, was Boston's wealthiest merchant.

MASH VS. M*A*S*H

So was life in the real MASH anything like the TV show? Well, yes and no.

The characters in the fictional 4077th M*A*S*H we all know and love first popped up in 1968 with the Richard Hooker novel *MASH: A Novel About Three Army Doctors*. The movie and the TV show followed. And while the 4077th was based on a real MASH unit—the 8076th—Dr. Otto Apel (an 8076th veteran, and author of a memoir of his experience) notes that like any work of fiction, it was a little removed from the truth. While the social lives of the TV show characters took center stage, almost everyone in the real MASH unit worked nonstop. Such intensity bred a deep and lifelong camaraderie, but not a lot of conversation—much less riotous sexual antics. Turnover in the units was fast-paced, so doctors and nurses would come and go before ever being formally introduced. Nobody ate meals at the same time, thanks to their work schedules. And while there were good times, the horrors of war were always minutes away.

But the television version was still pretty realistic. Apel was a consultant for the show, and many episodes were based on actual people and events. Although there was one other difference: The Korean War had no laugh track. M*A*S*H wouldn't have had one either, if the producers had gotten their way, but CBS insisted. As a compromise, only scenes in the operating room were shown without a laugh track—but thanks to DVDs, the entire laugh tracks can now be surgically removed.

* * * * *

BOMBS AWAY

In June 1944, the American army rolled into Rome as the Germans were retreating northward. In his book, *The Battle for Rome*, historian Robert Katz recounts the story of one American G.I., Thomas Garcia, who, on seeing the Roman Coliseum for the first time, said, "My God, they bombed that, too!"

THOSE HANDY BAGS

*Nowadays few men are willing to carry a purse,
but hundreds and even thousands of years ago it was
not unusual to see a man walking down the street,
through the forest or across a field swinging a purse.*

E arly purses—those used before the era of coin money—were actually pouches used to carry supplies. Egyptians used them. American Indians used them. So did the Greeks, Romans, and French. In fact, almost every culture used them, but it's the Greeks who are credited with the name "purse." But back then they called them *byrsas*. When the name was Latinized, it became *bursa*, and eventually the word evolved to *purse*.

The creation and use of coin money in Europe contributed to an increase in the popularity of little purses. Not much more than a basic drawstring bag, these purses were hung by a long string attached to a girdle or belt tied around a person's waist. Men and women of the upper classes soon began decorating their purses with jewels, embroidery, and bells as a sign of their wealth; the richer the person, the fancier the bag. These improved purses inspired the new, albeit shady, profession of cutpurses.

PURSES COME AND PURSES GO...

During the late 17th century, with the creation of built-in pockets, men stopped using purses. After the French Revolution women's fashions changed to reduce the number of undergarments they had to wear. So women too stopped using purses because they couldn't be hidden under layers of fancy underwear. Instead, ladies began carrying a new style of purse that became known as a "reticule." They had a special reticule for every function and many articles were written instructing women on how to wear them and what to put in one for each function.

In the early 19th century another change in fashion saw a waning in popularity of the purse. Larger skirts meant there was more room for pockets and many women chose to not carry a separate bag for their belongings.

But the creation of the hobble skirt in the early 20th century

Daniel Defoe (*Robinson Crusoe*) was the most pseudonymous writer in history.

saw a return of the purse. Hobble skirts were long and narrow, and not only made it difficult for women to walk, but they left no room for pockets. Large purses, inspired by the luggage bags often carried by men, and carried by long strings or chains became popular. The large purses became known as "handbags."

A DECADE-BY-DECADE STROLL THROUGH HANDBAGS

By the 1920s dresses were so skimpy that handbags became indispensable. Celluloid bags (the stuff many eyeglass frames are made out of today) became an accessory many fashionable women carried. Some of the most stylish ladies went so far as to carry an identically dressed miniature doll complete with a matching handbag.

The 1930s saw the creation of the clutch bag. During the 1940s, shoulder bags were designed to fix a dilemma of many female military personnel. No military woman was able to salute smartly while dangling a clutch purse from her hand, so shoulder bags became part of female military uniforms instead.

During World War II when metal and leather was in short supply, many purses were made out of wood and plastic. This trend carried on until the 1950s. In the 1960s designers made genuine reptile skin purses and silk handbags. The 1970s saw the creation of the brightly colored handbags, and the 1980s saw the innovation of designer-name purses. Today purse-making is a multi-billion-dollar business in America.

* * * * *

THE EVIL WEED

Sotweed was introduced to England in the 1600s and King James I wrote a booklet calling its use a "vile habit." This was the first government attempt to discourage smoking! Sotweed was a nickname for tobacco—and King James I's arguments failed to stop smokers from lighting up.

Cigarettes, matches, and lighters are among some of the most-common items found in women's handbags.

STAR SHINE

"I know it's only rock and roll"…
but it's given the world more than music.

Today, it's not uncommon to see celebrities, musicians, and sports stars channeling their fame and fortune for charitable causes. From the Michael Jordan Foundation to Steve Young's Forever Young Foundation, name recognition translates into big bucks for those in need. But, despite the current never-ending list of celebrity causes, star-fueled philanthropy gained global momentum in the mid-1980s, thanks to the gutsy efforts of a group of rock musicians.

Irish-born singer, activist, actor, and Nobel Peace Prize winner Bob Geldof took initiative for the international pop industry, adopting African famine as its humanitarian focus. Geldof had watched a news program about the plight of the poverty-stricken African people. The desperate situation and statistics prompted him to call friends and ask them to partake in a special recording session. High-profile friends included Boy George, Paul McCartney and Paul Young. Geldof teamed up with Ultravox singer Midge Ure to write the lyrics of "Do They Know It's Christmas." The group consisted of 40 of the United Kingdom's and Ireland's best-known pop stars and was aptly titled, Band Aid. The group assembled on November 25, 1984, for a 24-hour recording session. The hit single was released just in time for the 1984 holiday season. During its first 10 days of sales, it sold more than two million copies in England and one million copies in the United States. The proceeds of the song helped to raise money for Africa.

The success of the single spurred a Band Aid spin-off in the United States—USA for Africa. American musicians comprising a cross-section of pop, rock, and soul banded together for a similar cry for public awareness and recorded "We Are the World." Cowriters Michael Jackson, Lionel Richie, Bruce Springsteen, Kenny Rogers, and Stevie Wonder had solo bits throughout the jingle-like song.

Seventy percent of San Francisco Bay is less than 12 feet deep.

FROM BAND AID TO LIVE AID

Although Geldof's "Do They Know It's Christmas" was a huge
financial success, he had bigger ambitions for saving the world
from hunger. With the help of many musicians, he staged his Live
Aid concert, the biggest global event ever held at the time. The
16-hour event was held on two continents. In London, 72,000
fans packed a sun-drenched Wembley Stadium. John F. Kennedy
Stadium in Philadelphia, PA, attracted 90,000 fans. More than 60
acts featuring rock's elite, including Queen, David Bowie, Sting,
U2, Duran Duran, Phil Collins, Robert Plant, Ozzy Osbourne,
Elton John, Run DMC, Jimmy Page, Mick Jagger, Tina Turner,
Billy Joel, and Madonna, performed for free and covered their own
expenses. Geldof and his band, the Boomtown Rats, were the
third act featured in the British Live Aid. As Geldof was leaving
the stage, he was quoted as saying, "I just realized this is the best
day of my life." The event was watched by 1.4 billion people
worldwide from over 150 countries. The one-day event raised
more than $245 million (£136 million) for African famine relief.
Event organizers were still taking donations for several weeks later.
Half of the money raised was spent on food and half on long-term
development in Ethiopia and the surrounding areas. Geldof had
succeeded in drawing public attention to African poverty, which
paved the way for other celebrities to use their star power in a
wide variety of ways to support other causes.

SPORTS SPIRIT

In 1977, Yankees star, Dave Winfield, founded the Dave Winfield
Foundation. It was the first altruistic foundation ever created by a
sports celebrity, and it helped to chart new ground among athletes
wishing to give something back.

Famous followers include former Baltimore Oriole's star Cal
Ripken, who assists an oft-overlooked group—illiterate adults,
through his Ripken Learning Center in Baltimore. His center
offers free services to Baltimore residents in reading, writing, and
help locating job internships.

Tiger Woods sponsors inner-city golf clinics. Launched with
$500,000 from his own money and $1 million from American
Express, his clinics promote education and racial harmony. He
reached more than 12,000 children in six cities last year.

The twin towers of the Golden Gate Bridge were once taller than any building in San Francisco.

Dan Marino, of the Miami Dolphins, supports many charities in southern Florida. The superstar quarterback donates $500 for each touchdown pass and has raised more than $700,000 since instituting his "Touchdown for Tots" program.

And National Basketball Association (NBA) iron man, A.C. Green uses his foundation to preach for abstinence.

BEST SUPPORTING ACTRESSES
Famed actresses Whoopi Goldberg and Elizabeth Taylor lend their names and support to the Annual Angel Awards, sponsor of the project of Angel Food, which helps deliver meals to HIV/AIDS patients in Los Angeles.

THE BOTTOM LINE
Charitable foundations have an indisputable upside—celebrities with private charities can draw attention—and lots of money—to unique causes that might otherwise go ignored. And in the instance of Live Aid, an event can have a long-lasting legacy. A DVD of the marathon concert was recently released with the hopes of raising several million dollars for the humanitarian emergency that Africa is currently facing.

* * * * *

Stevie Wonder "signed" his contract to appear on "We Are the World" with two of his fingerprints instead of a signature.

* * * * *

SITTING PRETTY

For her 40th birthday, film producer Carlo Ponti presented his wife, actress Sophia Loren, with a toilet seat. She wasn't insulted, though—it was made of 14-karat gold.

"Sold down the river" entered the American idiom around 1850.

THE PRICE
OF FREE SPEECH

*Paul Robeson was one of the most gifted human beings who
ever lived. A lot of you may never have heard of him—and
there's a reason for that. They didn't want you to.*

The son of an American slave, Paul Leroy Bustill Robeson
was born in Princeton, New Jersey, in 1898. An outstand-
ing student in high school, he won an academic scholarship to Rutgers where he earned 12 letters (in track, baseball,
basketball, and football), graduated with honors, and was the class
valedictorian.

AND EVERYTHING HAD BEEN GOING SO WELL...
He financed his law studies at Columbia University in New York
City with the money he earned playing professional football. At
Columbia, he met and married biology student Eslanda Cordoza
Goode. It was Essie who convinced Paul to appear in an amateur
play that was staged by the Harlem YWCA. He got rave reviews
for his performance—but he stuck with the law.

After graduation, he got a job at a prestigious New York law
firm. But an incident there changed his life forever: A secretary
refused to work with him saying, "I never take dictation from a
n—." Robeson quit the firm and the law.

AN ACTOR'S LIFE FOR ME
From 1924 on, he appeared in a series of concerts, plays (including *Othello* in 1930), and movies (including *Show Boat* in 1936,
in which he sang what was to become his signature tune: "Ol'
Man River").

BLACK AND WHITE AND RED ALL OVER
He toured the United States and Europe in the 1930s and 1940s,
giving concerts and starring in plays, but one trip delivered
another life-changing whammy. In 1935, Robeson visited the
Soviet Union and was impressed with what he saw as a classless

It referred to sales of slaves along the Mississippi.

society where all races were treated equally. He wrote, "Here, for the first time in my life, I walk in full human dignity." Which, as great as it was for him, blinded him to the dark side of the Soviet version of communism.

UN-AMERICAN ACTIVITIES

After World War II, the cold war between the United States and the Soviet Union fueled a climate of fear and suspicion that Communists were trying to destroy America from within. When Robeson was called before the House Un-American Activities Committee, where it was demanded that he answer whether he was a Communist or not, Robeson, as was his right, refused to answer.

When asked about his trip to the Soviet Union, he said, "In Russia, I felt for the first time like a full human being—no color prejudice like in Mississippi, no color prejudice like in Washington."

ERASED FROM EXISTENCE

The committee rewarded Robeson's courage by taking away his passport and coercing other black leaders into testifying against him. Black and white leaders alike denounced him, and he was blacklisted in the entertainment industry. The mainstream media imposed a blackout on his activities and statements. Books, films, and articles about him disappeared from public view. All major concert halls in the United States were closed to him, and his records vanished from stores. It was as if he had never existed at all.

He could have worked outside the United States, but he couldn't leave the country without his passport.

A SHOCK TO THE SYSTEM

Despite the pressure, Robeson continued to speak out against oppression and inequality. That's why he suffered so much anguish when, in 1956, Soviet premier Nikita Khrushchev made the crimes of Joseph Stalin public: the forced famine, the genocide, the political purges. Robeson collapsed and was in and out of hospitals for the next few years being treated for depression and exhaustion.

HERE HE STOOD

When his autobiography, *Here I Stand*, was published in 1958, it wasn't reviewed by the mainstream press or widely distributed; just a few copies were sold. His passport was finally restored that year, but by then his show business career had evaporated. His health declined. In 1965, Essie died after a long bout with cancer. Robeson moved in with his sister, and his son took over his affairs. After fighting for justice and equality his entire life, Paul Robeson died in Philadelphia in 1976, the bicentennial year of the country that had given birth to him—and helped to ruin him.

****

"My father was a slave and my people died to build this country and I am going to stay here and have a part in it just like you. And no fascist-minded people will drive me from it. Is that clear?'"
—Paul Robeson's testimony before the House Un-American Activities Committee.

****

THE NAKED TRUTH

The famous abolitionist Sojourner Truth (born Isabella Baumfree in 1797 in Ulster County, New York) traveled throughout the United States giving personal testimony to her experiences as a slave. She was so often accused of being a man (she stood six feet tall), she once bared her breasts in public to prove that she was, in fact, a woman.

"Those are the same stars, and that is the same moon, that look down upon your brothers and sisters, and which they see as they look up to them, though they are ever so far away from us, and each other."

"Suppose a man's mind holds a quart, and a woman's don't hold but a pint; if her pint is full, it's as good as his quart."
—Sojourner Truth

THE WITCH OF WALL STREET

She walked up and down Wall Street in rags—but in her day she was the richest woman in America. Meet Hetty Green, financial genius and obsessive skinflint.

The employees at Manhattan's Chemical and National Bank were too intimidated to laugh at the strange woman who visited their vaults on a daily basis, even though she had a laundry list of eccentricities as long as your arm. She wore clothes so worn out they were falling apart on her body, she never washed her underwear because it was "too expensive," and she spent almost every day locked in the bank's vaults eating raw onions and counting her riches. Had Hetty Green been a different kind of woman, those who saw her marching down Wall Street might have snickered. But Hetty's reputation was every bit as formidable as her scowling, forbidding face.

BORN CHEAP
Stinginess came naturally to Hetty's family. Born in 1835 to a family of wealthy blue bloods, including a father who wanted his daughter to manage her fortune well, Hetty could read the daily financial papers to her dad at age six and opened her own savings account at age eight. By 21, she was so miserly that she didn't even want to light the birthday candles on her own cake because it would waste them. Eventually, the party guests convinced her to light them, but she blew them out immediately so she could return them to the grocery store for a refund.

SHE'S A RICH GIRL
This was the same birthday at which Hetty came into a multimillion-dollar trust. Almost a decade later, her father died and left her his vast estate. Hetty cleverly invested her money, increasing its value enormously. But she still wore secondhand clothes, took her meals in workingmen's dives, saw doctors at free charity clinics, and lived in cheap boardinghouses to avoid paying property taxes.

Montpelier, Vermont, is the only state capital with no McDonald's within city limits.

ON THE DOTTED LINE

She was suspicious of the many suitors who courted her, believing they were all after her money. But at age 33, she agreed to marry businessman Edward Henry Green—after he agreed to sign a prenuptial agreement renouncing all rights to her money. Two children and a lot of angst later, Edward Green divorced her. When he died in 1902, Hetty Green moved to Hoboken, New Jersey, with her children and commuted daily to her bank in New York City.

POOR LITTLE RICH KIDS

Vowing to make her son Ned the richest man in the world, Hetty saved every cent she could. She gave up washing her clothes, never changed or washed her sheets, tried to evade paying bills, and went to bed at sundown to avoid burning candles. She never turned on the heat or used hot water.

But she refused to spend any money on her kids, either. When Ned broke his leg, she wouldn't take him to the doctor, saying it was too pricey. His gangrenous leg later had to be amputated. She forced her daughter Sylvia to wear old clothes too, and she wouldn't let her date the "fortune hunters" Hetty believed were everywhere. When she finally let Sylvia marry, she forced the new husband to give up all rights to his wife's fortune.

SHE'S A RICHER GIRL

Through it all, Hetty made one shrewd financial decision after another. She made terrific investments, owned thousands of plots of land, and had enough cash to make loans to major businesses—even New York City itself—extracting heavy interest on each loan.

But Hetty's penny-pinching ways continued. She spent hours each day counting her money. Her habit of walking down to her bank each day in a ragged, black dress and with a scowl on her face earned her the nickname "the Witch of Wall Street."

THE DECLINE OF HETTY

Eventually, Hetty's health failed. She suffered from a painful hernia but refused to have an operation because it cost $150 (123 euros). She became even more paranoid and suspicious, believing kidnappers and murderers were after her and her fortune.

In old Rome, women were expected to cover their heads when walking outdoors.

Eventually, her bad temper was the end of her. She reportedly died of apoplexy, in 1916, after an argument with a servant (not one of her own, of course).

GIVING AWAY THE GREEN STUFF
Hetty Green left $100 million to her children, who, ironically, became some of the most generous philanthropists of their time, donating money to numerous museums, libraries, and civic institutions. Hetty Green would have been horrified to hear it.

* * * * *

MORE SALTY TIDBITS

- The colloquial phrase, "to salt [something] away," meaning "to store or save money or things," derives from the activity of packing and preserving with salt.

- It is thought that France's world famous cheese industry owes its existence to the presence of salt throughout the country. French cheeses were developed when dairy farmers used salt to preserve curdled milk.

- The adult human body contains 250 grams (8.8 ounces) of salt. Salt helps the heart contract and is instrumental in the transmission of nerve impulses to and from the brain.

- Vegetarians need more salt than carnivores because meat eaters get plenty of salt from animal tissue. Vegetarian animals instinctively seek out naturally occurring salt licks.

- Superstitious sailors would never mention salt while at sea, yet they were widely referred to as "old salts."

Kamikaze, the name adopted by World War II Japanese suicide pilots, means "Divine Wind."

EXTENDED SITTING SECTION

YOU GO GIRLS!

Old-fashioned laws permitted husbands to beat wives who refused to, ahem, submit to their spouses' demands. As if that wasn't insulting enough, governments granted only men the right to vote. Eventually, in America and England, groups of gutsy gals began demanding women's rights, especially suffrage (voting rights). Here's a sample of those rebellious females.

EARLY BLOOMERS

The women's suffrage movement attracted some unusual women. Take, for instance, Margaret Brent. In 1647 it was considered "not done" that a woman would remain unmarried, much less become a property owner. Brent managed to do both and accidentally became the first woman suffragist when she insisted—unsuccessfully—on being allowed to vote in the Maryland assembly.

Almost two centuries later, Harriet Tubman (1820–1913) escaped slavery through the Underground Railroad. Tubman should have been preoccupied after 19 trips across the Mason-Dixon Line, leading 300 other slaves 90 miles to freedom, which resulted in a $40,000 price tag for her head. Instead, she demanded the right to vote for *all* women while speaking out against slavery and racism. Not one to be idle, she also worked as a spy and nurse during the Civil War for the federal government, which rewarded her with a $20 monthly pension in the 1890s and her picture on postal stamps in 1995.

WHAT'S NEXT LIZ? VOTING RIGHTS FOR FURNITURE?

In 1848, Elizabeth Stanton (1815–1902) kicked off the "official" suffrage movement with the first United States convention for women's rights. As a young child, Stanton took scissors to certain paragraphs in law books owned by her daddy judge in an attempt to get rid of laws that essentially defined women as men's property. The judge, who often lamented that his only child wasn't a boy, stopped her by mentioning that such incisions wouldn't change a darn thing. To make up for being female, Stanton studied typically "male" courses, including Latin and Greek. Later on, she omitted the word "obey" from her wedding vows, giving her new husband a pretty good clue of what he was in for. Still, he called Stanton radical—as did several women's rights supporters—when she insisted that the early movement include voting rights for women.

NOBODY TELLS SUSAN B. TO HUSH UP
In 1851, Stanton stumbled into Susan B. Anthony's path at a street corner, igniting a 51-year relationship. Anthony (1820–1906) came from a Quaker family that included antislavery activists. Quakers supported equality of the sexes but also discipline and hard work, displayed by Anthony's severe expression flaunted later on by U.S. dollar coins. Anthony shifted from teaching to pushing for women's rights after being informed that females don't get to speak during political meetings. To make up for being silenced, she traveled about the country speaking for the women's cause.

In 1869, Stanton & Anthony separated from a national women's rights association that was waiting for black men to gain voting rights before pushing for woman suffrage. They created a new group with a "world-shattering" focus—voting rights for women *and* an end to male dominance.

VICTORIA'S UNMENTIONABLES
While both ladies initially embraced a new leader of the women's movement, Victoria Woodhull (1838–1927). Their efforts resulted in Woodhull only getting a tiny mention in a six-volume book series detailing the early women's movement because she used rather… unusual methods. Woodhull practiced spiritualism and magnetic healing, and often talked freely about sexual matters—something ladies of that era simply didn't do. In fact, during the 1800s, society prohibited words dealing with body parts in social conversation. Societal pressures did not stop "the Woodhull"; she not only became the first woman stockbroker in America, she also became the first woman to run for president.

Woodhull grew up poor, along with five siblings, in a family—led by a law-breaking father—that defined bizarre. By age 13 Woodhull and her sister conducted séances while their dad collected the money. After a disastrous marriage at age 15 to a drunken doctor, Woodhull befriends wealthy Cornelius Vanderbilt. Woodhull claimed that spirit guides Demosthenes, Napoleon and Josephine relayed insider stock market tips, which

Nearly 1,400 towns have been found of the mysterious ancient Indus civilization (2700–1750 B.C.).

she passed on to Vanderbilt. In turn, he passed her half of his considerable profits. With her sister, she created a new stock-brokerage, serving champagne and strawberries dipped in chocolate to customers.

At that point, Woodhull could have put her feet up and lived a life of luxury with her second hubby, but she believed spirits wanted her to lead a social revolution, cleaning up the mistreatment of women. This eventually flushes her career down the toilet. But first in 1871, while the two main factions of the women's movement kept busy criticizing each other, Woodhull ignored them and became the first woman to speak before the House Judiciary Committee. Her argument that the Constitution already gave women the right to vote didn't convince the majority of Congressmen.

After Woodhull announced her presidential bid in her new publication, the *Woodhull & Claflin Weekly*, the conservative faction of the women's movement began publicly to pooh-pooh her. In 1872 she was the first woman to run for president of the United States as a candidate of the new Equal Rights Party. Newspapers claimed that Woodhull had two husbands because she took in her drunken ex-husband. Her outcry against forcing women to stay in abusive marriages was interpreted as promoting "free love." Her refusal to condemn prostitutes—claiming that society drove them into selling themselves similar to the sexual submission that wives underwent—earned her a reputation as a tart.

In response, Woodhull published the love affairs of a famous *married* preacher, also president of the mud-slinging women's group. Woodhull spent Election Day in jail, charged with illegally printing "obscenity." In and out of jail, she apparently didn't have a get-out-of-jail-free card and lost her fortune to bail and lawyer's fees, until she was finally found innocent.

SOME LADIES LIKED IT ROUGH
Meanwhile, New Zealand in 1893 becomes the first country to give women the right to vote, but other countries refuse to do so. Since England's long time struggle for women's rights floundered by 1905, English suffragist Emmeline Pankhurst (1858–1928) and supporters had their fill of "ladylike" tactics and drew attention to the cause by disrupting government meetings, breaking windows, and setting fires. Pankhurst, responsible for the term "suffragette,"

It's mysterious largely because scientists have yet to decipher their pictographic scripts.

frequently ended up in jail with tubes up her nose filled with liquid food after refusing to eat.

Alice Paul (1885–1977) became a jailbird too after meeting Pankhurst while in England studying for a social work doctorate degree. Her crime? Dressed as a cleaning woman, she hid in a room waiting for the Prime Minister to speak. During a lull in his speech, she shouted, "How about votes for women?" Back in America, Paul disagreed with the statewide focus of the main women's group and instead resorted to civil disobedience to push a constitutional amendment. She started her "radical" tactics in 1913 by leading 8,000 protestors through Washington, D.C., streets. By 1917 Paul and others started picketing in front of Woodrow Wilson's White House. The women chained themselves to fences and held signs asking, "Mr. President, how long must women wait for liberty?" Paul's frequent jail time included force feedings and being assigned to the psychiatric ward where inmates nearly drove her crazy.

LEGAL EAGLE

A law university initially denied ex-teacher Belva Lockwood (1830–1917) her law diploma but she eventually got to use lawyerly skills to secure the right for women to vote in some states. Lockwood also became the first woman to practice law before the U.S. Supreme Court. Although Lockwood criticized Victoria Woodhull for being too radical, she too ran for president—in 1884 and 1888.

TALE ENDS OF AGING SUFFRAGISTS

- Stanton runs for Congress in 1866—receiving 24 votes. She presides over a new women's group in 1890, but the group spurns her in 1895 when, at age 80, she writes *The Woman's Bible*, which eliminates the original version's submissive role for females.
- Susan B. authors the 19th "Anthony" Amendment, but dies before it's finally added to the Constitution in 1920, finally allowing American women to vote.
- Woodhull is reported "dead" by newspaper headlines in 1873. Clearly alive, Woodhull eventually moves to England, marries hubby number three (after divorcing number two), and runs

Got indigestion? Crush a hog's tooth and put it inside four sugar cakes. Eat for four days.

briefly for U.S. president in 1879 and 1892 from across the Atlantic Ocean. Realizing the commute would be difficult, she stops campaigning. Instead, as a wealthy widow, she plays fairy godmother to residents in an English village until her death in 1927.

- Paul's picketing served as a warm-up for a lifetime of work on equal rights. She earns a bunch of law degrees and authors the Equal Rights Amendment, which Congress fails to pass every year until after her death. Before her death at age 92, she remains an activist—over the phone. In 1995, Paul's face shows up on 78-cent postal stamps.
- Pankhurst remains feisty—in and out of jail in her fifties—and dies in 1928, shortly after English women gain voting rights.
- Lockwood continues to argue cases—winning a big one in 1906—a $5 million lawsuit for eastern Cherokee people.

* * * * *

THAT LIVED IN LOOK

- What is believed to be the world's oldest artificial structure, was discovered in A.D. 2000, on a hillside at Chichibu, north of Tokyo, Japan. The discovery consists of 10 postholes, the remains of two huts, and stone tools. The shelter would have been built by a direct ancestor of humans, Homo erectus, who used stone tools. These huts date back half a million years!

- The oldest existing stone building was constructed over 4, 600 years ago in Sakkara, Egypt. It is a mastaba or tomb for kings and it honors Pharaoh Zoser, the first ruler of Egypt's Third Dynasty.

- The oldest continuously inhabited city is Damascus Syria, which has been lived in since 2000 B.C.

- Since there were no garbage collections in the early cities of Mesopotamia, refuse piled up in the streets and was then packed down by the traffic of people and animals—so the streets were paved with garbage.

That's how they did it in ancient Egypt, anyway, according to a medical text from 1552 B.C.

GREAT GIGS OF HISTORY

Ever wonder what you might have done for a living if you'd been born during the Middle Ages? Here are some suggestions.

ALCHEMIST

Multitasker Needed: You answered the ad: "Must be proficient in changing metals such as lead and copper into silver and gold. Also must be able to discover a universal cure for disease and a means for indefinitely prolonging life. We offer competitive wages and a full range of health benefits [such as the king's protection from marauding, murderous bandits]."

Welcome to My Lab: You got the job! Picture yourself as an alchemist in your medieval laboratory, hunched over bubbling flasks filled with foul-smelling fluids. It's a small, dark, cluttered place that stinks of smoke and mysterious chemicals. The room is filled with a grimy jumble of instruments, manuscripts, skulls, animal specimens, and assorted mystical objects. Like many of your colleagues, you work at home in order to save money and avoid outside interference. You do most of your experiments in the kitchen to take advantage of the cooking fire (though some others choose the attic or cellar, where late-night activity is less likely to be noticed by inquisitive neighbors). You've tried thousands of different experiments, yet success in reaching your ultimate goals continues to elude you.

Hanging With the Beautiful People: It's not surprising—given its heavy reliance on mystical notions and potions—that the profession of alchemy became increasingly populated with con artists and naive dabblers in the art. Despite the growing disrepute of the profession in the waning days of the Middle Ages, European kings and nobles continued to support their favorite alchemists. But sometimes, alchemists who failed to come through with the gold came to a bad end. It's said that Frederick of Wurzburg maintained a special gallows just for hanging alchemists.

France was the first country to adopt the 35-hour workweek.

Chemistry 101: Some of the alchemists' work was indispensable in the development of modern chemistry. They were the first to isolate a number of chemicals—from phosphorus to hydrochloric acid—and they developed new equipment and methods for distilling fluids, assaying metals, and controlling chemical reactions. Some of their devices, techniques, and concoctions are still used today. Chinese alchemists found that a mixture of saltpeter, sulfur, and carbon, when heated, did not immediately lead to immortality. But it did have a tendency to explode and set things on fire. Ironically, instead of finding the elixir of life, they had discovered a substance that would eventually lead to a whole lot of early mortality in the centuries to come: gunpowder.

TOWN CRIER

For Cryin' Out Loud!: The job of town crier can be traced back as far as 1066, when news of King William of Normandy's successful invasion of Britain was passed from town to town by men hired to call out the triumphant king's proclamation. In an age when newspapers were nonexistent and books were found only in the hands of a few clerics and the nobility, someone had to get the word out to the general populace. So proclamations, edicts, laws, and other news were usually passed on to the public by the town crier—the first talking newspaper. "Oyez, Oyez!" (roughly translated from the French as "hark" or "listen") became a familiar cry in town squares, markets, and other public meeting places, as townspeople gathered to listen to news of plagues, battles won in far-off lands, royal births, and deaths by execution.

Don't Shoot the Messenger: Town criers were strictly protected by law. "Don't shoot the messenger" was a very real command; anything nasty that was done to a town crier was deemed to be done to the king—and was, therefore, a treasonable offense punishable by death. Criers were usually people of some standing in the community because they had to be able to write and read the official proclamations. Often they were a husband and wife team, with the wife ringing the large handbell and the husband doing the shouting. Like today's mail carrier, the town crier had a regular route. He might read a proclamation at the door of the local inn, for example, then nail it to the doorpost of the establishment. The tradition resulted in the expression "posting a notice" and the naming of newspapers as "the Post."

FOOL

Surely You Jest!: The ancient profession of fool has been part of virtually every culture. An early form of the occupation was the court jester, a role that can be traced back to ancient Egypt. But it was in the Middle Ages that the fool, who was usually selected from the peasantry, came to prominence in society.

Besides the palaces of monarchs, fools also found gainful employment in the residences of the higher nobility, clergy, and even popes. And because the court jester was often summoned to try to lift his master out of an angry or melancholic mood, the requirements for the job included a quick wit, a sometimes wicked sense of humor, and a repertoire of humorous stunts and acrobatic feats. Though most jesters suffered from some physical or mental handicap and were often the butt of jokes, they were also among the only courtiers who could freely speak their minds to the monarch. And in the harsh world of medieval Europe, people who might not have been able to survive any other way managed to find themselves a social niche in the role of fool.

No Foolin'?: It was common practice for nobles to exchange their fools with one another. By the 13th century, the court fool was a regular institution; he was referred to in royal account books under the headings of wages, medical treatment, and clothes. One thing though: The popular perception of the way fools or jesters dressed—multicolored motley coat, tripointed hat with bells (the foolscap), and a scepter or sword—doesn't match up with histori-cal reality. Records suggest that, at least in the case of those who worked as professional court entertainers, fools in medieval times tended to dress much like the other fellows at court.

Natural-Born Fools: In contrast to these "professional" fools, some fools were clearly mad—or "touched by God," in the parlance of the Middle Ages. Historical records mention them dancing in a wild frenzy, tearing their clothes off, and speaking all manner of gibberish. This insane fool was called a "natural," and other fools, who entertained by their wit or other skills, were called "artificial" fools. Besides the royal court, many of the "artificials" were employed by businesses, including such finer establishments as taverns and brothels. They were also in great demand for pageants, processions, and festivals.

ROYAL FOOD TASTER

To the Bitter End: One point about taste is pretty well proven: Of all the basic taste sensations, the most critical is bitterness. Why? Well, for one thing, there is some wonderfully logical natural evidence: plant alkaloids are often bitter—and often poisonous. Therefore, it's not surprising that evolutionary pressures (one of the most important of these being the instinct toward self-preservation) would strongly favor acute sensitivity to bitter tastes. In fact, mammals are about a thousand times more sensitive to bitter substances than to sweet or salty ones.

"Try It, Sire, You'll Like It!": The importance of accurately tasting bitterness eventually evolved into one of the more risky professions of medieval times: professional food and drink tasters employed by nobles and monarchs. Their sole task was to sample food and drink long before it entered the royal mouth. These tasters underwent long and careful training to detect faint traces of bitterness. Often enough, in a kind of early arms race, the same dignitaries who needed tasters also employed alchemists to devise lethal compounds for their enemies, something apparently edible and harmless that would disguise the bitter taste. Generally, the tasters won out, saved by their acute mammalian sensitivities.

In fact, this particular arms race still continues—only now chemists are out to fool the taste buds of rodents, not royals. The hoped-for payoff: a truly successful rat poison.

ALE-CONNER

No Conning the Beer Guy: Hammurabi, the sixth king of ancient Babylon (1792–1750 B.C.), included provisions regulating the business of tavern keepers in his great and famous law code. The provisions covered the sale of beer and were designed to protect the consumer. The punishment for tavern keepers who violated the law was drowning.

In the Middle Ages, brewers were required to hang an alestake (usually a pole with some sort of sign at the end) out side their premises when they were ready to present a new batch of ale. This was a summons for the local ale tester, or conner, to drop by. The ale-conner was a civil servant—probably a very happy one—charged with ensuring the quality and quantity of beer served to the public.

"A Beer by Any Other Name Would Feel as Damp": William Shakespeare's father, John, was an ale-conner. The conner tested ale by pouring some on a bench and sitting in the resulting puddle (that's right) while drinking the rest. If there were sugar or impurities in the ale, the conner's leather trousers would stick after sitting for half an hour or so. Besides being able to drink for a living at a time when some folks routinely drank a gallon (almost 4 liters) of beer for breakfast, the ale-conner had considerable power to exact punishment on wrongdoers. Brewers caught short-measuring (a term that came to include pretty much any deficiency in either the quality or quantity of beer served to the customer) could expect punishment that included everything from fines to whipping, public humiliation in the stocks or pillory, or even worse, a turn in the cucking stool. This was a chair in the shape of a giant chamber pot in which the offender was repeatedly dunked in the river, to the delighted derision of his clientele.

Bitter Was Better: In the late Middle Ages, ale consisted of malt (usually made from barley, although other grains were also used), water, and yeast. But by the start of the 15th century, ale was being gradually replaced by beer, which was introduced to England and elsewhere from Flanders. Beer was "bittered" with hops and stayed fresher longer than English ale because of the preservative quality of the hops. By the end of the 15th century, beer had almost completely replaced the old English sweet ale.

BARBER-SURGEON

A Cutting-Edge Profession: In the Middle Ages, many barbers assumed the role of barber-surgeons. In England, for example, barbers attached to the army were tasked with cutting men's hair short—not because it was deemed particularly fashionable, but rather to get rid of lice. They were also detailed to perform dentistry, general surgery, and specific doctoring: the treatment of wounds received in battle. So not only could a barber remove your golden locks, but if need be, he could remove your left leg as well. As a result, a lot of blood tended to soak what little bandages the barber had at his disposal—hence, red merging with white, the design of the barber's pole.

No More Monking Around: So how did barbers end up in this dual-role profession in the first place? It turns out that, up until 1163, when Pope Alexander III finally put a stop to it, monks had been routinely performing surgical operations. The pope figured that hacking away at bodies wasn't something that God's lieutenants should be doing. Luckily for the monks (though not necessarily for their patients), barbers had been living in monasteries since the late 11th century (when another pope had decided he didn't like his priests with bushy beards or droopy moustaches). So the barbers got the surgery job.

This prime example of multitasking in the workplace lasted in Europe for around 600 years. It wasn't until 1745 that a guild of surgeons was formed that was distinct from the guild of barbers in England. Even then, the Royal College of Surgeons didn't receive its Royal Charter until 1800.

GONG FARMER

The Gong Show: During the Middle Ages, most castle privies (also called "gongs," "jakes," and the dignified-sounding "necessarium") were crude affairs. A lot of them consisted of a simple stone or wooden seat over a shaft that emptied into a moat or stream, but some larger castles had special latrine towers. It was the job of the gong farmer to climb down the deep, dank, and disgusting privy shafts to clean and empty the cesspits and ditches.

One of the strangest of professions, it was apparently better paying than many other medieval careers. Part of the gong farmers' income came from sorting through the excrement for dropped pennies, gloves, buttons, and the like, which they could then wash and either use or sell. Although it's highly unlikely that many gong farmers became, excuse the expression, stinking rich, it was definitely a classic example of medieval trickle-down economics.

* * * * *

SPEAKING YOUR LANGUAGE

You think politicians don't speak your language?

- Born and raised in Germany, King George I of England never bothered to learn how to speak English, even though he ruled the country from 1714 to 1727. He returned to Hanover as often as possible and, by leaving the running of the country to his ministers, created the first government cabinet.

- German was also the mother tongue of England's Queen Victoria who began her reign in 1837. Her mother was the daughter of a German duke and she spoke German with her daughter. Victoria ruled England for 64 years and never did get the hang of speaking English perfectly.

- On the other hand, the Holy Roman Emperor Charles V, crowned in 1519 had no trouble learning languages. He claimed he spoke Spanish to God, Italian to women, French to men, and German to his horse.

THE ENIGMA OF ENIGMA

In World War II one of the most vital but unsung roles performed by the intelligence services was that of cracking enemy codes. And the hardest code of all to crack was Enigma—that is, until Alan Turing and his team of scientists at Bletchley Park put their minds to it.

The Enigma story stretches out over almost 100 years, featuring a cast of peculiarly British eccentrics and geniuses, two unusual deaths, a pair of rock stars (one of them American), a TV journalist, and an audacious heist. Oh, and one world war, of course. Who said code breaking was boring?

BIRTH OF ENIGMA

The Enigma encryption and decryption machine was invented in Germany just after World War I by an engineer, Arthur Scherbius. He offered it to the German military, which was at first slow in recognizing the machine's worth. It was not until the late 1920s that the German army began using the machine, by which time the unfortunate Scherbius was dead—killed in a horse-riding accident in 1929.

The machine he left behind was portable and easy to operate. And the codes it created during World War II were an absolute nightmare to crack, despite the fact that as early as 1931 a German traitor passed on secrets of the device's design to the Brits.

THE ENIGMA VARIATIONS

The Enigma looked a bit like a typewriter crossed with an old-fashioned telephone switchboard. It had a keyboard; three rotors, with inner and outer rings on which were numbers to correspond to letters of the alphabet; circuits to scramble the movements of the rotors (which moved one position with every key press); and letters on the electric display. Each time a letter was typed into the keyboard, it was scrambled through the circuits powering the rotors, and its coded equivalent would pop up on the display.

Because of its shape on a map, Oklahoma has been called "the nation's largest meat cleaver."

Users at the other end would type the coded message in and, as if by magic, the original message would appear in the display. The one big complicating factor for would-be code breakers was that there were multiple sets of rotors used in the machine, and each set of three rotors had different configurations. To break the code, you had to know which set of three rotors was being used and in which configuration.

It was these multiple sets of rotors that made breaking the Enigma code so tricky: each rotor could be set in 26 different positions, across 26 different parts of the device. This may not sound like a huge number of potential permutations, but it meant that the chances of decoding just one letter were less than one in 150 million million million. Enough, the Germans figured, to keep even the best code breakers busy for a bit. If that weren't enough, the order of connections was changed at least once a day.

CRAZY NAME, CRAZY GUY
The British attempt to crack the Enigma codes was based at Bletchley Park, a country house in Buckinghamshire. The house was code named Station X, equipped out with the latest code-breaking equipment (well, plenty of pens and paper), and filled with the brightest and best analytical minds in Britain. These included the magnificently named Alfred Dillwyn Knox ("Dilly" to his fellow code breakers) and mathematical genius Alan Turing. Though there was no shortage of unconventional types working at Bletchley, Turing's habit of chaining his coffee mug to the radiator ensured that he stood out from the mass of eccentrics that populated the place.

DO NOT DISTURB
Despite the presence of so many unique personalities in one place, the locals were kept in the dark as to what went on at Bletchley Park. They were told it was being used for army personnel on rest and recuperation leave, and were told to keep away, the usual excuse being that they might disturb "Captain Ridley's shooting party." Even the code breakers' own friends and families weren't told where they were or what they were doing. Their role became even more secret and important when the war really got going in the spring of 1940, and the trickle of German signals became a

flood. The Nazis were convinced that their codes, supplied by the Enigma machine, were impenetrable.

BOMBE THE GERMANS

So smug were they about Enigma that the Germans didn't consider its one weakness: no letter could be encrypted to itself. That meant that the Allied operatives could tell when a code hadn't been correctly broken, simply by running a line of cracked code under the encrypted original. If any letter matched the one immediately below, they knew the crack had gone wrong. The task of doing this was sped up with the use of forerunners of computers called *bombes* (named for the ominous ticking noise they emitted), made by a Polish team in the 1930s. The Poles had almost cracked Enigma before the war, but when they were on the verge of doing so, the Germans had redesigned the machine.

IF THEY ONLY KNEW

Alan Turing played a vital part in refining and speeding up the work of the bombes. He worked on this side of the project with another mathematician, Joan Clarke. They worked so closely together that at one point Turing, who was gay, considered asking Clarke to marry him (homosexuality was illegal at the time, and marriage would have given Turing a fig leaf of respectability).

But even as the Bletchley scientists cracked the Enigma codes, they realized they would not be able to shout about it. By 1942, the Germans had more than 100,000 Enigma machines in operation throughout Europe, providing an endless stream of useful data. If Hitler found out that the Allies had been tapping into his army's intelligence, he would have withdrawn every machine. So, the Allies had to be selective about which Enigma information they acted on, so they would not arouse the suspicion of the Nazis and give away the fact that they were decoding German messages.

GOLDEN EGGS

The best of the flood of material that was deciphered was kept in a file called Ultra and was passed straight to Winston Churchill himself. Impressed by the level of success and secrecy at Bletchley, Churchill called the people at Station X: "my geese that laid the golden eggs and never cackled." The "geese" again came into their own in the Allied defense of the crucial Anglo-American supply lines across the Atlantic. Faced with a new breed of Enigma, with an extra rotor to make life that much more difficult, Turing and company worked around the clock to find a way in—helped enormously by the occasional capture of a German codebook or Enigma machine. One by one, coded messages used by German U-boats were broken, and the colossal losses they inflicted were stemmed. It's been postulated that the efforts of the Bletchley Park staff shortened the war by years.

SECRETS AND LIES

It's only recently that the story of the Enigma machine and the people around it has come out, as documents restricted under the Official Secrets Act have been declassified. One of the saddest tales to emerge was that of the postwar fate of Alan Turing.

A pioneer in the emerging and important field of computers, Turing should have been supported and protected by the intelligence services. Instead, because of his homosexuality, he was harried and persecuted. Turing was already in psychoanalysis attempting to deal with his sexuality. When he was arrested for soliciting sex from another man in 1950, he was driven over the edge. He lost his job at GCHQ (the successor to Bletchley Park) and was forced to undergo hormone treatment to "cure" him. Alienated and emotionally damaged, Turing committed suicide in 1954 by eating an apple that had been dipped in cyanide.

A MASTER PLAN

But the Enigma story didn't end there. If anything, it became more remarkable. By 2000, there were only three known Enigma machines left in the world. One of them was at Bletchley Park (now a museum). That year, it was stolen.

A reward was offered for the return of the machine, then valued at up to £100,000 ($185,000). Negotiations were carried out with its kidnappers by messages hidden in newspapers and Web pages, and "The Master" at a midnight graveyard rendezvous. Notes to the police from the machine's thief were signed "The Master." Then, in autumn of 2000, the police got a break. They were contacted by a mystery person who claimed he had bought the machine in good faith, and who, on hearing that there was a nationwide hunt for it, was prepared to give it back—but only via an intermediary.

DENNIS THE MENACE
In mid-October 2000, a parcel arrived at the office of *Newsnight* reporter Jeremy Paxman. As he was on vacation at the time, it sat unopened on his desk for a week. On his return, Paxman opened the package to find he was the lucky—if baffled—recipient of, you guessed it, the missing Enigma machine.

A few days later, Dennis Yates, a dealer in World War II memorabilia, was charged with offenses connected to the theft and was later sent to jail for handling the stolen machine. He'd been arrested while calling a national newspaper from a phone booth. His defense was that he was acting as an "honest broker" for an unnamed buyer in India ("The Master") and had no other knowledge of the theft.

REWRITING HISTORY
With all this renewed interest in Enigma, it was only a matter of time before the story made it into the movies. To date there have been not one but two films on the subject. First, in 2000, came *U-571*, a Hollywood blockbuster starring Bill Paxton, Harvey Keitel, and Jon Bon Jovi. If nothing else, this film wins an audacity award for its shameless rewriting of history. According to the film, it was the Americans—certainly not the Poles or the Brits—who were responsible for capturing the Enigma machine, so enabling the Allies to crack its code!

It was followed the next year by *Enigma*, featuring Kate Winslet. This was a murder mystery set at Bletchley Park, based on the book by Robert Harris. This adaptation also involved a famous figure from rock: it was produced by Mick Jagger.

The singer wasn't just there to finance the film. He had a genuine interest in the subject and actually owns one of the few existing examples of an Enigma machine.

There may not be many Enigma machines left, but their secret lives have been as exciting as anything James Bond ever got up to. Not bad for a machine and a governmental agency whose very existence was only admitted decades after they finished their most important work.

DREAMLAND
BY THE SEA

*The place that gave Mr. and Mrs. Joe Schmo the crazy
idea that happiness was just a few subway stops away.*

Between about 1880 and World War II, Coney Island was
the largest amusement park in the United States. But back
in 1609, when Dutch explorer Henry Hudson became the
first European to arrive on the premises, he found nothing more
than barren sand dunes and very unfriendly Native Americans.
After his petty officer was killed in a skirmish, Hudson moved on
to a much calmer and peaceful island later known as Manhattan.

At some point the island (which is five miles long and up
to one mile wide) was named *Konijn Eiland*, which is Dutch for
"Rabbit Island." *Konijn* became "Coney," possibly during the days
of Lady Deborah Moody, a London widow in her mid-50s, who
brought a group of religious dissenters to the island during a lull in
the Indian Wars. It was rough going—the local Native Americans
still weren't all that friendly—but the plucky group stayed on.

EASY ACCESS
Coney Island remained an island until 1829, when it was connected to mainland Long Island by Shell Road, a road made of—
you guessed it—shells. It's been a peninsula ever since. But lin-
guistically, it's still an island: one is said to be "on" Coney Island,
not "in" it.

HOLIDAY INN
Five years after Shell Road was built, a large hotel, Coney Island
House, opened for business in hopes of drawing a summer crowd to
the seaside. The hotel's success encouraged builders of even more
elegant hotels. What started as a genteel resort recommended by
doctors (sea bathing was considered to be healthy and invigorating), quickly became a hot spot with the upper classes. Before
long, hotels along the seashore welcomed such distinguished guests
as P. T. Barnum, Daniel Webster, and Washington Irving. Visitors

The first state to abolish capital punishment was Michigan, in 1847.

lingered on the hotels' long porches, ate their meals in posh dining rooms, and took dips in the Atlantic.

BATHING SUITS AND OTHER PURSUITS

The completion of Plank Road (made of planks, we assume) in 1850 made access easier and encouraged entrepreneurs like Peter Tilyou to set up shop: Tilyou not only sold beer for a nickel, but he also built bathhouses, so that visitors could change into their swimsuits right there on the beach—or, in those days of casual hygiene, rent them for the day.

Women's bathing costumes of the day were about the size of a modern-day conservative dress and, stockings included, weighed 15 pounds when wet. (A dress code was strictly enforced for nearly 100 years. For instance, in 1918 a hundred women were arrested for not wearing stockings on the beach. And in the early 1930s, men who exposed their chests on the beach could get a $50 fine and spend 10 days in jail.)

CONEY'S GREATEST GIFT TO HUMANITY

Frankfurters came to the United States via German immigrants. But they didn't really become popular until the 1880s, when Charles Feltman, a German baker, settled in Coney Island and decided to sell boiled frankfurters on heated buns from a cart. Each frankfurter sandwich was sold for a dime and was loaded with the traditional German toppings—mustard and sauerkraut.

Feltman was so successful that after a few years he opened his own restaurant, Feltman's German Beer Garden. In 1913, he hired Nathan Handwerker as a part-time delivery boy. But for $11 a week, Nathan wasn't too happy with his earnings. He began to plan for his own concession stand. In 1916, when he had saved $300, he made his dream a reality.

Nathan's stand offered a unique spiced meat frankfurter made from a recipe his wife, Ida, created. As a way to market his product, he promised free franks to the local doctors. His only condition was that they had to eat them in front of his stand wearing their white lab coats and stethoscopes. So when people saw the esteemed doctors eating Nathan's frankfurters, they automatically thought his franks must be of much better quality than his competitor's. And they were cheaper than Feltman's, since Nathan only charged a nickel apiece.

By the time Nathan opened his concession stand, frankfurters were commonly known as hot dogs—all because of an American cartoonist who couldn't spell. The story goes that one night in 1906, with a deadline looming, Tad Dorgan sketched a drawing of a dachshund smeared with mustard and squished in a bun. When it was time to caption the picture, poor Tad didn't know how to spell "dachshund," so he wrote, "Get your hot dogs!" instead.

LADIES AND GENTS OF LEISURE
But it was back in the late 1870s that island business really started booming: Five railroad lines ran to and from the island by then, bringing 50,000 to 60,000 visitors in 1878. For the first time in industrialized America, people were taking advantage of leisure time. Wearing their comparatively skimpy bathing suits and splashing in the surf was somehow liberating. Reporters of the day mention (and an early Edison Company film shows) the "jubilation" on the faces of Coney Islanders. The poor, working-class slob was learning how to have fun!

THERE GOES THE NEIGHBORHOOD
Gamblers, hookers, and card sharks were soon giving Coney Island a dubious reputation. Local residents were outraged. In hopes of cleaning up the place, they elected John Y. McKane as their police chief in 1868. But McKane ignored the misconduct (for a fee) and ended up behind bars himself when he was convicted of fixing elections.

TAKE THIS JOB AND SHOVE IT
In 1884, LaMarcus Adna Thompson opened the world's first roller coaster, the Switchback Railroad. It had 600 feet of wooden tracks, but unlike roller coasters of today, workers had to push it up to its highest point to get it going. Passengers paid a dime for a ride.

VIVA LUNA PARK!
Captain Paul Boyton had an even better idea. In 1895, he opened Sea Lion Park, the world's first enclosed amusement park. It featured a colony of sea lions and the ever-popular Shoot-the-Chutes, a waterslide that landed its riders in a man-made lagoon.

The first gold nugget found in the U.S. was in the Reed Gold Mine in North Carolina in 1799.

Sea Lion Park was redesigned in 1903 and transformed into Luna Park, the Las Vegas of its time. Besides elephant rides, camel rides, and a circus, the park featured the Dragon's Gorge, a tunnel ride that included a waterfall and scenes of the North Pole, Africa, the Grand Canyon, and the River Styx.

There was a simulated trip to the Moon. A live-action show, Fire and Flames, had the New York City fire department rescuing trapped residents of burning tenements, some of whom had to jump into nets to escape. This was an attraction that New Yorkers could identify with since a lot of them lived in real tenements. A real fire claimed Luna Park during the 1940s, and the site was eventually turned into a parking lot.

MEET ME TONIGHT IN DREAMLAND

Coney Island's most famous park, the completely white Dreamland, opened in 1904, and it duplicated a lot of Luna Park's ideas. Fighting the Flames was copied directly from Fire and Flames. There was a ride called Maxim's Flying Machine, a miniature railroad, a ballroom, and a Japanese teahouse. All watched over by the Dreamland Tower which stood 375 feet high and was covered with 100,000 lights.

Dreamland's most unusual attraction was the fully functional Incubator Hospital, which displayed actual premature babies in their incubators. This sounds a little less freaky when it's revealed that real doctors and nurses provided round-the-clock care for the little newborns. That's a relief, huh?

In 1911, a fire leveled Dreamland and all its spectacles in a matter of hours. The babies in the hospital were saved.

DAY-TRIPPING

By 1910 or so, the big hotels were closing, and the guests who used to come for weeks and months now only visited for weekends. And then they did not come at all. The island now belonged to the masses. The subway station built in 1918 cemented it. By the 1920s, one million people crowded the island on a single sunny day and walked the two-mile boardwalk, which had been completed in 1923.

During the Great Depression, Coney was the perfect escape; crowds averaging 35 million came each summer, but now the beaches were the primary draw because the masses couldn't afford

---

Maine is the largest U.S. producer of blueberries, with 99% of the country's production.

the fifty cents it took to buy a ride. Eventually the prices dropped to a nickel—for a hot dog, a ride, and the subway. But without an infusion of cash, the island started to decay.

THINGS ARE LOOKING UP—AND DOWN
On July 3, 1947, 1,300,000 people—one-fifth of the population of New York City—spent the day enjoying not just the beach and the rides, but also a fireworks show and an air show put on by the *New York Daily Mirror* and the U.S. Air Force. It's estimated that one in one hundred Americans visited Coney Island that weekend.

But that couldn't keep the decay away. By the 1950s, it looked like the island was doomed. Even while modern-day entrepreneurs were trying their hand at revitalizing the amusement parks on Coney, the island continued to decline. New amusement parks were going up around New York and the rest of the country, including Coney's biggest competitor: Disneyland in faraway California.

Some historians describe Coney as a ghost town in the 1970s. All of New York seemed a dangerous place then. On Coney Island the bathhouses closed, and the big hotels were torn down.

CONEY, REBORN
But you can't keep a good Coney Island down. In 1980, the New York Parks Department reported that concession revenues at the beach had been steadily rising for several seasons in a row.

Today, the rides and amusements are run by Astroland Amusement Park. The attractions include the Cyclone roller coaster, Go-Karts, the Tilt-a-Whirl, the Water Flume (a water-slide), and Dante's Inferno (with Spook-A-Rama, one of the park's two "dark" rides).

And let's not forget Astroland's Sideshows by the Seashore, featuring Insectavora, Serpentina, Bambi the Mermaid, Eak (the Illustrated Man), Scott Baker (the Twisted Shockmeister), Ravi (the Scorpion Mystic), Ula (the Rainproof Rubber Girl), and Todd Robbins (Amazement Is His Business).

* * * * *

The famous song "Under the Boardwalk," first popularized by the band the Drifters in 1964, is about Coney Island.

LEONARDO, THE SCIENCE GUY

A 15th-century man with 21st-century ideas.

He painted the *Mona Lisa*, the most famous painting in the world. He also painted *The Last Supper*—probably the most famous fresco in the world. But once you sit back and look at Leonardo da Vinci's entire body of work, you'd think that painting was just something he did in his spare time.

He was the true Renaissance man, and not just because he lived through it. While his countryman Christopher Columbus was out exploring the world, Leonardo was exploring everything that made the world tick. He's been called the first modern scientist.

A NICE ITALIAN BOY

Leonardo was born in 1452 in the town of Vinci. (Because he was illegitimate, he was named after his town rather than his father—his last name means "from Vinci.") He started out as a painter. Back then, the really good artists were usually employed by aristocrats, who expected them to design everything from pageant costumes to weapons. His impressive list of patrons included the Duke of Milan, a cardinal in the Vatican, and the king of France—not to mention a Borgia here, a Medici there.

TOP SECRET

Leonardo studied every scientific subject there was including anatomy, botany, physics, geology, optics, meteorology, aerodynamics...you name it. Like Albert Einstein, Leonardo wasn't great at math, but he made up for it in diligence; he used strict mathematical rules to test his ideas.

He wrote about everything he studied—with illustrations, of course. His notes and notebooks, all written backwards, were decipherable only with a mirror. This was probably because he was solitary and secretive by nature, and was afraid that someone would steal his ideas. But it's also possible that he wanted to hide his work from the authorities, who had already stopped his groundbreaking work in anatomy because dissection went against the teachings of the Roman Catholic Church. In fact, before he had to stop his anatomical research, Leonardo was the first person to draw an accurate picture of the human heart and describe its action.

MAKE A NOTE OF THAT

His curiosity was boundless, and Leonardo relied on intuition as much as intelligence. He predicted the invention of radio and the telephone. His notes on the subject say, "Men from the most remote countries shall speak to one another and shall reply," a prediction that relied on his work with waves. After noticing that water moves in waves, he extended the idea, deciding—with no physical evidence to back him up—that light and sound move in the same way. He used as an example the ripples caused by two stones dropped into the water. As the ripples grow larger and cross each other, they don't merge or change their shape. Aha! Just like the sounds of two bells that you can hear clearly and separately, even though one might be farther away from you than the other. This led him to the concept that everything gives off waves: a rock gives off heat, and food gives off an odor—all in waves.

The ideas would just pop: His notes are filled with reminders like, "Make glasses to magnify the Moon." But he never did get around to designing that telescope. So little time.

FOR GOOD MEASURE

Science can only be as exact as its measurements. In Leonardo's day, there were no reliable instruments for measuring speeds or distances—either on land or on sea—or for measuring the force of the wind, the moisture in the air, the amount of rainfall, and so on.

In Italy, educated men were still counting on their fingers. And to measure length, they used what was called a *braccio*, roughly an arm's length; but it varied from place to place, so that a man in Milan reading dimensions written by a man in Rome might interpret them differently.

So if our hero were going to throw himself wholeheartedly into science, he first had to improve some of the methods of measuring—and invent new ones. He sat down at the drawing board. Here are just some of the devices he came up with:

The frying pan built in 1950 for use at the Delmarva Chicken Festival is 10 feet in diameter.

- An adjustable drawing compass
- One of the first clocks that measured minutes as well as hours
- A scale that made it easier to read weights
- An odometer for wagons, which would measure the distance traveled
- A pedometer, to measure how far someone had walked
- An inclinometer, which would measure tilt, as in his flying machine
- A hygrometer, which measured absolute (zero) humidity
- An anemometer, to measure how fast the wind blew
- A device for measuring how much water expands when it turns to steam

THE HANDYMAN

And if the inventor were actually going to make some of his ideas into reality, he'd need the most cutting-edge tools he could invent or improve on. Like:

- An adjustable monkey wrench that looks a lot like the ones we use today
- A mechanical saw that looks like a modern power jigsaw
- A new design for the treadle lathe
- Automatic shears
- Machines for rolling copper and tin into thin sheets
- A screw-thread cutter that used a finished screw to guide the machine while it cut a new screw thread
- Designs for improvements on the chuck, drill, file, hammer, level, nail puller, pickax, pipe borer, posthole digger, and punch
- To lift heavy weights in construction jobs, he designed a ratchet jack that looked like an upside-down car jack. It hung inside a huge tripod, with the hook down, and it could raise a stone weighing half a ton.

FLYBOY

Once he had his measuring devices and his tools, the sky was the limit. And literally, the sky *was* Leonardo's limit. He was utterly fascinated by the idea of human flight. He was the first person to study it in a scientific way, but he got hung up on birds' wings. He spent years on the futile project of inventing a machine that

---

It holds 180 gallons of oil and 800 chicken quarters.

would imitate the flapping wings of birds. Experts speculate that if he'd worked on inventing a glider instead, he might have been the first person to fly.

Still, he was the first to think of a helicopter for human flight. He drew a design for what he called a "helix,' a huge screw really, that would be launched by four men whirling the vertical shaft, each pushing on one of the horizontal spokes that projected from it. This was absolutely correct in principle: the outer edge of the screw moved much faster, of course, than the central shaft, and this very rapid motion would compress the air below to lift the machine.

Then there was his parachute—which he conceived of as a means of transportation, not as a means of exiting an airplane. Leonardo's parachute was a tent 24 feet across and high. He supposedly tested it himself from a tower—nearly 300 years before the first recorded jump was made, in 1783, in France.

AND NOW, A WORD FROM OUR SPONSOR
Leonardo's longest gig, patron-wise, was the time he spent with the Duke of Milan from 1482 to 1499. Besides painting portraits and designing festivals for the duke, he also designed:
- Locks for the canals in the duke's neighborhood
- A pump that raised water from a stream and distributed it through the castle
- A heating system for the duchess's bath
- One of the world's first air-cooling systems (for the duchess's boudoir)
- War weapons that included:
  - Stink bombs mounted on arrows
  - An armored tank that looked like a flying saucer (because it could move in any direction, and the guns mounted on it could point anywhere)
  - An assault chariot (one of Leonardo's more dubious inventions, it was propelled by a man on horseback, and was equipped with projecting scythe blades so it could mow down the enemy as it moved forward)
  - A gadget for lighting cannon powder that worked just like, and was about the same size as, a (now vintage) Ronson cigarette lighter.

BURNING THE MIDNIGHT OIL

For his own use, Leonardo invented an oil lamp for working at night (which he often did). And just in case he slept late, he invented an alarm clock—which didn't keep time at all. It was kind of a Rube Goldberg contraption that worked with weights and water; instead of waking him with a "ring!" it would jerk at his foot to awaken him.

EVERYTHING BUT A KITCHEN SINK

A few of his miscellaneous inventions and designs, big and small:

- A coin-stamping machine
- A spotlight
- Ball bearings
- Portable bridges
- A well pump that used the same stream as a source of both supply and power
- A lazy Susan that worked between the kitchen and dining room
- Not one, but two, automatic roasting spits (one operated by mechanical power, the other by a fan set into the chimney)
- The prototype of an automobile: a wagon that propelled itself by means of springs and gears, with a transmission system that turned the wheels at different speeds when the wagon rounded a curve
- A diving suit (in leather) with an air reservoir
- A version of the bicycle
- Floats for walking on water

He was also the first person to draw maps giving an idea of the hills and valleys in the landscape. His maps were not truly topographic, but close enough.

IS THIS THE END OF LEO?

Leonardo spent his last years (1516–1519) in the service of Francis I, the king of France, and is, in fact, buried in Amboise, in central France.

There are a couple of 18th and 19th century paintings—based more on legend than truth—depicting Leonardo's death in the arms of King Francis. The king thought a lot of Leonardo: "no other man had been born into the world who knew as much as Leonardo," he supposedly said. But it's

---

The real name of Minnesota Fats, the billiards master, was Rudolf Wanderone.

doubtful that Francis thought enough of the artist to actually embrace him on his deathbed.

MONA MIGRATES
Leonardo painted the *Mona Lisa* in the first years of the 16th century, probably in 1506. He brought the painting with him when he left Italy to work in France. And that's why you'll find her still hanging around Paris—in the Louvre—today.

20TH-CENTURY POSTSCRIPT
In 1994, Bill Gates plunked down more than $30 million for one of Leonardo's notebooks: the Codex Leicester.

* * * * *

PATENT #6,449

One of the more interesting documents filed with the patent office, was U.S. patent number 6,469. Its title is "Buoying Vessels over Shoals." The invention, according to its creator, "is a new and improved manner of combining adjustable buoyant air chambers with a steamboat or other vessel for the purpose of enabling them to pass over bars or through shallow water."

The inventor whittled a 20-inch model to demonstrate how these buoyant chambers would look—but like many other inventors—Abraham Lincoln never did raise the funds to build a workable version of his idea.

THE QUEEN'S DWARF

The adventure-filled life of Jeffrey Hudson.
Here's the long and short of it. (Okay, mostly the short.)

Jeffrey Hudson was born, ironically, in the smallest county in England—Rutland County—on June 14, 1619. His father worked as a butcher, a not very well-paying position in those days. Mr. and Mrs. Hudson were both of ordinary stature, as were all their other children, which included three boys and a girl.

A GROWING CONCERN
As Jeffrey grew older, though, he simply didn't *grow*. At the age of seven, in fact, he stood a mere 18 inches tall. Jeffrey probably suffered from a condition common to dwarfs called hypopituitarism, a growth-hormone deficiency of the pituitary gland. In nearly every other respect, Jeffrey was quite normal; he was healthy, intelligent, and quite good-looking. He could have ended up spending most of his life as a sideshow in the local fair. But fate had something else in store.

FROM RAGS TO SILK BRITCHES
Everyone was curious about him, including the Duchess of Buckingham, whose husband was the best friend and principal advisor of King Charles I (1625–1649). At the request of the duchess, Jeffrey's parents dressed their son in his best Sunday clothes (such as they were), marched him the mile or so up the hill to the duchess's mansion, and handed him over. From then on, Jeffrey would be dressed in velvets, silks, and satins, with two servants to attend to his every need. He would still be on display, the subject of laughter and curiosity—but there was a big difference between dancing for a duchess and performing in front of the local yokels at the county fair.

MOVE OVER, PILLSBURY DOUGHBOY!
In early November 1626, the duke threw a series of lavish banquets at his palatial home in London, including one for King Charles and his queen, Henrietta Maria. Only the finest food in the land

The name Tehran, the capital of Iran, is derived from an old Persian word for "warm place."

was served, and all the guests were showered with gifts. Such fancy soirees called for culinary special effects: At the appointed hour, servants carried a huge, glistening pie to the royal table and set it down before the queen. Then, right on cue, a hand, then an arm, broke through the crust—followed by a small face peering out from beneath a shiny helmet. Finally, a tiny figure dressed in a miniature suit of armor emerged. It was Jeffrey Hudson.

THE QUEEN'S PET PROJECT
The queen took Jeffrey under her wing. The royal marriage wasn't going very well; young Henrietta Maria—the sister of Louis XIII, king of France—felt isolated and alone. And in a country that was largely Anglican, her passionate devotion to the Catholic faith only increased that sense of foreignness and isolation. So Henrietta Maria turned to her pets. To her menagerie of monkeys, dogs, and birds, she could now add her own little pet human, Jeffrey Hudson, who thereafter was known as the Queen's Dwarf.

FROM BAD TO NURSE
The queen had already lost one child shortly after childbirth; so when she became pregnant a second time, an expedition was mounted to fetch the finest nurse in all of France, Madame Peronne, to tend to the queen. Jeffrey had been included. So, on March 18, 1630, he and Madame Peronne set sail from Calais. A few hours after leaving port, the ship was taken over by pirates. But after a few days, realizing that the group they'd snatched was probably too hot to handle, the pirates released their captives and sent them on their way.

A DECADE OF DECADENCE
The decade starting in 1631 was surely the happiest time of Hudson's life. He was the hit of every social occasion; this was not just because of his curiosity value, but because of his wit, humor, and charm. He learned some new skills that were expected of young men at court, including shooting a pistol, riding, playing cards, and dancing. But while Jeffrey and his fellow courtiers were playing games inside the walls of the palace, some deadly serious games were being played outside them. The Puritans in Parliament

continued to grumble about the lavish spending of the monarchy and the high taxes that King Charles I continued to impose.

SEA-SICK AND TIRED

By 1641, the royal treasury was tapped out, and a desperate king was forced to reconvene the Parliament he had dismissed in 1629. The next January, Henrietta Maria, Jeffrey, and the rest of the queen's court fled London, through an angry crowd of Puritan sympathizers, and set sail for Holland.

The ship ran smack into a huge storm, which the queen and her entourage barely managed to survive. They finally reached Holland on March 1, 1642. On the return trip—nearly a year later, in what was becoming a depressingly familiar routine for poor Jeffrey—a huge storm hit the queen's convoy as soon as they lost sight of land. Several ships were lost in the storm, but the queen and Jeffrey managed to make it back to the Dutch coast.

NIGHTIE NIGHT

Back in Holland, the queen quickly raised more money and supplies, and she replaced the ships that had been lost in the storm. A year later, they sailed again for England—making it without a hitch. This time the trouble began *after* they landed, when the fishing village where they were staying overnight was bombarded by parliamentary ships. Dressed only in their nightgowns, the queen and her attendants were forced to flee their quarters. Meanwhile Jeffrey, armed with sword and pistol, joined the other male members of the queen's household down by the landing area, ready to repel the queen's enemies. At dawn, the tide carried the attacking ships out of range and the firing finally ceased.

NO HORSING AROUND

Henrietta Maria rewarded Jeffrey for his loyalty and bravery by conferring upon him the honorary title Captain of Horse. But by the summer of 1644, with the war against the parliamentary forces not going well at all, the queen and the royal entourage boarded a fleet of Dutch ships and hightailed it for France. Not surprisingly, they proceeded to run right into—yep, you guessed it!—another storm.

The composition of Wagner's German *Ring* cycle took over 20 years.

GO AHEAD, MAKE MY DAY

Henrietta Maria and company eventually made it to France. Once they'd settled in, they were joined there by William Crofts, the queen's Master of Horse, and several of the court's "young blades," aristocratic hangers-on whose principal occupation was hanging around the local saloons and getting sloshed. Once again, Jeffrey found himself the easy butt of cruel jokes. The now 25-year-old captain Hudson let it be known that the next person who insulted him would be challenged to a duel.

THE LITTLE SQUIRT

The final straw was an insult delivered by young Charles Crofts, brother of the aforementioned William. A duel was arranged, though, in all likelihood, no one—with the exception of Jeffrey Hudson—took it seriously. When the combatants were asked to choose their weapons, Crofts produced the 17th-century equivalent of a squirt gun (it was actually called a "squirt"), a large syringe that served in those days as a fire extinguisher. This apparently produced more than a few chuckles among the spectators. But in Jeffrey's mind, the time for jokes was over. The water pistol was put aside. The two duelists, 100 paces apart, faced each other on horseback. The horses charged, and when they were only a few yards apart, Jeffrey Hudson leveled his pistol and shot Crofts through the head. He died at the scene.

THIS LITTLE JEFFREY WENT TO MARKET

Though it's not clear exactly why, Jeffrey was banished from court (the queen may have been trying to protect Jeffrey, but there's also the factor that dueling was in disfavor at the moment in France).

In October 1644, Hudson packed up his things and left France. By ship. (Oh, no! Oh, yes.) Not long out of port Jeffrey's ship was boarded by Turkish corsairs—the dreaded Barbary pirates. Jeffrey was most likely taken to one of the slave-trade centers—Algiers, Tunis, or Tripoli—on the Barbary Coast, the group of North African states ruled by the Ottoman Turks. After their capture, slaves were taken down to a central market where they were put up for auction.

REACHING NEW HEIGHTS

Once a slave, it's likely that Hudson received his share of physical abuse. Along with a new regime of physical labor, his diet underwent a radical change: from rich, refined foods to much simpler fare, which would have been something like black bread and vinegar. It may have been this combination of extreme changes in his daily existence that brought about the most remarkable of changes: Jeffrey actually began to grow! Right after reaching the age of 30, he shot up from around two feet in height to three feet and nine inches (a little more than 1 meter).

LUCKLESS IN LONDON

Beginning in the mid-1660s, England made concerted efforts to buy back its citizens from the Barbary pirates. After nearly 25 years in slavery, Jeffrey Hudson finally obtained his freedom. He returned home to live with his only surviving brother, Samuel. In 1678, after seven or eight years living the quiet life, he decided to return to London. But anti-Catholic riots had broken out there, and his close identification with the fervently Catholic Henrietta Maria made him an easy target for the mob. He was thrown in prison and clapped in irons, with nothing to sleep on but boards. No heat was provided through the cold, damp English winters.

LARGER THAN LIFE

Jeffrey was released from prison in 1680, a tired and broken old man. His former connections at court helped him snag a little money from Henrietta Maria's son, King Charles II, who must have taken pity on the Queen's Dwarf. It's believed that Jeffrey died in the second half of 1681, but the exact date and place are unknown. There's no record of his final days. But in all probability, Jeffrey Hudson, a proud and adventurous spirit, died impoverished and alone.

* * * * *

"History is merely a list of surprises. It can only prepare us to be surprised yet again." —Kurt Vonnegut

The only marsupial native to North America is the opossum.

THE SPORT OF KINGS

*Read about the historic sport and then decide—
is there a falcon in your future?*

For about 800 years, the ancient Eastern art of falconry was Europe's favorite sporting pastime too. Kings walked away from battles in progress to exercise their hawks. Diplomacy was carried out with presents of particularly fine birds. Popes, priests, and even nuns were keen falconers, and many people took their hawks with them everywhere they went, perched on their shoulders or on the traditional leather glove. In fact, just about everybody who *could* keep a falcon *did*.

No-one knows when falcons were first tamed for hunting. It is only recently that advances in scientific understanding have made it possible to breed birds of prey in captivity with any kind of success. So throughout its history, falconry has been based on taking wild birds, either straight from the nest, or by catching young adults in nets. Early falconers used whatever birds of prey were available locally. In Central Asia today, which is perhaps where the sport originated, some falconers hunt on horseback using golden eagles, their birds plummeting down to earth to kill hares or pheasants for the pot, or to wipe out dangerous predators, like wolves.

A similar kind of sport still exists in the Arab world, where the traditional way of hunting with hawks is to go after a large, nutritious desert bird, the Houbara Bustard. Of course, today, falconers are likely to be oil-rich billionaires with fabulously expensive hawks from all over the world. But until recently, falconry was a practical method for desert nomads to get a rare taste of fresh meat.

Arab falconry was a major influence on Europe, because the Crusades exposed European nobles to the Arab tradition, with falcons and falconers being brought back by returning Crusaders. India, Persia, China, Japan, and other countries have traditions of falconry stretching back hundreds or thousands of years, and the pattern everywhere has been the same. Originally falconry was a reasonable if slightly impractical method of hunting, either for food or for sport, and usually in very remote and empty regions. It soon became mainly a status symbol, and the hunting aspect became a secondary consideration.

Raising goats to produce cashmere is one of the main occupations in Mongolia.

Even Japanese samurai received official instruction in the handling of hawks. When the 13th-century Chinese emperor Kublai Khan went hawking, he went with a retinue of 1,000 people. In the East, falconry had been practiced for a couple of thousand years, but it only reached Europe in about A.D. 800. But it didn't become popular in the Western world until the Crusaders returned from the Middle East and started the craze at home.

TRAINING YOUR FALCON

The methods used in falconry today, in Europe and the United States, are about the same as those established in medieval Europe, where falconry became insanely popular from about the ninth to the 17th centuries. First, you'll need a raptor (a bird of prey, like a hawk or an eagle). You could buy a captive-bred bird. But that spoils the fun of getting your bird, which is traditionally done by having yourself lowered down a cliff face on a rope so you can take a young bird from its nest. If you are not going to sew your bird's eyelids together (called seeling, which is meant to keep visual stimulation to a minimum but is hardly every practiced in the Western world anymore), you put a leather hood on its head to blind it anyway. You then begin a long, delicate, and labor-intensive period of training.

Hawks have an instinct to hunt, so the purpose of the training is not to teach them how to kill, but to modify their natural behavior until they will hunt with *you*, going after prey *you've* selected. The process is called manning. Apart from an elaborate system of training flights, it means carrying the falcon around on your wrist for several hours a day, every day, feeding it by hand (chopped mice, bits of dead songbirds, that sort of thing), and making sure it doesn't get frightened by strangers. You have to wear the same clothes every day so your bird doesn't get confused. If you upset your hawk, especially if it's one of the larger ones who kill with their feet, it will dig its razor-sharp talons into your flesh and refuse to let go. And that hurts.

JUST YOU AND YOUR BIRD

Of course, in the old days, kings and princes paid professional falconers to do all this, so that the birds would be ready when there was an important hunt on. The modern falconer, like you, has to rely on himself. For one thing, you'll have to quit your job. The sport needs full-time leisure; lots of fancy, special equipment; assistants; specially trained dogs; plus regular access to abundant game. Oh yes, and don't forget that each bird gets "wedded" to a particular kind of prey, each requiring a whole different technique. And when you finally get around to releasing your trained falcon after quarry, it is quite possible that one day it will take it into its head to fly off into the trees for some private enterprise hunting of its own and you will never see it again. In fact, a lot of birds are lost this way during training, before the hunting even begins.

THE GOOD OLD DAYS OF FALCONRY

One convention that has disappeared now is that particular kinds of falcons were associated with particular ranks in society. It isn't hard to guess how it worked: the rarer and more expensive a falcon was, the more important you had to be to have one. The eagle was the symbol of emperors, for instance, which is why the Habsburgs in Europe and czars in Russia had eagles on their coats of arms.

Next in importance came the beautiful white ice falcons from Greenland, sent in special falcon ships, and so rare that they were distributed to reigning monarchs only by a special international delivery system. (A single feather would be taken from the bird and sent ahead by separate messenger to make sure that there was no opportunity for fraud.) And so on through peregrines, merlins, and sparrow hawks, down the scale to the lowly kestrel, a common European bird which could be owned by anybody. The kestrel, in fact, will not hunt at all once it has been manned, preferring to live off the chopped mice.

Owning a bird representing a higher social status than your own was a felony, and more serious falcon-related crimes, like stealing birds from nests, could cost you a hand—or even your eyes. The first laws passed to protect wildlife were the laws to protect birds of prey.

OH, SHOOT!

Of course, once the shotgun was invented, hawking parties, as they were called, were replaced by shooting parties. The European

---

Galileo discovered that the surface of the moon was pitted, not smooth, in 1609

birds of prey suddenly went from being treasured symbols of beauty and power to being thought of as dangerous vermin, competing with sporting gun-owners for their precious targets. The raptors soon found the guns turned on them, and some species were actually wiped out.

FALCONRY, AMERICAN STYLE

American falconry has never had the aristocratic connotations of the European or Arabian versions. The European hawking craze was already dying out when America was colonized, and the Puritans weren't the kind of people who would have gone in for it. Few among the European aristocracy, who might still have practiced falconry, joined the migration to America.

But even though it's never been more than a minority interest sport, the different birds of prey available—and different kinds of landscape and prey species—have gradually created a distinctive American style of falconry, with Harris' Hawk being the most popular choice for American falconers. Harris' Hawk is much easier to train and to handle than traditional European hawks, and it also has the important advantage that it is not wedded to one prey species, but will fly at a wide variety of quarry. In fact, it is so much easier to keep that it has, for the first time ever, become possible to be a falconer and have a day job as well. Many European falconers are now switching to American-style falconry, using captive-bred Harris' Hawks, and turning this all-embracing passion into a more normal kind of weekend sporting interest.

In many countries, the natural prey of the species used in the sport have either been severely reduced through pollution or are protected by law, and organized resistance to the sport from wildlife protection organizations has caused some national falconry associations to shut down completely. There are a few scattered enthusiasts still trying to keep the old traditions alive, with private facilities of their own. Mostly, though, falconry has survived by adapting to modern conditions. This means that there are falconry centers where you can do short courses, gawk at some big imported raptors, and watch expert displays from professionals living off ticket sales. Old-fashioned hunting of wild game is only likely to happen in a few places where a fal-

Maud Gonne, Yeats's lover, was a founder of the Irish party Sinn Fein (We Ourselves).

conry center has an arrangement for private land with special breeding of prey species.

This is a far cry from the origins of the sport.

* * * * *

Some wordsmiths think the word "hobby," meaning "pastime," comes from the use, during the Middle Ages, of the Eurasian hobby (a kind of falcon).

YUMMY

The Romans thought that dormice, small rodents, were a big delicacy. The upper classes raised them at home. They fed nuts to the dormice and then ate the dormice.

THANKS FOR READING OUR BOOK!

We hope you had as much fun reading it as we did writing it.

Language	"Thank you"
Afrikaans	*dankie*
Australian	*ta*
Chinese, Cantonese	*do jeh*
Chinese, Mandarin	*xie xie*
Danish	*tak*
French	*merci*
German	*danke*
Greek	*efharisto*
Hindi	*sukria*
Italian	*grazie*
Japanese	*arigato*
Korean	*kamsa hamnida*
Norwegian	*takk tahk*
Polish	*dziekuje*
Portuguese	*obrigado*
Russian	*spasibo*
Spanish	*gracias*
Swahili	*asante*
Swedish	*tack*

Count Ferdinand von Zeppelin's first airship took flight in Germany on July 2, 1900.

QUIZ ANSWERS

ALL THAT JAZZ (page 265)

1. d: Nightclub attendance.
That night, everyone in town showed up to see the winning band, while the losers played to an empty house.

2. e: All of 'em, baby.
Like a funky casserole, jazz also includes elements of gospel, banjo music, syncopated brass, and other eclectic roots.

3. d: Memphis.
Memphis had Elvis and the blues.

4. e: All of 'em, baby.
Compared to the mathematically ho-hum sounds of turn-of-the-century America, jazz was technically complex and challenging for musicians.

5. b: Jazz-proof furniture.
It may have looked like plain old furniture, but it was said to resist the evil and intrusive sounds of jazz, which corrupted people—making them crazy and uninhibited. Woo-hoo!

6. 1 (d), 2(a), 3(e), 4(c), 5(b)

7. d: The goatee.
The goatee first became associated with jazz through Dizzy Gillespie. But he was still in school in the 1920s, and the goatee-as-counterculture symbol began post-WWII. The jazz–goatee connection was permanently secured in the American psyche in the 1960s by TV's *Dobie Gillis* and its goatee-wearing beatnik Maynard G. Krebs (played by future Gilligan, Bob Denver).

8. c: Houses of ill repute.
Many jazz musicians made big bucks at these then-thriving establishments, designed especially for "entertainment districts" in New Orleans and other jazz hot spots. The management left them alone to play and experiment in their own musical directions.

9. a: Tap jazz.

Sometimes tap dancers perform to jazz music, but it's not a real jazz style. Hard bop jazz has freight train tempos and thunderstorm solos; fusion jazz mixes jazz with rock and roll; free jazz is wild and experimental; and cool jazz has a slow, laid-back groove.

TEMPEST OVER A TEA PARTY (page 289)

c. The British national debt of 130 million pounds was the largest in its history up to that time. Much of the debt had been incurred in defending the colonies during the French and Indian War, so Parliament thought the colonies should shoulder some of the cost of their defense. Previous taxes on glass, lead, and paper had been repealed after colonial protests, but the tax on tea was to remain to show that Parliament had the power to enforce taxation. The East India Company, Britain's largest commercial enterprise, imported tea from India. But the company was almost bankrupt, couldn't pay its taxes, and had huge stockpiles of tea going stale in their warehouses—largely due to the colonists' boycott of British tea.

c. Remember "no taxation without representation"? The Tea Act of 1773 would actually have *lowered* the cost of tea; the East India Company could sell the tea directly, eliminating the middleman. Its tea would have been cheaper than the Dutch tea the colonists were illegally smuggling in through the Dutch West Indies. And the tax on tea wasn't high, at least in modern terms. The tax was only 3 pence per pound of tea. Ben Franklin estimated that the average household drank no more than 10 pounds of tea a year, making the average family's tea tax bill an affordable 30 pence. The Bostonians were just agitating against England's right to impose taxes.

c. Contrary to some schoolbook pictures, none of the men are reported to have worn feathers and darkened their skin with ashes or burnt cork. Go figure.

c. There was no violence or burning, and some of the ships' crews even helped the colonists hoist the tea chests up from the holds. The disposal of the tea was done in such an orderly fashion that the ship' officers were called on deck to witness that no damage had been done to anything but the tea. A replacement for a broken lock was sent for. Emptying 342 cases of tea took about three hours—from six to nine o'clock in the evening. And the patriots took care that none of their party pilfered any tea. All men were required to take off their shoes and turn them upside down to empty out any tea that may have collected there. A crowd of hundreds watched the whole thing in silence. Although it was suggested that the ships be set ablaze, there was fear that the fire would spread to town so the suggestion was abandoned.

c. The Boston Tea Party took place at low tide so the ships' bottoms were resting on muck. The water at Griffin's Wharf that night was only two feet deep. Consequently, tea piled up above the water's surface like sand dunes or haystacks. So much tea that it clogged the harbor's channel, and sailors had to row out to break up the water-logged clumps and push them out to sea.

a. Sam Adams had been a tax collector, but a very lenient one.

c. In today's dollars, the value of the trashed tea was $1,000,000.

b. Darjeeling tea from India, the most popular variety.

c. None of the tea partiers was ever punished for the vandalism. There was such a strict code of secrecy regarding who participated that it's still unclear who took part. One man kept his participation secret until finally telling the story when he was 104. One loose-lipped barber, a Mr. Eckley, hinted at his involvement. The man who squealed on Eckley to the authorities was stripped naked and tarred and feathered. No one else ever came forward with incriminating information.

a. Ben Franklin, in London at the time, offered to reimburse the East India Company for its losses at the hands of the patriots. But he conditioned the offer on Parliament's repealing of the Port Act, which had closed the port of Boston. Parliament refused. No one ever paid for the lost tea.

INDEX

Bancroft Library, 389–392
Band Aid, 432
Bank, Aaron, 237
bank failures, 106
banking, history of, 109–111,
   320
Banting, Frederick, 283–285
Bara, Theda, 122
Barbary pirates, 474–475
barbecue, history of, 148–150
barbers, 62, 453
Barrymore, Maurice, 114
bartering, 108
baseball, 420–423
Bataan Death March, 34
Bates, Peg Leg, 117
bathing suits, 462
Battle of Bull Run, 79
Battle of El Guettar, 142
Battle of Gettysburg, 224–227
Battle of the Marne, 90–91
Bay of Biscay, 119
Beauregard, P. G. T., 79
Beautiful Mind, A, 22
Beckwith, Charles, 263
beer, 452
Beethoven, Ludwig van, 171–172
Belgium, 308
Bell, Alexander Graham, 229
Ben-Hur, 231, 232
Bennett, James Gordon, 325
Bergerac, Savinien Cyrano de,
   244–245
Berlin Wall, 180–183
Bernhardt, Sarah, 114
Berra, Yogi, 412
Berryman, John, 219
Best, Charles, 284, 285
Bible Communism, 163

Bill of Rights, 129
Billy the Kid, 232
bird flu, 250
birds of prey, 476–480
Birdseye, Clarence, 105
birthing process, 408–410
Black, Greene Vardiman, 235
Black Like Me (Griffin), 10–11
Blackbeard, 144
blacklisting, 436
blacksmiths, 6
Blechynden, Richard, 287
Bletchley Park, 456–457, 458
blistering, 17
bloodletting, 62
Bludworth, Thomas, 1–2
Boesch, Rudy, 293
Bolger, Ray, 114–115
Bolton, Herbert E., 389–392
bombs, balloon, 200–201
Bond, James, 71, 145
Boniface VIII, 375
Boomtown Rats, 433
Booth, John Wilkes, 122
bootleggers, 72, 74
Borges, Jorge Luis, 413
borrowing, 108
Boston Tea Party, 287, 289–290
Boudreaux, Edith, 104
Boyton, Paul, 462
Bradbury, Ray, 12
Brahmanism, 411
Brand, Bernie, 102
Brazil, 111, 308
breeding, dog, 206
Brent, Margaret, 443
brewers, 451–452
Brice, Fanny, 116
Bronze Age, 5

PLUNGE INTO MORE BATHROOM READER TITLES

The best-selling *Uncle John's Plunges into...* Series:

*Uncle John's Bathroom Reader
Plunges into History*
Copyright © 2001.
504 pages, $16.95

*Uncle John's
Bathroom Reader
Plunges into the Universe*
Copyright © 2002.
504 pages, $16.95

*Uncle John's Bathroom Reader
Plunges into Great Lives*
Copyright © 2003.
504 pages, $16.95

*Uncle John's Bathroom
Reader Plunges into
The Presidency*
Copyright © 2004.
324 pages, $12.95

*Uncle John's Bathroom
Reader Plunges into
Texas*
Copyright © 2004.
320 pages, $12.95

UNCLE JOHN'S PRESENTS

Uncle John's Presents
Book of the Dumb
Copyright © 2003.
320 pages, $12.95

Uncle John's Presents
Book of the Dumb 2
Copyright © 2004.
320 pages, $12.95

Uncle John's Presents
Mom's Bathtub Reader
Copyright © 2004.
320 pages, $12.95

Uncle John's Presents
Blame it on the Weather
Copyright © 2002.
240 pages, $12.00

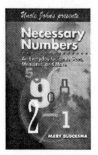

Uncle John's Presents
Necessary Numbers
Copyright © 2002.
280 pages, $12.00

UNCLE JOHN'S BATHROOM READER PUZZLE BOOKS

Uncle John's
Bathroom Reader
Puzzle Book 1
Copyright © 2003.
240 pages, $12.95

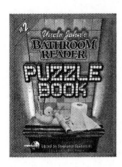

Uncle John's
Bathroom Reader
Puzzle Book 2
Copyright © 2004.
240 pages, $12.95

FOR KIDS ONLY!

Uncle John's Bathroom Reader
For Kids Only!
Copyright © 2002.
288 pages, $12.95

Uncle John's Electrifying
Bathroom Reader
For Kids Only!
Copyright © 2003.
288 pages, $12.95

Uncle John's Top Secret
Bathroom Reader
For Kids Only!
Copyright © 2004.
288 pages, $12.95

TO ORDER

Contact:
Bathroom Readers' Press
P.O. Box 1117,
Ashland, OR 97520
Phone: 541-488-4642
Fax: 541-482-6159
brorders@mind.net
www.bathroomreader.com

Shipping & Handling Rates:
- 1 book: $3.50
- 2 – 3 books: $4.50
- 4 – 5 books: $5.50
- 5 + books: $1.00/ book

Priority shipping also
available.
We accept checks &
credit card orders.
Order online, or by fax, mail,
e-mail, or phone.

Wholesale Distributor
Publishers Group West (U.S.):
800-788-3123
Raincoast Books (Canada):
800-663-5714

THE LAST PAGE

S it down and be counted!
Become a member of the Bathroom Readers' Institute!
No join-up fees, monthly minimums or maximums, organized dance parties or quilting bees, solicitors or annoying phone calls (we only have one phone line), Spam—or any other canned meat product—to worry about...just the chance to get our fabulous monthly newsletter (and if you want) some extremely cool Uncle John stuff.

So send us a letter at:

The Bathroom Readers' Institute
P.O. Box 1117
Ashland, OR 97520

Or email us at www.BathroomReader.com

Hope you enjoyed the book—and if you're skipping to the end, what are you doing reading this page? Go back and finish!